CRIMINAL FAIR TRIAL RIGHTS

The Article 6 fair trial rights are the most heavily-litigated Convention rights before the European Court of Human Rights, generating a large and complex body of case law. With this book, Goss provides an innovative and critical analysis of the European Court's Article 6 case law.

The category of 'fair trial rights' includes many component rights. The existing literature tends to chart the law with respect to each of these component rights, one by one. This traditional approach is useful, but it risks artificially isolating the case law in a series of watertight compartments.

This book takes a complementary but different approach. Instead of analysing the component rights one by one, it takes a critical look at the case law through a number of 'cross-cutting' problems and themes common to all or many of the component rights. For example: how does the Court view its role in Article 6 cases? When will the Court recognise an implied right in Article 6? How does the Court assess Article 6 infringements, and when will the public interest justify an infringement?

The book's case-law-driven approach allows Goss to demonstrate that the European Court's criminal fair trial rights jurisprudence is marked by considerable uncertainty, inconsistency, and incoherence.

Volume 11 in the Criminal Law Library series

Criminal Law Library

Volume 1: Self-Defence in Criminal Law
Boaz Sangero

Volume 2: Evidence of Bad Character
John Spencer

Volume 3: The Management and Enforcement of Community-Based Sentences: A Practitioner's Guide
Clare Fazal

Volume 4: Fair Trials: The European Criminal Procedural Tradition and the European Court of Human Rights
Sarah Summers

Volume 5: Hearsay Evidence in Criminal Proceedings
John Spencer

Volume 6: Homicide Law in Comparative Perspective
Edited by Jeremy Horder

Volume 7: Case Management in the Crown Court
HH Judge Roderick Denyer QC

Volume 8: The Presumption of Innocence: Evidential and Human Rights Perspectives
Andrew Stumer

Volume 9: Inquests
John Cooper

Volume 10: The Privilege Against Self-Incrimination and Criminal Justice
Andrew L-T Choo

Criminal Fair Trial Rights

Article 6 of the European Convention on Human Rights

Ryan Goss

·HART·
PUBLISHING
OXFORD AND PORTLAND, OREGON
2016

Published in the United Kingdom by Hart Publishing Ltd
16C Worcester Place, Oxford, OX1 2JW
Telephone: +44 (0)1865 517530
Fax: +44 (0)1865 510710
E-mail: mail@hartpub.co.uk
Website: http://www.hartpub.co.uk

Published in North America (US and Canada) by
Hart Publishing
c/o International Specialized Book Services
920 NE 58th Avenue, Suite 300
Portland, OR 97213-3786
USA
Tel: +1 503 287 3093 or toll-free: (1) 800 944 6190
Fax: +1 503 280 8832
E-mail: orders@isbs.com
Website: http://www.isbs.com

First published in hardback 2014
Paperback edition, 2016

Hart Publishing is an imprint of Bloomsbury Publishing plc.

British Library Cataloguing in Publication Data
Data Available

ISBN: HB: 978-1-84946-550-2
PB: 978-1-50990-986-5

Typeset by Hope Services, Abingdon
Printed and bound in Great Britain by
Lightning Source UK Ltd

For my parents,
Roisin and Wayne Goss

ACKNOWLEDGMENTS

The Article 6 case law of the European Court of Human Rights is a fascinating and important body of law, permeated by intellectual puzzles, and it is my hope that this book furthers our understanding of some of those puzzles. But if this book is about 'doing human rights law better', then my own efforts to 'do human rights law' in this book would not have been possible without the assistance and encouragement of many others.

I must acknowledge Lincoln College, the University of Oxford, and the Australian National University, for their extensive support throughout this project. In addition, I could not have completed this research without the Rhodes Trust's generous backing, and I am grateful to all at Rhodes House, especially Sir Colin Lucas, Don Markwell, and Mary Eaton, for their counsel and friendship.

This book is, in part, a descendant of my Oxford BCL studies and doctoral thesis, *Rethinking Article 6*. I thank Andrew Ashworth for supervising that thesis, and for his ongoing advice, trust, and encouragement; he has been a superb supervisor. For examining and giving formal feedback on my research at various stages, my gratitude goes to Liora Lazarus, Conor Gearty, and Steven Greer. For the inspiring BCL seminars that partly provoked this project, I thank, in addition to those already named, Christopher McCrudden, Paul Craig, John Gardner, Leslie Green, Alison Young, Ben Goold, and Nicholas Barber. For discussions and advice over the years about this book and its ancestor thesis I am grateful to Peter Cane, Roisin Goss, Wayne Goss, Caitlin Goss, Eric Heenan, Miles Jackson, Amy King, Johannes Krebs, Nicholas Luke, Travers McLeod, Robert Mullins, Joshua Neoh, Lionel Nichols, Don Rothwell, Simon Quinn, Natasha Simonsen, Andrew Stumer, and my students at Oxford and the ANU. For their support and advice, I must also thank Richard Hart, Rachel Turner, Mel Hamill, and everyone at Hart Publishing, who have all been terrific to work with on this book. All of that having been said, the usual disclaimer applies.

Even in the age of the invaluable HUDOC and BAILII databases, I am indebted to the Bodleian Libraries, the Codrington Library at All Souls College, the Lincoln College Library, the Oxford Union Library, and the ANU Law Library. For hosting me during the research and writing of this book, my thanks go to Lincoln College, Jael Rogers House, the Healy family, and all at Western Road. And for their support, good humour, and patience, I thank my family and friends, and, especially, Amy King.

The law is current to St Patrick's Day, 2014.

RA GOSS

Canberra, March 2014

NOTE ON METHODOLOGY

This book is the result of an extensive survey of the European Court's Article 6 criminal fair trial rights case law. This short note explains the methodology used to identify the cases forming the basis of that survey.

Primary research for the book was conducted using multiple overlapping searches via the European Court's very useful HUDOC database, and involved reviewing and reading well over 1,500 decisions of the Court ranging from the inception of the Strasbourg institutions through to 17 March 2014. HUDOC 'tags' cases with various codings (as some examples, judgments will often be coded with the Article(s) considered in the case, any keywords describing the major issues in the case, and an 'importance' level from '1' to '3' based on the Bureau of the Court's assessment of the case).[1] This coding is not always done consistently, and so one must run several searches if one wishes to have a reasonably exhaustive set of results.

As part of that series of searches, every decision of the Court tagged as 'Article 6' and which included the word 'criminal' in the text was reviewed, as was every decision tagged as 'Article 6(2)' or 'Article 6(3)'. Every decision of the Court tagged as 'Article 6(1)' with an importance level of '1' was also reviewed, as were many of the decisions tagged as 'Article 6(1)' with importance levels '2' and '3'. In addition to these searches, a series of cross-cutting searches were also conducted for appearances of key words and phrases such as 'proceedings as a whole' or 'irretrievably' in Article 6 cases, and for relevant material discussed in the context of provisions related to Article 6 (for example, Article 5(4)). Cases available only in French were reviewed and translated as appropriate. In all, these searches identified well over 1,500 'hits', which included some civil cases, some less relevant cases; some cases generated more than one 'hit' due to the overlapping nature of the searches.

As noted in the acknowledgments, this book is in part a revised descendant of a doctoral thesis submitted and examined at the University of Oxford; since the time of the thesis' submission more than 500 recent cases have been surveyed, read, and added to the book as appropriate.

There are limitations to this methodology. It does not comprise a statistical survey, and cannot lead to any quantitative conclusions. It was, instead, a way of facilitating that method of legal research which may be summarised as 'try to read all the cases'.

[1] The two HUDOC User Manuals provide useful background information on these matters and are an invaluable guide for anyone conducting research in this area: see http://tinyurl.com/HUDOCmanuals. Note that importance level '1' usually includes, but is not limited to, cases reported in the official reports.

CONTENTS

TABLE OF CASES

TABLE OF TREATIES

Introduction

This book is a critique of the European Court of Human Rights' case law dealing with the right to a fair trial in criminal cases.[1] It explores the extent to which the European Court's case law in this area is consistent, predictable, transparent, and coherent.

Article 6 of the European Convention for the Protection of Human Rights and Fundamental Freedoms ('the Convention') provides protection for the right to a fair trial in civil and criminal proceedings. Article 6 includes multiple 'component' rights, some explicitly listed in the Convention, and others recognised by the European Court as implicit in the text. The explicitly listed component rights range from the right 'to a fair and public hearing within a reasonable time by an independent and impartial tribunal established by law' to the rights, for those 'charged with a criminal offence', to 'be presumed innocent until proved guilty according to law' and have 'the free assistance of an interpreter'. Examples of implicit rights include the accused's right 'to communicate with [the accused's] advocate out of hearing of a third person'[2] and the right 'to silence and . . . not to incriminate oneself'.[3]

Article 6 occupies a prominent place in the Convention system: between 1959 and 2009, more than half of the European Court judgments in which a violation was found included an Article 6 violation, either criminal or civil.[4] In 2013, the most recent year for which statistics are available, nearly one-third of the judgments in which a violation was found included a violation of Article 6; this was more than for any other Article.[5] This book looks at the case law concerning criminal proceedings from the beginning of the Court's operation through to 2014.[6] This Introduction frames the scope of the book's argument and outlines the ways in which that argument will be developed.

[1] The European Court of Human Rights will hereafter be referred to as 'the European Court' or 'the Court' as appropriate.

[2] *S v Switzerland* (App 12629/87) (1992) 14 EHRR 670, para 48.

[3] *Saunders v United Kingdom* (App 19187/91) (1997) 23 EHRR 313, para 68.

[4] European Court of Human Rights, *The European Court of Human Rights: Some Facts and Figures: 1959–2009* (Council of Europe, 2009) 6. See D Harris, M O'Boyle and C Warbrick, *Law of the European Convention on Human Rights*, 2nd edn (Oxford University Press, 2009) 202.

[5] European Court of Human Rights, *The European Court of Human Rights in Facts and Figures: 2013* (Council of Europe, 2014) 7.

[6] The case law is up to date as of 17 March 2014.

1.1 Framing the Scope of the Argument

There is significant scholarship on Article 6, either focusing directly on Article 6,[7] or dealing with it in the course of a broader Convention survey.[8] Usually, these works approach Article 6 as a series of component rights, and their treatment is divided into chapters or sections, each devoted to one or several component rights. These works are important and useful. This book does not aspire to be an exhaustive guide to any of Article 6's components, let alone to all of them. Instead, it takes a different approach. The book pursues an original doctrinal approach to the Article 6 material, and aims to provide a complement to the existing scholarship that will be of use to practitioners and scholars alike. It does so in the following ways.

First, the doctrinal approach in this book is one that is best described as 'cross-cutting' rather than a right-by-right analysis. It aims to consider those ideas, difficulties and debates that are common to many, or all, of the Article 6 component rights and to examine how the European Court deals with those challenges. By examining these cross-cutting issues, it is hoped that the book will more easily contextualise, and emphasise points of similarity and difference among, the Court's approaches to the Article 6 rights. In this way the book aims to act as a *complement* to, and not a *replacement* for, the work of other doctrinal authors such as Trechsel, van Dijk and van Hoof, or Harris, O'Boyle and Warbrick, by uncovering new points of contention and disagreement in the way that the Court approaches Article 6 criminal fair trial case law.

It is also hoped that the cross-cutting approach allows the book to function, in part, as a reference work. If a practitioner preparing submissions for a case wishes to identify the cases in which the 'fourth instance rule' has been circumvented, for example, she might turn to part B.5 and find fodder for her arguments; if a scholar wishes to argue for the recognition of a new implied right within the Article 6 framework, part D.3 will provide him with arguments which may be useful in formulating the right; if a judge wonders whether it is appropriate to utilise a balancing analysis in an Article 6 case, part E provides examples of case law for and

[7] See, eg, Stephanos Stavros, *The Guarantees for Accused Persons under Article 6 of the European Convention on Human Rights* (Martinus Nijhoff, 1993); Stefan Trechsel, *Human Rights in Criminal Proceedings* (Oxford University Press, 2006); Sarah J Summers, *Fair Trials: The European Criminal Procedural Tradition and the European Court of Human Rights* (Hart Publishing, 2007); Ben Emmerson, Andrew Ashworth and Alison Macdonald, *Human Rights and Criminal Justice*, 3rd edn (Sweet & Maxwell, 2012).

[8] See, eg, Pieter van Dijk and GJH van Hoof, *Theory and Practice of the European Convention on Human Rights*, 4th edn (Intersentia, 2006); Harris, O'Boyle and Warbrick, *Law of the European Convention on Human Rights* (n 4 above); R Clayton and H Tomlinson (eds), *The Law of Human Rights*, 2nd edn (Oxford University Press, 2009); Clare Ovey and Robin White, *Jacobs and White: The European Convention on Human Rights*, 4th edn (Oxford University Press, 2006); Steven Greer, *The European Convention on Human Rights: Achievements, Problems and Prospects*, 2nd edn (Cambridge University Press, 2006); C Gearty, *Principles of Human Rights Adjudication* (Oxford University Press, 2004); Kai Möller, *The Global Model of Constitutional Rights* (Hart Publishing, 2012).

against the use of such an analysis. In this way this book acts as a complementary volume to the more traditional reference works.

Second, the book is critical of the Court. It challenges suggestions that 'the judgments of the Court are exceptionally well reasoned'[9] and that the Court 'has developed an impressive case law' on Article 6.[10] Indeed, my central argument in this book is that the Article 6 criminal fair trial case law of the European Court is incoherent, under-theorised, and poorly explained. The book establishes that there are inconsistencies in the way that the Court approaches issues, and that the Court often does not acknowledge the significant complexity inherent in its own judgments. Later in this Introduction, this central argument is outlined further.

Third, this is a doctrinal book rooted in the detail of the European Court's case law. It focuses almost exclusively on the Court's case law, and is the result of an extensive survey of Article 6 criminal cases identified through the Court's HUDOC database system;[11] readers will find a short note summarising the methodology used in conducting this survey before the book's introduction. Well over 1,000 cases were reviewed in preparing the book, and some 500 are cited in its text. This broad research base allows the book to describe and critique the European Court's case law in innovative ways, and to identify a greater range of inconsistencies than that which has previously been described. It should be acknowledged, however, that this focus on the European Court's case law means that the book does not consider the ways in which domestic courts have applied Article 6, or the ways in which domestic courts apply European Court case law. The targeted focus on the case law itself also means that the book does not attempt to identify political or sociological explanations for the approaches taken by the European Court: there is considerable analysis and debate elsewhere in the scholarly and policy literature on the theoretical and institutional functioning of the Court,[12] and on the Court's

[9] Francois Ost, 'The Original Canons of Interpretation of the European Court of Human Rights' in Mireille Delmas-Marty and Christine Chodkiewicz (eds), *The European Convention for the Protection of Human Rights: International Protection Versus National Restrictions* (Martinus Nijhoff, 1992) 284.

[10] Paul Lemmens, 'The Right to a Fair Trial and its Multiple Manifestations' in E Brems and J Gerards (eds), *Shaping Rights in the ECHR* (Cambridge University Press, 2013) para 2.3.4.

[11] HUDOC is accessible at http://cmiskp.echr.coe.int/tkp197/search.asp?skin=hudoc-en. The book focuses on European Court decisions rather than Commission decisions or the Committee of Ministers' practice, but reference to Commission decisions is made wherever relevant. Similarly, the focus is on Article 6 criminal fair trial rights decisions, but reference is made to civil Article 6 cases and other European Convention cases where such reference is necessary in order to understand the criminal Article 6 cases.

[12] See, as some examples, Marie-Benedicte Dembour, '"Finishing Off" Cases: the Radical Solution to the Problem of the Expanding European Court of Human Rights Caseload' [2002] *EHRLR* 604; M-B Dembour and M Krzyzanowska-Mierzewska, 'Ten Years On: The Voluminous and Interesting Polish Case Law' [2004] *EHRLR* 517; S Greer and L Wildhaber, 'Reflections of a Former President of the European Court of Human Rights' [2010] *EHRLR* 165; Robin White, *Judgments in the Strasbourg Court: Some Reflections*, SSRN Working Paper Series (2009); A Lester, 'The European Court of Human Rights after 50 Years' [2009] EHRLR 461; C Gearty, *Civil Liberties* (Oxford University Press, 2007); C Gearty, 'The European Court of Human Rights and the Protection of Civil Liberties: An Overview' (1993) 52 *Cambridge Law Journal* 89; Gearty, *Principles of Human Rights Adjudication* (n 8 above) 33–114; K Möller; R White and I Boussiakou, 'Separate Opinions in the European Court of Human Rights' (2009) 9(1) *Human Rights Law Review* 37; G Letsas, *Judge Rozakis's Separate Opinions and the Strasbourg Dilemma*, SSRN Working Paper Series (2011); K Dzehtsiarou, *Consensus from Within the Palace Walls*,

relationship with the courts of Council of Europe states.[13] Such debates are of great interest, but they are beyond the limits of this book. This book's focus is, instead, on the detail of the case law.

Fourth, to the extent that the book offers a normative argument, it may be broadly described as an argument that the Court should adopt a rejuvenated approach to Article 6 criminal cases. As will be further explained in greater detail in the next section of this Introduction, this book calls for an approach that is more consistent, more coherent, and better explained. Where that is not possible or desirable, I argue for greater and plainer explanation of why. At the conclusion of each of the parts of this book I offer some more specific normative recommendations as examples of ways in which the broader normative argument might begin to be implemented by the European Court. It is hoped that these constructive suggestions, taken together with the criticisms made throughout the book, will provide foundations for further descriptive and normative work by scholars, by those preparing arguments in Article 6 litigation, and by the Court. But even if the European Court prefers not to adopt these *specific* arguments, it is hoped that recognition of the more *general* concerns about coherence and predictability will produce an Article 6 case law that is better able to provide a sense of guidance.

It is worth emphasising at the outset that this book does not make a normative argument that the European Court should implement or seek out a *broader, more expansive* protection of criminal fair trial rights. Equally, it does not make a normative argument that the Court should implement or seek out a *narrower or more restrictive* approach to criminal fair trial rights. Instead, this book considers the degree to which the European Court's case law in these areas provides citizens, lawyers, and officials with a consistent, coherent, and theorised approach to the law.

University College Dublin Working Papers in Law, Criminology and Socio-Legal Studies Paper 40/2010; Erik Voeten, 'The Impartiality of International Judges: Evidence from the European Court of Human Rights' (2008) 102(4) *American Political Science Review* 417; Yonatan Lupu and Erik Voeten, 'Precedent in International Courts: A Network Analysis of Case Citations by the European Court of Human Rights' (2011) *British Journal of Political Science* 1; B Cali, 'The Purposes of the European Human Rights System: One or Many?' [2008] *EHRLR* 299.

[13] See, as some examples, N Bratza, 'The Relationship between the UK Courts and Strasbourg' [2011] *EHRLR* 505; CC Murphy, *Human Rights Law and the Challenges of Explicit Judicial Dialogue*, Jean Monnet Working Paper No 10/2012; M Lasser, *Judicial Transformations: the Rights Revolution in the Courts of Europe* (Oxford University Press, 2009) 90–115; Gearty, *Principles of Human Rights Adjudication* (n 8 above); C Gearty, 'The Human Rights Act: an Academic Sceptic Changes his Mind but not his Heart' [2010] *EHRLR* 582; A Lester, 'The ECtHR and the HRA: British Concerns' (2012) 17 *Judicial Review* 1; Lord Hoffman, 'The Universality of Human Rights' (Judicial Studies Board Annual Lecture, 19 March 2009); Lord Neuberger, 'The British and Europe' (Cambridge Freshfields Annual Law Lecture, 12 February 2014); C Gearty, *Can Human Rights Survive?* (Cambridge University Press, 2006); M Pinto-Duschinsky, *Bringing Rights Back Home* (Policy Exchange, 2011); J Sumption QC, 'Judicial and Political Decision-Making: the Uncertain Boundary' (FA Mann Lecture, 8 November 2011); Mark Coen, '"With Cat-like Tread": Jury Trial and the European Court of Human Rights' (2014) Human Rights Law Review (Advance Access) 1, 21–25; G Clayton and H Wray, 'Editorial: Othman v United Kingdom (2012)' (2012) 26 *Journal of Immigration, Asylum and Nationality Law* 2; S Briant, 'Dialogue, Diplomacy and Defiance: Prisoners' Voting Rights at Home and in Strasbourg' [2011] *EHRLR* 243.

1.2 Framing the Measuring Stick Against which the European Court's Case Law will be Tested

This book is critical of the European Court's treatment of Article 6 criminal fair trial cases. In order to structure that criticism, a measuring stick is needed. As is foreshadowed above, the measuring stick in this book is: to what extent does the Court's case law provide a clear, stable, predictable, consistent and understandable sense of the current state of European human rights law? To what extent does the case law provide citizens, lawyers and officials with adequate guidance as to their position under the law?

This book does not aspire to be a work of legal theory or of philosophy, but it draws support for these criteria from the accounts that a number of legal philosophers have provided of the indicia of the rule of law. Any reference to 'the rule of law' inevitably conjures up a variety of politically- and legally-charged meanings.[14] It is, as Jennings wrote, 'apt to be rather an unruly horse'.[15] This book does not attempt to tame the horse, but instead draws upon formalist accounts of the rule of law to explain the measuring stick against which the European Court's case law is to be assessed.[16] If one looks at the work of Joseph Raz and Lon Fuller, for example, one can identify factors which 'can be derived from the basic idea of the rule of law'[17] or which are 'distinct standards by which excellence in legality may be tested'.[18] Importantly for present purposes, both Raz and Fuller argue that law should be prospective, open, clear, and relatively stable.[19] Indeed, as Raz explains, law '*must be capable of guiding the behaviour of its subjects*. It must be such that they can find out what it is and act on it'.[20] Of course, such insights are not those of Raz and Fuller alone. Hayek, for example, highlighted the importance of 'rules fixed and announced beforehand':

[14] The rule of law is also, of course, an idea inherent in the fair trial, and has been used by the European Court in several cases: see, eg, Gearty, *Principles of Human Rights Adjudication* (n 8 above) 68 *et seq*; Steve Foster, *Human Rights and Civil Liberties*, 2nd edn (Pearson Education, 2008) 54, citing *Thynne, Wilson and Gunnell v United Kingdom* (App 11787/85) (1990) 13 EHRR 666; *T and V v United Kingdom* (App 24724/94; 24888/94) (2000) 30 EHRR 121; and *Stafford v United Kingdom* (App 46295/99) (2002) 35 EHRR 32. It is also 'a core concept in international human rights instruments jurisprudence': ME Badar, 'Basic Principles Governing Limitations on Individual Rights, and Freedoms in Human Rights Instruments' (2003) 7 *International Journal of Human Rights* 63, 65.

[15] Ivor Jennings, *The Law and the Constitution*, 5th edn (University of London Press, 1959) 60.

[16] The reference to 'formalist' accounts is made while acknowledging that it conceals some complexity; see B Tamanaha, *On the Rule of Law* (Cambridge University Press, 2004) 92; NW Barber, 'Must Legalistic Conceptions of the Rule of Law have a Social Dimension?' (2004) 17 *Ratio Juris* 474.

[17] Joseph Raz, *The Authority of Law: Essays on Law and Morality* (Clarendon Press, 2002) 214.

[18] Lon Fuller, *The Morality of Law* (Yale University Press, 1964) 42.

[19] Raz, *The Authority of Law* (n 17 above) 214; Fuller, *The Morality of Law* (n 18 above) 49–65, 79. On the similarities, and differences, between Fuller and Raz, see Kristen Rundle, *Forms Liberate: Reclaiming the Jurisprudence of Lon L Fuller* (Hart Publishing, 2012) 148–54; Tamanaha, *On the Rule of Law* (n 16 above) 93–94. Further on desiderata of this sort, see also T Bingham, *The Rule of Law* (Penguin, 2011).

[20] Raz, *The Authority of Law* (n 17 above) 214 (emphasis in original).

> [G]overnment in all its action is bound by *rules fixed* and *announced beforehand* – rules which make it *possible to foresee* with fair certainty how the authority will use its coercive powers in given circumstances, and to plan one's individual affairs on the basis of this knowledge.[21]

It is not the aim of this book to provide an exhaustive account of different views on the rule of law or the consequences of non-compliance with those views, or to deal with the complexities involved in that area of legal philosophy. Instead, these statements provide a useful tool with which to analyse the case law of the European Court, and with which to consider the extent to which the European Court's case law is capable of providing guidance and reasonable certainty as to the state of the law.

This account of a rule of law measuring stick may be qualified and clarified in five ways. First, one can acknowledge that no legal system can be perfect,[22] but that, as Endicott argues, these rule of law factors are ideals to aspire to, even if they cannot be attained.[23] Second, and as a related point, we can consider the notion of 'guidance' more closely. In assessing the extent to which the European Court's case law is capable of providing guidance, this book's standards are not overly demanding: as Endicott puts it, we are concerned with the extent to which the case law may be used 'as a guide', and not the extent to which the case law 'dictate[s] an outcome in every possible case'.[24] As will become apparent, the book argues that the case law lacks these characteristics in a number of crucial respects, and that this undermines its ability to provide the sort of guidance that Endicott describes.

Third, the accounts of the rule of law outlined above may be thought to have special application in the human rights context. Indeed, in the human rights context there can be said to be an 'onus of justification' on 'the judiciary and all public authorities to justify limitations of human rights'; the rule of law requires that limitations on rights comply with principles of legality and be 'accessible, certain, and foreseeable'.[25] Liora Lazarus argues that this onus of justification requires that

> judicial reasoning around human rights is transparent, consistent and clear. If citizens are to engage fully and critically with rights reasoning – be it legislative, executive or judicial – they must at the very least know why rights are asserted or limited.[26]

[21] Friedrich Hayek, *The Road to Serfdom* (Routledge Classics, 2001) 75–76 (emphasis added).

[22] Raz, *The Authority of Law* (n 17 above) 222; Fuller, *The Morality of Law* (n 18 above) 41–42.

[23] Timothy Endicott, 'The Impossibility of the Rule of Law' (1999) 19 *Oxford Journal of Legal Studies* 1.

[24] ibid 18.

[25] L Lazarus, 'Conceptions of Liberty Deprivation' (2006) 69 *Modern Law Review* 738, 740–41, drawing on H Mountfield, 'The Concept of a Lawful Interference with Fundamental Rights' in J Jowell and J Cooper (eds), *Understanding Human Rights Principles* (Hart Publishing, 2001).

[26] L Lazarus, 'Mapping the Right to Security' in B Goold and L Lazarus (eds), *Security and Human Rights*, 2nd edn (Hart Publishing, 2007) 326. See also Etienne Mureinik, 'A Bridge to Where? Introducing the Interim Bill of Rights' (1994) 10 *South African Journal on Human Rights* 31, 32 ('a culture in which every exercise of power is expected to be justified'); Andrew Legg, *The Margin of Appreciation in International Human Rights Law* (Oxford University Press, 2012) 4.

Thus, if the onus of justification is seen as a particular manifestation of the desiderata of the rule of law, and is taken together with the more general statements about the rule of law outlined earlier, a clear picture is formed of what is required of the European Court's case law: reasoning that is transparent, consistent, clear, coherent, and capable of providing guidance.

Fourth, in terms of the particular importance of coherence, a point on which it will be argued that the European Court's case law falls down all too often, there is considerable philosophical and theoretical scholarship.[27] Without summarising that scholarship here, it may be emphasised that my real concern is with what Raz describes as 'local coherence', what Levenbook describes as 'area-specific' coherence, and what Tobin terms 'internal system coherence'.[28] That is to say, the concern is with the application of a test of coherence to 'a subset, to a group of legal standards and decisions constituting a branch of law' rather than any more 'global' sense of coherence.[29] The goal of local coherence is one that 'judges with limitations of knowledge and time can be expected to achieve'.[30] Raz also makes the point that while the application of local coherence can overlap with a doctrine of *stare decisis*, that should not disguise the fact that a concern for coherence is applicable 'even in countries which do not have a formal doctrine of precedent'.[31]

Fifth, and related to the previous point, it must be emphasised that there is no part of the argument in this book that relies on common law principles of *stare decisis*. Indeed, the European Court does not operate under any binding system of precedent.[32] Nonetheless, as the Court said in *Stafford v United Kingdom* (and in many cases subsequently):

> While the Court is not formally bound to follow any of its previous judgments, it is in the interests of legal certainty, foreseeability and equality before the law that it should not depart, without cogent reason, from precedents laid down in previous cases.[33]

[27] See, as examples, Joseph Raz, 'The Relevance of Coherence' in Joseph Raz (ed), *Ethics in the Public Domain: Essays in the Morality of Law and Politics* (Clarendon Press, 1995); BB Levenbook, 'The Role of Coherence in Legal Reasoning' (1984) 3 *Law and Philosophy* 355; Gearty, *Principles of Human Rights Adjudication* (n 8 above) 174; L Moral Soriano, 'A Modest Notion of Coherence in Legal Reasoning: a Model for the ECJ' (2003) 16 *Ratio Juris* 296; J Tobin, 'Seeking to Persuade: a Constructive Approach to Human Rights Treaty Interpretation' (2010) *Harvard HR Journal* 1.

[28] See Raz, 'The Relevance of Coherence' (n 27 above) 317–19; Levenbook, 'The Role of Coherence in Legal Reasoning' (n 27 above) 371; Tobin, 'Seeking to Persuade' (n 27 above) 37.

[29] Levenbook, 'The Role of Coherence in Legal Reasoning' (n 27 above) 371; Raz, 'The Relevance of Coherence' (n 27 above); cf Dworkin on 'local priority': R Dworkin, *Law's Empire* (Hart Publishing, 1998) 250–54.

[30] Levenbook, 'The Role of Coherence in Legal Reasoning' (n 27 above) 371.

[31] Raz, 'The Relevance of Coherence' (n 27 above) 318.

[32] A McHarg, 'Reconciling Human Rights and the Public Interest: Conceptual Problems and Doctrinal Uncertainty in the Jurisprudence of the European Court of Human Rights' (1999) 62 Modern Law Review 671, 673; Gearty, *Principles of Human Rights Adjudication* (n 8 above) 197, 200; A Mowbray, 'An Examination of the European Court of Human Rights' Approach to Overruling its Previous Case Law' (2009) 9 *Human Rights Law Review* 179, 180–87; Paul Roberts, 'Does Article 6 of the European Convention on Human Rights Require Reasoned Verdicts in Criminal Trials?' (2011) *Human Rights Law Review* 1. cf Lupu and Voeten, 'Precedent in International Courts' (n 12 above).

[33] *Stafford v United Kingdom* (n 14 above) para 68. See, eg, also *Micallef v Malta* (App 17056/06) (15 October 2009) para 81; *Bayatyan v Armenia* (App 23459/03) (2012) 54 EHRR 15, para 98; *Scoppola v*

Similarly, as Roberts put it, even if the Court does not operate under any 'strict doctrine of precedent', that does not discount

> the inherent (pre-judicial) rationality of treating like cases alike, and different cases differently, or the impact of collegiate judicial culture and institutional incentives, all of which promote consistency in decision-making.[34]

The point of this clarification is this: the book *does* focus on the Court's case law, and makes arguments on the lack of coherence, consistency, and predictability in that case law. To adapt Gearty's phrase, the book makes arguments exploring the Court's 'more relaxed approach to the challenge of internal consistency'.[35] Those arguments are not, however, grounded in any common law notion of *stare decisis.*

There are, of course, many alternative ways in which one might assess the case law of a court. A rule of law measuring stick is by no means the only choice one could make in writing a book such as this. For example, one might ask, instead, whether the body of case law does a good job of pursuing broader European geopolitical goals, or whether the case law tends to succeed at doing justice in the individual case.[36] An assessment of the Article 6 case law against those benchmarks might well provide fertile ground for future research by lawyers, sociologists, and political scientists. In this book, however, the focus is on the rule of law, a choice made not least because of the central importance of the rule of law to law itself. As Raz puts it:

> It is of the essence of law to guide behaviour through rules and courts in charge of their application. Therefore, the rule of law is the specific excellence of the law.[37]

The rule of law is, additionally, a standard to which the European Court itself, in a variety of contexts, has held itself.[38] Of course, the rule of law also provides a framework which will be of considerable interest, and it is hoped practical utility, to practitioners and scholars seeking to make sense of the European Court's corpus of case law and to apply it to the case in front of them.

And so, the question posed by this book is this: to what extent does the European Court's criminal fair trial case law measure up against the book's measuring stick? To what extent is the case law consistent, predictable, locally

Italy (No 3) (App 126/05) (2013) 56 EHRR 19, para 94. This statement is often qualified by an acknowledgment of the Court's 'evolutive' approach to interpretation, considered in part A.

[34] Roberts, 'Does Article 6 of the European Convention on Human Rights Require Reasoned Verdicts in Criminal Trials?' (n 32 above) 10–11.

[35] Gearty, *Principles of Human Rights Adjudication* (n 8 above) 179.

[36] Some authors may, of course, regard broader considerations such as these as forming part of a more substantive conception of the rule of law. See, eg, the discussion in Tamanaha, *On the Rule of Law* (n 16 above) 102–13. Such a substantive conception is not adopted for the purposes of this book.

[37] Raz, *The Authority of Law* (n 17 above) 225.

[38] See, eg, *Malone v United Kingdom* (App 8691/79) (1985) 7 EHRR 14; *Khan v United Kingdom* (App 35394/97) (2001) 31 EHRR 45; *Liberty and others v United Kingdom* (App 58243/00) (2009) 48 EHRR 1; *Thynne, Wilson and Gunnell v United Kingdom* (n 14 above); *T and V v United Kingdom* (n 14 above); and *Stafford v United Kingdom* (n 14 above).

coherent, and capable of acting as a guide to citizens, lawyers, officials, and judges? As will be seen in the next section, and throughout this book, the argument made here is that the case law does not measure up well.

1.3 Outlining the Structure of the Book and How the Argument is Developed

Having described the scope of the argument, and having delineated some theoretical foundations for the measuring stick that will be used to assess the Court's case law, I turn now to sketching the course of the argument in this book. In this subsection I first outline the thematic cross-cutting issues that are addressed in the book, and then the broad arguments that run through these thematic issues.

The book is divided into two sections. In section I, there are four principal parts, each dealing with a cross-cutting theme that is of relevance to all of the various Article 6 component rights. The parts are, of course, interrelated. Part A is foundational, and begins the book by considering the interpretative techniques used by the European Court in Article 6 criminal cases. It assesses a variety of techniques deployed by the Court, including what will be described as the 'democratic catchphrase', and analyses the extent to which the Court has made clear the content of each of those techniques and the relationship between them. In part B, the focus is on how the Court describes its own role in Article 6 criminal fair trial cases. Part B critiques various manifestations of the ostensibly deferential approach of the Court against the book's measuring stick. It also includes extensive analysis of the Court's 'fourth instance doctrine', ultimately arguing that the doctrine is riddled with exceptions in a way that significantly undermines its coherence and utility. The complexity of the internal structure of Article 6 is the focus of part C, as the book assesses a number of ways in which the European Court has explained the relationships between the various component provisions and rights that make up Article 6, and demonstrates significant incoherence in this area of law. The examination of the Court's views on the internal dynamics of Article 6 continues in part D, which looks at the Court's implied rights jurisprudence. After briefly outlining the implied rights, part D focuses on assessing the various foundations on which the Court has grounded the implied rights, and argues that its treatment of those foundations fails to meet the rule of law and legality standards.

Section II contains one part, part E, which deals with the Court's approach to assessing alleged infringements or violations of Article 6. Part E is the largest of the book's five parts and builds on the work done in parts A–D to consolidate many of the book's core arguments. It begins by setting out what I describe as 'the puzzle of Article 6': the complexity created by uncertainty over how to assess Article 6 violations. It then considers a number of tools used by the Court in this context: the assessment of the 'proceedings as a whole'; the use of counterbalancing and defect curing; the notion that some infringements render proceedings irretrievably unfair; and the Court's 'sole or decisive' test in the context of evidence, and argues that these tools do not measure up favourably against the standards set out above. As I will show, not only do the tools demonstrate radical uncertainty within themselves, but they also form part of an overall system that is incoherent. Finally, part E considers the Court's willingness (or reluctance) to engage in 'attempts to limit Article 6 rights by reference to the community interest'.[39] This final section of part E examines the inconsistencies plaguing the Court's case law and the use of tools such as proportionality reasoning and references to 'the very essence of the right'.

In terms of the arguments that run through these cross-cutting thematic areas, there are two broad classes of argument that are used to substantiate the book's central thesis. The first relates to the Court's explanation of the details of how individual analytical approaches or interpretative tools work, what their content is, and what their limits are. The individual tools and approaches are often under-theorised, opaque, and poorly explained. As a result, I argue, they are insufficient to provide guidance of the sort outlined above. It is difficult to imagine how a potential applicant might begin to make sense of this case law.

Further, and in the alternative, is the second broad class of argument. If the first of the broad arguments related to the *inner workings* of each of the various analytical approaches and tools, the second broad argument relates to the Court's explanations of how those tools and approaches *relate to one another*. Here, I argue that the Court often deploys a variety of inconsistent approaches and tools, and does so without acknowledging or attempting to reconcile the inconsistency. As such, I will demonstrate, the Court provides insufficient guidance to those who seek predictability, consistency, and transparency from its judgments with respect to the various cross-cutting themes. Thus, for example, there is significant uncertainty of this sort as to the Court's views on the internal structure of Article 6 (part C) or as to the Court's approach to when the public interest may be taken into account in assessing a violation of Article 6 (part E). The Court's case law, as described in this book, provides the Court with what I might term *irrational flexibility*: the ability to apply different tests or approaches without explaining why one test or approach is appropriate in one situation but not in another. It should be emphasised here that the book accepts that the European Court *could* elect to adopt a highly nuanced series of analytical approaches or interpretative tools, each carefully chosen and adapted to the context of a particular right or a particular factual matrix; or that the Court *could* elect to adopt and explain a nuanced approach on the basis of its position as an arbiter of the philosophical and theoretical place of human rights in European democracy. What the book demonstrates, however, is that in key respects the Court has failed to make and explain any such choice, and that it has failed to explain or acknowledge the inconsistencies where they exist.

[39] Andrew C Stumer, *The Presumption of Innocence* (Hart Publishing, 2010) 110.

These two arguments manifest themselves in different ways in the book's various parts. But taken together, and across the sum of these parts, they demonstrate significant incoherence and uncertainty in the European Court's Article 6 criminal fair trial rights case law.

SECTION I

A

Interpreting Article 6

Stavros wrote that the 'interpretation of Article 6 has proved from the outset a very difficult task for the European Convention organs'.[1] In a sense, this book is entirely about the European Court's approach to interpreting Article 6. This part, however, is more focused: here, I consider the general statements the Court has made in terms of identifying the principles that guide its interpretation of Article 6, what practices it has appeared to employ in its interpretation, and the interpretative importance that the Court places on the role of Article 6 in a democratic society. Part A thus provides a preliminary foundation for the book's analysis of how the European Court approaches Article 6 in criminal cases. It is intimately connected to, and should be read with, parts B to E.

It has been said that the Court has chosen to view 'the task of interpretation as a single complex operation', and as a task for which it is inappropriate to organise interpretative tools into a hierarchy.[2] This may be the case. But, I will argue, this is no excuse for incoherence. Moreover, as Greer notes, this 'unstructured approach' has been the subject of little rigorous discussion.[3] While authors such as Greer have done valuable general theoretical work on interpretative approaches under the Convention, in this part the focus is on Article 6 criminal cases, and on the detail of those cases. It makes two broad arguments.

First, this part argues that while the European Court has used a variety of interpretative techniques and tools in Article 6 cases, it has rarely explained *why* it uses a particular technique or tool in a particular case or type of case. This lack of explanation of why one technique is preferred over another in some cases, but not others, generates uncertainty. Second, this part argues that when one focuses in on each of the interpretative techniques or tools in isolation, the jurisprudence explaining the individual techniques is also marked by considerable uncertainty. As will be seen in this part and subsequent parts, this uncertainty undermines the transparency and predictability of the Court's decisions.

[1] Stephanos Stavros, *The Guarantees for Accused Persons under Article 6 of the European Convention on Human Rights* (Martinus Nijhoff, 1993) 327.

[2] See Clare Ovey and Robin White, *Jacobs and White: The European Convention on Human Rights*, 4th edn (Oxford University Press, 2006) 40; Steven Greer, *The European Convention on Human Rights: Achievements, Problems and Prospects*, 2nd edn (Cambridge University Press, 2006) 194; Francois Ost, 'The Original Canons of Interpretation of the European Court of Human Rights' in Mireille Delmas-Marty and Christine Chodkiewicz (eds), *The European Convention for the Protection of Human Rights: International Protection Versus National Restrictions* (Martinus Nijhoff, 1992) 285.

[3] Greer, *The European Convention on Human Rights* (n 2 above) 194.

A.1 The European Court Sometimes Seeks Guidance from the Vienna Convention in Interpreting Article 6

While this book does not focus on issues of public international law, nor on the law of treaty interpretation in general, in this section I briefly consider the ways in which the law of treaties has shaped the European Court's interpretative approach. More detailed analysis of treaty law relevant to the Convention can be found elsewhere.[4]

The Convention predates the Vienna Convention on the Law of Treaties ('the Vienna Convention').[5] The European Convention is, moreover, considered to be 'a treaty of a special kind',[6] a 'lawmaking treaty',[7] and one that favours individuals' rights rather than state sovereignty.[8] Notwithstanding these factors, the position has been, since *Golder* at least, that the European Court considers its interpretative approach to be guided by the Vienna Convention:

> The Court . . . should be guided by Articles 31 to 33 of the Vienna Convention . . . [which] enunciate in essence generally accepted principles of international law.[9]

Shortly after *Golder*, in *Luedicke, Belkacem and Koc*, the European Court considered the interpretation of Article 6:

> For the purposes of interpreting Article 6(3)(e), the Court will be guided . . . by Articles 31 to 33 of the Vienna Convention . . . In order to decide the issue arising in the present proceedings, the Court will therefore seek to ascertain 'the ordinary meaning to be

[4] R Clayton and H Tomlinson (eds), *The Law of Human Rights*, 2nd edn (Oxford University Press, 2009) 302–8; Ovey and White, *Jacobs and White* (n 2 above) 38–40; Franz Matscher, 'Methods of Interpretation of the Convention' in R Macdonald, F Matscher and H Petzold (eds), *The European System for the Protection of Human Rights* (Martinus Nijhoff, 1993) 65–68.

[5] Vienna Convention on the Law of Treaties 1969, 1155 UNTS 33 (adopted 23 May 1969, entered into force 27 January 1980). See *Golder v United Kingdom* (App 4451/70) (1979–80) 1 EHRR 524, paras29–30.

[6] Clayton and Tomlinson, *The Law of Human Rights* (n 4 above) 307. See J Tobin, 'Seeking to Persuade: A Constructive Approach to Human Rights Treaty Interpretation' (2010) *Harvard HR Journal* 1, 20.

[7] *Golder v United Kingdom* (n 5 above) para 36. See Pieter van Dijk and GJH van Hoof, *Theory and Practice of the European Convention on Human Rights*, 4th edn (Intersentia, 2006) 557–58; Jonas Christoffersen, *Fair Balance: Proportionality, Subsidiarity and Primarity in the ECHR* (Martinus Nijhoff, 2009) 50–51.

[8] See R Bernhardt, 'Thoughts on the Interpretation of Human-Rights Treaties' in Franz Matscher (ed), *Protecting Human Rights: The European Dimension*, 2nd edn (Carl Heymanns Verlag KG, 1990) 70–71.

[9] *Golder v United Kingdom* (n 5 above) para 29. See Ost, 'The Original Canons of Interpretation of the European Court of Human Rights' (n 2 above) 288; Ben Emmerson, Andrew Ashworth and Alison Macdonald, *Human Rights and Criminal Justice*, 3rd edn (Sweet & Maxwell, 2012) 79–80; Clayton and Tomlinson, *The Law of Human Rights* (n 4 above) 302–8; Ovey and White, *Jacobs and White* (n 2 above) 38–40; Heribert Golsong, 'Interpreting the European Convention on Human Rights Beyond the Confines of the Vienna Convention' in R Macdonald, F Matscher and H Petzold (eds), *The European System for the Protection of Human Rights* (Martinus Nijhoff, 1993) 147–51; Julian Arato, 'Constitutional Transformation in the ECtHR: Strasbourg's Expansive Recourse to External Rules of International Law' (2012) 37(2) *Brooklyn Journal of International Law* 304.

> given to the terms' of Article 6(3)(e) 'in their context and in the light of its object and purpose' (Art. 31(1) of the Vienna Convention).[10]

As will be seen, the Court tends to focus, ostensibly at least, on ascertaining an Article 6 provision's 'object and purpose'; much more rarely does the Court seek to identify the 'ordinary meaning' of Article 6 terms.

The *Golder* approach was also referred to in *Deumeland v Germany*[11] and in *Loizidou v Turkey*, in which the Court 'recalled'

> that the Convention must be interpreted in the light of the rules of interpretation set out in the Vienna Convention . . . In the Court's view, the principles underlying the [European] Convention cannot be interpreted and applied in a vacuum. Mindful of the Convention's special character as a human rights treaty, it must also take into account any relevant rules of international law when deciding on disputes concerning its jurisdiction.[12]

It should be noted that it was unclear in *Loizidou*, and subsequently, what effect being 'mindful' of this 'special character' was intended to have on the Court's interpretative approach.

The European Court has also used *Golder* as one of the foundations for its 'evolutive' interpretative approach to Article 6.[13] One example of this approach is evident in the concurring opinion of Judge Morenilla in *Hornsby v Greece*:

> the opinion of the majority is consistent with our case-law, which interprets [Article 6(1)] in accordance with the principles established in its Preamble and in Article 3 of the Vienna Convention . . . that is to say in a teleological, autonomous and evolutive manner, adapted to social needs.[14]

It is now accepted orthodoxy that the European Court adopts a dynamic, living instrument approach to interpretation of the Convention.[15]

[10] *Luedicke, Belkacem and Koc v Germany* (App 6210/73) (1979–80) 2 EHRR 149, para. 39, citing *Golder v United Kingdom* (n 5 above) para 29, and quoting from Art 31(1) of the Vienna Convention. This approach was applied in *Luedicke*, para 46, considered in Stavros, 342–43; Stefan Trechsel, *Human Rights in Criminal Proceedings* (Oxford University Press, 2006) 331–32.

[11] *Deumeland v Germany* (App 9384/81) (1986) 8 EHRR 448, para 12.

[12] *Loizidou v Turkey* (App 15318/89) (1997) 23 EHRR 513, para 43. Similar passages have appeared in cases including *Fogarty v United Kingdom* (App 37112/97) (2002) 34 EHRR 12, para 35; *McElhinney v Ireland* (App 31253/96) (2002) 34 EHRR 13, para 36; *Al-Adsani v United Kingdom* (App 35763/97) (2002) 34 EHRR 11, para 55. See also Greer, *The European Convention on Human Rights* (n 2 above) 195; van Dijk and van Hoof, *Theory and Practice of the European Convention on Human Rights* (n 7 above) 517, 571.

[13] JG Merrills, *The Development of International Law by the European Court of Human Rights*, 2nd edn (Manchester University Press, 1995) 69.

[14] *Hornsby v Greece* (App 18357/91) (1997) 24 EHRR 250, para 12 of the Concurring Opinion of Judge Morenilla; cf *Feldbrugge v Netherlands* (App 8562/79) (1986) 8 EHRR 425, para 12 of Joint Dissenting Opinion of Judges Ryssdal, Bindschedler-Robert, Lagergren, Matscher, Sir Vincent Evans, Bernhardt and Gersing. See van Dijk and van Hoof, *Theory and Practice of the European Convention on Human Rights* (n 7 above) 581.

[15] See, eg, E Brems, *Human Rights: Universality and Diversity* (Martinus Nijhoff, 2001) 396–97; Christoffersen, *Fair Balance* (n 7 above) 54–55; Emmerson, Ashworth and Macdonald, *Human Rights and Criminal Justice* (n 9 above) 88–94; Ovey and White, *Jacobs and White* (n 2 above) 46–47; Clayton and Tomlinson, *The Law of Human Rights* (n 4 above) 304, 308–12; G Letsas, 'The ECHR as Living

Article 32 of the Vienna Convention allows for *travaux préparatoires* to be consulted as a supplementary means of interpretation. A detailed study of the Article 6 *travaux* is not possible within the limitations of this book.[16] For present purposes, it suffices to note that the *travaux* provide only limited guidance on Article 6: 'no very specific and exact ideas on the scope of [Article 6] emerge from the *travaux*'.[17] That being said, the *travaux* do indicate considerable uncertainty on the part of the drafters as to the role of the European Court, and particularly as to the extent to which it would be prevented from assuming the powers of a supranational appellate court.[18] The drafters appeared to conclude that the Court's purview would be limited to a narrow band of cases,[19] and that its powers would be limited.[20] Uncertainty about the role of the European Court will be a theme that is returned to in part B.

Taking into account the limited guidance provided by the *travaux*, and the European Court's evolutive approach, it is perhaps unsurprising that the Court rarely expressly relies on the *travaux* in interpreting Article 6.[21] The cases in which

Instrument: Its Meaning and Legitimacy' in A Follesdal, B Peters and G Ulfstein (eds), *Constituting Europe* (Cambridge University Press, 2013); Marie-Benedicte Dembour, *Who Believes in Human Rights?* (Cambridge University Press, 2006) 21, 170–76; A Mowbray, 'An Examination of the European Court of Human Rights' Approach to Overruling its Previous Case Law' (2009) 9 *Human Rights Law Review* 179, 193–94; Greer, *The European Convention on Human Rights* (n 2 above) 214; Arato, 'Constitutional Transformation in the ECtHR' (n 9 above); Matscher, 'Methods of Interpretation of the Convention' (n 4 above) 68–70; Ost, 'The Original Canons of Interpretation of the European Court of Human Rights' (n 2 above) 302–3; Paul Mahoney, 'Judicial Activism and Judicial Restraint in the ECHR' (1990) 11 *Human Rights Law Journal* 57, 61–68; Lord Hoffman, 'The Universality of Human Rights' (Judicial Studies Board Annual Lecture, 19 March 2009) para 35; Aoife Daly, 'The Right of Children to be Heard in Civil Proceedings and the Emerging Law of the ECHR' (2010) *International Journal of Human Rights* 1. But cf Bernhardt, 'Thoughts on the Interpretation of Human-Rights Treaties' (n 8 above) 70; and, as noted by Christoffersen, the warning in Joint Dissenting Opinion of Judges Wildhaber, Costa, Lorenzen, Kovler and Jebens in *Hirst v United Kingdom (No 2)* (Grand Chamber) (App 74025/01) (2006) 42 EHRR 41, para 6. The first reference to a 'living instrument' approach in the Court's case law came in *Tyrer*, an Art 3 case: *Tyrer v United Kingdom* (App 5856/72) (1979–80) 2 EHRR 1, para 31; see also *Dudgeon v United Kingdom* (App 7525/76) (1981) 4 EHRR 149, para 60; *Marckx v Belgium* (App 6833/74) (1979–80) 2 EHRR 330, para 41. See, on *Marckx*, Heribert Golsong, 'The European Court of Human Rights and the National Law-maker' in Franz Matscher (ed), *Protecting Human Rights: The European Dimension*, 2nd edn (Carl Heymanns Verlag KG, 1990) 242–43.

16 Further discussion of the *travaux* contents can be found, on particular points, in E.1.4 below and elsewhere: AW Brian Simpson, *Human Rights and the End of Empire* (Oxford University Press, 2001); D Nicol, 'Original Intent and the European Convention on Human Rights' (2005) *Public Law* 152; Emmerson, Ashworth and Macdonald, *Human Rights and Criminal Justice* (n 9 above) 99–100; Merrills, *The Development of International Law by the European Court of Human Rights* (n 13 above) 90–95.

17 *Konig v Germany (No 1)* (App 6232/73) (1979–80) 2 EHRR 170, Separate Opinion of Judge Matscher. See Nicol, 'Original Intent and the European Convention on Human Rights' (n 16 above) esp 170–72.

18 See, eg, European Commission on Human Rights, *Preparatory Work on Article 6 of the European Convention* (DH(56)11, Council of Europe, 1956); European Court of Human Rights, *Preparatory Work on Article 6 of the European Convention* (CDH(68)3, Council of Europe, 1968).

19 European Court of Human Rights, CDH(68)3 (n 18 above) 10; European Commission on Human Rights, DH(56)1, (n 18 above) 6–7.

20 European Commission of Human Rights, DH(56)11 (n 18 above) 6–8; European Court of Human Rights, CDH(68)3 (n 18 above) 8.

21 See Emmerson, Ashworth and Macdonald, *Human Rights and Criminal Justice* (n 9 above) 88; Ovey and White, *Jacobs and White* (n 2 above) 40–41; Clayton and Tomlinson, *The Law of Human Rights* (n 4 above) 307; cf Tobin, 'Seeking to Persuade' (n 6 above) 22.

the *travaux* are even mentioned are few in number and fall into one of several groups. First, some cases acknowledge that the *travaux* provide little useful guidance,[22] or expressly state that it is unnecessary to resort to the *travaux*.[23] Second, there are cases in which the European Court draws on the *travaux* to aid understanding of the meaning of 'civil' in Article 6.[24] Third, there are cases where passing reference is made without engaging in analysis of any depth, or passing reference is made to emphasise a point.[25]

A.2 Object and Purpose: the Court's Attempts at Teleological Interpretation are Marked by Incoherence

As we saw above, the Vienna Convention provides an interpretative framework that the European Court applies to the Convention. In this section, the focus is on the Court's attempts in the context of Article 6 to implement part of the interpretative approach expressed in Article 31(1) of the Vienna Convention: that a treaty 'shall be interpreted' among other things, 'in the light of its object and purpose'.[26] The argument is straightforward: while the European Court is enthusiastic in invoking the 'object and purpose' of Article 6, it rarely explains why the 'object and purpose' approach is used in a particular case in preference to some of the other interpretative approaches outlined in this part, and it seldom identifies or explains what the object and purpose of the Article are. Ultimately, it is argued that the Court's interpretative approach in this regard is incoherent and under-theorised, with consequences for the ability of the case law to provide guidance.[27]

[22] *Pakelli v Germany* (App 8398/78) (1984) 6 EHRR 1, para 31; *Axen v Germany* (App 8273/78) (1984) 6 EHRR 195, para 31; *Pretto v Italy* (App 7984/77) (1984) 6 EHRR 182, para 26; *Sutter v Switzerland* (App 8209/78) (1984) 6 EHRR 272, para 33; *B and P v United Kingdom* (App 36337/97) (2002) 34 EHRR 19, Concurring Opinion of Judge Sir Nicolas Bratza.

[23] *Maaouia v France* (App 39652/98) (2001) 33 EHRR 42, Dissenting Opinion of Judge Loucaides joined by Judge Traja; *Jorgic v Germany* (App 74613/01) (2008) 47 EHRR 6, para 68. See also *Golder v United Kingdom* (n 5 above) para 36; Nicol, 'Original Intent and the European Convention on Human Rights' (n 16 above) 167–68. See also Pieter van Dijk, 'The Interpretation of Civil Rights and Obligations by the European Court of Human Rights' in Franz Matscher (ed), *Protecting Human Rights: The European Dimension*, 2nd edn (Carl Heymanns Verlag KG, 1990) 140.

[24] *Deumeland v Germany* (n 11 above) para 20 of the Joint Dissenting Opinion of Judges Ryssdal, Bindschedler-Robert, Lagergren, Matscher, Sir Vincent Evans, Bernhardt and Gersing; *Feldbrugge v Netherlands* (n 14 above) para 20 of Joint Dissenting Opinion of Judges Ryssdal, Bindschedler-Robert, Lagergren, Matscher, Sir Vincent Evans, Bernhardt and Gersing; *Ferrazzini v Italy* (App 44759/98) (2002) 34 EHRR 45, Dissenting Opinion of Judge Lorenzen; *Neumeister v Austria* (App 1936/63) (1979–80) 1 EHRR 91, para 14; *Pellegrin v France* (App 28541/95) (2001) 31 EHRR 26, para 5 of Joint Dissenting Opinion of Judges Tulkens, Fischbach, Casadevall and Thomassen.

[25] *Golder v United Kingdom* (n 5 above) Separate Opinion of Judge Zekia; *Saunders v United Kingdom* (App 19187/91) (1997) 23 EHRR 313, Concurring Opinion of Judge Walsh. See *Markovic and others v Italy* (App 1398/03) (2007) 44 EHRR 52, Dissenting Opinion of Judge Zagrebelsky; Ost, 'The Original Canons of Interpretation of the European Court of Human Rights' (n 2 above) 289–90.

[26] See also Merrills, *The Development of International Law by the European Court of Human Rights* (n 13 above) 76–78; Siobhan McInerney-Lankford, 'Fragmentation of International Law Redux: the Case of Strasbourg' (2012) 32(3) *OJLS* 609, 624.

[27] cf the early view of Ost, 'The Original Canons of Interpretation of the European Court of Human Rights' (n 2 above) 292–302.

In *Sutter v Switzerland*, for example, the Court prioritised a purposive interpretive approach:

> Whilst the member States . . . all subscribe to this principle of publicity, their legislative systems and judicial practice reveal some diversity as to its scope and manner of implementation, as regards both the holding of hearings and the 'pronouncement' of judgments. The formal aspect of the matter is, however, of secondary importance as compared with *the purpose underlying the publicity required* by [Article 6(1)].[28]

The *Sutter* Court does not, in this passage or elsewhere, expressly identify what is, in fact, the purpose underlying the publicity requirement or how that purpose assists interpretation of the provision. As remarkable as it may seem to fail to identify the 'object and purpose' relied upon, *Sutter* is not the only case in which the Court has done just that.[29]

Similarly, in *DeCubber v Belgium*, the Court adopted an 'object and purpose' approach to an impartiality question:

> the Court recalls that a restrictive interpretation of Article 6(1) . . . would not be consonant with the object and purpose of the provision, bearing in mind the prominent place which the right to a fair trial holds in a democratic society.[30]

As with *Sutter*, the *DeCubber* Court does not explain why an object and purpose approach was appropriate in this case.[31] The European Court also fails again to identify or explain the actual 'object and purpose' on which it relies. As will be seen throughout this section, this failure to explain makes it harder to predict the likely outcomes of future cases, and adds to the general sense of incoherence in this area.

In *Colozza*, the European Court was willing to derive object and purpose of the Article as a whole in order to ground an implied right:

> Although this is not expressly mentioned in [Article 6(1)], *the object and purpose* of the Article *taken as a whole* show that a person 'charged with a criminal offence' is entitled to take part in the hearing.[32]

[28] *Sutter v Switzerland* (n 22 above) para 27 (emphasis added), citing *Pretto v Italy* (n 22 above) para 21 and *Axen v Germany* (n 22 above) para 26.

[29] It may also be noted here that the European Court declined to adopt an autonomous meaning of the word 'publicity' despite its willingness to do so when interpreting other terms in the Convention, and did so without explanation. cf, eg, *Engel v Netherlands* (App 5100/71) (1979–80) 1 EHRR 647, para 81; Matscher, 'Methods of Interpretation of the Convention' (n 4 above) 70–73. Detailed consideration of the 'autonomous meaning' jurisprudence is not within the scope of this book.

[30] *DeCubber v Belgium* (App 9186/80) (1985) 7 EHRR 236, para 30; Ost, 'The Original Canons of Interpretation of the European Court of Human Rights' (n 2 above) 293–94.

[31] The only explanation is a citation of *Delcourt v Belgium* (App 2689/65) (1979–80) 1 EHRR 355, para 25. See similarly, *Allen v United Kingdom* (App 25424/09) (12 July 2013) para 92.

[32] *Colozza v Italy* (App 9024/80) (1985) 7 EHRR 516, para 27 (emphasis added). See van Dijk and van Hoof, *Theory and Practice of the European Convention on Human Rights* (n 7 above) 589; Trechsel, *Human Rights in Criminal Proceedings* (n 10 above) 252. The *Colozza* passage is referred to in a number of subsequent cases, eg, *Brozicek v Italy* (App 10964/84) (1990) 12 EHRR 371, para 45; *Hermi v Italy* (App 18114/02) (2008) 46 EHRR 46, para 59; *Somogyi v Italy* (App 67972/01) (2008) 46 EHRR 5, para 65; *T v Italy* (App 14104/88) (12 October 1992) para 26; *FCB v Italy* (App 12151/86) (1992) 14 EHRR 909, para 33; *Belziuk v Poland* (App 23103/93) (2000) 30 EHRR 614, para 37.

This book returns to the specific issue of implied rights in part D; for now, it may be noted that in *Colozza* and subsequent cases, the Court invokes 'object and purpose' as 'show[ing]' that an applicant is entitled to take part in a criminal hearing. I do not cavil with the latter principle. The objection, instead, is to the Court's cavalier use of 'object and purpose': at no point does *Colozza* identify what the object and purpose of Article 6 *are*, nor does it explain why these defined factors lead to the conclusion that the Court outlined.

If cases like *Sutter, DeCubber,* and *Colozza* purported to invoke the 'object and purpose' of Article 6, in *John Murray v United Kingdom*, the European Court demonstrated a willingness to interpret Article 6 in accordance with its 'aims' in the context of the right to silence and the privilege against self-incrimination:

> By providing the accused with protection against improper compulsion by the authorities these immunities contribute to avoiding miscarriages of justice and to securing the aims of Article 6.[33]

In *Allan v United Kingdom*, the European Court repeated the *John Murray* language, stating that the purpose of the immunities is

> to provide an accused with protection against improper compulsion by the authorities and thus to avoid miscarriages of justice and secure *the aims of Article 6*.[34]

Despite the Court drawing on 'the aims of Article 6' as a partial basis for its interpretative approach in these cases, at no stage did it specify what these aims *are*, or explain why this sort of case warranted this particular interpretative approach.[35] Moreover, the Court gave no explanation for the proposition that Article 6 should be interpreted in a way that avoids miscarriages of justice, nor does it make it clear whether avoiding miscarriages of justice is, in fact, one of the aims of Article 6.

In addition to sometimes referring to 'object', 'purpose', and 'aim,' the Court has also referred to the 'spirit of Article 6'.[36] In still other cases, such as *Medenica v Switzerland*, the Court described its task as being 'to determine whether the *result*

[33] *John Murray v United Kingdom* (App 18731/91) (1996) 22 EHRR 29, para 45.

[34] *Allan v United Kingdom* (App 48539/99) (2003) 36 EHRR 12, para 44 (emphasis added), citing *John Murray v United Kingdom* (n 33 above) para 45. This passage appears almost verbatim in cases including *JB v Switzerland* (App 31827/96) [2001] Crim LR 748, para 64; *Shannon v United Kingdom* (App 6563/03) (2006) 42 EHRR 31, para 39; *Shabelnik v Ukraine* (App 16404/03) (19 February 2009) para 55; *Bykov v Russia* (App 4378/02) (10 March 2009) para 92; *Tarasov v Ukraine* (App 17416/03) (31 October 2013) para 82.

[35] In a similar passage in *Martin v Estonia* (App 35985/09) (30 May 2013) para 80, the European Court appears to suggest that one of the aims of Article 6 is 'equality of arms', which seems to risk confusing *a right protected by Article 6* with the *aim* of Article 6.

[36] See *Marziano v Italy* (App 45313/99) (28 November 2002) para 31 (*l'esprit de l'Article 6*); *Sejdovic v Italy* (App 56581/00) (10 November 2004) para 33. See also *Sejdovic v Italy* (App 56581/00) (1 March 2006) para 86; *Hermi v Italy* (n 32 above) para 73; *Talat Tunc v Turkey* (App 32432/96) (27 March 2007) para 59; *Salduz v Turkey* (App 36391/02) (2009) 49 EHRR 19 para 59; *Demebukov v Bulgaria* (App 68020/01) (28 February 2008) para 47; *Sakhnovskiy v Russia* (App 21272/03) (5 February 2009) para 44; *Protopapa v Turkey* (App 16084/90) (24 February 2009) para 82; *Krestovskiy v Russia* (App 14040/03) (28 October 2010) para 28; *Sakhnovskiy v Russia* (App 21272/03) (2 November 2010) para 90; *Cani v Albania* (App 11006/06) (6 March 2012) para 54.

called for by the Convention has been achieved'.[37] It is unclear whether notions of 'spirit' and 'result' are meant to be used mutually exclusively from an approach that looks at the 'object and purpose' of a provision, or when one approach should be used in preference to the other. Even if one assumes that there is no conflict between a 'result-oriented' or 'spirit-orientated' interpretation and other interpretative approaches, the Court crucially gives no explanation of what it actually considers to be 'the result called for by the Convention' or the 'spirit of Article 6' in these cases or more generally.

This semantic confusion arguably reached a crescendo in *Kolu v Turkey*, in which, in the space of a single paragraph, the European Court relied on 'the concept of fairness enshrined in Article 6(1)', 'the concept of fair trial', and 'the aims of Article 6'.[38] The Court may have intended that the reader regard these three phrases as synonymous or interchangeable, but such an intention is not clear. Alternatively, the European Court may have carefully chosen three different phrases for three different purposes, but did so without indicating why each phrase is appropriate for each different purpose. In judgments such as this, the European Court hinders transparency and the predictability of its judgments by not making its interpretative reasoning process completely clear: when should we invoke the concept of fairness? When should the concept of a fair trial be invoked? And when are we able to consider the aims of Article 6? What are those aims and concepts? The Court's work in these cases leaves much unexplained.[39] Of course, there may well be eminently sensible reasons why the European Court might choose to adopt one interpretative approach in one class of case, and another in another class of case. What is lacking is any explanation of the interpretative choices, and any elaboration on how those choices work in a given case.

It must be acknowledged that there are some cases in which the European Court has attempted to identify the aim or object or purpose of Article 6. Thus, for example, in *Stefanelli v San Marino*, the Court attempted to identify at least one of the aims of Article 6, but with minimal interpretative utility:

> By rendering the administration of justice transparent, publicity contributes to the achievement of the aim of Article 6(1), namely *a fair trial*, the guarantee of which is one of the principles of any democratic society.[40]

[37] *Medenica v Switzerland* (App 20491/92) (14 June 2001) para 55 (emphasis added). See also *Somogyi v Italy* (n 32 above) para 67; *Colozza v Italy* (n 32 above) para 30; Yutaka Arai-Takahashi, *The Margin of Appreciation Doctrine and the Principle of Proportionality in the Jurisprudence of the ECHR* (Intersentia, 2002) 34; Christoffersen, *Fair Balance* (n 7 above) 299–300.

[38] *Kolu v Turkey* (App 35811/97) (2 August 2005) para 51 (translated). In the original, 'la notion d'équité consacrée par l'Article 6(1)'; 'la notion de procès équitable'; and 'les buts de l'Article 6'. See similarly, those cases expressing the view that 'the key principle governing the application of Article 6 is fairness', eg, *Gregacevic v Croatia* (App 58331/09) (10 July 2012) para 49.

[39] On the links between 'object and purpose' and dynamic interpretation, see Golsong, 'Interpreting the European Convention on Human Rights Beyond the Confines of the Vienna Convention' (n 9 above) 149; Ost, 'The Original Canons of Interpretation of the European Court of Human Rights' (n 2 above) 292–93.

[40] *Stefanelli v San Marino* (App 35396/97) (2001) 33 EHRR 16, para 19 (emphasis added), citing, 'as the most recent authority', *Serre v France* (App 29718/96) (29 September 1999) para 21.

In so doing, the Court has identified that one of the aims of Article 6(1)'s fair trial guarantee is, in fact, 'a fair trial'. This circumlocution contributes little to the Court's analysis. The Court has also identified the purpose of Article 6 as 'enshrining the fundamental principle of the rule of law', without elaborating on how that principle might apply.[41] Another attempt came in *Salduz v Turkey*, in which the Court addressed the 'purpose' of Article 6:

> [E]ven if the primary purpose of Article 6, as far as criminal proceedings are concerned, is to ensure a fair trial by a 'tribunal' competent to determine 'any criminal charge', it does not follow that the Article has no application to pre-trial proceedings.[42]

In this passage, therefore, the European Court strongly implies that the 'primary' purpose of Article 6 'is to ensure a fair trial by a "tribunal" competent to determine "any criminal charge"'. However uncontroversial this statement may appear, by identifying a 'primary' purpose, the Court implicitly relegates all other purposes to lesser 'secondary' status, and has done so without explanation and without defining what those secondary purposes might be.

A.3 The European Court Uses Several Techniques to Overcome Ordinary Literal Meanings

As was noted above, Article 31(1) of the Vienna Convention places significance on the 'ordinary meaning' of a provision. It is rare, however, for the European Court to engage in detailed analysis of the ordinary meaning of Article 6, or any component part thereof. One example of such detailed analysis appeared in *Pakelli v Germany*, in which the Court examined Article 6(3)(c) and linguistic differences between the French and English texts.[43] While such examples exist, they are not common.[44] Indeed, the Court has often demonstrated a willingness to overlook apparently straightforward literal analysis.[45] This section considers three

[41] *Salabiaku v France* (App 10519/83) (1991) 13 EHRR 379 para 28.

[42] *Salduz v Turkey* (n 36 above) para 50. On *Salduz*, see R Pattenden, 'Case Comment: Right to Counsel at the Police Station' (2011) 15(1) *International Journal of Evidence and Proof* 70; TAHM van de Laar and RL de Graaff, '*Salduz* and *Miranda*: Is the US Supreme Court Pointing the Way?' [2011] *EHRLR* 304; W Wu, 'Interrogational Fairness under the European Convention on Human Rights' (2011) 39 *International Journal of Law, Crime and Justice* 37; E Bjorge, 'Exceptionalism and Internationalism in the Supreme Court: *Horncastle* and *Cadder*' (2011) *Public Law* 475; N Bratza, 'The Relationship between the UK Courts and Strasbourg' [2011] *EHRLR* 505. On the application of the guarantees to the investigation stage, see, eg, Sarah J Summers, *Fair Trials: The European Criminal Procedural Tradition and the European Court of Human Rights* (Hart Publishing, 2007) 129–31.

[43] *Pakelli v Germany* (n 22 above) para 31. See van Dijk and van Hoof, *Theory and Practice of the European Convention on Human Rights* (n 7 above) 636–37.

[44] See also *Luedicke, Belkacem and Koc v Germany* (n 10 above) paras 42–46; Merrills, *The Development of International Law by the European Court of Human Rights* (n 13 above) 70–71. An additional example of linguistic difference is the presence of the word 'contestations' in the French version of Art 6(1): see, eg, R Clayton and H Tomlinson (eds), *Fair Trial Rights*, 2nd edn (Oxford University Press, 2010) 126–28.

[45] cf Golsong, 'Interpreting the European Convention on Human Rights Beyond the Confines of the Vienna Convention' (n 9 above) 23.

examples of techniques the Court has used to overcome ordinary literal meanings in Article 6 cases. Crucially, in terms of the broader argument of this part, the Court rarely explains when it will use any one of these techniques in preference to any other, or when it will use any one of these techniques rather than the interpretative techniques outlined elsewhere in this part.

The first technique is to dismiss an apparently ordinary meaning by reference to the Convention's drafters' intentions, even if those intentions are not ascertainable. This approach appears, for example, in *Axen v Germany*, where the Court considered the public pronouncement of judgment:

> However, many member States . . . have a long-standing tradition of recourse to other means, besides reading out aloud, for making public the decisions of . . . their courts . . . The authors of the Convention cannot have overlooked that fact, even if concern to take it into account is not so easily identifiable in their working documents as in the *travaux préparatoires* of the [International Covenant on Civil and Political Rights]. The Court therefore does not feel bound to adopt a literal interpretation.[46]

In this way, the Court avoids a literal interpretation by hypothesising what the drafters' intentions must have been. One may note that the Court does not explain when a drafters' intention approach is to be preferred to the Court's 'living instrument' view of the Convention, or how the two might interact.[47]

The second and third techniques are, in a sense, both examples of the Court drawing on what Article 31(1) of the Vienna Convention describes as the 'context' of the provision under consideration.[48] Context provides the Court with an array of interpretative options that allow it to sidestep a literal interpretation. Thus, the second technique is to overcome literal obstacles by reference to aspects of the relationship between different component parts of Article 6. In *Bonisch v Austria*, considering the Article 6(3)(d) right to call and examine witnesses, the Court overcame a literal obstacle by reference to the internal structure of Article 6:

> Read literally, [Article 6(3)(d)] relates to witnesses and not experts. In any event, the Court would recall that the guarantees contained in [Article 6(3)] are constituent elements, amongst others, of the concept of a fair trial . . . In the circumstances of the instant case, the Court, whilst also having due regard to the [Article 6(3)] guarantees, including those enunciated in sub-paragraph (d), considers that it should examine the applicant's complaints under the general rule of [Article 6(1)].[49]

In this way the European Court avoids having to deal with a potentially inconvenient Article 6(3)(d) issue by instead addressing the same issue under the broader

[46] *Axen v Germany* (n 22 above) para 31. See Ost, 'The Original Canons of Interpretation of the European Court of Human Rights' (n 2 above) 288–89.

[47] Mahoney, 'Judicial Activism and Judicial Restraint in the ECHR' (n 15 above) 69–70. cf A.1.

[48] See, eg, Ost, 'The Original Canons of Interpretation of the European Court of Human Rights' (n 2 above) 290.

[49] *Bonisch v Austria* (App 8658/79) (1987) 9 EHRR 191, para 29. Article 6(3)(d) states: 'Everyone charged with a criminal offence has the following minimum rights: . . . to examine or have examined witnesses against him and to obtain the attendance and examination of witnesses on his behalf under the same conditions as witnesses against him'.

auspices of Article 6(1). This approach raises questions about the internal structure of Article 6, and, in particular, about the relationship between the various component rights and the overarching fair hearing guarantee contained in Article 6(1). Often, the European Court's treatment of the internal structure of Article 6 is marked by a lack of clarity and an undeveloped sense of how the different component parts interrelate; the internal structure of Article 6 is considered in greater detail in part C. For now, however, it is worth marking this technique as a way of circumventing a potentially inconvenient literal interpretation of one component part of Article 6.

If the second technique involved looking beyond a particular provision in favour of Article 6 as a whole, the third technique looks beyond Article 6 to the context of the Convention system as a whole. An example is *Maaouia v France*, in which the Court considered 'the applicability of Article 6(1) to procedures for the expulsion of aliens'.[50] In describing its interpretative approach, the Court focused not on Article 6 in isolation, but rather on the Convention system *as a whole*:

> 36. The Court points out that the provisions of the Convention must be construed in the light of the entire Convention system, including the Protocols. In that connection, the Court notes that Article 1 of Protocol No 7 . . . contains procedural guarantees applicable to the expulsion of aliens. In addition, the Court observes that the preamble to that instrument refers to the need to take 'further steps to ensure the collective enforcement of certain rights and freedoms by means of the Convention'. Taken together, those provisions show that the States were aware that Article 6(1) did not apply to procedures for the expulsion of aliens and wished to take special measures in that sphere . . .
>
> 37. The Court therefore considers that by adopting Article 1 of Protocol No 7 containing guarantees specifically concerning proceedings for the expulsion of aliens the States clearly intimated their intention not to include such proceedings within the scope of Article 6(1) of the Convention.[51]

In light of earlier discussion, this passage raises questions. For example, if Convention provisions 'must be construed in light of the entire Convention system', then when is it appropriate for the Court to focus specifically on the object and purpose of *Article 6*, as opposed to the object and purpose of the *entire* Convention system? In what ways do the two differ? If the object and purpose of Article 6 are not in fact different to those of the entire Convention system, it is unclear why the Court would refer to the Article in some cases and the Convention system in others.[52]

As Ovey and White note, the difficulty with using context as an interpretative tool is that it can 'vary considerably', from consisting 'solely of paragraphs of the

[50] *Maaouia v France* (n 23 above) para 35.

[51] ibid paras 36–37. See Ovey and White, *Jacobs and White* (n 2 above) 45; Andrew Legg, *The Margin of Appreciation in International Human Rights Law* (Oxford University Press, 2012) 125.

[52] Moreover, if it is to be a general principle that the provisions of the Convention must be construed in light of the entire Convention system, it remains unclear what impact such a principle might have on the Court's jurisprudence in areas such as the admissibility of evidence obtained through breach of a Convention right: see also B.6 below.

same article' to 'the whole Convention, including its Preamble and Protocols'.[53] This interpretative flexibility, unaccompanied by explanation, leads to incoherence in the Court's interpretative framework and makes it difficult to predict the likely outcome of future cases.

This section considered three techniques that the Court has utilised to overcome literal interpretations of Article 6. In the next section, I consider the Court's exhortation that rights protection should be 'practical and effective' in the Article 6 context.

A.4 The European Court Inconsistently Cites the Need for 'Practical and Effective' Interpretation

The European Court has frequently expressed the view that the Convention 'is intended to guarantee not rights that are theoretical or illusory but rights that are practical and effective'.[54] This view was first articulated in the Article 6 civil context by *Airey v Ireland*,[55] and in the criminal context by *Artico v Italy*.[56] Thus, for example, in *Lala v Netherlands*, the Court used the 'practical and effective' test to dismiss 'unduly formalistic' conditions:

> Everyone charged with a criminal offence has the right to be defended by counsel. For this right to be practical and effective, and not merely theoretical, its exercise should not be made dependent on the fulfilment of unduly formalistic conditions.[57]

[53] Ovey and White, *Jacobs and White* (n 2 above) 45. See also Ost, 'The Original Canons of Interpretation of the European Court of Human Rights' (n 2 above) 290.

[54] *Artico v Italy* (App 6694/74) (1980) 3 EHRR 1, para 33. See also cases such as *Imbrioscia v Switzerland* (App 13972/88) (1994) 17 EHRR 441, para 38; *Bertuzzi v France* (App 36378/97) (13 February 2003) paras 23–25; *Allenet de Ribemont v France* (App 15175/89) (1995) 20 EHRR 557 para [35]; *Panteleyekno v Ukraine* (App 11901/02) (29 June 2006) para 65; *Nerattini v Greece* (App 43529/07) (18 January 2009) para 23; *Riepan v Austria* (App 35115/97) (14 November 2000) para 29; *Peltier v France* (App 32872/96) (21 May 2002) para 36; *Bakan v Turkey* (App 50939/99) (12 June 2007) para 71; *Boldea v Romania* (App 19997/02) (15 February 2007) para 28; *Sakhnovskiy v Russia* (2009) (n 36 above) para 41; *Assanidze v Georgia* (App 71503/01) (2004) 39 EHRR 32, paras 181–82; *Mostacciuolo Giuseppe v Italy (No 2)* (App 65102/01) (29 March 2006) para 81; *Vanjak v Croatia* (App 29889/04) (14 January 2010) para 39; *Gabrielyan v Armenia* (App 8088/05) (10 April 2012 para 65; *Niculescu v Romania* (App 25333/03) (25 June 2013) para 112; *Allen v United Kingdom* (n 31 above) para 92; cf *R v Big M Drug Mart Ltd* [1985] 1 SCR 295, para 117. See further, Greer, *The European Convention on Human Rights* (n 2 above) 197; C Gearty, *Principles of Human Rights Adjudication* (Oxford University Press, 2004) 72–73; Christoffersen, *Fair Balance* (n 7 above) 55–56; Ost, 'The Original Canons of Interpretation of the European Court of Human Rights' (n 2 above) 294; Merrills, *The Development of International Law by the European Court of Human Rights* (n 13 above) 98–122; Dembour, *Who Believes in Human Rights?* (n 15 above) 21; E Brems, 'Conflicting Human Rights: an Exploration in the Context of the Right to a Fair Trial in the European Convention on Human Rights' (2005) 27 *Human Rights Quarterly* 294, 298; Tobin, 'Seeking to Persuade' (n 6 above) 25.

[55] *Airey v Ireland* (App 6289/73) (1979–80) 2 EHRR 305, para 24.

[56] *Artico v Italy* (n 54 above) para 33; Trechsel, *Human Rights in Criminal Proceedings* (n 10 above) 194–95.

[57] *Lala v Netherlands* (App 14861/89) (1994) 18 EHRR 586, para 34. The decision in *Pelladoah*, delivered the same day as Lala, repeats this passage virtually verbatim, and also lacks explanation or doctrinal support: *Pelladoah v Netherlands* (App 16737/90) (1995) 19 EHRR 81, para 41.

The 'practical and effective' approach has also been employed, again without much in the way of explanation, in cases concerning Article 6(2) and Article 6(3).[58] Of course, it may well be defensible for the Court to adopt a 'practical and effective' approach. The difficulty arises in the Court's inability to explain when it will resort to a practical and effective interpretation and when it will prefer a more restrictive text- or context-focused interpretation. In all these cases, there is at least an argument that can be made that the 'practical and effective' approach provides the Court with an *ex post facto* justification for interpretations that might otherwise be in tension with the provision's literal meaning or in tension with, for example, a more purposive interpretation.

Such an argument is strengthened if one considers the cases that do *not* utilise the 'practical and effective' approach as well as considering those that do. For example, in *Lamanna* the European Court adopted a purposive approach. It held that even though judgment had not been pronounced publicly in two lower court hearings, the purpose of Article 6(1) had been served 'by the public delivery of the appellate court's judgment'.[59] In so doing, the European Court overlooked the plain failure of the lower courts to render judgment in public, and demonstrated a willingness to focus on a purposive approach. The European Court did so without explaining its approach. One wonders what the result in this case might have been if the European Court had, instead, adopted the view that interpretation should aspire to guarantee 'rights which are practical and effective as opposed to theoretical and illusory'[60] at the lower court level.

In other instances, the Court appears to acknowledge the 'practical and effective' doctrine before resiling from it. In *Czekalla*, and *Bogumil*, the European Court considered alleged violations of Article 6(3)(c).[61] In *Czekalla* (and in a similar passage in *Bogumil*), the Court stated:

> While it has frequently observed that the Convention is designed to guarantee not rights that are theoretical or illusory but rights that are practical and effective, assigning counsel does not in itself ensure the effectiveness of the assistance he may afford an accused . . . The competent national authorities are required under Article 6(3)(c) to intervene only if a failure by legal-aid counsel to provide effective representation is manifest or sufficiently brought to their attention in some other way.[62]

[58] See, eg, *Allenet de Ribemont v France* (n 54 above) para 35, citing *Artico v Italy* (n 54 above) 33; *Soering v United Kingdom* (App 14038/88) (1989) 11 EHRR 439, para 34; and *Cruz Varas v Sweden* (App 15576/89) (1992) 14 EHRR 1, para 99; *Protopapa v Turkey* (n 36 above) para 80.

[59] *Lamanna v Austria* (App 28923/95) (10 July 2001) para 34. See also Trechsel, *Human Rights in Criminal Proceedings* (n 10 above) 132; see part E.

[60] *Allenet de Ribemont v France* (n 52 above) para 35.

[61] *Czekalla v Portugal* (App 38830/97) (10 October 2002); *Bogumil v Portugal* (App 35228/03) (7 October 2008).

[62] *Czekalla v Portugal* (n 61 above) para 60; see also *Bogumil v Portugal* (n 61 above) para 46. *Czekalla* cites *Daud v Portugal* (App 22600/93) (2000) 30 EHRR 400, para 38; see also *Artico v Italy* (n 54 above) para 36; *Kamasinski v Austria* (App 9783/82) (1991) 13 EHRR 36, para 65; van Dijk and van Hoof, *Theory and Practice of the European Convention on Human Rights* (n 7 above) 641; Trechsel, *Human Rights in Criminal Proceedings* (n 10 above) 205–6, 287–90.

This passage involves the European Court acknowledging that 'practical and effective' is the overarching approach, but that there are exceptions to that approach, exceptions defined seemingly by the inconvenience of the approach's application. But in the absence of a general and explained theory of the 'practical and effective' doctrine, in future cases involving Article 6(3)(c), or indeed involving any other Article 6 right, it is difficult to know whether the European Court will adopt its usual 'practical and effective' approach, or if it will recognise an exception.

The Court ought to explain more clearly why particular cases, or classes of case, justify a generous 'practical and effective' interpretation rather than a more restrictive interpretation. Without such explanation, the risk is that it will appear to be selecting interpretative approaches in an arbitrary, and perhaps even opportunistically incoherent, fashion.

A.5 The European Court's Use of Extrinsic Materials is Opaque

In addition to the interpretative catchphrases identified above, the European Court has also drawn on extrinsic material (often, documents of the Council of Europe) in interpreting Article 6. Thus, in *Sander v United Kingdom*, for example, the Court considered the extent to which a juror's reportedly racist comments might violate the applicant's Article 6(1) rights. In finding a violation, the Court considered the alleged racism:

> 23. . . . to be a very serious matter given that . . . eradication of racism has become a common priority goal for all Contracting States (see, inter alia, Declarations of the Vienna and Strasbourg Summits of the Council of Europe) . . .
>
> 34. . . . Given the importance attached by all Contracting States to the need to combat racism (see [23] above), the Court considers that the judge should have reacted in a more robust manner.[63]

Of course, this book does not dispute the abhorrence of racism, but it is important to note that the Court provides no explanation of the criteria it uses to determine when it is appropriate to draw on this sort of extrinsic material to elucidate the meaning of Article 6.

Indeed, if the Court intended that the Vienna and Strasbourg declarations become guides to interpreting the Convention, one might wonder why the Court has not elsewhere drawn on passages such as this from the Strasbourg declaration:

> Sharing the concern of citizens about the new dimension of threats to their security and the dangers which these threats constitute for democracy: . . . [we] decide to seek com-

[63] *Sander v United Kingdom* (App 34129/96) (2001) 31 EHRR 44, paras 23, 34. On *Sander*, see Mark Coen, '"With Cat-Like Tread": Jury Trial and the European Court of Human Rights' (2014) *Human Rights Law Review* (Advance Access) 1, 4–5.

> mon responses to the challenges posed by the growth in corruption, organised crime and drug trafficking throughout Europe.[64]

Such a passage might justify all manner of state restrictions on rights in the name of fighting corruption, organised crime and drugs. An advocate before the Court could legitimately cite this passage from the Strasbourg declaration, following the example of *Sander*. This book makes no comment on the normative desirability of such a possible argument. Instead, it seeks to emphasise that unexplained and unjustified use of extrinsic materials as an aid to interpretation may lead to greater incoherence and uncertainty.

The problems with extrinsic materials are not confined to these two conventions. A broadly similar approach was evident in *Ramanauskas v Lithuania*, in which the Court drew on the Council of Europe's Criminal Law Convention on Corruption ('the Corruption Convention'):[65]

> 50. . . . authorises the use of special investigative techniques, such as undercover agents, that may be necessary for gathering evidence in this area, provided that the rights and undertakings deriving from international multilateral conventions concerning 'special matters', for example human rights, are not affected.
>
> 51. That being so, *the use of special investigative methods* – in particular, undercover techniques – *cannot in itself infringe the right to a fair trial.* However . . . their use must be kept within clear limits.[66]

The Court provided no further reasoning in support of the proposition that interpretation of the Convention should be constrained by the Corruption Convention. While subsequent conventions may prevail over a previous convention to the extent of any inconsistency, the Court identifies no inconsistency, and identifies no provision in the Corruption Convention justifying such a cursory treatment of the issue. The Corruption Convention, it may be noted, mentions 'human rights' only once, in its Preamble.

The use of extrinsic materials is not limited to Council of Europe documents.[67] In *Ergin v Turkey (No 6)*, the Court used extrinsic materials to aid its interpretation in a case involving military tribunals with jurisdiction over civilians. The Court derived support for

> its approach from developments over the last decade at [the] international level . . . which confirm the existence of a trend towards excluding the criminal jurisdiction of military courts over civilians.[68]

[64] Second Summit of Heads of State and Government of the Council of Europe, *Final Declaration* (Strasbourg, 10–11 October 1997).

[65] European Criminal Law Convention on Corruption, ETS 173 (adopted 27 January 1999, entered into force 1 July 2002).

[66] *Ramanauskas v Lithuania* (App 74420/02) [2008] Crim LR 639, paras 50–51 (emphasis added).

[67] See also E Brems, 'The Margin of Appreciation Doctrine in the Case-Law of the ECtHR' (1996) 56 *Zeitschrift für Ausländisches Öffentliches Recht und Völkerrecht* 240, 286–87.

[68] *Ergin v Turkey (No 6)* (App 47533/99) (2008) 47 EHRR 36, para 45.

The Court derived support for its conclusion from 'the situation at [the] international level'.[69] The international developments to which the European Court referred included UN Human Rights Committee comment and observations,[70] reports to the Commission on Human Rights,[71] and Inter-American Court of Human Rights case law.[72] The Court does not explain why such use of extrinsic materials is justified. Even if one accepts that such material may be useful, it is important that the Court more fully explain how it chooses which material to use, and when it is appropriate to use extrinsic material. For example, should extrinsic material only be used when the object and purpose of a provision is unclear? May it be used if the European Court has not yet applied the 'practical and effective' test?

My argument is *not* that the Court should never take into account extrinsic materials in interpreting Article 6, or that such materials may never be useful. But there are Council of Europe conventions on topics ranging from television[73] and cinema[74] to human trafficking[75] and 'cybercrime'.[76] Unless it is clear when these conventions may be invoked, and what interpretative work they may be used for, the European Court's interpretative approach to Article 6 will remain opaque and potentially arbitrary.

A.6 Democracy and Article 6

This section examines a number of ways in which the European Court uses the assertion that Article 6 rights hold an 'important' or 'prominent' place in a democratic society, and the extent to which the Court explains those usages.[77] In this

[69] ibid para 54.
[70] ibid paras 22–23.
[71] ibid para 24.
[72] ibid para 25.
[73] European Convention on Transfrontier Television, ETS 132 (adopted 5 May 1989, entered into force 1 May 1993).
[74] European Convention on Cinematographic Co-Production, ETS 147 (adopted 2 October 1992, entered into force 1 April 1994).
[75] Council of Europe Convention on Action against Trafficking in Human Beings, ETS 197 (adopted 16 May 2005, entered into force 1 February 2008).
[76] European Convention on Cybercrime, ETS 185 (adopted 23 November 2001, entered into force 1 July 2004).
[77] For the European Court's consideration of 'democracy' generally, see C Gearty, 'Democracy and Human Rights in the European Court of Human Rights: A Critical Appraisal' (2000) 51 *Northern Ireland Legal Quarterly* 381; A Mowbray, 'The Role of the ECHR in the Promotion of Democracy' (1999) *Public Law* 703; S Marks, 'The European Convention on Human Rights and its "Democratic Society"' (1995) 66 *British Yearbook of International Law* 209; Greer, *The European Convention on Human Rights* (n 2 above) 199–200; Ost, 'The Original Canons of Interpretation of the European Court of Human Rights' (n 2 above) 300–1; Merrills, *The Development of International Law by the European Court of Human Rights* (n 13 above) 125–49; Steve Foster, *Human Rights and Civil Liberties*, 2nd edn (Pearson Education, 2008) 53–54. On the links between proportionality and democracy, see Christoffersen, *Fair Balance* (n 7 above) 195. In some ways, the analysis in this section overlaps with the European Court's 'object and purpose' analysis considered above, but it is worthy of examination insofar as it is one of the particular interpretative mainstays that the European Court relies on in its Art 6 case law.

section I argue that the way in which the Court has made repeated use of this assertion has rendered its judicial reasoning opaque. This lack of satisfactory explanation undermines the extent to which the case law can be said to be consistent with the rule of law ideals outlined above.

Of the cases that refer to the role of fair trial rights in a democratic society, one may begin with *Delcourt*.[78] In considering the applicability of Article 6 to appellate proceedings, *Delcourt* included the following passage:

> In a democratic society within the meaning of the Convention, the right to a fair administration of justice holds such a prominent place that a restrictive interpretation of Article 6(1) would not correspond to the aim and the purpose of that provision.[79]

While it may be self-evident to some extent, it may be noted that the European Court does not articulate why it views the right to a fair trial as holding such a prominent place in a democratic society, or why the centrality of fair trial rights to a democratic society rules out a restrictive interpretation. Indeed, surely it could just as easily be said that the centrality of fair trial in a democratic society meant Article 6 should be read strictly literally,[80] or should be read strictly in accordance with its framers' intentions? Furthermore, how does this sort of expansive interpretation approach fit with the interpretative approaches outlined earlier in this part? The judgment in *Delcourt* does not answer these questions expressly or explain its reasoning process.[81]

Moreover, the *Delcourt* Court does not explain, or elaborate on, its assertion that fair trial rights hold a *special* place in a democratic society. Why does this matter? Predictability and consistency demand that the Court explain why Article 6 holds *particular* significance in a democratic society that justifies a different interpretative approach from that which might be used when considering, for example, the prohibition on torture[82] or the freedom of expression.[83] If, in the alternative, the Court is articulating a more general approach to interpretation of the Convention as a whole, then transparency demands that the Court not cloud its reasoning through reference to any attributes peculiar to Article 6.

[78] *Delcourt v Belgium* (n 31 above).

[79] ibid para 25, citing *Wemhoff v Germany* (App 2122/64) (1979–80) 1 EHRR 55, 75 (para 8 of 'As to the Law'); see similarly, *Gregacevic v Croatia* (n 38 above) para 49; cf *Wersel v Poland* (App 30358/04) (13 September 2011) para 41. See David Harris, M O'Boyle and C Warbrick, *Law of the European Convention on Human Rights*, 2nd edn (Oxford University Press, 2009) 201; Trechsel, *Human Rights in Criminal Proceedings* (n 10 above) 82–83; van Dijk and van Hoof, *Theory and Practice of the European Convention on Human Rights* (n 7 above) 514, 582. While *Borgers* arguably had the effect of overruling *Delcourt* (see, eg, Dembour, *Who Believes in Human Rights?* (n 15 above) 166–68; Summers, *Fair Trial* (n 42 above) 108–9), the passage is nonetheless of interest.

[80] To some extent this was the position of the Concurring Opinion of Judge Bernhardt, joined by Judge Bindschedler-Robert and Judge Matscher in *Sutter v Switzerland* (n 22 above) (see Trechsel, *Human Rights in Criminal Proceedings* (n 10 above) 83).

[81] While *Delcourt* (n 31 above) refers to *Wemhoff v Germany* (n 79 above) 75 (para 8 of 'As to the Law'), *Wemhoff* refers to Art 5 and makes no reference to the 'democratic society'.

[82] Article 3 of the Convention.

[83] Article 10 of the Convention.

These references to democracy have become, perhaps, the catchphrase that launched a thousand interpretative approaches. So, for example, after *Delcourt*, there were a number of cases which used the prominent place of fair trial rights in a democratic society as the basis for an interpretative approach that emphasised substance over form in determining whether Article 6 had been infringed.[84] Similarly, other cases used the 'democratic society' catchphrase to justify an interpretative approach in accordance with the maxim that the Convention is intended to guarantee rights that are 'practical and effective'.[85] At no stage in these cases does the European Court explain why the place of fair trial rights in a democratic society means that it should adopt *this particular interpretative approach*.[86]

There are also instances in which the Court uses the 'democratic society' catchphrase to justify rather *particular* interpretative outcomes. In *Somogyi v Italy*,[87] the Court made this statement about the obligation that Article 6 imposes on contracting states:

> The Court considers that, in view of the prominent place held in a democratic society by the right to a fair trial, Article 6 of the Convention imposes on every national court an obligation to check whether the defendant has had the opportunity to apprise himself of the proceedings against him where, as in the instant case, this is disputed on a ground that does not immediately appear to be manifestly devoid of merit.[88]

A different particular interpretative outcome was evident in *Zagaria v Italy*,[89] where the Court stated that:

> [G]iven the prominent place occupied by the right to good administration of justice in a democratic society, any measures restricting the rights of the defence must be absolutely necessary. Once a less restrictive measure can suffice, it must be applied.[90]

[84] See *DeWeer v Belgium* (App 6903/75) (1979–80) 2 EHRR 439, para 44, citing *Airey v Ireland* (n 55 above) para 24; *Sutter v Switzerland* (n 22 above) para 27; *Subinski v Slovenia* (App 19611/04) (18 January 2007) para 62; *Hanzevacki v Croatia* (App 17182/07) (16 April 2009) para 28. See also Olivier Jacot-Guillarmod, 'Rights Related to Good Administration of Justice' in R Macdonald, F Matscher and H Petzold (eds), *The European System for the Protection of Human Rights* (Martinus Nijhoff, 1993).

[85] See discussion in A.4 above and, eg, *Bertuzzi v France* (n 54 above) para 24 (which appears to regard some Art 6 rights as more important than others in this regard: 'This is particularly so of the right of access to the courts in view of the prominent place held in a democratic society by the right to a fair trial'), citing *Airey v Ireland* (n 55 above) para 24, referring to *Delcourt v Belgium* (n 31 above) para 25; *Gabrielyan v Armenia* (n 54 above) para 65.

[86] Little is gained by analysing the cases cited by the European Court, directly or indirectly: see *DeWeer v Belgium* (n 84 above) para 44; *Airey v Ireland* (n 55 above) para 24; *Sutter v Switzerland* (n 22 above) para 27; *Pretto v Italy* (n 22 above) para 22; *Axen v Germany* (n 22 above) para 26; *Adolf v Austria* (App 8269/78) (1982) 4 EHRR 313, para 30; *Subinski v Slovenia* (n 84 above) para 62. See van Dijk and van Hoof, *Theory and Practice of the European Convention on Human Rights* (n 7 above) 596–97.

[87] *Somogyi v Italy* (n 32 above).

[88] ibid para 72, citing, inter alia, *Delcourt v Belgium* (n 31 above). And see, citing the *Somogyi* passage, *Seyithan Demir v Turkey* (App 25381/02) (28 July 2009) para 42.

[89] *Zagaria v Italy* (App 58295/00) (27 November 2007).

[90] ibid para 31, citing *Van Mechelen and others v Netherlands* (App 21363/93) (1998) 25 EHRR 647, para 58 (translation).

Once again, neither of these passages explains *why* the democratic concern leads to the particular interpretative outcome, or whether the democratic concern is somehow of relevance to Article 6 rights but not to other Convention rights.[91]

In yet other cases the focus is not on the proposition that fair trial rights *per se* are central to democracy, but rather that *inspiring public confidence in the courts* is central to democracy. This approach has been most common in cases arising out of Article 6(1)'s 'impartial tribunal' guarantee.[92] Thus in *Piersack v Belgium*, for example, the European Court stated that, in an impartiality case: 'What is at stake is the confidence which the courts must inspire in the public in a democratic society'.[93]

This analysis may lead one to suspect that the European Court's use of the democratic catchphrase is more about rhetoric than precise legal analysis. Indeed, even more so than the examples cited above, there are many cases in which the European Court peppers its judgments with passing references to the place of fair trial rights in a democratic society that appear to be little more than rhetorical flourishes.[94] In *Belziuk*, for example, democracy is drawn upon casually as a preamble to a list of basic principles:

> Bearing in mind the prominent place which the right to a fair trial holds in a democratic society, the Court recalls at the outset the fundamental principles which emerge from its jurisprudence relating to Article 6(1) in conjunction with (3)(c), relevant to the instant case.[95]

In most such cases, this is done without any explanation of why it is pertinent to the analysis at hand, and without explanation of how the catchphrase might affect

[91] Nor is explanation provided by the cases cited by the European Court. See *Remli v France* (App 16839/90) (1996) 22 EHRR 253, paras 47–48; *Van Mechelen and others v Netherlands* (n 90 above) para 58.

[92] See Harris, O'Boyle and Warbrick, *Law of the European Convention on Human Rights* (n 79 above) 290–97; cf Trechsel, *Human Rights in Criminal Proceedings* (n 10 above) 56–57.

[93] *Piersack v Belgium* (App 8962/79) (1983) 5 EHRR 169, para 30. See also *DeCubber v Belgium* (n 30 above) para 30, citing *Delcourt v Belgium* (n 31 above) para 30; *Hauschildt v Denmark* (App 10486/83) (1990) 12 EHRR 266, para 48, citing *DeCubber v Belgium* (n 30 above) para 26; *Sander v United Kingdom* (n 63 above) para 22; *Sahiner v Turkey* (App 29279/95) (25 September 2001) para 37; *Cooper v United Kingdom* (App 48843/99) (2004) 39 EHRR 8, para 104; *Ocalan v Turkey* (App 46221/99) (2005) 41 EHRR 45, para 116; *Kyprianou v Cyprus* (App 73797/01) (2007) 44 EHRR 27, para 118, citing *Padovani v Italy* (App 13396/87) (26 February 1993) para 27; *Chmelir v Czech Republic* (App 64935/01) (2007) 44 EHRR 20, para 55; *Farhi v France* (App 17070/05) (2009) 48 EHRR 34, para 23. Related reasoning has been adopted in some Art 6(1) 'publicity' cases: *Jan-Ake Andersson v Sweden* (App 11274/84) (1993) 15 EHRR 218, para 49, cited in *Jussila v Finland* (App 73053/01) (2007) 45 EHRR 39, para O–II5 of the Dissenting Judgment of Judge Loucaides (and joined by Judges Zupancic and Spielmann).

[94] See, eg, *Campbell and Fell v United Kingdom* (App 7819/77) (1985) 7 EHRR 165, para 69; *Soering v United Kingdom* (n 58 above) para 113; *Riepan v Austria* (n 54 above) para 27; *Ocalan v Turkey* (n 93 above) para 133, citing *S v Switzerland* (App 12629/87) (1992) 14 EHRR 670, para 48; *Olaechea Cahuas v Spain* (App 24668/03) (2009) 48 EHRR 24, para 60, citing *Soering v United Kingdom* (n 58 above) para 113; *Marcello Viola v Italy* (App 45106/04) (5 October 2006) para 61; *Walchli v France* (App 35787/03) (26 July 2007) para 37; *Kulikowski v Poland* (App 18353/03) (19 May 2009) para 58. See also Trechsel, *Human Rights in Criminal Proceedings* (n 10 above) 21–23, 83; van Dijk and van Hoof, *Theory and Practice of the European Convention on Human Rights* (n 7 above) 545.

[95] *Belziuk v Poland* (n 32 above) para 37. On *Belziuk*, see R Kolb, 'The Jurisprudence of the ECHR on Detention and Fair Trial in Criminal Matters from 1992–1998' (2000) 21 *Human Rights Law Journal* 348, 358–59.

the analytical outcome. These references could, perhaps, be considered harmless rhetoric. But the use of the democratic catchphrase in this way risks suggesting that there is something incapable of articulation that is special about Article 6 compared to other Convention rights, and risks lending the veneer of rhetorical authority to passages in judgments that might otherwise be lacking.

A.7 Building the Foundations for a New Approach to Interpreting Article 6

This part considered the European Court's interpretative approaches to Article 6 criminal cases, and in doing so laid the foundations for the analysis to follow. The part considered a number of interpretative approaches and demonstrated that there was uncertainty about the rationales for these approaches, as well as uncertainty as to when one should be preferred over another.

In light of the criticisms made in this part, how, then, ought the Court approach the interpretation of Article 6? As throughout this book, the principal normative argument to be made here is that the European Court ought to articulate its reasoning more clearly, to avoid inconsistencies wherever possible and, where this is not possible, to explain the reasons why apparent inconsistencies are unavoidable. More specifically, the criticism in this part gives rise to a number of particular normative arguments. The European Court, I suggest, ought to prefer interpretations giving effect to the ordinary meaning of the Convention in light of its object and purpose wherever possible, consistently with Article 31 of the Vienna Convention, and to prefer such interpretations more often than it does at present. But the European Court ought not to invoke the 'object and purpose' of Article 6, or the 'object and purpose' of any component element of Article 6, without articulating the precise object or purpose on which it relies. As a corollary, whenever the European Court opts for a meaning other than the ordinary meaning of an Article 6 provision, the Court ought to explicitly acknowledge this and explain why that meaning has been adopted in preference to the ordinary meaning of the provision. Similarly, if the Court wishes to continue to rely on the 'practical and effective' interpretative technique in general, it ought to explain why that technique is not used whenever another technique is used in its place. Taking into account the criticisms made in this part, the 'democratic catchphrase' should be used sparingly if it is used at all. If it is used at all, its relevance should be explained. These normative arguments are, of course, directed at enhancing the overall ability of the European Court to provide guidance with its Article 6 case law.

In the next part, I develop the analysis further by looking at how the Court defines its own role in Article 6 criminal fair trial cases.

B

The European Court's Role in Article 6 Cases

If part A considered the tools that the European Court has used, part B considers the tasks for which those tools are used: here the focus is on the Court's view of its own institutional, jurisdictional and procedural role in Article 6 cases. I explore the extent to which the European Court's stated view of its own role matches what seems to happen in reality. The cross-cutting themes in this part are, of course, closely interrelated with the themes of interpretation discussed in part A: the role a court carves out for itself will shape the way it interprets cases, and the interpretative approaches adopted by a court will shape its role. Both parts should thus be read together, and also read together with subsequent parts. By adding the analysis in this part to that in part A, a fuller picture is built of how the European Court operates in Article 6 criminal fair trial cases.

There are two broad arguments in this part. The first is that the European Court's sense of its own role is poorly defined and poorly explained. The second is that there is a disconnect between the Court's stated view of its own role and the way in which the Court seems to operate in practice. This is particularly the case, as will be seen, in the context of the Court's 'fourth instance doctrine'. Indeed, it will be shown that there are real questions as to the extent to which the Court's 'fourth instance doctrine' case law bears out its rhetoric.

The European Court's failure to conceptualise its role clearly, and the gap between its rhetoric and its practice, undermine the predictability and coherence of the Court's case law.[1]

At the outset of any investigation of the European Court's view of its own role, it must be acknowledged that the Court faces an array of political and institutional difficulties.[2] While this book does not explore those political and institutional difficulties in depth, it must be acknowledged that the European Court's caseload generally, and its Article 6 caseload specifically, is immense.[3] Similarly, it

[1] For general discussion of how the European Court conceives of the Strasbourg system, see, eg, JG Merrills, *The Development of International Law by the European Court of Human Rights*, 2nd edn (Manchester University Press, 1995) 44–67.

[2] See, eg, A Lester, 'The European Court of Human Rights after 50 Years' [2009] *EHRLR* 461, 467–70; S Greer and L Wildhaber, 'Reflections of a Former President of the European Court of Human Rights' [2010] *EHRLR* 165.

[3] In January 2014, the President of the Court celebrated the successful impact of Protocol 14 to the European Convention, demonstrated by the fact that the total number of pending cases has been

cannot go unnoticed that the Court is also under a variety of competing political pressures, which are in no small part the product of debate over the appropriate role for a regional human rights court.[4] It might be argued that these pressures provide justification for the proposition that the rule of law values of clarity, coherence and transparency should give way to other values (political expediency, or institutional self-defence, for example) in a particular case.[5] Such arguments may well prove compelling to the political scientist or the diplomat. But for the lawyer working in this field there is an alternative that does not involve any withdrawal from the rule of law principles. Put simply in the words of a former President of the Court, 'a court should always try to look like a court'.[6] If, in a given case, the Court feels obliged to take political factors or institutional difficulties into account, far better for it to articulate those factors or difficulties, so as to avoid distorting the rest of the court's case law through disingenuous interpretative gymnastics, so as to facilitate understanding of those difficulties, and so as to provide guidance to those seeking to understand the reasoning of the court in a given case. As will become clear, however, all too often the European Court has instead elected to employ incoherent and under-explained reasoning in explaining its own role in Article 6.

B.1 The European Court Adopts an Ostensibly Modest and Deferential Approach in Article 6 Cases

From an early stage, the European Court has tended to adopt an approach that is ostensibly deferential in Article 6 cases. Thus, for example, in the 1970 *Delcourt* case, the Court demonstrated an extremely deferential approach to Belgian domestic law.[7] Indeed, in *Delcourt* the Court deferred to established practice because of its

reduced 'below the symbolic figure of 100,000 pending cases' (to 90,900 cases) from a high of 160,000 cases in September 2011: Registrar of the Court, Press Release, 'President Spielmann highlights the Court's very good results in 2013' (Council of Europe, 30 January 2014); note, at 7, that 'Nearly a third of the judgments in which the Court found a violation included a violation of Article 6'. See also Registrar of the Court, Press Release, 'Reform of the Court: filtering of cases successful in reducing backlog' (Council of Europe, 24 October 2013); Paul Mahoney et al, *Statement on Case-Overload at the ECtHR* (European Law Institute, 2012); R Wolfrum and U Deutsch (eds), *The European Court of Human Rights Overwhelmed by Applications: Problems and Possible Solutions* (Springer, 2009).

[4] See, eg, N Watt and Owen Bowcott, 'David Cameron calls for reform of ECtHR', *The Guardian*, 26 January 2012, available at www.theguardian.com/law/2012/jan/25/david-cameron-reform-human-rights; BBC News, 'Human rights row: UK quitting would be disaster – ECHR head', 14 January 2014, available at www.bbc.co.uk/news/uk-politics-25726319; 'ECtHR decisions may become invalid in Russia', *Russia Today*, 24 December 2013, available at http://rt.com/politics/court-constitution-echr-law-726/; M Pinto-Duschinsky, *Bringing Rights Back Home* (Policy Exchange, 2011).

[5] On the idea of institutional self-defence, see NW Barber, *Self-Defence for Institutions*, Oxford Legal Studies Research Paper No 61/2012.

[6] Greer and Wildhaber, 'Reflections of a Former President of the European Court of Human Rights' (n 2 above) 173.

[7] *Delcourt v Belgium* (App 2689/65) (1979–80) 1 EHRR 355, para 36. *Delcourt* was a 1970 independence and impartiality case concerning the role of the Belgian Procureur-Général's department in the Court of Cassation's deliberations.

longevity ('more than a century and a half'), to a democratically-elected national parliament ('a parliament chosen in free elections has deliberately decided to maintain the system'), and to Belgian lawyers and citizens (the system was 'never ... put in question by the legal profession or public opinion in Belgium').[8]

The European Court's more recent case law provides examples that indicate that the general deferential tone has continued. This will be expanded upon incidentally in various ways in subsequent sections, but one useful example is *Koval v Ukraine*. In *Koval*, the Court gave this view of its own role:

> The Court, having regard to its subsidiary role in relation to the domestic authorities, which are better placed and equipped as fact-finding tribunals, finds that there has accordingly been no violation of Article 6(1) ... in respect of the failure of the domestic authorities to conduct a thorough and adversarial review of the applicant's submissions as to the allegedly unlawful forfeiture of his bail.[9]

I shall return to specific aspects of *Koval* below; for now, however, it may simply be noted that the Court has here expressly described its position as 'subsidiary'.[10] Ostensible deference of this sort is evident throughout the Court's descriptions of its role in Article 6 cases, perhaps partly so as 'not to alienate the respondent governments'.[11]

The Court also emphasises the modesty of its powers. Thus, for example, in the Article 50 hearing arising out of the Article 6 issues in *LeCompte, Van Leuven and DeMeyere*, the Court recalled

> that it is not empowered under the Convention to direct the Belgian State – even supposing that the latter could itself comply with such a direction – to annul the disciplinary sanctions imposed on the three applicants and the sentences passed ... in criminal proceedings.[12]

In so doing, the Court emphasises the narrow ambit of its powers. While this book is not about the jurisdiction and powers of the European Court in general, and indeed this section focuses on the European Court's *statements about* its own role, this sort of modesty must be borne in mind.

In a sense, this ostensible modesty and deference is similar to the modesty expressed by the Court through its margin of appreciation case law. This doctrine, described by Lester as 'slippery and ... elusive',[13] is typically but not exclusively

[8] ibid para 36.

[9] *Koval v Ukraine* (App 65550/01) (2009) 48 EHRR 5, para 118, citing *McShane v United Kingdom* (App 43290/98) (2002) 35 EHRR 23, para 103 (an Art 2 case).

[10] See also *Flueras v Romania* (App 17520/04) (9 April 2013) para 46; *Hogea v Romania* (App 31912/04) (29 October 2013) para 43; H Petzold, 'The Convention and the Principle of Subsidiarity' in R Macdonald, F Matscher and H Petzold (eds), *The European System for the Protection of Human Rights* (Martinus Nijhoff, 1993).

[11] Stephanos Stavros, *The Guarantees for Accused Persons under Article 6 of the European Convention on Human Rights* (Martinus Nijhoff, 1993) 83.

[12] *LeCompte, Van Leuven and DeMeyere v Belgium* (App 6878/75) (1983) 5 EHRR 183, para 13. See also *Taxquet v Belgium* (Grand Chamber) (App 926/05) (2012) 54 EHRR 26, para 83.

[13] Cited in R Clayton and H Tomlinson (eds), *The Law of Human Rights*, 2nd edn (Oxford University Press, 2009) 320.

used by the European Court when considering the extent to which a government's interference with a right is justifiable under the provisions of Articles 8(2), 9(2), 10(2) and 11(2).[14] Greer notes that 'no simple formula can describe how it works' and 'its most striking characteristic remains its casuistic, uneven, and largely unpredictable nature'.[15] The margin of appreciation jurisprudence and scholarly analysis can thus be quite complex.[16] Although it is very rare for the Court to discuss the margin of appreciation in the Article 6 criminal context,[17] there are isolated occasional references.[18] In this part, however, the focus is on the various much more common ways in which the European Court frequently expresses ostensible modesty and deference in the Article 6 context.

[14] See, eg, D Harris, M O'Boyle and C Warbrick, *Law of the European Convention on Human Rights*, 2nd edn (Oxford University Press, 2009) 349–59.

[15] Steven Greer, *The European Convention on Human Rights: Achievements, Problems and Prospects*, 2nd edn (Cambridge University Press, 2006) 223.

[16] See, eg, ibid 222–26; Jonas Christoffersen, *Fair Balance: Proportionality, Subsidiarity and Primarity in the ECHR* (Martinus Nijhoff, 2009), generally, and 227–357; Ben Emmerson, Andrew Ashworth and Alison Macdonald, *Human Rights and Criminal Justice*, 3rd edn (Sweet & Maxwell, 2012) 130–43; Steve Foster, *Human Rights and Civil Liberties*, 2nd edn (Pearson Education, 2008) 60–63; Clare Ovey and Robin White, *Jacobs and White: The European Convention on Human Rights*, 4th edn (Oxford University Press, 2006) 52–54; N Lavender, 'The Problem of the Margin of Appreciation' [1997] 4 *EHRLR* 380, generally; Merrills, *The Development of International Law by the European Court of Human Rights* (n 1 above) 151–75; Yutaka Arai-Takahashi, 'The Margin of Appreciation Doctrine: a Theoretical Analysis of Strasbourg's Variable Geometry' in A Follesdal, B Peters and G Ulfstein (eds), *Constituting Europe* (Cambridge University Press, 2013); E Brems, *Human Rights: Universality and Diversity* (Martinus Nijhoff, 2001) 341–422; E Brems, 'The Margin of Appreciation Doctrine in the Case-Law of the ECtHR' (1996) 56 *Zeitschrift für Ausländisches Öffentliches Recht und Völkerrecht* 240, esp 252–53; MR Hutchinson, 'The Margin of Appreciation Doctrine in the European Court of Human Rights' (1999) 48 *International and Comparative Law Quarterly* 638; CS Feingold, 'The Doctrine of Margin of Appreciation and the European Convention on Human Rights' (1977–78) 53 *Notre Dame Lawyer* 90; Franz Matscher, 'Methods of Interpretation of the Convention' in R Macdonald, F Matscher and H Petzold (eds), *The European System for the Protection of Human Rights* (Martinus Nijhoff, 1993) 75–78; Mireille Delmas-Marty, 'The Richness of Underlying Legal Reasoning' in Mireille Delmas-Marty and Christine Chodkiewicz (eds), *The European Convention for the Protection of Human Rights: International Protection Versus National Restrictions* (Martinus Nijhoff, 1992); Paul Mahoney, 'Judicial Activism and Judicial Restraint in the ECHR' (1990) 11 *Human Rights Law Journal* 57, 78–85; J Schokkenbroek, 'The Basis, Nature and Application of the Margin of Appreciation Doctrine in the Case Law of the European Court of Human Rights' (1998) 19 *Human Rights Law Journal* 30; J Tobin, 'Seeking to Persuade: a Constructive Approach to Human Rights Treaty Interpretation' (2010) *Harvard HR Journal* 1, 42.

[17] Lavender, 'The Problem of the Margin of Appreciation' (n 16 above) 383; Greer, *The European Convention on Human Rights* (n 15 above) 225, 251. There are some references in the Art 6 civil context: see, eg, *Ashingdane v United Kingdom* (App 8225/78) (28 May 1985) para 57; *Waite and Kennedy v Germany* (App 26083/94) (2000) 30 EHRR 261, para 59; *Stubbings and others v United Kingdom* (App 22083/95) (1996) 23 EHRR 213, para 50; *Tinnelly & Sons Ltd and others and McElduff and others v United Kingdom* (App 20390/92) (1998) 27 EHRR 24, para 72; *Seal v United Kingdom* (App 50330/07) (2012) 54 EHRR 6, para 75; *Boyajyan v Armenia* (App 38003/04) (22 March 2011) para 42. See also Yutaka Arai-Takahashi, *The Margin of Appreciation Doctrine and the Principle of Proportionality in the Jurisprudence of the ECHR* (Intersentia, 2002); Pieter van Dijk and GJH van Hoof, *Theory and Practice of the European Convention on Human Rights*, 4th edn (Intersentia, 2006) 570.

[18] See, eg, *Croissant v Germany* (App 13611/88) (1992) 16 EHRR 135, para 27; *Medenica v Switzerland* (App 20491/92) (14 June 2001) paras 58–59; Stavros, *The Guarantees for Accused Persons* (n 11 above) 354–55; van Dijk and van Hoof, *Theory and Practice of the European Convention on Human Rights* (n 17 above) 600; Arai-Takahashi, *The Margin of Appreciation Doctrine* (n 17 above) 34; Schokkenbroek, 'The Basis, Nature and Application of the Margin of Appreciation Doctrine (n 16 above) 32.

B.2 The European Court States that Its Role is Not to Enunciate General Doctrines

The European Court's view of its role as limited and modest is evident in its decision-making. This section focuses on the Court's insistence that it is not its role to situate its rulings on particular cases within broader general theories.

Harmsen notes that the 'established jurisprudential practice' of the European Court is to make decisions 'on a strict case-by-case basis, without the enunciation of more general doctrine'.[19] This view is evident in *Golder v United Kingdom*. *Golder* was an Article 6 civil case, but it contained a passage subsequently drawn upon in criminal cases:

> It is not the function of the Court to elaborate a general theory of the limitations admissible in the case of convicted prisoners, nor even to rule *in abstracto* on the compatibility of [certain provisions of the Prison Rules] . . . with the Convention. Seised of a case which has its origin in a petition presented by an individual, the Court is called upon to pronounce itself only on the point whether or not the application of those Rules in the present case violated the Convention to the prejudice of Golder.[20]

In *Golder*, therefore, the European Court outlined two propositions. First, its job was to decide the case in front of it (something which will be returned to in the next section). Second, the first proposition meant it was not appropriate for the Court to attempt to elaborate a general theory. With respect, the second does not flow from the first. Indeed, deciding the dispute before the Court will often require explanation of how that case fits with the other case law of the European Court, and such an explanation will often necessitate a generalised sense of how the case law fits together. Without such explanation and generality, the case law risks becoming incoherent and inconsistent.

The Court's reluctance to pronounce on matters not before the Court has clouded its sense of the extent to which it is able to make general pronouncements. The *Golder* view is repeated in *DeWeer*, where the Court firmly stated what its role is *not*:

> The 'right to a court' . . . is subject to implied limitations, two examples of which are given [in] the Commission's report . . . it is not the Court's function, though, to elaborate a general theory of such limitations.[21]

[19] R Harmsen, 'The European Convention on Human Rights after Enlargement' (2001) 5 *International Journal of Human Rights* 18, 32. See also A McHarg, 'Reconciling Human Rights and the Public Interest: Conceptual Problems and Doctrinal Uncertainty in the Jurisprudence of the European Court of Human Rights' (1999) 62 *Modern Law Review* 671, 673; Matscher, 'Methods of Interpretation of the Convention' (n 16 above) 63–64.

[20] *Golder v United Kingdom* (App 4451/70) (1979–80) 1 EHRR 524, para 39, citing *DeBecker v Belgium* (App 214/56) (27 March 1962) (para 14 of 'As to the Request . . . to Strike the Case Out').

[21] *DeWeer v Belgium* (App 6903/75) (1979–80) 2 EHRR 439, para 49. See also, eg, *Colozza v Italy* (App 9024/80) (1985) 7 EHRR 516, para 29. On implied limitations, see, eg, Christoffersen, *Fair Balance* (n 16 above) 78–81.

Thus in cases like *DeWeer*, the European Court expressly states that its role is not to place isolated implied limitations in the context of a more general theory. In these passages, the Court denies any responsibility for creating a coherent, reasoned, broadly consistent body of law. This raises two concerns.

First, this approach suggests there may be *no* general theory underpinning these limitations. This may not necessarily be a problem, but the Court's reluctance to even engage with the issue hints at a broader uncertainty over the path that the Court is treading. Second, it makes it difficult to gain a sense of the trajectory of the Court's case law. Specifically, it makes it difficult to determine when implied limitations are likely to be recognised, developed or expanded upon, something to which I return in more detail in part D. This difficulty reduces certainty about the state of the law, and decreases the case law's ability to provide guidance. If the European Court's concern is focusing on the case in front of it, that concern can be addressed without abdicating any responsibility for situating its decision in context.[22]

Moreover, as will be seen throughout this book, there are many instances in which the European Court *is* willing to articulate general theories.[23] The unexplained basis on which the European Court will be willing to identify and explain general theories in some cases, but not others, adds to the sense that the Court's case law is marked by incoherence.

B.3 The European Court Makes Incoherent Claims about Avoiding Abstract Challenges

This section considers the European Court's insistence that, as was stated in *Minelli v Switzerland*, the Court

> has to confine itself, as far as possible, to an examination of the concrete case before it . . . Accordingly, it has to give a ruling not on the [domestic] legislation and practice *in abstracto* but solely on the manner in which they were applied to the applicant.[24]

[22] cf Merrills, *The Development of International Law by the European Court of Human Rights* (n 1 above) 38.

[23] See, as one example, the general theory about the presumption of innocence articulated by the Grand Chamber in *Allen v United Kingdom* (App 25424/09) (12 July 2013) para 103 ('the Court would formulate the principle of the presumption of innocence in this context as follows . . .').

[24] *Minelli v Switzerland* (App 8660/79) (1983) 5 EHRR 554, para 35, citing *Adolf v Austria* (App 8269/78) (1982) 4 EHRR 313, para 36. See also *Fruni v Slovakia* (App 8014/07) (21 June 2011) para 133; Harris, O'Boyle and Warbrick, *Law of the European Convention on Human Rights* (n 14 above) 303–6; Stefan Trechsel, *Human Rights in Criminal Proceedings* (Oxford University Press, 2006) 186–91; van Dijk and van Hoof, *Theory and Practice of the European Convention on Human Rights* (n 17 above) 625; cf Steven Greer, 'Constitutionalising Adjudication under the European Convention on Human Rights' (2003) *Oxford Journal of Legal Studies* 405, 406–7; Andrew C Stumer, *The Presumption of Innocence* (Hart Publishing, 2010) 90–91; and the European Court's pilot judgment process, discussed in, eg, *Broniowski v Poland (Friendly Settlement)* (App 31443/96) (2006) 43 EHRR 1, paras 34–37.

To adapt the American terminology, the concern in *Minelli* could be said to be a reluctance to rule on the application as though the applicant sought a facial challenge rather than an 'as applied' challenge.[25]

In *Minelli* the Court offered no explanation for this approach, apart from referring to its previous decision in *Adolf v Austria*.[26] Neither these decisions, nor the decisions to which they refer, explain *why* the Court purports to abstain from abstract analysis.[27] Thus at no point in this group of cases does the Court offer explanation or doctrinal support for the proposition that focusing on 'the concrete case before it' means that the Court cannot conduct abstract analysis. Passing reference to Article 25 of the Convention does not illuminate the European Court's reasoning.[28] Even if the Court cannot or does not wish to draw on doctrinal support for the propositions on which it relies, the interests of predictability, clarity and consistency call for an explanation of *why* a given approach is justified, what its limits might be, and whether there are circumstances in which the Court might be willing to conduct facial analysis. A similar lack of explanation is evident in cases such as *Hauschildt*, *John Murray*, *Brogan*, *Sahiner*, *Fey*, *Incal*, *Thorgerisson*, and *Valentino Acatrinei*.[29]

And there are cases in which the Court purports to disclaim abstract analysis before going on to do precisely that. Thus in *Malige v France* the Court stated that it:

> 30. . . . considers that it is not its task to rule on the French system of deductible-point driving licences as such, but to determine whether, in the circumstances of the case, Mr Malige's right of access to a tribunal, within the meaning of Article 6(1) of the Convention, was respected . . .
>
> 31. In the first place, the Court must determine whether the sanction of deducting points from driving licences is a punishment, and accordingly whether it is 'criminal' within the meaning of Article 6(1).[30]

[25] In a facial challenge, 'the challenger must establish that no set of circumstances exists under which the Act would be valid': *United States v Salerno* 481 US 739, 745 (1987). See Harmsen, 'The European Convention on Human Rights after Enlargement' (n 19 above) 33.

[26] *Adolf v Austria* (n 24 above) para 36. See Trechsel, *Human Rights in Criminal Proceedings* (n 24 above) 159–60; van Dijk and van Hoof, *Theory and Practice of the European Convention on Human Rights* (n 17 above) 580.

[27] More than that, at least two of the decisions cited in fact countenance the possibility of abstract challenges: see *X v United Kingdom* (App 7215/75) (1982) 4 EHRR 188, paras 41–42; *Marckx v Belgium* (App 6833/74) (1979–80) 2 EHRR 330, para 27. See also *Guzzardi v Italy* (App 7367/76) (1981) 3 EHRR 333, para 88.

[28] As in *Schiesser v Switzerland* (App 7710/76) (1979–80) 2 EHRR 417, para 32.

[29] See *Hauschildt v Denmark* (App 10486/83) (1990) 12 EHRR 266, para 45; *John Murray v United Kingdom* (App 18731/91) (1996) 22 EHRR 29, para 44; *Brogan and others v United Kingdom* (App 11209/84) (1989) 11 EHRR 117, para 53; *Sahiner v Turkey* (App 29279/95) (25 September 2001) para 43; *Fey v Austria* (App 14396/88) (1993) 16 EHRR 387, para 27; *Incal v Turkey* (App 22678/93) (2000) 29 EHRR 449, para 70; *Thorgeir Thorgeirson v Iceland* (App 13778/88) (1992) 14 EHRR 843, para 48; *Valentino Acatrinei v Romania* (App 18540/04) (25 June 2013) para 68.

[30] *Malige v France* (App 27812/95) (1999) 28 EHRR 578, paras 30–31. See van Dijk and van Hoof, *Theory and Practice of the European Convention on Human Rights* (n 17 above) 553.

In one paragraph, the Court dismisses the idea of abstract analysis; in the following paragraph the Court commences facial *Engel*-style analysis of the sanction in the abstract.[31] There is no indication that the Court has a clear understanding of when, if ever, facial abstract analysis is appropriate. The articulation of a reasoned, explained theory of why and when facial or abstract review was inappropriate would enhance the extent to which future decisions could be predicted, and past decisions understood.[32]

A final point should be made in this analysis of the Court's ostensible reluctance to engage in abstract analysis. This reluctance is difficult to reconcile with the repeated occasions on which the European Court *mandates* abstract analysis in one form or another. Two Article 6 examples will suffice for now. When the Court ruled, as it did in *Jalloh*, that evidence obtained through a breach of the Article 3 prohibition on torture is inadmissible,[33] it ruled in the abstract, insofar as any future case involving that issue will theoretically be governed by the rule in *Jalloh* regardless of the facts of that individual case. When the Court ruled, as it did in *Benham*, that 'where deprivation of liberty is at stake, the interests of justice in principle call for legal representation', it was ruling in the abstract.[34] Neither of these statements is normatively undesirable or incapable of justification. What is troubling is that the Court can vehemently distance itself from abstract analysis in some cases, while enthusiastically embracing it in others, without offering any explanation for the disparity in either class of case. Unless the Court articulates a clear vision of its role with respect to facial challenges and as-applied challenges, and articulates and explains deviations from that vision where necessary, it will be difficult to rationalise past decisions and predict future decisions.

B.4 The European Court Describes Its Role as Limited by the 'Fourth Instance' Doctrine

The European Court frequently describes its role in Article 6 cases in contradistinction to the role of domestic appellate courts: the Court emphasises that it is not a court of fourth instance.[35] It is not for the Court, according to many judg-

[31] A similarly odd combination of passages is evident in *Bouamar*, an Art 5 case cited directly or indirectly in this context in Art 6 cases such as *Pham Hoang v France* (App 13191/87) (1993) 16 EHRR 53, para 33 and *Salabiaku v France* (App 10519/83) (1991) 13 EHRR 379, paras 25 and 30. The *Bouamar* Court explained that its role was not to conduct general abstract analysis but then followed this with several examples of detailed abstract analysis. See *Bouamar v Belgium* (App 9106/80) (1989) 11 EHRR 1, paras 48–53, citing *Lithgow and others v United Kingdom* (App 9006/80) (1986) 8 EHRR 329.

[32] See Harmsen, 'The European Convention on Human Rights after Enlargement' (n 19 above) 33–34.

[33] *Jalloh v Germany* (App 54810/00) (2007) 44 EHRR 32, para 105. See B.6 below.

[34] *Benham v United Kingdom* (App 19380/92) (1996) 22 EHRR 293, para 61.

[35] See, eg, Harris, O'Boyle and Warbrick, *Law of the European Convention on Human Rights* (n 14 above) 202; Ovey and White, *Jacobs and White* (n 16 above) 159; Trechsel, *Human Rights in Criminal Proceedings* (n 24 above) 83–84, 257; Emmerson, Ashworth and Macdonald, *Human Rights and Criminal Justice* (n 16 above) 129–30; Andrew Legg, *The Margin of Appreciation in International Human*

ments, to review the factual or legal analysis of domestic courts in the way that such analysis is performed by domestic appellate courts. An example of this sentiment is evident in *Schenk v Switzerland*, in which the Court made this statement about the intensity of its review powers:

> According to Article 19 . . . of the Convention, the Court's duty is to ensure the observance of the engagements undertaken by the Contracting States in the Convention. In particular, it is not its function to deal with errors of fact or of law allegedly committed by a national court unless and in so far as they may have infringed rights and freedoms protected by the Convention.[36]

In so doing, the European Court emphasised that it is not a supranational appellate court with free-ranging jurisdiction. Greer states that the doctrine means the Court is not to act as 'final court of appeal or fourth instance'.[37] Stavros argued that this doctrine 'has limited quite drastically [the European Court's] competence to review the merits of a criminal charge'.[38] Indeed, in 2009, the President of the Court stated that:

> Although we must not set ourselves up as a fourth instance rehearing what has already been heard in the domestic courts, we do have a duty to oversee the requirements of fair trial as guaranteed by Article 6 of the Convention.[39]

This section and the next section examine the tension inherent in this statement: the tension between the Court purporting not to be a fourth instance court but simultaneously attempting to 'oversee the requirements of fair trial'. In so doing I explore the fourth instance doctrine, the extent to which it has been explained and applied by the European Court, and the extent to which it actually prevents the European Court reviewing the merits of a domestic court decision. Two broad arguments run through this section.

First, it will be shown that the fourth instance doctrine is often invoked but poorly explained and under-theorised. Second, I will demonstrate that the fourth

Rights Law (Oxford University Press, 2012) 167–74; Petzold, 'The Convention and the Principle of Subsidiarity' (n 10 above) 50; Christoffersen, *Fair Balance* (n 16 above) 238–39; S Wallace, 'The Empire Strikes Back: Hearsay Rules in Common Law Legal Systems and the Jurisprudence of the ECtHR' [2010] *EHRLR* 408, 409; L Hoyano, 'What is Balanced on the Scales of Justice? In Search of the Essence of the Right to a Fair Trial' [2014] Crim LR 4, 7–8; Bill O'Brian, *Confrontation: the Defiance of the English Courts*, University of Warwick School of Law Legal Studies Research Paper 2010-09 (2010) 1, 24.

[36] *Schenk v Switzerland* (App 10862/84) (1991) 13 EHRR 242, para 45. See also *Khametshin v Russia* (App 18487/03) (4 March 2010) para 29; *Gafgen v Germany* (Grand Chamber) (App 22978/05) (2010) 52 EHRR 1, para 163; *Oao Neftyanaya Kompaniya Yukos v Russia* (App 14902//04) (20 September 2011) para 534; *Aigner v Austria* (App 28328/03) (10 May 2012) para 33; *Yefimenko v Russia* (App 152/04) (12 February 2013) para 118; *CB v Austria* (App 30465/06) (4 April 2013) paras 35, 39; *Erkapic v Croatia* (App 51198/08) (25 April 2013) para 70; *Botea v Romania* (App 40872/04) (10 December 2013) para 31.

[37] Greer, *The European Convention on Human Rights* (n 15 above) 216. See also Legg, *The Margin of Appreciation in International Human Rights Law* (n 35 above) 167.

[38] Stavros, *The Guarantees for Accused Persons* (n 11 above) 45.

[39] Jean-Paul Costa, 'The Authority of the Jurisprudence of the ECtHR' in Steering Committee for Human Rights (ed), *Reforming the European Convention on Human Rights: A Work in Progress* (Council of Europe Publishing, 2009) 292.

instance doctrine is, in fact, riddled with a series of exceptions that render the doctrine incoherent and internally inconsistent. Ultimately, I argue that the fourth instance doctrine is not as straightforward as is commonly assumed, and that the exceptions to the doctrine are of sufficient number and breadth to raise the possibility that the exceptions may, in fact, have become the rule. But, to begin, a basic account of the European Court's fourth instance doctrine.

A version of the fourth instance doctrine appears to have been commonly accepted in the Convention's *travaux*.[40] One of the earliest statements of this doctrine by the European Court may be in *Ringeisen v Austria (Merits)*, which stated, without referring to any doctrinal support:

> It is not the function of the European Court to pronounce itself on the interpretation of Austrian law on which the said judgment is based or to express an opinion on the manner in which it was substantiated; on the other hand, it is the Court's duty to examine the grounds relied upon by Ringeisen and to determine whether or not the Regional Commission respected the rule of impartiality laid down in [Article 6(1)].[41]

Much more recently, in *Karpenko v Russia* the Court stated that

> it is not its task to act as a court of appeal or, as is sometimes stated, as a court of fourth instance, in respect of the decisions taken by domestic courts. It is the role of the domestic courts to interpret and apply the relevant rules of procedural or substantive law.[42]

Similar sentiments were frequently expressed in the four decades between *Ringeisen* and *Karpenko*. In cases such as *Bernard v France* we see the Court's general reluctance to engage in appellate-style analysis:

> It is admittedly not the Court's task to substitute its own assessment of the facts and the evidence for that of the domestic courts and, as a general rule, it is for these courts to assess the evidence before them. The Court's task is to ascertain whether the proceedings considered as a whole, including the way in which the evidence was taken, were fair.[43]

Later, in *Miragall Escolano and others v Spain*, the European Court expressed the same idea in a slightly different way:

[40] See discussion in A.1.

[41] *Ringeisen v Austria (Merits)* (App 2614/65) (1979–80) 1 EHRR 504, para 97. On *Ringeisen*, see Harris, O'Boyle and Warbrick, *Law of the European Convention on Human Rights* (n 14 above) 293; van Dijk and van Hoof, *Theory and Practice of the European Convention on Human Rights* (n 17 above) 613. *Ringeisen* was applied in, eg, *Winterwerp v Netherlands* (App 6301/73) (1979–80) 2 EHRR 387, para 46; *Vaudelle v France* (App 35683/97) (2003) 37 EHRR 16, para 55; *Jakub v Slovakia* (App 2015/02) (28 February 2006) para 48. See also *Kemmache v France (No 3)* (App 17621/91) (1995) 19 EHRR 349, para 44, which was applied in, eg, *Perlala v Greece* (App 17721/04) (22 February 2007) para 25; *Melich and Beck v Czech Republic* (App 35450/04) (24 July 2008) para 48; *Paraponiaris v Greece* (App 42132/06) (25 September 2008) para 24.

[42] *Karpenko v Russia* (App 5605/04) (13 March 2012) para 80. See also *Ghirea v Moldova* (App 15778/05) (26 June 2012) para 30.

[43] *Bernard v France* (App 22885/93) (2000) 30 EHRR 808, para 37, citing *Edwards v United Kingdom* (App 13071/87) (1993) 15 EHRR 417, para 34 and *Mantovanelli v France* (App 21497/93) (1997) 24 EHRR 370, para 34. cf van Dijk and van Hoof, *Theory and Practice of the European Convention on Human Rights* (n 17 above) 587; Trechsel, *Human Rights in Criminal Proceedings* (n 24 above) 176.

> The Court reiterates . . . that *it is not its task to take the place of the domestic courts.* It is primarily for the national authorities, notably the courts of appeal and of first instance, to resolve problems of interpretation of domestic legislation. The role of the Court is limited to verifying whether the effects of such interpretation are compatible with the Convention.[44]

At first glance, therefore, the European Court's approach is clear.[45] It is not the role of the Court to act as an appellate court – a term effectively defined as engaging in review of the national courts' legal and factual analysis. But the reality of the case law is more complex, as is evident in the caveat expressed in *Schenk* above: 'unless and in so far as they may have infringed rights and freedoms protected by the Convention'.[46] The general rule, therefore, is that review of legal and factual analysis is not within the Court's purview. The caveat, in turn, creates a class of exceptions to the general rule. Such a caveat may be thought logical in isolation. Difficulties arise, however, when this caveat is applied.

The reality is that in order for the caveat to be effective, the Court must recognise that the caveat implicitly requires that *every* Article 6 criminal fair trial case coming before it be scrutinised to determine whether there have been any errors infringing rights and freedoms protected by the Convention. That scrutiny may be strong or weak, but it *is* scrutiny. Moreover, the interests of transparency and accountability call for an explanation of how that initial scrutiny should be conducted, and the level of intensity appropriate to such a review. Put another way, the Court cannot conclude that a national court's legal and factual analysis does not 'infringe rights and freedoms' *unless* it engages with and assesses the national court's analysis in some preliminary way. Of course, as soon as that preliminary assessment has been conducted, the trap has been sprung, and the Court has engaged with the national courts' factual and legal analysis.

There is, however, no indication of what test the Court applies, nor of a realisation on its part that the caveat necessarily involves some level of engagement with the legal and factual analysis of every case it considers. An example of this tension is evident in *Walchli v France*, where the Court stated that

[44] *Miragall Escolano and others v Spain* (App 28366/97) (2002) 34 EHRR 24, para 33 (emphasis added), citing *Brualla Gomez de la Torre v Spain* (App 26737/95) (2001) 33 EHRR 57, para 31 and *Edificaciones March Gallego SA v Spain* (App 28028/95) (2001) 33 EHRR 46, para 33; van Dijk and van Hoof, *Theory and Practice of the European Convention on Human Rights* (n 17 above) 572–73. See also *Gruais and Bosquet v France* (App 67881/01) (10 January 2006) para 27; *Vitan v Romania* (App 42084/02) (25 March 2008) para 55.

[45] For a non-critical explanation and acceptance of the fourth instance rule, see the discussion of *Rowe and Davis v United Kingdom* (App 28901/95) (2000) 30 EHRR 1 in Legg, *The Margin of Appreciation in International Human Rights Law* (n 35 above) 168–69.

[46] *Schenk v Switzerland* (n 36 above) para 45; Petzold, 'The Convention and the Principle of Subsidiarity' (n 10 above) 50. See also, eg, *Bernard v France* (n 43 above) para 37; *Miragall Escolano and others v Spain* (n 44 above) para 33; *Ringeisen v Austria (Merits)* (n 41 above) para 97; *Orlov v Russia* (App 29652/04) (21 June 2011) para 98; *Niculescu v Romania* (App 25333/03) (25 June 2013) para 113.

> [it is] the primary responsibility of national authorities, including courts . . . to *interpret the legislation*. The Courts role is limited to *ensuring compatibility with the Convention of the effects of such an interpretation*.[47]

In the absence of further guidance from the Court on how to distinguish between analysis of the *interpretation* of legislation and analysis of the *effects* of the interpretation of legislation, the Court's stance is opaque. There is no attempt, for example, to differentiate the nature of an appeal from the nature of a review. In these ways the Court sets itself to walk an interpretative high-wire without acknowledging that the high-wire even exists.

The European Court thus repeatedly frames its role as different from that of the appellate courts, *except* to the extent that the proceedings have engaged Article 6's fair trial protections. But the Court does not provide the formula for approaching the question of how, and at what level of intensity, it reviews a national court's factual and legal analysis in order to determine whether that analysis has triggered Article 6 engagement. In *Goktepe v Belgium*, the Court stated

> in principle it is for national courts to assess the evidence gathered by them. The task of the Court is to determine whether the procedure as a whole, including the presentation of evidence, has been fair.[48]

Versions of this formulation have been used frequently.[49] It is noteworthy that the European Court does not, in any of these cases, provide guidance as to how it determines which cases demand that the European Court itself engage with the national court's factual and legal analysis in order to determine whether a breach of the Convention has occurred.[50]

As the analysis above has shown, at no stage has the Court recognised that the caveat may implicitly require that *every* Article 6 criminal fair trial case coming before it be scrutinised to determine whether there have been any errors infringing rights and freedoms protected by the Convention. Such preliminary scrutiny is a logical precursor to the more thorough scrutiny that the caveat envisages.

[47] *Walchli v France* (App 35787/03) (26 July 2007) para 27 (translated) (emphasis added).

[48] *Goktepe v Belgium* (App 50372/99) (2 June 2005) para 25 (translated), citing *Van Mechelen and others v Netherlands* (App 21363/93) (1998) 25 EHRR 647, para 50.

[49] See, eg, *Garcia Ruiz v Spain* (App 30544/96) (2001) 31 EHRR 22, para 28; *Mostacciuolo Giuseppe v Italy (No 2)* (App 65102/01) (29 March 2006) para 80 (civil); *Jakumas v Lithuania* (App 6924/02) (18 July 2006) para 54; *Mamidakis v Greece* (App 35533/04) (11 January 2007) para 29; *Perlala v Greece* (n 41 above) para 25; *Gorgievski v FYROM* (App 18002/02) (16 July 2009) pars 46–47; *Gladyshev v Russia* (App 2807/04) (30 July 2009) paras 74–75; *Khametshin v Russia* (n 36 above) para 29; *Nicoleta Gheorghe v Romania* (App 23470/05) (3 April 2012) para 34.

[50] The European Court's lack of explanation for the fourth instance doctrine, and of the way in which that doctrine works, is compounded by the lack of any jurisprudential or case authority for the doctrine. See, eg, *Bernard v France* (n 43 above) para 37; *Gocmen v Turkey* (App 72000/01) (17 October 2006) para 70; *Edwards v United Kingdom* (n 43 above) para 34; *Vidal v Belgium* (App 12351/86) (22 April 1992) para 33; *Barbera, Messegue and Jabardo v Spain* (App 10588/83) (1989) 11 EHRR 360, para 68. The cases are also marked by curious contradictions. In *Unterpertinger*, eg, referred to in many fourth instance doctrine cases, the European Court makes no express statement whatsoever about the European Court's role and in fact conducts analysis consisting of an assessment of the evidence before the national court, something the doctrine purports to prohibit: see *Unterpertinger v Austria* (App 9120/80) (1991) 13 EHRR 175, para 33.

Moreover, the European Court provided no guidance on how that initial scrutiny should be conducted, or on the level of intensity appropriate to such review. We thus have considerable evidence in support of the first broad argument, namely that the fourth instance doctrine is often invoked but poorly explained and under-theorised.

In the 2007 decision of *Dumitru Popescu v Romania*, the European Court appeared to express regret that it could not function as an appellate court:

> [H]owever regrettable it may be, it should be noted that it is not generally for the Court to deal with errors fact or law allegedly committed by a domestic court.[51]

The next section considers the extent to which the Court does, in reality, conduct appellate-style analysis.

B.5 The Fourth Instance Doctrine is Riddled with Exceptions to the Point of Incoherence

In this section, the focus is less on the question of how the caveat is *triggered*, and instead on how the caveat is *applied*. Here, I argue that the range of exceptions applied via the caveat is so great that it may be more accurate to frame the exceptions as the rule, and to describe the ostensible reluctance to conduct appellate-style review as the exception. In this section, as in the last, the term 'appellate-style review' is used in the way that the European Court uses that concept: conducting review of factual or legal analysis or conclusions of domestic courts.

The first subsection (B.5.1) considers the way in which the European Court's jurisprudence on the right to a reasoned judgment constitutes an exception to the general rule prohibiting interference with factual and legal analysis. In the following subsection (B.5.2), I consider other ways in which the Court has identified exceptions in a range of areas of Article 6 case law. Finally, I draw conclusions about how best to accurately summarise the fourth instance doctrine in subsection B.5.3. Overall, this section challenges the notion that the Court has 'studiously and properly followed' the fourth instance doctrine.[52]

The distinction between an analysis of the fairness of 'the proceedings as a whole', and an appellate-style factual and legal analysis, is a slippery one. This book accepts that an assessment of the fairness of proceedings as a whole will often involve review of the factual and legal conclusions reached by a domestic court. Indeed, that was the conclusion reached by the analysis of 'the caveat' above. But the focus of my criticism is that the Court fails to acknowledge this reality; as will be seen in this section, its rhetoric about not engaging in appellate-style review is not matched by its practice. Indeed, what will be demonstrated in the following sections is that the Court has repeatedly engaged in extensive review

[51] *Dumitru Popescu v Romania (No 2)* (App 71525/01) (26 April 2007) para 102 (translated).

[52] Harris, O'Boyle and Warbrick, *Law of the European Convention on Human Rights* (n 14 above) 202.

of domestic courts' factual and legal analysis. This is not to say that the Court in these cases was *not also* involved in a review of the fairness of the proceedings as a whole, but it is to emphasise that the Court *was* involved in appellate-style review.[53]

B.5.1 The Right to Reasons Provides a Major Exception to the Fourth Instance Doctrine

The right to a reasoned judgment is one of the component elements of Article 6.[54] The argument here is that, in many cases, consideration of the adequacy of a national court's reasons blurs into what reads like appellate review. Of course, the Court's ability to engage in such consideration is enlivened by the caveat: it can engage in this sort of analysis only where the fairness of the trial is in question. I argue here that right to reasons analysis has the potential to be appellate-style review in the clothing of the caveat. If all it takes to enliven the caveat is an argument alleging inadequate reasons, then virtually every case has the potential to trigger appellate-style review. Moreover, I argue that the Court provides little guidance to indicate how it determines the adequacy of reasons, and, in particular, the intensity of review it applies to a given set of reasons when considering their adequacy. In the absence of such guidelines, the risk is that the Court's decisions on the right to reasons may appear arbitrary, and that the fourth instance doctrine may not be as secure as the Court's rhetoric suggests.

Of course, as was stated in *Salov v Ukraine*, 'the question whether a court has failed to fulfil its obligation to state reasons can only be determined in the light of the circumstances of the particular case'.[55] Nevertheless, determining a case on the facts of that particular case should not disguise the need for the Court to identify a general standard against which it measures the adequacy of reasons.

In *Hadjianastassiou*, for example, there is reasons review that appears to come close to appellate review:

> 33. . . . The national courts must . . . indicate with sufficient clarity the grounds on which they based their decision. It is this, inter alia, which makes it possible for the

[53] See E.2 for detailed consideration, and critique, of the European Court's references to the 'proceedings as a whole'.

[54] See, eg, van Dijk and van Hoof, *Theory and Practice of the European Convention on Human Rights* (n 17 above) 595–96; Trechsel, *Human Rights in Criminal Proceedings* (n 24 above) 102–10; Ovey and White, *Jacobs and White* (n 16 above) 179; Harris, O'Boyle and Warbrick, *Law of the European Convention on Human Rights* (n 14 above) 268–69; *Taxquet v Belgium* (Grand Chamber) (n 12 above); Paul Roberts, 'Does Article 6 of the European Convention on Human Rights Require Reasoned Verdicts in Criminal Trials?' (2011) *Human Rights Law Review* 1. See also *Taxquet v Belgium* (Grand Chamber) (n 12 above) paras 90–92. See also D.1.

[55] *Salov v Ukraine* (App 65518/01) (2007) 45 EHRR 51, para 89, citing *Ruiz Torija v Spain* (App 18390/91) (1995) 19 EHRR 553, para 29. See also *Backes v Luxembourg* (App 24261/05) (8 July 2008) para 65 and *Taxquet v Belgium* (App 926/05) (13 January 2009) para 40; *Taxquet v Belgium* (Grand Chamber) (n 12 above); and Harris, O'Boyle and Warbrick, *Law of the European Convention on Human Rights* (n 14 above) 268.

> accused to exercise usefully the rights of appeal available to him. The [European] Court's task is to consider whether the method adopted in this respect has led in a given case to results which are compatible with the Convention.
>
> 34. In this instance the judgment read out . . . contained no mention of the questions as they appeared in the record of the hearing . . . Admittedly it referred to . . . the Military Criminal Code . . . and described the information communicated as of minor importance, but it was not based on the same grounds as the decision of the Permanent Air Force Court.[56]

In this passage, the excerpted section of paragraph 34 constitutes appellate-style review as the Court explains that term, insofar as it involves reviewing the national court's conclusions of fact and law. The right to reasons affords the Court the opportunity to act in a thoroughly appellate-style manner. Moreover, significantly, there is no indication in this judgment of what constitutes 'sufficient clarity' of reasons, or of how intensively to conduct the review that reaches a conclusion on the question of clarity.

The adequacy of a domestic court's reasons was also considered in *Khudobin v Russia*, in which the Court stated bluntly:

> [A]lthough . . . the domestic court had reason to suspect that there was an entrapment, it did not analyse the relevant factual and legal elements which would have helped it to distinguish entrapment from a legitimate form of investigative activity. It follows that the proceedings which led to the applicant's conviction were not 'fair'.[57]

In this way the Court directly challenges the 'factual and legal' analysis of the domestic court, and does so without identifying the standard or intensity of review that is appropriate in such cases.[58] Similarly, in *Kuznetsov*, the Court cited the importance of reasons,[59] and then engaged in lengthy legal and factual analysis, including this passage:

> The Court is struck by the inconsistent approach of the Russian courts, on the one hand finding it established that the Commissioner and her aides had come to the applicants' religious meeting and that it had been terminated ahead of time, and on the other hand refusing to see a link between these two elements without furnishing an alternative explanation for the early termination of the meeting. Their findings of fact appear to suggest that the Commissioner's arrival and the applicants' decision to interrupt their religious service had simply happened to coincide. That approach permitted the domestic courts to avoid addressing the applicants' main complaint, namely that neither the Commissioner nor the police officers had had any legal basis for interfering with the conduct of the applicants' religious event. The crux of the applicants' grievances – a

[56] *Hadjianastassiou v Greece* (App 12945/87) (1993) 16 EHRR 219, paras 33–34. See also van Dijk and van Hoof, *Theory and Practice of the European Convention on Human Rights* (n 17 above) 635; Trechsel, *Human Rights in Criminal Proceedings* (n 24 above) 108–9.

[57] *Khudobin v Russia* (App 59696/00) (2009) 48 EHRR 22, para 137.

[58] See also Trechsel, *Human Rights in Criminal Proceedings* (n 24 above) 106–7.

[59] *Kuznetsov and others v Russia* (App 184/02) (2009) 49 EHRR 15, para 83.

> violation of their right to freedom of religion – was thus left outside the scope of review by the domestic courts.[60]

This lengthy extract demonstrates the extent to which the European Court engages in rigorous factual and legal analysis of the national court's reasons.[61] This book readily recognises that such analysis may be essential to determining whether the applicant's right to reasons was infringed. The interests of predictability and consistency demand, however, that the Court make clear the appropriate standard of review to apply in reviewing reasons cases. Moreover, and perhaps more importantly for present purposes, the Court needs to indicate why this sort of reasons analysis could not be invoked in virtually *every* Article 6 criminal case, thus rendering every case subject to appellate-style review and neutralising the fourth instance doctrine.

It is important to emphasise, therefore, that despite the Court's definition of its own role as not acting like an appellate court, its case law provides it with the opportunity to be precisely that.[62] The right to reasons case law provides a gaping exception to the general rule. Moreover, it does so in an understructured way. In *Nechiporuk and Yonalko v Ukraine*, for example, the Court engaged in extensive factual and legal review of the national courts' reasons. This passage is an excerpt from that analysis:

> 277. The [European Court] finds the responses of both the first-instance court and the Supreme Court to those arguments to be *strikingly scant and inadequate.* While dismissing as unfounded the first applicant's allegations about pressure on the witness and noting that 'there [was] no information from which it could be discerned [otherwise]', the courts *failed to comment on* the undisputed fact of the administrative detention of Mr K. and *ignored* the existence of the audiotape referred to by the applicant even though it had been included in the case-file materials. . . .
>
> 279. Turning to the present case, the Court notes that: firstly, the courts decided to attach weight to the accusatory statements of Mr K. *in disregard of specific and pertinent facts* with a potential to undermine their reliability and accuracy; secondly, it was *never established in a convincing manner* that Mr K. had made those statements of his own free will – the fact that he had pursued that approach in the court might merely have resulted from continuing intimidation; and, lastly, the statements of Mr K. became consistently unfavourable for the first applicant from the time of his questioning, coinciding with his own detention.

[60] ibid para 84.

[61] This passage has been cited in support of this sort of review: see *Haxhia v Albania* (App 29861/03) (8 October 2013) para 3 of Partly Dissenting Opinion of Judge De Gaetano.

[62] For examples of the many similar reasons cases in which the fourth instance doctrine has been invoked and then circumvented, see *Gradinar v Moldova* (App 7170/02) (8 April 2008) paras 112–115; *Vanjak v Croatia* (App 29889/04) (14 January 2010) paras 60–61; *Mamikonyan v Armenia* (App 25083/05) (16 March 2010) paras 35–37; *Vetrenko v Moldova* (App 36552/02) (18 May 2010) paras 55–59; *Bulfinsky v Romania* (App 28823/04) (1 June 2010) paras 44–48; *Nechiporuk and Yonalko v Ukraine* (App 42310/04) (21 April 2011) paras 268–281; *Mitrofan v Moldova* (App 50054/07) (15 January 2013) paras 50–55; cf Trechsel, *Human Rights in Criminal Proceedings* (n 24 above) 104–6 and *Segame SA v France* (App 4837/06) (7 June 2012) para 64.

> 280. The Court has held, in the context of its examination of the fairness of civil proceedings, that by ignoring a specific, pertinent and important point of the applicant, the domestic courts fall short of their obligations under [Article 6(1)] of the Convention. It observes a similar issue in the present case, where that requirement, although being even more stringent in the context of criminal proceedings, was not met.
>
> 281. . . . there has been a violation of [Article 6(1)] of the Convention.[63]

This sort of reasoning gives the European Court the opportunity to review the factual and legal analysis of national courts in virtually any Article 6 criminal fair trial case. An applicant who feels unsatisfied by their domestic appellate system may be well advised to allege violations of the right to reasons in order to allow the Court to trigger thorough review of the domestic system's factual and legal analysis. As a dissenting opinion in *Vetrenko v Modlova* stated, in these cases the Court has assumed 'the role of a court of appeal and seeks to substitute its own view for that of the national courts'.[64] This book takes no position on whether or not such intrusive appellate-style review is desirable; the crucial point for my argument is that this situation gives rise to incongruence between the law as stated and the law as applied, and significantly undermines the coherence of the Court's case law.

B.5.2 The European Court's Case Law Discloses Numerous Additional 'Exceptions' to the Fourth Instance Doctrine

This subsection considers seven further classes of exception through which the Court is able to conduct appellate-style review of domestic courts' factual and legal analysis. Together with the right to reasons exception above, these loopholes combine to provide the Court with an array of ways to conduct appellate-style analysis, notwithstanding its protestations that such analysis is beyond its ambit. Additionally, these loopholes constitute further examples of incongruence between the law as stated and the law as applied.

The first exception arises in the context of presumptions of fact and law of the kind considered in *Salabiaku*.[65] *Salabiaku* warned that contracting states must 'confine [presumptions of fact or of law] within reasonable limits which take into account the importance of what is at stake and maintain the rights of the defence'.[66]

[63] *Nechiporuk and Yonalko v Ukraine* (n 62 above) paras 277–281 (emphasis added), applied in *Vyerentsov v Ukraine* (App 20372/11) (11 April 2013) para 88.

[64] *Vetrenko v Moldova* (n 62 above) paras 2–5 of Joint Dissenting Opinion of Judges Bratza, Garlicki and David Thor Bjorgvinsson.

[65] *Salabiaku v France* (n 31 above). For more on *Salabiaku*, see Stumer, *The Presumption of Innocence* (n 24 above) 98–102; van Dijk and van Hoof, *Theory and Practice of the European Convention on Human Rights* (n 17 above) 628–29; Ovey and White, *Jacobs and White* (n 16 above) 199–200; Trechsel, *Human Rights in Criminal Proceedings* (n 24 above) 168–70; Harris, O'Boyle and Warbrick, *Law of the European Convention on Human Rights* (n 14 above) 301–2; Alan Norrie, 'Criminal Justice, Judicial Interpretation, Legal Right' in T Campbell, KD Ewing and A Tomkins (eds), *Sceptical Essays on Human Rights* (Oxford University Press, 2001) 265.

[66] *Salabiaku v France* (n 31 above) para 28. cf Lord Hoffmann in *R v G* [2008] UKHL 37, [2009] 1 AC 92, para 5.

In *Pham Hoang*, therefore, the Court considered several such presumptions in order to determine whether they had been confined within reasonable limits. This analysis led the Court to review directly the factual and legal analysis of the domestic courts:

> Furthermore, in its judgment . . . the Court of Appeal did not cite in the reasons for its decision any of the impugned provisions of the Customs Code when it ruled on the accused's guilt, even if it in substance took Articles 399 and 409 as its basis for holding that he had had 'an interest in customs evasion' and that he was guilty of an attempted customs offence . . . The court set out the circumstances of the applicant's arrest and took account of a cumulation of facts. It noted that during the afternoon of 3 January 1984 he had, in his own car, driven an important drug trafficker to several shops in order to buy hydrochloric acid; a little earlier, it added, he had been present in the flat where the head of the trafficking network had brought 5kg of caffeine and he had agreed to take Tran and Ngo to where the heroin was to be delivered. Lastly, it noted that although he had 'not physically come into possession' of the heroin, this was due only to the intervention of the police and was thus for reasons beyond his control . . .
>
> It therefore appears that the Court of Appeal duly weighed the evidence before it, assessed it carefully and based its finding of guilt on it. It refrained from any automatic reliance on the presumptions created in the relevant provisions of the Customs Code and did not apply them in a manner incompatible with [Article 6(1) and (2)] of the Convention.[67]

The lengthy quote is necessary to demonstrate the level of detail that the Court's analysis includes. My argument is not that this detail and depth is normatively undesirable for the purposes of *Salabiaku* analysis. But it must be noted that such analysis falls squarely within the appellate-style analysis that the Court states it does not conduct as a general rule; this is concrete detailed analysis of the domestic court's reasoning.

A similar presumptions case was *Telfner v Austria.* In that case, the Court warned that

> as a general rule, it is for the national courts to assess the evidence before them, while it is for the [European] Court to ascertain that the proceedings considered as a whole were fair.[68]

Nevertheless, several paragraphs after this warning, the Court's analysis engaged directly with the way in which the national court had assessed the evidence:

> In addition, the Court notes that both the District Court and the Regional Court speculated about the possibility of the applicant having been under the influence of alcohol which was, as they admitted themselves, not supported by any evidence. Although such speculation was not directly relevant to establishing the elements of the offence with

[67] *Pham Hoang v France* (n 31 above) paras 35–36; Trechsel, *Human Rights in Criminal Proceedings* (n 24 above) 170.

[68] *Telfner v Austria* (App 33501/96) (2002) 34 EHRR 7, para 15. See also Harris, O'Boyle and Warbrick, *Law of the European Convention on Human Rights* (n 14 above) 301; Ovey and White, *Jacobs and White* (n 16 above) 198–99; van Dijk and van Hoof, *Theory and Practice of the European Convention on Human Rights* (n 17 above) 626–27.

> which the applicant had been charged, it contributes to the impression that the courts had a preconceived view of the applicant's guilt.[69]

Here, the Court found that certain speculation was 'not supported by any evidence'. This plainly involves 'assess[ing] the evidence'. While the national courts here 'admitted' their evidentiary flaw, there is nothing in the Court's logic that would prevent it from reviewing the evidence in a case where the national courts made no such admission. Once again, the Court demonstrated a willingness to engage in review of factual and legal analysis in cases involving presumptions of law or of fact.

The second of the exceptions in this section is drawn from *CG v United Kingdom*. In *CG*, the central question was 'whether the nature and frequency of the trial judge's interventions, combined with the deficiencies . . . in his summing-up' violated Article 6.[70] In the course of determining whether the judge's actions infringed Article 6(1), the Court engaged in intensive review of the trial transcript:

> The next interruptions came in the course of the applicant's own examination-in-chief by her counsel. The Court notes that these were again frequent in number, appearing on twenty-two of the thirty-one pages of the transcript, and that they commenced very early in the course of the examination. The judge effectively took over the examination for a short time (between pages 2 and 4 of the transcript), and his interruptions led the applicant's counsel to seek a short adjournment, which the judge granted (at page 6).[71]

Indeed, the Court went so far as to say:

> While the Court accepts the assessment of the Court of Appeal that the applicant's counsel found himself incommoded and disconcerted by these interruptions, it also agrees with the Court of Appeal, from its own examination of the transcript of the evidence, that the applicant's counsel was never prevented from continuing with the line of defence that he was attempting to develop either in cross-examination or through his own witness.[72]

These passages demonstrate that the Court engaged in close review of the domestic courts' factual and legal analysis. It may be that this is the normatively desirable course for the Court to take in resolving an Article 6(1) complaint, but it does not sit well with the Court's frequent protestations that it does not conduct appellate-style review.

The third exception arises out of *Walchli v France*, in which the European Court considered whether certain procedural rules infringed the applicant's Article 6 rights. The Court warned that national courts

> must, in applying the rules of procedure, avoid both excessive formalism which would impair the fairness of the procedure, and an excessive flexibility that would remove the procedural requirements established by law.[73]

[69] *Telfner v Austria* (n 68 above) para 19.
[70] *CG v United Kingdom* (App 43373/98) (2002) 34 EHRR 31, para 35. See Harris, O'Boyle and Warbrick, *Law of the European Convention on Human Rights* (n 14 above) 270.
[71] *CG v United Kingdom* (n 70 above) para 38.
[72] ibid para 41.
[73] *Walchli v France* (n 47 above) para 29 (translated).

The Court thus effectively stated that any Article 6 case involving procedural rules could trigger a review of the national court's application of those rules, in order to ensure that the national courts had avoided excessive formalism and excessive flexibility. Such a requirement gives the Court considerable scope for review in cases involving procedural rules, and runs against the ostensibly general approach.

The fourth exception arises out of some of the cases concerning evidence and witnesses. The applicant in *Koval v Ukraine* complained that a witness (his wife) had not been examined, contrary to Article 6(3). The Court first 'note[d]'

> that the applicant's wife was not examined by the domestic courts in connection with the issue of forfeiture of bail, despite being present throughout the court proceedings. However, the applicant initially did not request to have evidence taken from her in court. Furthermore, he has failed to explain what he intended to prove with the witness evidence that would have been produced and how this evidence could have been relevant to the determination of the charge of interfering with a witness.[74]

Thus the Court considered, in some detail, the course of evidence in the domestic courts and how that course may have been different if the applicant's wife had been examined. Similar analysis was conducted in *Bricmont*, *Maresti*, *Vanjak*, and *Tseber*.[75] In so doing, the Court engages with and reviews the domestic courts' factual and legal conclusions.

Another case concerning witnesses was *Vladimir Romanov*. The applicant complained that he had been denied 'adequate opportunity to put questions to witnesses against him'.[76] The Court engaged in extensive review of the national courts' factual and legal analysis:

> 101. Turning to the facts of the present case . . . It is also true that the applicant admitted to having been present at the crime scene with the intention of beating Mr I. up and that the courts relied on that admission, but under Russian law a conviction cannot rest solely on the admission of the accused . . . *The Court is not convinced that the applicant's avowal that he had intended to beat the victim up amounted to an admission that he had wanted to rob him too . . .*
>
> 102. As to the three witnesses, they had made no observations on the alleged acts and gave evidence only on the fact that they had seen some four men running from the crime scene. Furthermore, the witnesses were unable to identify those men . . . As regards the confessions, the Court notes that the co-defendants retracted them at the trial, alleging coercion on the part of the investigator. Leaving aside the investigation techniques and the alleged interrogation of the co-defendants in a state of drug intoxication, *the Court reiterates that a higher degree of scrutiny should be applied to assessment of statements by co-defendants, because the position in which the accomplices find them-*

[74] *Koval v Ukraine* (n 9 above) para 116.

[75] *Bricmont v Belgium* (App 10857/84) (1990) 12 EHRR 217, para 89 (considered in Ovey and White, *Jacobs and White* (n 16 above) 207; Petzold, 'The Convention and the Principle of Subsidiarity' (n 10 above) 50; Trechsel, *Human Rights in Criminal Proceedings* (n 24 above) 103; *Maresti v Croatia* (App 55759/07) (25 June 2009) paras 36–41; *Vanjak v Croatia* (n 62 above) paras 47–56; *Tseber v Czech Republic* (App 46203/08) (22 November 2012) paras 67–69.

[76] *Vladimir Romanov v Russia* (App 41461/02) (24 July 2008) para 92.

> *selves while testifying is different from that of ordinary witnesses* . . . For the guarantees of Article 6 of the Convention to be respected on account of the admissibility of a guilty plea from a co-accused, such a plea should only be admitted to establish the fact of a commission of a crime by a pleading person, and not the applicant, and a judge should make it clear to the jury that the guilty plea by itself did not prove that the applicant was involved in that crime.[77]

The italicised excerpts, in particular, constitute direct engagement with the national courts' factual and legal analysis. This form of analysis undermines the Court's frequent insistence that, in general, it is not its role to review national courts' factual and legal conclusions.

Similarly, in the self-incrimination case of *Condron*, the Court engaged in detailed factual-legal review of the proceedings in the national courts:

> 63. . . . the Court of Appeal had no means of ascertaining whether or not the applicants' silence played a significant role in the jury's decision to convict. The Court of Appeal had regard to the weight of the evidence against the applicants. However it was in no position to assess properly whether the jury considered this to be conclusive of their guilt.
>
> 64. The Court is not persuaded either that the fact that the co-accused, Mr Curtis, who also remained silent during police interview . . . was acquitted indicates that the jury attached little weight to the applicants' silence in finding them guilty. It cannot be excluded that the jury accepted Mr Curtis' explanation for his silence and did not therefore draw an adverse inference against him; it cannot be excluded either that the jury may have accepted the applicants' defence to the charges, for example their claim that the police had planted incriminating evidence in their flat . . . and that the evidence against them was not as overwhelming as the Court of Appeal considered. In any event, it is a speculative exercise which only reinforces the crucial nature of the defect in the trial judge's direction and its implications for review of the case on appeal.[78]

Once again, the European Court's frequent insistence that it is not its role to review national courts' factual-legal analysis is rendered more incoherent whenever it engages in this sort of review of the national court's factual-legal analysis.

A fifth exception, one related to those above, is evident in *Brennan v United Kingdom*, where the Court states that, 'as a general rule', it would not

> substitute its own assessment of the evidence made by a domestic court, *save in circumstances where* the domestic court's assessment was arbitrary or capricious, or the system of guarantees or safeguards which applied in the assessment of the reliability of confession evidence was manifestly inadequate.[79]

[77] ibid paras 101–102 (emphasis added).

[78] *Condron v United Kingdom* (App 35718/97) (2001) 31 EHRR 1, paras 63–64.

[79] *Brennan v United Kingdom* (App 39846/98) (2002) 34 EHRR 18, para 51 (emphasis added), citing *Edwards v United Kingdom* (n 43 above) para 34 (note that *Edwards* makes no reference whatsoever to 'arbitrary or capricious', nor to the 'system of guarantees or safeguards' standard). See extensive appellate-style analysis under the guise of the review of 'arbitrary' decision-making in *Ajdaric v Croatia* (App 20883/09) (13 December 2011) paras 29–53. For reference to the European Court's willingness to intervene in cases of arbitrary interpretation of legal provisions, see *Sahin and Sahin v Turkey* (App 13279/05) (2012) 54 EHRR 20, paras 84–90.

One may note that this passage allows the Court a sizeable loophole to engage in appellate-style review of the domestic court's assessment of the evidence. Further, it is also plain that the *Brennan* judgment does not provide guidance on whether the Court should test *every* domestic court's factual assessments against the 'arbitrary or capricious' standard before deciding to review them, or if there is another appropriate 'gatekeeper' standard. In any event, granting the Court the power to review 'arbitrary or capricious' domestic court rulings sounds very close indeed to the appellate-style review from which the Court has distanced itself.

The sixth exception is evident in *DeWeer*. In that case, the Court considered the validity of the applicant's purported waiver of 'his right to have his case dealt with by a tribunal'.[80] The Court stated:

> [I]n a democratic society too great an importance attaches to the 'right to a court' . . . for its benefit to be forfeited solely by reason of the fact that an individual is a party to a settlement reached in the course of a procedure ancillary to court proceedings. In an area concerning the public order (*ordre public*) of the member States . . . any measure or decision alleged to be in breach of Article 6 calls for particularly careful review.[81]

It is unclear whether the force of this statement is that 'particularly careful review' will be conducted of any waiver case,[82] or whether 'particularly careful review' is called for in any case in which a contracting state asserts a public order interest. Regardless of whether these statements are directed at waiver or at public order, this exception imposes on the Court an obligation to conduct 'particularly careful review', which would conceivably include review of the domestic court's legal and factual conclusions with respect to a waiver or public order.

Our seventh exception involves the European Court simply stating that it is unable to endorse the factual or legal analysis of a national court and, as such, that analysis is questioned or overturned by the Court. Thus, for example, in *Hanzevacki*, the Court considered the arguments of an applicant whose lawyer had fallen ill during the hearing. The national court had 'concluded that the counsel's presence was not necessary in view of the evidence . . . and the features of the crime'.[83] The Court, however, stated:

> 25. The Court *cannot endorse the views of the appellate court* for the following reasons. The Court notes that one of the most important aspects of a concluding hearing in criminal trials is an opportunity for the defence, as well as for the prosecution, to present their closing arguments, and it is the only opportunity for both parties to orally present their view of the entire case and all the evidence presented at trial and give their assessment of the result of the trial. The Court considers that the choice made by the

[80] *DeWeer v Belgium* (n 21 above) para 49.

[81] ibid para 49, citing *De Wilde and others v Belgium* (App 2832/66) (1979–80) 1 EHRR 373, para 65. See, analogously, van Dijk and van Hoof, *Theory and Practice of the European Convention on Human Rights* (n 17 above) 601.

[82] See Clayton and Tomlinson, *The Law of Human Rights* (n 13 above) 859; Harris, O'Boyle and Warbrick, *Law of the European Convention on Human Rights* (n 14 above) 245; C Gearty, *Principles of Human Rights Adjudication* (Oxford University Press, 2004) 192.

[83] *Hanzevacki v Croatia* (App 17182/07) (16 April 2009) para 24.

> prosecution not to attend the concluding hearing in the case against the applicant cannot have any effect on the right of the accused to be represented by a lawyer of his own choosing.[84]

Virtually identical language appeared in *Maresti*.[85] Similarly, in *Sebalj*, the European Court restated the fourth instance doctrine and then, three paragraphs later, openly indicated that it was unwilling to accept the analysis of the national courts:

> The national courts based their conclusion that the applicant was questioned in a lawyer's presence on the fact that a statement to this effect had been given by State officials who had a duty to act in accordance with the laws well known to them. However, *the Court cannot endorse such a conclusion* in the light of the fact that the national courts failed to examine the obvious discrepancy between the alleged time of the presence of lawyer . . . and the time of the applicant's actual questioning.[86]

In such cases, the European Court does not don even the thinnest of veils in questioning the analysis of the national courts.

B.5.3 Have the 'Exceptions' Become the Rule?

In the two preceding subsections, therefore, eight groups of examples point to ways in which the European Court routinely engages in review of domestic courts' factual and legal analysis. If one accepts this case law on its face, then the state of the law could be summarised in the following way. In the course of an Article 6 criminal application, the Court's role is not to review domestic courts' factual or legal analysis, unless the application:

- concerns the right to reasons;
- concerns *Salabiaku* presumptions;
- is an Article 6(1) application considering the role of the trial judge;
- concerns rules of procedure;
- concerns witnesses;
- arises out of an arbitrary or capricious assessment by a domestic court or out of a confession for which there were inadequate reliability-assessment safeguards;
- involves either a waiver of the right of access to a court or involves *ordre public* considerations; or
- involves domestic courts' reasoning that the European Court 'cannot endorse'.

Taken together, these exceptions provide the European Court with an array of ways in which it can review domestic courts' factual and legal analysis.[87] An applicant in any Article 6 criminal application, if unsatisfied with domestic appellate

[84] ibid para 25 (emphasis added).

[85] *Maresti v Croatia* (n 75 above) para 41.

[86] *Sebalj v Croatia* (App 4429/09) (28 June 2011) para 262 (emphasis added). The fourth instance doctrine is outlined at para 259.

[87] cf van Dijk and van Hoof, *Theory and Practice of the European Convention on Human Rights* (n 17 above) 572–73.

processes, would be well advised to raise one or more of the categories identified above in order to provide the Court with the trigger to review domestic proceedings. The right to reasons could be invoked in many Article 6 criminal applications; rules of procedure and witnesses would similarly be able to be invoked on a regular basis. Thus, the two broad arguments with respect to the fourth instance doctrine – the first about internal coherence and the second about the incongruence between rhetoric and practice – combine to undermine the Court's approach in this area.

If the European Court is willing to review factual and legal analysis in so many situations, it risks giving the appearance that the default position is, in fact, that the Court regards itself as *empowered* to engage in appellate-style analysis *unless* the application is a rare one that is incapable of being brought within one of the categories above. This may well be a desirable outcome, insofar as it can be interpreted as reflecting judicial expertise about legal procedures and legal interpretation.[88] If that were to be the case, however, the interests of transparency, congruence and predictability demand that the Court reformulate its approach to appellate-style review to reflect the reality that is plainly evident in the case law.[89] Alternatively, the European Court might choose to reduce the extent to which it engages in appellate-style review, and in doing so recognise that some instances of what would have previously been regarded as unfair trials would thenceforth go unremarked upon by the Court. Either course would reduce the incongruence between the law as stated and the law as applied.

The Court may wish, instead, to preserve the unarticulated fiction of the fourth instance rule in an attempt to consolidate its own institutional or geopolitical position within Europe. As was outlined above, this book will leave such suggestions to the political scientists and diplomats, and focus instead on the doctrinal detail of the case law. Nonetheless, it may be noted that if the European Court elects to perpetuate the uncertainty in the existing case law in pursuit of unarticulated political objectives, it will only serve to inhibit the Court's ability to provide the people, judges, and officials of Europe with guidance as to the Court's role in Article 6 cases. Better, surely, for the Court to 'always try to look like a court'.[90]

B.6 The European Court's Approach to the Law of Evidence is Marked by Incoherence

In defining its role in Article 6 criminal cases, the European Court is frequently called upon to engage with issues related to the law of evidence. This section looks

[88] See, more generally on these rationales, Legg, *The Margin of Appreciation in International Human Rights Law* (n 35 above) 167–74.

[89] There may also be institutional or logistical implications, of the sort discussed by Trechsel, *Human Rights in Criminal Proceedings* (n 24 above) 84.

[90] Greer and Wildhaber, 'Reflections of a former President of the European Court of Human Rights' (n 2 above) 173.

at the Court's approach to rules of admissibility. This section is not an exhaustive survey of the Court's approach to issues related to the law of evidence, or even of its approach to rules of admissibility. Some particular aspects of those general issues have been touched on above, and others are dealt with in subsequent parts.[91] For now, however, a brief overview of the Court's approach is appropriate insofar as it constitutes part of the way that the Court generally defines its role in Article 6 criminal cases. Here I argue that the Court's approach is incoherent, poorly explained, and that it fails to appreciate the complexity of the framework outlined in its own case law.

The starting point is *Schenk*, where the Court outlined its inability to consider rules of admissibility:

> While Article 6 . . . guarantees the right to a fair trial, it does not lay down any rules on the admissibility of evidence as such, which is therefore primarily a matter for regulation under national law. The Court therefore cannot exclude as a matter of principle and in the abstract that unlawfully obtained evidence of the present kind may be admissible. It has only to ascertain whether Mr Schenk's trial as a whole was fair.[92]

It may be worthwhile to disaggregate the way in which the European Court has considered several ideas in this passage. First, the Court states that because Article 6 does not lay down any rules on evidence, *therefore* it is primarily a matter for national law (one wonders whether this logic would defeat most of the Article 6 implied rights).[93] Second, the Court states that the logical consequence of this being primarily a matter for national law is that the Court cannot rule that such evidence will never be admissible (it is unclear why the Court's inability to rule in the abstract follows from something being primarily a matter of national law). Notwithstanding these tensions, *Schenk* has proven extremely influential, and has repeatedly been referred to directly or indirectly.[94]

[91] For analysis of how the European Court's jurisprudence interacts with the domestic law of evidence of, eg, the United Kingdom, see I Dennis, *The Law of Evidence*, 3rd edn (Sweet & Maxwell, 2007); P Murphy, *Murphy on Evidence*, 10th edn (Oxford University Press, 2008); Colin Tapper, *Cross and Tapper on Evidence*, 12th edn (Oxford University Press, 2010).

[92] *Schenk v Switzerland* (n 36 above) para 46. See Trechsel, *Human Rights in Criminal Proceedings* (n 24 above) 293–94; Harris, O'Boyle and Warbrick, *Law of the European Convention on Human Rights* (n 14 above) 202, 256; van Dijk and van Hoof, *Theory and Practice of the European Convention on Human Rights* (n 17 above) 585–86; Petzold, 'The Convention and the Principle of Subsidiarity' (n 10 above) 54; Arai-Takahashi, *The Margin of Appreciation Doctrine* (n 17 above) 49.

[93] See also *Foldes and Foldesne Hajlik v Hungary* (App 41463/02) (2008) 47 EHRR 11, para 28; cf *Jalloh v Germany* (n 33 above) para 94. See also Trechsel, *Human Rights in Criminal Proceedings* (n 24 above) 293–94; see part D.

[94] *Garcia Ruiz v Spain* (n 49 above) para 28; *Allan v United Kingdom* (App 48539/99) (2003) 36 EHRR 12, para 42; *Diamantides v Greece (No 2)* (App 71563/01) (19 May 2005) para 46; *Foldes and Foldesne Hajlik v Hungary* (n 93 above) para 28; *Jalloh v Germany* (n 33 above) para 94; *Soylemez v Turkey* (App 46661/99) (21 September 2006) para 121; *Shabelnik v Ukraine* (App 16404/03) (19 February 2009) para 54; *Pelissier and Sassi v France* (App 25444/94) (2000) 30 EHRR 715, para 45; *PG and JH v United Kingdom* (App 44787/98) (2008) 46 EHRR 51, paras 76–78; *Solakov v FYROM* (App 47023/99) (31 October 2001) para 57; *AM v Italy* (App 37019/97) (14 December 1999) para 24; *Van Mechelen and others v Netherlands* (n 48 above) para 50; *Doorson v Netherlands* (App 20524/92) (1996) 22 EHRR 330, para 67; *Kostovski v Netherlands* (App 11454/85) (1990) 12 EHRR 434, para 39; *Bracci v Italy* (App 36822/02) (13 October 2005) para 51; *Luca v Italy* (App 33354/96) (2003) 36 EHRR 46, para

Crucially, however, *Schenk* sets up a false dichotomy: the Court's job is *not* to rule on admissibility, especially in the abstract, but its job *is* to ascertain whether the trial as a whole was fair.[95] But the two are not mutually exclusive. *Schenk* failed to establish a mechanism for how to deal with cases where an admissibility issue may render the 'trial as a whole' unfair. If one accepts the premise of *Schenk*, then to determine whether a 'trial as a whole' is fair, the logical course may well be to examine the evidence admitted by the national court and to consider whether or not it should have been admitted. On the other hand, if *Schenk* warns against ruling on admissibility and urges that it be the province of domestic courts, then perhaps the Court should not engage with issues of admissibility at all, even in considering the fairness of the 'trial as a whole'. The Court's role in such cases is left radically unclear by *Schenk*. For example, in order to determine whether the admission of certain evidence rendered any particular trial unfair, the Court may potentially need to review the admission of evidence in *every* Article 6 criminal fair trial case to ensure that the trial under consideration was fair at first glance. What standard should be used on such a review? Should the standard on any such preliminary review be different to that which might be used on a subsequent closer look?

There is an additional problem. *Schenk* exhibits the European Court's general reluctance to make abstract rulings, stating that it could not 'exclude as a matter of principle and in the abstract that unlawfully obtained evidence of the present kind may be admissible'.[96] But, as will be seen, the European Court has repeatedly taken decisions contrary to this general statement. Often, these decisions take precisely the form of 'exclud[ing] as a matter of principle and in the abstract that' certain kinds of evidence 'may be admissible'.

A useful case study to illustrate these criticisms is provided by those cases relating to the admissibility of evidence obtained in breach of a Convention right. A forceful statement of the European Court's view of its role with respect to evidence was made in *Jalloh* (similar statements were made in cases such as *Khan, Allan, PG and JH,* and *Gafgen*[97]):

38; *Khan v United Kingdom* (App 35394/97) (2001) 31 EHRR 45, para 34; *Teixeira de Castro v Portugal* (App 25829/94) (1999) 28 EHRR 101, para 34; *Gafgen v Germany* (Grand Chamber) (n 36 above) para 162; *Orlov v Russia* (n 46 above) para 99; *Tseber v Czech Republic* (n 75 above) para 42; *CB v Austria* (n 36 above) para 35; *Erkapic v Croatia* (n 36 above) para 70; *Sica v Romania* (App 12036/05) (9 July 2013) para 56; *Botea v Romania* (n 36 above) paras 31–32; see Trechsel, *Human Rights in Criminal Proceedings* (n 24 above) 294.

[95] See E.2 for more on the 'proceedings as a whole'.

[96] *Schenk v Switzerland* (n 36 above) para 46. We have met this general reluctance before: see B.3 above.

[97] *Khan v United Kingdom* (n 94 above) para 34; *Allan v United Kingdom* (n 94 above) para 42; *PG and JH v United Kingdom* (n 94 above) para 76; *Gafgen v Germany* (App 22978/05) (2009) 48 EHRR 13, para 97; *Gafgen v Germany* (Grand Chamber) (n 36 above) para 163. See Andrew Ashworth, 'The Exclusion of Evidence Obtained by Violating a Fundamental Right: Pragmatism before Principle in the Strasbourg Jurisprudence' in P Roberts and J Hunter (eds), *Criminal Evidence and Human Rights* (Hart Publishing, 2012); M Spurrier, '*Gafgen v Germany*: Fruit of the Poisonous Tree' [2010] *EHRLR* 513; Steven Greer, 'Should Police Threats to Torture Suspects Always be Severely Punished? Reflections on the *Gafgen* Case' (2011) 11(1) *Human Rights Law Review* 67; H Sauer and M Trilsch, '*Gafgen v Germany*

> It is therefore not the role of the Court to determine, as a matter of principle, whether particular types of evidence – for example, evidence obtained unlawfully in terms of domestic law – may be admissible or, indeed, whether the applicant was guilty or not. The question which must be answered is whether the proceedings as a whole, including the way in which the evidence was obtained, were fair.[98]

Thus *Jalloh* repeats the dichotomy that determining whether certain types of evidence are admissible is *not* the role of the Court, but determining the fairness of the proceedings as a whole *is* the role of the Court. This dichotomy obscures the possibility that a ruling on the fairness of proceedings might, implicitly or explicitly, involve ruling on admissibility.

The difficulties with this dichotomy were evident, in fact, in *Jalloh*. In a passage worth excerpting at length, the Court ruled on the admissibility of certain evidence in the course of determining the fairness of the proceedings as a whole:

> 105. . . . the use of evidence obtained in violation of Article 3 in criminal proceedings raises serious issues as to the fairness of such proceedings . . . *In [the European Court's] view, incriminating evidence – whether in the form of a confession or real evidence, obtained as a result of acts of violence or brutality or other forms of treatment which can be characterised as torture – should never be relied on as proof of the victim's guilt, irrespective of its probative value.* Any other conclusion would only serve to legitimate indirectly the sort of morally reprehensible conduct which the authors of Article 3 of the Convention sought to proscribe . . .
>
> 106. Although the treatment to which the applicant was subjected did not attract the special stigma reserved to acts of torture, it did attain in the circumstances the minimum level of severity covered by the ambit of the Article 3 prohibition. *It cannot be excluded that on the facts of a particular case the use of evidence obtained by intentional acts of ill-treatment not amounting to torture will render the trial against the victim unfair* irrespective of the seriousness of the offence allegedly committed, the weight attached to the evidence and the opportunities which the victim had to challenge its admission and use at his trial.[99]

The logical result of this passage is that if contracting states wish to comply with the European Court's case law, certain types of evidence *must* become inadmissible regardless of the individual circumstances of a particular case. A plainer demonstration of the flaws of the *Schenk* dichotomy is difficult to imagine.

The question then becomes why the Court's role with respect to evidence changes when evidence was obtained in breach of Article 3. The Court's explanation is that

(Case Comment)' (2011) 105 *American Journal of International Law* 313; S Ast, 'The *Gafgen* Judgment of the ECtHR: On the Consequences of the Threat of Torture for Criminal Proceedings' (2010) 11(12) *German Law Journal* 1393; Ovey and White, *Jacobs and White* (n 16 above) 193–96.

[98] *Jalloh v Germany* (n 33 above) para 95, citing *Khan v United Kingdom* (n 94 above) para 34, *PG and JH v United Kingdom* (n 94 above) para 76, and *Allan v United Kingdom* (n 94 above) para 42.

[99] *Jalloh v Germany* (n 33 above) paras 105–106 (emphasis added), citing *Rochin v California* 342 US 165 (1952). See also *Grigoryev v Ukraine* (App 51671/07) (15 May 2012) para 84; Trechsel, *Human Rights in Criminal Proceedings* (n 24 above) 88; cp *Alchagin v Russia* (App 20212/05) (17 January 2012) paras 69–74.

> Article 3 enshrines one of the most fundamental values of democratic societies. Even in the most difficult circumstances, such as the fight against terrorism and organised crime, the Convention prohibits in absolute terms torture and inhuman or degrading treatment or punishment, irrespective of the victim's conduct. Unlike most of the substantive clauses of the Convention, Article 3 makes no provision for exceptions and no derogation from it is permissible.[100]

Several points should be made with respect to this series of justifications and the extent to which they justify unique treatment for Article 3. First, there is at least an argument that *every* Convention right enshrines fundamental values of democratic societies.[101] Second, there are other Articles not providing for exceptions (Article 5, for example).[102] Third, there are other non-derogable Articles (Articles 2, 4(1) and 7).[103] These three factors indicate the potential for incoherence in the European Court's case law: if these factors justify interfering with admissibility rules in certain cases, why not in others? This area of the law is also rendered more complex by rulings on the inadmissibility of, for example, evidence obtained 'as a result of incitement by state agents'.[104] I return to *Jalloh* in later parts.[105] But of course neither this section, nor this book, is concerned directly with the admissibility of evidence obtained in breach of a Convention right. The broader concern is that the Court's stated position may not always be reflected in the substance of its decisions.

B.7 Building the Foundations for a New Approach to How the European Court Describes Its Own Role

Part B demonstrated that although the Court often describes its role in forceful and unequivocal terms, those terms are often undermined by a series of under-theorised exceptions. The Court's sense of its own role is poorly defined and poorly explained, and there is a disconnect between the Court's stated view of its own role and the way in which the Court operates in practice.

Given these criticisms, therefore, how ought the European Court to define and explain its role in Article 6 cases? In addition to this book's broader normative arguments with respect to consistency and coherence, the criticism in this part also gives rise to several more specific normative arguments. Indeed, the critical

[100] *Jalloh v Germany* (n 33 above) para 99; cf Spurrier, '*Gafgen v Germany*: Fruit of the Poisonous Tree' (n 97 above).

[101] Indeed, see the Preamble to the European Convention.

[102] Although cf *Austin v United Kingdom* (App 39692/09) (2012) 55 EHRR 14.

[103] See Andrew Ashworth, 'Security, Terrorism and the Value of Human Rights' in B Goold and L Lazarus (eds), *Security and Human Rights*, 2nd edn (Hart Publishing, 2007).

[104] *Khudobin v Russia* (n 57 above) para 133.

[105] Relevant passages of *Jalloh* have also been drawn upon in a number of cases, eg, *Soylemez v Turkey*at (n 94 above) paras 122–125; *Haci Ozen v Turkey* (App 46286/99) (12 April 2007) paras 99–101; *Sacettin Yildiz v Turkey* (App 38419/02) (5 June 2007) paras 46–48; *Gafgen v Germany* (n 97 above) paras 98–99; *Levinta v Moldova* (App 17332/03) (16 December 2008) paras 99–100.

arguments above form the foundation for a normative argument that the Court ought to articulate its role more honestly and openly: to acknowledge that considering whether or not Article 6 has been violated will often involve conducting appellate-style analysis, and may well require the enunciation of general doctrines or the consideration of abstract challenges. Such an acknowledgment would provide helpful guidance to would-be applicants, and to contracting states, about how the European Court views its own role in Article 6 cases.[106] Any such acknowledgment ought to be framed as a necessary corollary of the assessment of whether or not there has been a violation of Article 6, which need not constitute a vast intrusion into the domestic affairs of contracting states. It is best, surely, to reduce the extent to which the European Court is disingenuous about its own role.

Those who study the institutional and political difficulties faced by the European Court, however, may suggest that those difficulties make it impossible for the Court to admit squarely to the reality of its role in Article 6 cases. This book's focus, of course, is on enhancing the ability of the Court to provide guidance, and the above criticisms proceed from that starting point. But even if some believe that political reality would win out over the need for clearer guidance in this area of law, and the Court therefore wishes to maintain the fourth instance doctrine, I suggest that the interests of clarity and predictability demand that the European Court honestly situate the exceptions to the fourth instance doctrine *as exceptions* and explain why those exceptions might apply to one class of case but not another. Explanation of this sort would help foster a greater degree of certainty about the current state, and likely future direction, of the Court's Article 6 case law.

[106] This acknowledgment need not generate fears of widespread interventionism by the European Court across the Convention's various rights: there are good reasons for a less deferential approach by the Court when it comes to matters, such as criminal procedure, about which its judges may have particular expertise. See, eg, Legg, *The Margin of Appreciation in International Human Rights Law* (n 35 above) 167–74.

C

Out of One, Many? The Internal Structure of Article 6

This part considers how the Court analyses the relationships between the various component parts of Article 6. In this book, I refer to these relationships as comprising the *internal* structure of Article 6.

In considering the European Court's analysis of Article 6's internal structure, this part asks a big-picture question about how the Court views Article 6: do its component elements amount to *one* guarantee or do they constitute *multiple independent* guarantees? Put another way, does Article 6 provide protection for the right to a fair trial (a single right, the definition of which is elaborated on by the provisions of Article 6(1), Article 6(2), and Article 6(3)), or does Article 6 provide protection for a collection of related but independent rights, all of which are housed together in the omnibus provision of Article 6? Confusion between the umbrella description of Article 6 rights as the 'right to a fair trial', and the specific 'fair and public hearing' right protected by Article 6(1), may add complexity and uncertainty to attempts to conceptualise the internal structure of Article 6.[1]

Generalisations are commonly made about the internal structure of Article 6. In this part, I challenge some of these generalisations. For example, in its Grand Chamber decisions in cases such as *Salduz* and *Al-Khawaja and Tahery*, the Court asserted as uncontroversial the proposition that the individual Article 6(3) guarantees were merely elements of the Article 6(1) fair trial guarantee.[2] This part demonstrates that such statements were oversimplifications by the Grand Chamber.[3] Less of an oversimplification was Greer's statement that the 'standard

[1] For a possible example of this confusion, see Olivier Jacot-Guillarmod, 'Rights related to Good Administration of Justice' in R Macdonald, F Matscher and H Petzold (eds), *The European System for the Protection of Human Rights* (Martinus Nijhoff, 1993) 381, where Jacot-Guillarmod misquotes a key passage from *Golder v United Kingdom* (App 4451/70) (1979–80) 1 EHRR 524, para 28. *Golder* refers to Art 6(1) but Jacot-Guillarmod's rendering of the quote has *Golder* referring to Art 6 more generally. Note, in passing, that the 'Right to a fair trial' heading to Art 6 was not added to the text of the European Convention until 1998, when Protocol No 11 entered into force. Among other things, Protocol No 11 prescribed various headings to be inserted into the European Convention's Articles. See also Sarah J Summers, *Fair Trials: The European Criminal Procedural Tradition and the European Court of Human Rights* (Hart Publishing, 2007) 102–3.

[2] *Salduz v Turkey* (App 36391/02) (2009) 49 EHRR 19, para 50; *Al-Khawaja and Tahery v United Kingdom* (Grand Chamber) (App 26766/05) (2012) 54 EHRR 23, paras 142–146.

[3] As another example of such a generalisation, it is sometimes asserted that 'the requirement that a trial be fair [is] absolute' and that 'the contents of the right are not cut and dried': ADP Brady, *Proportionality and Deference under the UK HRA: An Institutionally Sensitive Approach* (Cambridge

of fairness for criminal trials embraces the same general Article 6(1) criteria as apply in civil proceedings, but also includes the more detailed specifications found in Article 6(2) and (3)'.[4] Statements of this sort may well be accurate so far as they go, but, as will be seen, they conceal considerable complexity in terms of the functioning of the Court's case law.

Moreover, this part and subsequent parts (especially part E) will demonstrate the consequences that arise out of oversimplifications of this sort. Indeed, by analysing how the Court describes Article 6's internal relationships, this part attempts to explain something even more crucial about the Court's approach to Article 6: an understanding of the way that the European Court approaches the internal structure of Article 6 is crucial to understanding the way that the Court deals with the question of when Article 6 has been violated. Simply put, when determining whether there has been a violation, the Court will need to conduct that analysis within certain boundaries (if, for example, an application is considered separately under Article 6(1) alone and then under Article 6(3)(a) alone, those boundaries may be different to an application considered under Article 6(1) and Article 6(3)(a) 'taken together'). Choosing to deal with an application by asking 'has there been a fair trial?' involves asking a very different question indeed from, for example, 'has the accused person been informed promptly, in a language which the person understands and in detail, of the nature and cause of the accusation against them?'. This part, then, is about how the Court describes those boundaries, and how the internal structure of Article 6 affects them; part E will deal with how to make the assessments within those boundaries. Part D addresses in greater depth matters relating to the internal structure of Article 6 in the context of the implied rights. As such, the discussion of Article 6's internal structure in this part is vitally linked to the discussion in subsequent parts.

In this part, I argue that the Court has adopted a number of approaches to the internal structure of Article 6, and that these approaches are not always compatible. Crucially, the Court does not explain its use of different approaches in different cases in any meaningful way. Moreover, this part argues that these approaches are often lacking internal consistency. In order to illuminate a discussion on these questions of internal structure, much of the discussion in this part relates to applications that involve alleged infringements of more than one of Article 6's provisions. How the European Court deals with an application alleging violations of *both* Article 6(1) and Article 6(3)(a), for example, provides an insight to how the European Court views the internal relationship between those two provisions and the internal structure of Article 6 more generally.

University Press, 2012) 171, citing, inter alia, *Brown v Stott* [2000] UKPC D 3, [2003] 1 AC 681. The detail of the European Court case law is less commonly examined.

[4] Steven Greer, *The European Convention on Human Rights: Achievements, Problems and Prospects*, 2nd edn (Cambridge University Press, 2006) 253.

C.1 The European Court has Adopted Several Approaches to the Internal Structure of Article 6

The Court has adopted a variety of descriptions of the internal relationships of Article 6. This part considers some of those descriptions. At the outset, it should be noted that while some of these descriptions may be in tension with one another, or even contradict each other, others are not mutually exclusive. After beginning with the 1961 description adopted by the European Commission in *Nielsen v Denmark*, the approaches considered by this part include:

- that each of the different component parts constitute distinct minimum requirements;
- that the requirements of Article 6(2) and Article 6(3) represent more-specifically-defined aspects of Article 6(1) and, as such, the focus of the European Court's analysis in a given case should be on assessing complaints under the more general provision of Article 6(1) rather than the specific terms of Article 6(2) and/or Article 6(3). Under this view, Article 6(2) and Article 6(3) are most useful insofar as they provide guidance on how to define and apply the Article 6(1) guarantee;
- that the requirements of Article 6(2) and Article 6(3) represent more specifically defined aspects of Article 6(1) and, as such, the focus of the European Court's analysis in a given case should be on assessing complaints under the more specific provision(s) rather than the general terms of Article 6(1); and
- that the requirements of Article 6(2) and Article 6(3) represent more specifically defined aspects of Article 6(1) and, as such, the European Court's analysis in a given case should involve assessing complaints by 'taking together' the terms of Article 6(1) and Article 6(3) (or Article 6(1) and Article 6(2), as the case may be).

The existing literature does not always acknowledge the complexity, and potential for inconsistency, inherent in these various approaches.[5] As this part will demonstrate, these approaches provide various examples of the Court's irrational flexibility that features throughout this book.

[5] See, eg, P van Dijk and GJH van Hoof, *Theory and Practice of the European Convention on Human Rights*, 4th edn (Intersentia, 2006) 631–32; D Harris, M O'Boyle and C Warbrick, *Law of the European Convention on Human Rights*, 2nd edn (Oxford University Press, 2009) 246, 306; E Brems, 'Conflicting Human Rights: an Exploration in the Context of the Right to a Fair Trial in the European Convention on Human Rights' (2005) 27 *Human Rights Quarterly* 294; cf Stefan Trechsel, *Human Rights in Criminal Proceedings* (Oxford University Press, 2006) 210. In one judgment, the European Court purported to adopt two of these options in a single paragraph without acknowledging even the possibility of a contradiction: 'The Court . . . often examines the complaints under both provisions taken together. Where the applicant complains of numerous procedural defects, the Court may examine the various grounds . . . in turn in order to determine whether the proceedings, considered as a whole, were fair': *Blokhin v Russia* (App 47152/06) (14 November 2013) para 156.

C.2 The European Commission's Decision in *Nielsen* Provided a Reasonably Clear Approach

In 1961, the European Commission handed down its decision in *Nielsen v Denmark.* It was one of the first 20 matters dealt with by the Strasbourg institutions for which there exist published decisions, and it provides an interesting model of one way to approach Article 6's internal structure. The applicant challenged his indictment on the ground that 'the text of [the] indictment was not set out in detail sufficient to give him the possibility of adequately defending himself' in violation of Article 6(3)(a).[6] In analysing the complaint, the Commission considered the internal structure question.

The Commission noted 'that neither the Convention nor the relevant "*travaux preparatoires*" furnish any guide as to the interpretation of the words' of Article 6(3).[7] The Commission, therefore, described its task as being 'to interpret this provision in accordance with the general aim of Article 6'.[8] The Commission went on to state (for ease of reference, this will be 'passage A'):

> Article 6 of the Convention does not define the notion of 'fair trial' in a criminal case. [Article 6(3)] enumerates certain specific rights which constitute essential elements of that general notion, and [Article 6(2)] may be considered to add another element. The words 'minimum rights', however, clearly indicate that the six rights specifically enumerated in [Article 6(3)] are not exhaustive, and that a trial may not conform to the general standard of a 'fair trial', even if the minimum rights guaranteed by [Article 6(3)] – and also the right set forth in [Article 6(2)] – have been respected.[9]

The reasoning in this passage deserves close analysis. First, the Commission stated that Article 6 does not *define* the general notion of a fair trial. Second, the Commission indicates that the rights in Article 6(2) and Article 6(3) constitute essential elements of the general notion of a fair trial. Third, the Commission stated that the wording of Article 6(3) 'clearly' indicated that the rights listed in Article 6(3) are *not* an exhaustive list of what constitutes a fair trial. Fourth, as a result, the Commission states that compliance with all of the Article 6(3) rights does not necessarily result in compliance with the broader Article 6 fair trial guarantee. The passage, which rests on a close reading of the text of Article 6, was only the first stage of the Commission's analysis.

[6] *Nielsen v Denmark* (App 343/57) (1961) 4 YB 494, 534. The full text is not available on the European Court's 'HUDOC' database.

[7] ibid 534.

[8] ibid 534. See A.2.

[9] ibid 548. Note that the 'Right to a fair trial' heading to Article 6 was not added to the text of the European Convention until 1998, when Protocol No 11 entered into force. As such, the Commission's references in this passage to 'fair trial' may be understood as referring to either the 'fair hearing' guarantee in Art 6(1), or to the general protection provided by Art 6. It is not immediately clear what the European Commission is referring to when it mentions the 'six rights' in Art 6(3).

Having established this initial foundation for its understanding of the internal structure of Article 6, the Commission continued to describe that internal structure in this way (for ease of reference, this will be 'passage B'):

> The relationship between the general provision of [Article 6(1)] and the specific provisions of [Article 6(3)], seem[s] to be as follows: In a case where no violation of [Article 6(3)] is found to have taken place, the question whether the trial conforms to the standard laid down by [Article 6(1)] must be decided on the basis of a consideration of the trial as a whole, and not on the basis of an isolated consideration of one particular aspect of the trial or one particular incident. Admittedly, one particular incident or one particular aspect even if not falling within the provisions of [Article 6(2)] or [Article 6(3)], may have been so prominent or may have been of such importance as to be decisive for the general evaluation of the trial as a whole. Nevertheless, even in this contingency, it is on the basis of an evaluation of the trial in its entirety that the answer must be given to the question whether or not there has been a fair trial.[10]

The formula adopted by the Commission in these passages in *Nielsen*, therefore, clearly indicates that, if it is possible for an alleged violation to be considered under the specific guarantees of Article 6(3), then it should be so considered. If no violation of Article (3) 'is found to have taken place', then 'the question whether the trial conforms to the [more general] standard laid down by [Article 6(1)] must be decided on the basis of a consideration of the trial as a whole'. It should be emphasised that, under this approach, the analysis of the 'trial as a whole' or of 'the trial in its entirety' is only triggered if there is no violation of Article 6(2) or Article 6(3).[11]

The approach adopted by the Commission in *Nielsen* involved close analysis and explication of the text of Article 6, and provided an account of the internal structure of Article 6 that provided meaning to each of its component parts. That is, the *Nielsen* approach provided a plausible and coherent explanation for why Article 6 contained a series of individually-articulated guarantees rather than a single unelaborated guarantee. The *Nielsen* approach also made plain that, while there may be overlap between the ideas in Article 6(1), and Article 6(2) and Article 6(3), such overlap does not mean that any of Article 6's provisions deserve greater or lesser protection. For the Commission, Article 6(2) and Article 6(3) did not merely serve the purpose of helping to define the 'fair hearing' guarantee in Article 6(1): they were *guarantees in and of themselves* and should be analysed as such. Thus, *Nielsen* expressed a firm view on the crucial distinction between, on the one hand, regarding Article 6(2) and Article 6(3) as stand-alone guarantees and, on the other hand, regarding Article 6(2) and Article 6(3) as helpful definitional elaborations or examples of situations in which Article 6(1)'s 'fair hearing' guarantee might be triggered. As will be seen, there is significant tension in the case law of the European Court between these two approaches, to the detriment of the coherence and consistency of the European Court's case law.

[10] *Nielsen v Denmark* (n 6 above) 548, 550.

[11] A broadly similar approach is advocated by Hoyano (albeit without making reference to *Nielsen*): L Hoyano, 'What is Balanced on the Scales of Justice? In Search of the Essence of the Right to a Fair Trial' [2014] Crim LR 4, 27–28.

Thus, despite its place early in the life of the Strasbourg institutions, *Nielsen* provided a clear and readily understood model of how to consider an application in which multiple violations of Article 6 are alleged, and more generally of the internal structure of Article 6. It is a model worthy of close attention by the European Court. Notwithstanding these analytical strengths, however, the reasoning in *Nielsen* has been cited directly by the Strasbourg institutions only sporadically.[12] Indeed, as will become clear, other approaches to the internal structure are more prevalent.[13] Some of these other approaches are radically different to that outlined in *Nielsen*'s passage B and are often in tension with one another. In its case law more generally, the European Court has essentially ignored the reasoning proposed and adopted in *Nielsen*, especially that in passage B. To be clear, this is *in no way* a criticism made on *stare decisis* grounds: instead, my criticism is of the unexplained choice to ignore a reasoned, explained approach to the internal structure of Article 6 in favour of a multiplicity of incoherent and inconsistent approaches lacking any underlying theory. In this sense, *Nielsen* offers a counterfactual example of what might have been, and a model for an alternative approach which it is not too late for the European Court to adopt.

C.3 The European Court Sometimes Describes the Components of Article 6 as Independent Minimum Requirements

The first contemporary approach involves the European Court describing the internal structure of Article 6 by focusing on the nature of the Article 6(3) rights. In these cases, the Court frames the Article 6(3) rights as requiring protection in their own right regardless of what protection may or may not be provided by Article 6(1). More specifically, in a number of cases, the Court has described the Article 6(3) guarantees as stand-alone independent rights, or as 'minimum rights'. It is this approach that is the closest, of the more contemporary approaches, to

[12] See, eg, *Blastland v United Kingdom* (Commission) (App 12045/86) (7 May 1987); *AB v Germany* (Commission) (App 11863/85) (4 May 1987); *F v United Kingdom* (Commission) (App 11058/84) (13 May 1986).

[13] See, eg, *DeWeer v Belgium* (App 6903/75) (1979–80) 2 EHRR 439, para 56, citing *Nielsen v Denmark* (n 6 above). For background on *DeWeer*, see, eg, Trechsel, *Human Rights in Criminal Proceedings* (n 5 above) 114, 163; Harris, O'Boyle and Warbrick, *Law of the European Convention on Human Rights* (n 5 above) 209; van Dijk and van Hoof, *Theory and Practice of the European Convention on Human Rights* (n 5 above) 540–41. *DeWeer* referred to in, eg, *Artico v Italy* (App 6694/74) (1980) 3 EHRR 1, para 32; *Quaranta v Switzerland* (App 12744/87) (24 May 1991) para 27; *Imbrioscia v Switzerland* (App 13972/88) (1994) 17 EHRR 441, para 37; *Goddi v Italy* (App 8966/80) (1984) 6 EHRR 457, para 28; *Colozza v Italy* (App 9024/80) (1985) 7 EHRR 516, para 26; *Bonisch v Austria* (App 8658/79) (1987) 9 EHRR 191, para 29; *Unterpertinger v Austria* (App 9120/80) (1991) 13 EHRR 175, para 29; *Barbera, Messegue and Jabardo v Spain* (App 10588/83) (1989) 11 EHRR 360, para 67; *Kostovski v Netherlands* (App 11454/85) (1990) 12 EHRR 434, para 39; *Windisch v Austria* (App 12489/86) (1991) 13 EHRR 281, para 23; *Isgrò v Italy* (App 11339/85) (21 January 1991) para 31; *Asch v Austria* (App 12398/86) (1993) 15 EHRR 597, para 25; *Artner v Austria* (App 13161/87) (25 June 1992) para 19; *Pullar v United Kingdom* (App 22399/93) (1996) 22 EHRR 391, para 45; *Foucher v France* (App 22209/93) (1998) 25 EHRR 234, para 30.

that outlined in *Nielsen* above. Indeed, in *Luedicke, Belkacem and Koc v Germany*, in the course of finding a violation of Article 6(3)(e), the European Court went on to accept that

> for the purpose of ensuring a fair trial, [Article 6(3)] enumerates certain rights ('minimum rights'/'*notamment*') accorded to the accused.[14]

As simple a point as it may seem, it is rare for the Court to draw attention to the status of Article 6(3) rights as 'minimum rights', or even to consider that status.[15] In *Luedicke* the German government argued for a particular interpretation of Article 6(3)(e) by referring to the wording of other Article 6(3) rights.[16] The Court, however, rejected any such argument:

> The Court is not called on in the current proceedings to interpret [Article 6(3)(c)] and [Article 6(3)(d)], which are not concerned with the same situation as [Article 6(3)(e)] . . . The Court restricts itself to the following remark: whatever the doubts that might be prompted by the interpretation of [Article 6(3)(c)] and [Article 6(3)(d)], such doubts cannot be relied on in opposition to the clear meaning of the adjective 'free' in [Article 6(3)(e)].[17]

In *Luedicke*, therefore, the European Court was firm in emphasising the independent and stand-alone nature of the Article 6(3)(e) guarantee. This approach stands in contrast to some of the cases that will be considered later in this part. In a sense, this is the tension at the heart of Article 6: to what extent is Article 6 a single guarantee, and to what extent is it a series of guarantees?

More than three decades after *Luedicke*, the Court's 2009 Chamber decision in *Al-Khawaja and Tahery v United Kingdom* included an unusually lengthy statement on the internal structure of Article 6. This statement emphasises the 'minimum rights' approach noted in *Luedicke*:

> As with the other elements of [Article 6(3)], [Article 6(3)(d)] is one of the *minimum rights which must be accorded to anyone who is charged with a criminal offence.* As minimum rights, the provisions of [Article 6(3)] constitute *express guarantees* and cannot be read, as it was by the [England and Wales] Court of Appeal in *Sellick*, as illustrations of matters to be taken into account when considering whether a fair trial has been held. Equally, even where those minimum rights have been respected, the general right to a fair trial guaranteed by [Article 6(1)] requires that the Court ascertain whether the proceedings as a whole were fair. Hence, in *Unterpertinger v Austria*, the Court held that the reading out of statements of witnesses without the witness being heard in a public hearing could not be regarded as being inconsistent with [Article 6(1)] and [Article 6(3)(d)] of the Convention but it went on to emphasise that the use made of this in evidence

[14] *Luedicke, Belkacem and Koc v Germany* (App 6210/73) (1979–80) 2 EHRR 149, para 42. On *Luedicke*, see, eg, Trechsel, *Human Rights in Criminal Proceedings* (n 5 above) 331–39; van Dijk and van Hoof, *Theory and Practice of the European Convention on Human Rights* (n 5 above) 649–50; Harris, O'Boyle and Warbrick, *Law of the European Convention on Human Rights* (n 5 above) 327.

[15] See Hoyano, 'What is Balanced on the Scales of Justice?' (n 11 above) 7.

[16] *Luedicke, Belkacem and Koc v Germany* (n 14 above) para 43.

[17] ibid para 44.

> had nevertheless to comply with the rights of the defence which it was the object and purpose of Article 6 to protect.[18]

This statement is unusual in describing the internal structure of Article 6 in considerable detail, and as such is worth disaggregating. First, the *Al-Khawaja* Chamber Court notes that Article 6(3) rights are 'minimum rights' and 'express guarantees' that stand alone. Second, their status as minimum express guarantees means that the Article 6(3) rights are *not* simply criteria to be considered as part of an Article 6(1) analysis. Third, the relationship between Article 6(3) and Article 6(1) is such that an Article 6(1) analysis may take place even where there is no Article 6(3) violation. Fourth, the logical extension of this third point is that there may not be complete or partial overlap between the content and modes of analysis adopted in Article 6(1) and Article 6(3). These statements reflect some of the *Nielsen* reasoning and may appear, on their face, uncontroversial. As will be seen later in this part, however, the European Court has frequently adopted radically different approaches to that adopted here in *Al-Khawaja*. Indeed, as we shall see, a contrary approach was adopted in the *Al-Khawaja* Grand Chamber decision.[19]

In decisions such as *Luedicke* and the Chamber decision in *Al-Khawaja*, as well as the decision in *Nielsen v Denmark*, the European Court has indicated clearly that the internal structure of Article 6 is such that the rights identified in Article 6(3) are independent minimum rights, worthy of protection regardless of what protection may or may not be provided by Article 6(1), and at least partly autonomous from Article 6(1).[20] In following sections, I consider some of the European Court's other, competing, approaches to this interpretative task.

C.4 The European Court has Used Three Approaches Based on the 'Specific Aspects' Maxim

The text of Article 6 states that the rights identified in Article 6(3) are 'minimum rights' for every person 'charged with a criminal offence'. Notwithstanding that text, the European Court has chosen, in many decisions, to emphasise the status of the Article 6(3) rights as also representing 'specific aspects' of the more general

[18] *Al-Khawaja and Tahery v United Kingdom* (App 26766/05) (2009) 49 EHRR 1, para 34 (emphasis added), referring to *R v Sellick and Sellick* [2005] EWCA Crim 651, [2005] Crim LR 722. See also Bill O'Brian, *Confrontation: the Defiance of the English Courts*, University of Warwick School of Law Legal Studies Research Papers 2010–09 Paper 1, esp 12; Mark Coen, 'Hearsay, Bad Character and Trust in the Jury: Irish and English Contrasts' (2013) 17 *International Journal of Evidence and Proof* 250, esp 264.

[19] See *Al-Khawaja and Tahery v United Kingdom* (Grand Chamber) (n 2 above) paras 143–146 and the Joint Partly Dissenting and Partly Concurring Opinion of Judges Sajo and Karakas.

[20] This view of Art 6's internal structure is also evident in discussion of whether a waiver of one Art 6 right might constitute a waiver of another Art 6 right (see, eg, *Navone and others v Monaco* (App 62880/11) (24 October 2013) para 74) and cases in which the European Court finds a violation of one paragraph of Art 6 and then goes on to find another. For example, cases like *Fatullayev*, in which the European Court found a violation of Art 6(1) on impartiality grounds and then went on to find a separate violation of Art 6(2): *Fatullayev v Azerbaijan* (App 40984/07) (22 April 2010) paras 133–163. This approach contrasts with others we will consider below.

'fair hearing' guarantee contained in Article 6(1). In this section, I consider three ways in which the Court has used the 'specific aspects' maxim to describe the internal structure of Article 6.

Three macro-arguments run throughout this section: first, that some of these three ways are in tension with the minimum rights approaches considered above. Second, these three ways are in tension with *each other*. Finally, it is argued that the European Court has failed to provide an explanation of how each of the three ways work, and why the three different ways are used at different times. Of course, if the Court wished to adopt a finely-calibrated system in which it chose different approaches for different cases on the basis of identifiable criteria, it could do so. As will be seen, the difficulty here arises when the Court adopts approaches that are in tension with one another with very little explanation or justification at all.

C.4.1 Approach One: 'The Rights are Specific Aspects of Article 6(1), So the Focus Should be on Article 6(1)'

In a series of cases, the European Court has stated that because the guarantees contained in Article 6(3) are elements or aspects of the broader general guarantee contained in Article 6(1), the complaint should be addressed exclusively under Article 6(1). At times, the European Court's jurisprudence under this approach seems to suggest that Article 6(2) and Article 6(3) are merely ancillary definitional advice for the purposes of construing Article 6(1). Thus, for example, in *Colozza v Italy*, the Court stated that the Article 6(3) guarantees

> are constituent elements, amongst others, of the general notion of a fair trial. In the circumstances of the case, the Court, whilst also having regard to those guarantees, considers that it should examine the complaint under [Article 6(1)].[21]

Often, as in *Colozza*, the European Court will state that it had 'regard' to the Article 6(3) guarantees, but examined the complaint under Article 6(1). Another classic example of this approach is evident in *Bonisch v Austria*. In *Bonisch*, the Court adopted an approach that notionally gave 'due regard' to the Article 6(3) guarantees as part of the Article 6(1) analysis:

> [T]he guarantees contained in [Article 6(3)] are constituent elements, amongst others, of the concept of a fair trial set forth in [Article 6(1)]. In the circumstances of the instant case, the Court, whilst also having due regard to the [Article 6(3)] guarantees, including those enunciated in [Article 6(3)(d)], considers that it should examine the applicant's complaints under the general rule of [Article 6(1)].[22]

[21] *Colozza v Italy* (n 13 above) para 26, citing *Goddi v Italy* (n 13 above)para 28. *Goddi* cites *Artico v Italy* (n 13 above) para 32. *Artico* cites *DeWeer v Belgium* (n 13 above) para 56. *DeWeer* cites *Nielsen v Denmark* (n 6 above). For more on *Colozza*, see, eg, van Dijk and van Hoof, *Theory and Practice of the European Convention on Human Rights* (n 5 above) 589; Trechsel, *Human Rights in Criminal Proceedings* (n 5 above) 252–56; Harris, O'Boyle and Warbrick, *Law of the European Convention on Human Rights* (n 5 above) 248.

[22] *Bonisch v Austria* (n 13 above) para 29. See van Dijk and van Hoof, *Theory and Practice of the European Convention on Human Rights* (n 5 above) 584.

Notwithstanding the European Court's undertaking to have regard to the Article 6(3) guarantees, however, the Court conducted no detailed consideration of Article 6(3), and went so far as to say that there was *no need* to reach a conclusion on the Article 6(3) violation in this case.[23] But beyond the terms of this specific case, it should be noted that it is unclear what the Court means by saying 'whilst also having due regard to the [Article 6(3)] guarantees': how much regard should be had? What analytical purpose does this regard serve? If there is a conflict between two provisions, will the European Court prioritise the provision it is 'having regard to', or the provision it is 'examining under'?

Nevertheless, in case after case, the European Court adopted this formulation. Thus in *Barbera, Messegue and Jabardo v Spain*, the Court recalled

> that the guarantees in [Article 6(2) and Article 6(3)(d)] are specific aspects of the right to a fair trial set forth in [Article 6(1)]; it will therefore have regard to them when examining the facts under [Article 6(1)].[24]

Later, in *Hennings v Germany*, the European Court reiterated

> that the guarantees contained in Article 6(3) are constituent elements, amongst others, of the general notion of a fair trial. In the circumstances of the case, whilst also having regard to those guarantees, . . . the complaint should be examined under [Article 6(1)].[25]

Versions of the approach have also appeared more recently in cases such as *Salduz* and the Grand Chamber's *Al-Khawaja and Tahery* decision.[26]

An extreme example of this approach can be found in the European Court's decision in *IJL, GMR and AKP v United Kingdom*. In *IJL*, the European Court dismissed alleged violations of Article 6(3) on the basis that they all amounted to a violation of Article 6(1) anyway:

> [T]he guarantees of [Article 6(3)] are specific aspects of the right to a fair trial set out in [Article 6(1)]. In the circumstances of the case, it does not find it necessary to examine the applicants' allegations separately from the standpoint of [Article 6(3)(a)–(d)], since they amount to a complaint that the applicants did not receive a fair trial.[27]

This statement, breathtaking in its brevity, risks drastically simplifying the state of the law. Indeed, such a statement effectively reduces the provisions of Article 6(1), Article 6(2), and Article 6(3)(a)–(e) to a two-word 'fair trial' guarantee.

[23] See *Bonisch v Austria* (n 13 above) paras 28–37.

[24] *Barbera, Messegue and Jabardo v Spain* (n 13 above) para 67. For more on *Barbera*, see, eg, Trechsel, *Human Rights in Criminal Proceedings* (n 5 above) 86, 128–29, 164–65; Harris, O'Boyle and Warbrick, *Law of the European Convention on Human Rights* (n 5 above) 246–47, 300–1; C Gearty, 'The European Court of Human Rights and the Protection of Civil Liberties: an Overview' (1993) 52 *Cambridge Law Journal* 89, 104.

[25] *Hennings v Germany* (App 12129/86) (1993) 16 EHRR 83, para 25.

[26] *Salduz v Turkey* (n 2 above) para 50; *Al-Khawaja and Tahery v United Kingdom* (Grand Chamber) (n 2 above) para 145.

[27] *IJL, GMR and AKP v United Kingdom* (App 29522/95) (2001) 33 EHRR 11, para 77, citing *Edwards v United Kingdom* (App 13071/87) (1993) 15 EHRR 417, para 33. For discussion of *IJL* in a slightly different context, see Andrew Ashworth, 'Self-Incrimination in European Human Rights Law: a Pregnant Pragmatism?' (2008) 30 *Cardozo Law Review* 751, 756.

Subsequently, in *Dowsett v United Kingdom*, the European Court took matters a step further and disregarded an Article 6(3) complaint in favour of a broad 'fairness' question:

> As the guarantees in [Article 6(3)] are specific aspects of the right to a fair trial set out in [Article 6(1)], the Court has not examined the applicant's allegations separately from the standpoint of [Article 6(3)(b)]. It has addressed the question whether the proceedings in their entirety were fair. [28]

Such analysis not only fails to provide a plausible role for Article 6(2) and Article 6(3) that is distinct from that of Article 6(1), but is also in tension with the European Court's other case law on this topic. It is not clear whether the *IJL* and *Dowsett* Courts would even go so far as to 'have regard' to Article 6(2) and Article 6(3). As O'Brian argued in a different context, 'whatever the merits of a Convention that merely included Article 6(1) and not the rest of Article 6, that is not the Convention we have'.[29]

Another aspect of this approach is evident in cases where the Court reaches a conclusion on an alleged violation of Article 6(1), and then states that is unnecessary to reach a further conclusion on an alleged violation of Article 6(2) or Article 6(3). Thus, for example, in *Coeme v Belgium*, the European Court found an Article 6(1) violation and then stated:

> That [violation] being so, the Court considers that it is not necessary to rule on the alleged violation of [Article 6(2)] and [Article 6(3)(b)], since the arguments put forward on the latter point coincide, in substance, with those examined under [Article 6(1)].[30]

And in *Bonisch v Austria*, the Court stated:

> [T]here has been a breach of [Article 6(1)]. This conclusion dispenses the Court from giving a separate ruling on the alleged violation of [Article 6(3)(d)].[31]

Thus there is some ambiguity over the extent to which it is unnecessary to rule on violations of sub-articles other than Article 6(1). More specifically, especially in *Bonisch*, there is some suggestion that such a ruling is unnecessary if there has been a violation of Article 6(1). This suggestion goes unexplained (and we know, from *Nielsen*'s passage B, that there is an equally compelling argument to be made for the opposite view). Moreover, the *Coeme* Court seems to indicate that such a ruling is unnecessary because of overlap of the *arguments* relating to the two

[28] *Dowsett v United Kingdom* (App 39482/98) (2004) 38 EHRR 41, para 40, citing *Edwards v United Kingdom* (n 27 above) paras 33–34.

[29] Bill O'Brian, *Confrontation: the Defiance of the English Courts*, University of Warwick School of Law Legal Studies Research Paper 2010–09 (2010), 35.

[30] *Coeme v Belgium* (App 32492/96) (22 June 2000) para 104. For more on *Coeme*, see Trechsel, *Human Rights in Criminal Proceedings* (n 5 above) 110; van Dijk and van Hoof, *Theory and Practice of the European Convention on Human Rights* (n 5 above) 624.

[31] *Bonisch v Austria* (n 13 above) paras 28–29, 35. See also *Peltier v France* (App 32872/96) (21 May 2002) paras 41–43.

provisions.[32] And yet this does not take into account the possibility that the *arguments and factual analysis* could be the same, but the *standard and content of the legal guarantees* could be different. Thus, even if two arguments could be dismissed as 'coinciding in substance', that dismissal does not account for differing legal standards.

There are many examples of this approach. In *Kypiranou v Cyprus*, the European Court upheld the applicant's allegation of an Article 6(1) impartiality violation.[33] The Court went on to rule that, in 'view of the grounds on which it . . . found a violation of [Article 6(1)], . . . no separate issue' arose under Article 6(2) or Article 6(3)(a).[34] Similarly, in *Caplik v Turkey*, the European Court found a violation of Article 6(1) on independence and impartiality grounds, and considered it unnecessary to assess other alleged violations of Article 6(1) and Article 6(2).[35] In *Hatun and others v Turkey*, the European Court considered that a finding of a violation on impartiality-independence grounds made it unnecessary to consider more general complaints of an unfair procedure.[36] And in *Golinelli and Freymuth v France*, the applicants alleged a violation of the rights of the defence and an impartiality violation;[37] the European Court held that the matter should be considered only under Article 6(1), and that no separate issue arose under Article 6(3).[38] In *Demicoli v Malta*, the European Court found a violation of Article 6(1) and considered that it was 'not necessary to examine' Article 6(2).[39]

An illustration of the particular difficulties with this approach is provided by comparing a number of cases that considered domestic hearings held *in absentia*. In *Osu v Italy*, the European Court found a violation of Article 6(1) and, as such, considered it 'not necessary to examine the matter under the provisions of' Article 6(3).[40] In contrast, in *Hu v Italy*, decided less than five years later, the Court found that a trial *in absentia* amounted to a violation of Article 6(1) *and* Article 6(3), and it was held unnecessary to address the question of a separate Article 6(2) violation.[41] There is no explanation of why it was necessary in *Hu* to address the alleged violations of Article 6(1) *and* Article 6(3) but *not* the alleged violation of Article

[32] See also *Evrenos Onen v Turkey* (App 29782/02) (15 February 2007) para 29.

[33] *Kyprianou v Cyprus* (App 73797/01) (2007) 44 EHRR 27, paras 122–135.

[34] ibid paras 136–141.

[35] *Caplik v Turkey* (App 57019/00) (15 July 2005) paras 32–33.

[36] *Hatun and others v Turkey* (App 57343/00) (20 October 2005) paras 29–30.

[37] *Golinelli and Freymuth v France* (App 65823/01) (22 November 2005) para 25.

[38] ibid para 25 (translated). In support of this proposition, the European Court cited *Reinhardt and Slimane-Kaid v France* (App 23043/93) (1999) 28 EHRR 59; *Meftah and others v France* (App 32911/96) (26 July 2002); and *Richen and Gaucher v France* (App 31520/96) (23 January 2003). On *Reinhardt* see Summers, *Fair Trials* (n 1 above) 120.

[39] *Demicoli v Malta* (App 13057/87) (1992) 14 EHRR 47; see van Dijk and van Hoof, *Theory and Practice of the European Convention on Human Rights* (n 5 above) 552; Trechsel, *Human Rights in Criminal Proceedings* (n 5 above) 53. See E.4 which returns to the 'never fair' notion.

[40] *Osu v Italy* (App 36534/97) (11 July 2002) paras 40–41. Citing the same reason, the European Court also held it unnecessary to consider an alleged violation of Art 13: paras 42–43.

[41] *Hu v Italy* (App 5941/04) (28 September 2006) paras 58–62, citing *RR v Italy* (App 42191/02) (9 June 2005) para 64, which, in turn, did not refer to doctrinal support.

6(2). In contrast to *Osu* and *Hu*, other hearing *in absentia* cases have simply found a violation of Article 6 without specifying which provision of Article 6 had been infringed.[42] The risk that the European Court takes is that it appears to be picking and choosing when it is 'necessary' to consider different provisions of Article 6, and that without an explanation or rationalisation for these choices, its decisions become very difficult to predict or analyse. As we have seen already, and will continue to see, these discrepancies affect the scope of inquiry and the type of arguments that may be used in any given situation.

One final, and particularly unusual, example of the European Court's view that Article 6(2) and Article 6(3) are specific aspects of Article 6(1) was evident in its decision in *Anatoliy Tarasov v Russia*.[43] In that case, the applicant alleged violations of Article 6(3)(b)–(d); the Court stated without explanation that it would 'examine the applicant's complaint under *Article 6(1) and* Article 6(3)(b)–(c)'.[44] Having thus redefined the scope of the applicant's complaint, the Court went on to find that there had been an Article 6(1) violation and that it was 'not necessary' to examine the alleged Article 6(3) violations 'separately'.[45] In so doing, this case and the others discussed in this section involve the European Court indicating that the provisions of Article 6(2) and Article 6(3) are specific aspects of Article 6(1), and that as such the real analysis should be done under Article 6(1), with reference to Article 6(2) or Article 6(3) only where necessary.

C.4.2 Approach Two: 'The Rights are Specific Aspects of Article 6(1), So the Focus Should be on Article 6(2) or (3)'

In other cases, the European Court has stated that because the guarantees contained in Article 6(2) and Article 6(3) are elements or aspects of the broader general guarantee contained in Article 6(1), the complaint should be addressed under Article 6(2) or Article 6(3), respectively. Thus, for example, in *Pakelli v Germany*, the Court considered the relationship between Article 6(1) and Article 6(3)(c). The Court recalled

> that the provisions of Article 6(3)(c) represent specific applications of the general principle of a fair trial, stated in [Article 6(1)]. Accordingly, the question whether [Article 6(1)] was observed has no real significance in the applicant's case; it is absorbed by the question whether [Article 6(3)(c)] was complied with. The finding of a breach of the

[42] See, eg, *Poitrimol v France* (App 14032/88) (1994) 18 EHRR 130, paras 28–39; *Somogyi v Italy* (App 67972/01) (2008) 46 EHRR 5, paras 61–76, and *Sejdovic v Italy* (App 56581/00) (1 March 2006) para 106.

[43] *Anatoliy Tarasov v Russia* (App 3950/02) (18 February 2010).

[44] ibid para 42 (emphasis added).

[45] ibid paras 48–49. cf *Fedorenko v Russia* (App 39602/05) (20 September 2011) para 88, 93; *Tsonyo Tsonev v Bulgaria (No 3)* (App 21124/04) (16 October 2012) paras 46, 48, 53; *Hikmet Yilmaz v Turkey* (App 11022/05) (4 June 2013) paras 15, 23; *Konak v Turkey* (App 3042/05) (3 September 2013) paras 17, 21, 22.

> requirements of [Article 6(3)(c)] dispenses the Court from also examining the case in the light of [Article 6(1)].[46]

Intriguingly, the only explanation offered by the Court for adopting this approach was a reference to *DeWeer v Belgium*, '*mutatis mutandis*'.[47] The relevant passage of *DeWeer* in fact expresses a view somewhat in tension with that adopted in *Pakelli*:

> The finding of a breach of the requirements of [Article 6(1)] dispenses the Court from also examining the case in the light of [Article 6(2)] and [Article 6(3)], a course which might have been incumbent on it in different circumstances.[48]

This discrepancy exemplifies the difficulties with the European Court's approach to the internal structure of Article 6. In some cases, it seems, Article 6(1) will trump Article 6(2) or Article 6(3) (as in *DeWeer*), and in others Article 6(1) will be trumped by Article 6(2) or Article 6(3) (as in *Pakelli*).[49] The difficulty is knowing when the European Court is likely to analyse a case as falling under one or the other theory, and understanding what the rationale is for the differing approaches. That incoherence, of course, takes on significant implications when it is remembered that the framing of the scope of any case inevitably affects the arguments and modes of analysis relevant to an assessment of any violation or infringement of Article 6.[50]

Similarly to *Pakelli*, in *Daud v Portugal*, the European Court adopted a curious description of its analytical process:

> As the requirements of [Article 6(3)] are to be seen as particular aspects of the right to a fair trial guaranteed by [Article 6(1)], the Court will examine the applicant's complaints successively under [Article 6(3)(c)] and [Article 6(3)(e)] without isolating [Article 6(3)] from the common core to which it belongs.[51]

Under this formulation, the European Court appears to require analysis under the relevant subparagraph of Article 6(3), with resort to the broader context of Article 6 (including Article 6(1)) only a subsidiary concern. The European Court does not explain what the 'common core' is, its interpretative relevance, or how it is to be applied.[52]

[46] *Pakelli v Germany* (App 8398/78) (1984) 6 EHRR 1, para 42. For additional background on *Pakelli*, see van Dijk and van Hoof, *Theory and Practice of the European Convention on Human Rights* (n 5 above) 636–37; Harris, O'Boyle and Warbrick, *Law of the European Convention on Human Rights* (n 5 above) 315, 317; Trechsel, *Human Rights in Criminal Proceedings* (n 5 above) 251, 271–72, 276–77.

[47] *Pakelli v Germany* (n 46 above) para 42, citing *DeWeer v Belgium* (n 13 above) para 56.

[48] *DeWeer v Belgium* (n 13 above) para 56.

[49] Additional evidence of the latter approach is provided by those cases in which the European Court finds a violation of an Art 6(2) or Art 6(3) right and then considers it unnecessary to go on to consider a separate alleged violation of Art 6(1). See, eg, *Bok v Netherlands* (App 45482/06) (18 January 2011) paras 48–50. This contrasts with approaches outlined in sections above and below.

[50] See especially E.2.

[51] *Daud v Portugal* (App 22600/93) (2000) 30 EHRR 400, para 33, citing *Artico v Italy* (n 13 above) para 32 and *FCB v Italy* (App 12151/86) (1992) 14 EHRR 909, para 29. See Trechsel, *Human Rights in Criminal Proceedings* (n 5 above) 289.

[52] The French equivalent of 'common core' ('tronc commun') appears in a small number of Art 6 cases: see the French versions of *Artico v Italy* (n 13 above) para 32; *Cardot v France* (App 11069/84)

A variation on this approach is evident in *Radio France v France*, in which the European Court 'point[ed] out':

> that the complaint under [Article 6(1)] overlaps with the complaint under [Article 6(2)], so that it is not necessary to examine the facts complained of from the standpoint of [Article 6(1)] taken alone.[53]

The Court concluded that there had been 'no violation' of Article 6(2).[54] But there was no statement whatsoever about whether there had been a breach of Article 6(1), implying that such analysis was unnecessary in light of the conclusion reached on Article 6(2).

These formulations are very different from that offered in the cases discussed in the previous subsection. Indeed, in these cases the European Court simply 'recalls' and 'points out' its approach in a way that is in tension with the views it has expressed elsewhere, and in no way acknowledges or explains this serious inconsistency. As the next subsection demonstrates, the Court has yet another approach altogether.

C.4.3 Approach Three: 'The Rights are Specific Aspects of Article 6(1), So Consider the Provisions "Taken Together"'

Under a third approach flowing from the 'specific aspects' maxim, the European Court *takes the different provisions together*, assesses an alleged violation under both provisions, and produces a result. This is an approach touched on by Trechsel, who criticises the Court's

> tendency not to examine whether a specific minimum guarantee has been respected or not, but to combine at the outset the specific guarantees with the general right to a fair trial and to deal with them together without proper distinction... there is no justification for the Court's policy of blurring the application of [Article 6(1)] and [Article 6(3)].[55]

This approach, Trechsel argues, leaves 'Article 6 in a cloud of ambiguity'.[56] Stumer, who focuses on Article 6(2), argues that:

> To regard the presumption of innocence in Article 6(2) as a right subsumed within the right to a fair trial in Article 6(1) is contrary to the structure of the [Convention] which places the presumption of innocence in a separate paragraph . . . [and] also belies the drafting history of the [Convention].[57]

(1991) 13 EHRR 853, Dissenting Opinion of Judge Morenilla; *Van Geyseghem v Belgium* (App 26103/95) (2001) 32 EHRR 24, Dissenting Opinion of Judge Pellonpaa; and *Meftah and others v France* (n 38 above) para 40. See also C.4.3 below in the context of *Meftah*.

[53] *Radio France and others v France* (App 53984/00) (30 March 2004) para 24, citing *Salabiaku v France* (App 10519/83) (1991) 13 EHRR 379, para 31.

[54] *Radio France and others v France* (n 53 above) para 24.

[55] Trechsel, *Human Rights in Criminal Proceedings* (n 5 above) 87–88.

[56] ibid 87. See also, Hoyano, 'What is Balanced on the Scales of Justice?' (n 11 above) 8.

[57] Andrew C Stumer, *The Presumption of Innocence* (Hart Publishing, 2010) 95–98. cf *Shuvalov v Estonia* (App 39820/08) (29 May 2012) para 75; *Maksim Petrov v Russia* (App 23185/03) (6 November 2012) para 102.

In this section, I expand upon these criticisms and outline the incoherence and lack of explanation that characterises the Court's 'taken together' approach. Very rarely does the Court explain how this hybridisation should take place, or what structure its analysis should follow. Moreover, the Court offers no real explanation of when this approach should be adopted in preference to the approaches identified in previous sections of this part.

As an example, in *Monnell and Morris v United Kingdom*, the European Court conflates Article 6(1) and Article 6(3) under the 'taken together' approach:

> The guarantees contained in [Article 6(3)(c)] are constituent elements, amongst others, of the general notion of a fair trial in criminal proceedings stated in [Article 6(1)]. The Court . . . considers that the nature of the applicants' complaints makes it appropriate to take [Article 6(1)] and [Article 6(3)(c)] together.[58]

Having conducted its analysis, the European Court reached a conclusion on both provisions taken together, finding that neither applicant 'was denied a fair procedure as guaranteed by [Article 6(1)] and [Article 6(3)(c)]' and that there was thus 'no breach of either of these provisions of the Convention'.[59]

In *Hadjianastassiou v Greece*, the Court adopted another formulation:

> As the requirements of [Article 6(3)] constitute specific aspects of the right to a fair trial, guaranteed under [Article 6(1)], the Court will examine the complaint under both provisions taken together.[60]

Similarly, in *Foucher v France*, the Court conflated the Article 6(3) guarantees and the Article 6(1) guarantee:

> [T]he guarantees in [Article 6(3)] are specific aspects of the right to a fair trial set forth in general in [Article 6(1)]. For this reason, it considers it appropriate to examine this complaint under the two provisions taken together.[61]

In lieu of an explanation for this position, the Court referred to a series of cases that ultimately lead to *Nielsen v Denmark*.[62]

[58] *Monnell and Morris v United Kingdom* (App 9562/81) (1988) 10 EHRR 205, para 53. For more on *Monnell and Morris*, see, eg, Harris, O'Boyle and Warbrick, *Law of the European Convention on Human Rights* (n 5 above) 314; Trechsel, *Human Rights in Criminal Proceedings* (n 5 above) 276, 442–43.

[59] *Monnell and Morris v United Kingdom* (n 58 above) para 70.

[60] *Hadjianastassiou v Greece* (App 12945/87) (1993) 16 EHRR 219, para 31. See Trechsel, *Human Rights in Criminal Proceedings* (n 5 above) 87–88.

[61] *Foucher v France* (n 13 above) para 30. See Trechsel, *Human Rights in Criminal Proceedings* (n 5 above) 212–15.

[62] See *Foucher v France* (n 13 above) para 30; *Artner v Austria* (n 13 above) para 19; *Asch v Austria* (n 13 above) para 25; *Isgrò v Italy* (n 13 above) para 31; *Delta v France* (App 11444/85) (1993) 16 EHRR 574, para 35; *Windisch v Austria* (n 13 above) para 23; *Kostovski v Netherlands* (n 13 above) para 39; *Barbera, Messegue and Jabardo v Spain* (n 13 above) para 67; *Unterpertinger v Austria* (n 13 above) para 29; *Bonisch v Austria* (n 13 above) para 29; *Artico v Italy* (n 13 above) para 32; *Goddi v Italy* (n 13 above) para 28; *Colozza v Italy* (n 13 above) para 26. This group of cases included cases approaching the point in different ways: while *Foucher* appears to require the Court to *combine* the two provisions for the purposes of its analysis, a case like *Barbera* requires the European Court to consider them all through the lens of Art 6(1): *Barbera, Messegue and Jabardo v Spain* (n 13 above) para 67.

On some occasions, the Court has adopted a slightly different phrasing for this approach, referring to 'both texts combined', as in *GB v France*:

> In view of the fact that the requirements of [Article 6(3)(b)] of the Convention can be broken down into separate elements of the right to a fair hearing, guaranteed under [Article 6(1)], the court studied the set of grievances in the light of both texts combined.[63]

In *Melich and Beck v Czech Republic*, the European Court took this approach a step further, and combined the 'three texts' of Article 6(1), Article 6(2) *and* Article 6(3):

> Noting that, in this case, the objections raised by the petitioners on the ground of [Article 6(1), (2) and (3)(d)] overlap, it considers it appropriate to consider in terms of the three texts combined.[64]

Similarly, in *Coeme v Belgium*, the European Court stated that it would take Article 6(1) together with other Articles 'where necessary', without specifying for what such regard would have to be necessary:

> The requirements of [Article 6(2)] and [Article 6(3)(b)] are to be seen as particular aspects of the right to a fair trial guaranteed by [Article 6(1)]. The Court considers that it is appropriate to examine the complaints in the light of [Article 6(1)], taken in conjunction, where necessary, with its other paragraphs and the other provisions of the Convention [Articles 13 and 14].[65]

It may be noted, therefore, that for this analysis the *Coeme* Court apparently regarded it as important to take Article 6(1) together with not only Article 6(2) and Article 6(3), but also Article 13 and Article 14.

The European Court has adopted the 'taken together' approach on many occasions.[66] There are even curious cases (such as *Salduz* and *Boke and Kandemir*) in

[63] *GB v France* (App 44069/98) (2002) 35 EHRR 36, para 57.

[64] *Melich and Beck v Czech Republic* (App 35450/04) (24 July 2008) para 47, citing *GB v France* (n 63 above) para 57, in support of the proposition that the Art 6(3) requirements are aspects of Art 6(1), and invoking *Janosevic v Sweden* (App 34619/97) (2004) 38 EHRR 22, para 96 in support of the proposition that the Art 6(2) presumption of innocence is one of the elements required by Art 6(1). A similar taking together of Art 6(1), (2) and (3) occurred in *Vaquero Hernandez and others v Spain* (App 1883/03) (2 November 2010) para 123. On the presumption of innocence in the European Court's case law, see, eg, Stumer, *The Presumption of Innocence* (n 57 above) 88–151.

[65] *Coeme v Belgium* (n 30 above) para 93.

[66] *Panasenko v Portugal* (App 10418/03) (22 July 2008) para 41 (translated); *Paraponiaris v Greece* (App 42132/06) (25 September 2008) para 23; *Rupa v Romania* (App 58478/00) (16 December 2008) paras 221, 234; *Vladimir Romanov v Russia* (App 41461/02) (24 July 2008) paras 96, 106; *Luca v Italy* (App 33354/96) (2003) 36 EHRR 46, para 37; *Medenica v Switzerland* (App 20491/92) (14 June 2001) paras 53]and 60; *Solakov v FYROM* (App 47023/99) (31 October 2001) para 56; *Bernard v France* (App 22885/93) (2000) 30 EHRR 808, para 37; *Matyjek v Poland* (App 38184/03) (24 April 2007) para 54; *Demebukov v Bulgaria* (App 68020/01) (28 February 2008) para 43; *Hulki Gunes v Turkey* (App 28490/95) (2006) 42 EHRR 27, paras 87, 96; *Bracci v Italy* (App 36822/02) (13 October 2005) para 49; *Popov v Russia* (App 26853/04) (13 July 2006) paras 169, 189; *Grigoryevskikh v Russia* (App 22/03) (9 April 2009) para 75; *Sibgatullin v Russia* (App 32165/02) (23 April 2009) para 38; *Rasmussen v Poland* (App 38886/05) (28 April 2009) para 41; *Seyithan Demir v Turkey* (App 25381/02) (28 July 2009) para 39; *Prezec v Croatia* (App 48185/07) (15 October 2009) para 25; *Caka v Albania* (App 44023/02)

which the applicant argued their case under Article 6(3), but for which the European Court took that allegation together with Article 6(1) to find a violation of both Article 6(3) and Article 6(1).[67] Most recently, referring to *Salduz*, the Grand Chamber in *Al-Khawaja* adopted a 'taken together' approach and went so far as to state that it had *always* considered alleged Article 6(3) violations as part of an 'overall examination of the fairness of the proceedings' in which Article 6(3) guarantees were 'one element, amongst others' of the Article 6(1) guarantee.[68] The Grand Chamber's boldness is reflected in its assertion that it had 'always' adopted such an approach (contrary to the analysis elsewhere in this part) and is underlined in the Joint Partly Dissenting and Partly Concurring Opinion of Judges Sajo and Karakas.[69]

Some scholars have sought to explain particular instances of the 'taken together' approach. Thus, for example, it is said that the Article 6(3)(d) guarantees are linked to the 'equality of arms' guarantee, which can be grounded in Article 6(1); as such, alleged violations are often taken together.[70] Such analysis does not, however, probe beyond the superficial. Indeed, importantly, in all these cases, it is unclear exactly *what* is being 'taken together'. The Court does not articulate whether it is taking together the factual analysis relevant to the two articles, the legal analysis, or both. It is not clear whether the two provisions retain their identity while being 'taken together' or if they are completely hybridised. Further, the European Court provides no guidance on which of the provisions should take priority, within the 'taken together' analysis, in the event of tension or contradiction. As an example, in *Barbera, Messegue and Jabardo v Spain*, we can see what

(8 December 2009) para 77; *Penev v Bulgaria* (App 20494/04) (7 January 2010) paras 35–36; *Luchaninova v Ukraine* (App 16347/02) (9 June 2011) para 60; *Breukoven v Czech Republic* (App 44438/06) (21 July 2011) para 42; *Balitskiy v Ukraine* (App 12793/03) (3 November 2011) para 28; *Damir Sibgatullin v Russia* (App 1413/05) (24 April 2012) para 44; *Neziraj v Germany* (App 30804/07) (8 November 2012) para 45; *Gani v Spain* (App 61800/08) (19 February 2013) para 36; *CB v Austria* (App 30465/06) (4 April 2013) para 38; *Vyerentsov v Ukraine* (App 20372/11) (11 April 2013) para 72; *Chorniy v Ukraine* (App 35227/06) (16 May 2013) para 36; *Valentino Acatrinei v Romania* (App 18540/04) (25 June 2013) para 66; *Kozlitin v Russia* (App 17092/04) (14 November 2013) para 58; *Vararu v Romania* (App 35842/05) (3 December 2013) para 29; *Siyrak v Russia* (App 38094/05) (19 December 2013) para 25; cf the approach in *Cani v Albania* (App 11006/06) (6 March 2012) para 48 ('the applicant's complaint will be examined under the overall fairness requirements of Article 6') and, similarly, *Leas v Estonia* (App 59577/08) (6 March 2012) para 76.

[67] *Salduz v Turkey* (n 2 above) paras 45, 50, 63; *Boke and Kandemir v Turkey* (App 71912/01) (10 March 2009) paras 69, 71. On *Salduz*, see R Pattenden, 'Case Comment: Right to Counsel at the Police Station' (2011) 15(1) *International Journal of Evidence and Proof* 70; TAHM van de Laar and RL de Graaff, '*Salduz* and *Miranda*: Is the US Supreme Court Pointing the Way?' [2011] *EHRLR* 304; W Wu, 'Interrogational Fairness under the European Convention on Human Rights' (2011) 39 *International Journal of Law, Crime and Justice* 37; E Bjorge, 'Exceptionalism and Internationalism in the Supreme Court: *Horncastle* and *Cadder*' (2011) *Public Law* 475; N Bratza, 'The Relationship between the UK Courts and Strasbourg' [2011] *EHRLR* 505.

[68] *Al-Khawaja and Tahery v United Kingdom* (Grand Chamber) (n 2 above) paras 143–146.

[69] ibid.

[70] van Dijk and van Hoof, *Theory and Practice of the European Convention on Human Rights* (n 5 above) 644. See also Harris, O'Boyle and Warbrick, *Law of the European Convention on Human Rights* (n 5 above) 306.

'taking together' may mean in practice. In considering whether certain witnesses' evidence was heard in circumstances that complied with Article 6, the European Court stated:

> 80. . . . The evidence of the various witnesses was heard in circumstances that complied with the requirements of Article 6(1) taken in conjunction with [Article 6(3)(d)], because the witnesses were examined at a public hearing under an adversarial procedure.[71]

Statements of this sort risk confusing the content of the guarantees provided by Article 6(1) and Article 6(3)(d), respectively, and also leave some ambiguity over the extent to which the result reached would have been the same had the analysis been done solely under Article 6(1) or solely under Article 6(3)(d).

It is very rare, moreover, for the European Court to provide an explanation of *why* it combines texts, or takes them together. In *Meftah v France*, the European Court provided a longer-than-usual analysis of the relationship between Article 6(1) and Article 6(3) in the course of explaining its 'taken together' analysis:

> The various rights of which a non-exhaustive list appears in [Article 6(3)] reflect certain of the aspects of the notion of a fair trial in criminal proceedings. When compliance with [Article 6(3)] is being reviewed, its basic purpose must not be forgotten nor must it be severed from its roots. The Court therefore considers complaints under [Article 6(3)] under those two provisions taken together.[72]

This passage, therefore, suggests that the reason the provisions should be 'taken together' is that the European Court should not forget the 'basic purpose' of Article 6(3) and that it should not be 'severed from its [Article 6(1)] roots'. One author has gone so far as to identify the 'risk of isolating the specific guarantees . . . from the [Article 6(1)] "root"'.[73] This seems to reflect a remarkable lack of confidence in the European Court's interpretative skills. The *Meftah* Court does not identify or explain the 'basic purpose' of Article 6(3), nor does it explain its theory of 'roots'. Indeed, one could just as easily say that the basic purpose and roots of *Article 6(3)* demand that any alleged violation be assessed solely within the parameters of Article 6(3) itself without reference to any other provision.[74] The *Meftah* Court's explanation is lacking.

An alternative explanation for the 'taken together' approach is offered in *Melich and Beck*, as noted above:

> Noting that, in this case, the objections raised by the petitioners on the ground of [Article 6(1), (2) and (3)(d)] overlap, it considers it appropriate to consider in terms of the three texts combined.[75]

[71] *Barbera, Messegue and Jabardo v Spain* (n 13 above) para 80.

[72] *Meftah and others v France* (n 38 above) para 40. See also Jacot-Guillarmod, 'Rights related to Good Administration of Justice' (n 1 above) 383–84; van Dijk and van Hoof, *Theory and Practice of the European Convention on Human Rights* (n 5 above) 638.

[73] Jacot-Guillarmod, 'Rights related to Good Administration of Justice' (n 1 above) 384.

[74] On the 'roots' terminology, see also the discussion of *Daud v Portugal* in C.4.2 above.

[75] *Melich and Beck v Czech Republic* (n 64 above) para 47.

This approach risks confusing the nature of the guarantees provided by Article 6(1), Article 6(2) and Article 6(3), respectively: it involves assuming that overlapping arguments warrant merging several distinct legal standards. If the European Court is happy for them to be merged where the facts are convenient to do so, then the content of Article 6 risks being boiled down to a single, simple 'fair trial' guarantee. Such a simplification does not sit well with the detailed provisions of Article 6(1), Article 6(2), and Article 6(3).

Furthermore, while much of this section has focused primarily on the European Court's descriptions of the 'taken together' doctrine itself, it must be emphasised that the way in which the European Court *applies* this doctrine is also marked by uncertainty and a lack of explanation. There are two uncertainties worth highlighting. The first is that the European Court does not spell out what legal test it is actually applying. That is, the European Court does not specify whether 'taking together' two provisions involves simply applying both of them at once, or first one and then another, or whether it involves some element of combination or hybridisation. The second is that, when conducting analysis of the facts of a particular case, the Court does not explain which facts are relevant to which provision, which facts are relevant to both provisions, or why.

Instead, the practice of the European Court seems to be this: at the outset of any Article 6 'taken together' analysis it indicates that it is taking together two or more provisions.[76] It does not provide further definition or articulation of how these different legal tests combine. It then proceeds to recount and analyse the facts of the case, usually without specifying expressly or implicitly which facts are relevant to which provisions or subset of provisions.[77] More rarely, sometimes the European Court will identify facts that are relevant for a particular legal test, but on these occasions it often does so without indicating how the test interrelates with the rest of its legal analysis, or without indicating how a series of unstructured legal tests feed in to an ultimate conclusion in any structured sense.[78] It then proceeds to reach a conclusion, almost always finding either a violation of *all* of the provisions that had been taken together or no violation of *any* of the provisions that had been taken together.[79] In other cases, such as *Coeme*, the focus of

[76] See, eg, *Monnell and Morris v United Kingdom* (n 58 above) para 53; *Hadjianastassiou v Greece* (n 60 above) para 31; *Foucher v France* (n 13 above) paras 26, 30; *GB v France* (n 63 above) para 57; *Rupa v Romania* (n 66 above) para 221; *Luca v Italy* (n 66 above) para 37; *Medenica v Switzerland* (n 66 above) para 53; *Bernard v France* (n 66 above) para 37; *Matyjek v Poland* (n 66 above) para 54; *Demebukov v Bulgaria* (n 66 above) para 43.

[77] Sometimes there may be reference to a particular implied right, but without explanation of the basis of the implied right, and without explanation of whether the implied right relates to one or all of the 'taken together' provisions. See, generally as examples, *Hadjianastassiou v Greece* (n 60 above) paras 31–37; *Foucher v France* (n 13 above) paras 31–38; *GB v France* (n 63 above) paras 57–70; *Paraponiaris v Greece* (n 66 above) paras 23–27; *Luca v Italy* (n 66 above) paras 37–45; *Medenica v Switzerland* (n 66 above) paras 53–60; *Bernard v France* (n 66 above) paras 37–40; *Matyjek v Poland* (n 66 above) paras 55–65; *Hulki Gunes v Turkey* (n 66 above) paras 87–96.

[78] See, eg, *Monnell and Morris v United Kingdom* (n 58 above) paras 55–70; *Rupa v Romania* (n 66 above) paras 218–234; *Demebukov v Bulgaria* (n 66 above) paras 44–59.

[79] See, eg, *Hadjianastassiou v Greece* (n 60 above) para 37; *Monnell and Morris v United Kingdom* (n 58 above) para 70; *Foucher v France* (n 13 above) para 38; *GB v France* (n 63 above) para 70;

the 'taken together' analysis appears to be almost exclusively on one particular provision (in *Coeme*, Article 6(1)), such that it is difficult to distinguish a 'taken together' analysis from an analysis focusing exclusively on one provision alone.[80] This method of reasoning is problematic, and poses difficulties for those who seek some sense of guidance and predictability from the Court's judgments.

A closely related theme to the 'taken together' approach appears in those European Court decisions that state that a violation of one provision of Article 6 will be sufficient to trigger finding a violation of another provision. For example, in *Heaney and McGuinness v Ireland*, the European Court identified a 'close link' between the 'rights guaranteed by' Article 6(1) and the 'presumption of innocence guaranteed by' Article 6(2), and very matter-of-factly found a violation of Article 6(2) on the basis of the Article 6(1) violation:

> [T]here has been a violation of the applicants' right to silence and their right not to incriminate themselves guaranteed by [Article 6(1)] . . . Moreover, given the close link, in this context, between those rights guaranteed by [Article 6(1)] and the presumption of innocence guaranteed by [Article 6(2)], the Court also concludes that there has been a violation of the latter provision.[81]

In *Quinn v Ireland*, too, the Court used similar language to find an Article 6(2) violation on the basis of an Article 6(1) violation. [82] The corollary was evident in *Averill v United Kingdom*, when the Court used a conclusion as to an Article 6(1) violation to justify its decision not to conduct Article 6(2) analysis:

> Having found that [Article 6(1)] has not been breached, the Court considers that for the same reasons there has been no violation of Article 6(2).[83]

This approach renders the relationship between Article 6(1) and Article 6(2) more opaque, and does not assist in understanding the content of Article 6(2), nor how that content may be distinguished from Article 6(1) or, indeed, Article 6 as a whole.[84]

A similar variation is evident in cases in which the European Court has indicated that it will attempt to interpret parts of Article 6 'in light of' other parts of the Article. In *Pelissier and Sassi v France*, for example, there are several statements about the structure and importance of Article 6. These statements indicate that Article 6(3)(a) must be interpreted in light of Article 6(1), *and* that Article 6(3)(a) must be interpreted in light of Article 6(3)(b):

Paraponiaris v Greece (n 66 above) para 27; *Bernard v France* (n 66 above) para 41; *Demebukov v Bulgaria* (n 66 above) para 59; *Hulki Gunes v Turkey* (n 66 above) para 96.

[80] See *Coeme v Belgium* (n 30 above) paras 91–141. See also *Solakov v FYROM* (n 66 above) with reference to Art 6(3)(d): paras 66–67.

[81] *Heaney and McGuinness v Ireland* (App 34720/97) (2001) 33 EHRR 12, para 59. See also Trechsel, *Human Rights in Criminal Proceedings* (n 5 above) 359; Harris, O'Boyle and Warbrick, *Law of the European Convention on Human Rights* (n 5 above) 262.

[82] *Quinn v Ireland* (App 36887/97) (21 December 2000) paras 59–60.

[83] *Averill v United Kingdom* (App 36408/97) (2001) 31 EHRR 36, para 52.

[84] Further discussion of the Court's implied rights jurisprudence follows in part D.

> The scope of [Article 6(3)(a)] must in particular be assessed in the light of the more general right to a fair hearing guaranteed by [Article 6(1)] . . . Lastly, as regards the complaint under [Article 6(3)(b)] of the Convention, the Court considers that [Article 6(3)(a) and (b)] are connected and that the right to be informed of the nature and the cause of the accusation must be considered in the light of the accused's right to prepare his defence.[85]

The Court used a similar form of analysis in *Sadak* and *Gouget.*[86] In cases of this type, therefore, the European Court indicates a willingness to emphasise the links between the different Article 6 guarantees when examining or explaining the definition or content of those guarantees. This analysis does not necessarily amount to the European Court conflating the Article 6 guarantees into one single guarantee. Importantly, however, the European Court does not make clear what it means when it assesses one provision in light of another, or what impact that may have on the interpretative task.

C.5 Building the Foundations for a New Approach to the Internal Structure of Article 6

This part considered the European Court's approach to the internal structure of Article 6. It was demonstrated that, instead of opting for the *Nielsen* approach, the European Court has adopted a series of different approaches to Article 6, and that these approaches involve considerable incoherence and inconsistency. It is difficult to identify any reasoned, rational, predictable explanation of why certain classes of case fall within one of the three limbs, while other classes are treated differently. The European Court certainly articulates no such explanation. As was established at the beginning of this part, all of this matters, because the European Court's approach to Article 6's internal structure shapes the boundaries for any inquiry as to whether there has been a violation of Article 6.

If the European Court wishes to deploy different approaches in similar situations – or different approaches in different situations – the interests of predictability and consistency demand that it explain *why.* As matters stand, the European Court risks creating the appearance that it classifies cases on a random or convenient mix-and-match basis, where it assesses one complaint under Article 6(1), another under Article 6(3), and yet another under Article 6(1) and Article 6(3) 'taken together'. In no available decision does the European Court explain why one of these choices would be legitimate in one type of case, but another preferable in another type of case.

[85] *Pelissier and Sassi v France* (App 25444/94) (2000) 30 EHRR 715, paras 52–54. In support of the first sentence in para 52, the European Court cited *DeWeer v Belgium* (n 13 above) para 56; *Artico v Italy* (n 13 above) para 32; *Goddi v Italy* (n 13 above) para 28; and *Colozza v Italy* (n 13 above) para 26. See also van Dijk and van Hoof, *Theory and Practice of the European Convention on Human Rights* (n 5 above) 632–33; Trechsel, *Human Rights in Criminal Proceedings* (n 5 above) 203–4.

[86] *Sadak and others v Turkey* (App 29900/96) (2003) 36 EHRR 26, paras 49–50; *Gouget and others v France* (App 61059/00) (24 January 2006) para 28.

What, then, ought to be the approach of the European Court? The Court's aim, I suggest, ought to be to avoid interpretations that collapse the 258 words of Article 6 into a simple two-word 'fair trial' guarantee. If that aim is considered together with the goals furthering consistency and coherence of reasoning, I propose that the Court ought to revive what has been described in this part as the *Nielsen* approach. The analysis of any alleged violation of any component right of Article 6, most notably those explicitly or implicitly protected in Article 6(2) and Article 6(3), ought to begin with an analysis of that alleged violation *in isolation from any other violations which happen to be alleged by the same applicant.*[87] The European Court's inquiry would be strictly limited to, for example, whether or not the applicant had been 'informed promptly . . . of the nature and cause of the accusation against him',[88] or whether the applicant had 'adequate time and facilities for the preparation' of her defence.[89] Reference to broader notions of a fair trial, or to taking the Article 6(3) violation 'together' with Article 6(1) in order to assess a violation, ought to be avoided entirely at this stage.

Confining the inquiry at this stage would, I suggest, have a number of benefits. First, it would reflect the text of the Convention more faithfully than most of the current case law, and in this way this approach also accords with the normative arguments made in part A. Second, it would assist the European Court's efforts to provide guidance as to the various Article 6 rights by forcing focused thought and argument onto the contents of the individual components, rather than allowing the Court to avoid that thought by reference to more general concepts of a fair trial. There would be less scope for the ordinary meaning of the text of Article 6, and especially the text of Article 6(2) and Article 6(3), to be subverted by reference to considerations extraneous to that text. Third, as will become clear when the analysis in this part is read in conjunction with the analysis in part E, this way of approaching an alleged violation of Article 6 would also minimise the room for irrational flexibility in the judgments of the Court. For reasons that will become clear in part E, there would be less call for fuzzy notions of 'the proceedings as a whole',[90] 'counterbalancing', 'defect curing',[91] or 'irretrievable unfairness'[92] if the inquiry at this stage is confined to assessing whether or not a specific defined right has been violated.

Of course, it is entirely possible that, after assessing each allegation of a violation of a specific component right of Article 6, the European Court would conclude there has been no violation on the facts. In such a case, I suggest, the Court should then be able to have recourse to assessing whether, notwithstanding the absence of a violation of Article 6(3)(a), the broader Article 6 guarantee of a fair trial has been violated. Such analysis may well be subject to the analytical pitfalls

[87] A broadly similar approach to that outlined here is supported by Hoyano, albeit without reference to *Nielsen*: see Hoyano, 'What is Balanced on the Scales of Justice?' (n 11 above) 27–28.

[88] If the applicant alleged a violation of Art 6(3)(a).

[89] If the applicant alleged a violation of Art 6(3)(b).

[90] See E.2.

[91] See E.3.

[92] See E.4.

that characterise the existing case law, many of which will be explored in part E, but at least those analytical pitfalls will no longer be able to infect the Court's interpretation of the individual component rights of Article 6.

Even if, however, the European Court is unconvinced by the details of this *Nielsen*-inspired approach, I submit that it is incumbent upon the Court to consider carefully the broader normative arguments made in this part about the need for some form of enhanced sense of coherence and consistency within the case law relating to the internal structure of Article 6.

D

The Implied Rights

This part considers the origins of the implied rights, their scope and limits, and identifies indications in the European Court's case law that may suggest the basis for 'new' implied rights in the future. When I refer to 'implied rights' I am referring to those rights that the European Court has recognised as falling within the terms of Article 6, but which are not expressly provided for in the text of that provision.[1] In this context, identifying and analysing the implied rights is, to some extent, an exercise in considering how best to approach the definition and interpretation of Article 6.

In recent years, the European Court's Article 6 implied rights jurisprudence has taken on an energetic life of its own, and has been central to many high-profile Article 6 cases.[2] Given the role of the implied rights in fleshing out the context of the Article 6 guarantees, an understanding of how the Court identifies, explains, and applies the implied rights is crucial to assessing the Court's Article 6 case law. And of course the discussion of the implied rights is intimately linked to the consideration elsewhere in the book of approaches to interpretation, to the internal structure of Article 6, and to how the European Court assesses infringements of Article 6.

This part begins by briefly identifying the implied rights that have been recognised by the European Court and in the literature (D.1). It then moves on to consider the European Court's 1993 decision in *Funke*, which may be regarded as the starting point for consideration of the implied rights (D.2). The part then considers the various foundations on which the European Court has based its recognition of implied rights since *Funke*, and the foundations on which the European Court has been unwilling to base implied rights (D.3). This part then turns to consider some of the difficulties that the European Court has faced in defining the scope and limits of the implied rights (D.4).

Overall, this part's argument is that the European Court's implied rights jurisprudence is marked by significant uncertainty and incoherence, raising doubts over the extent to which that jurisprudence can provide guidance to courts, lawyers and citizens.

[1] See, eg, Steven Greer, *The European Convention on Human Rights: Achievements, Problems and Prospects*, 2nd edn (Cambridge University Press, 2006) 198; Ben Emmerson, Andrew Ashworth and Alison Macdonald, *Human Rights and Criminal Justice*, 3rd edn (Sweet & Maxwell, 2012) 101–4, 106–10.

[2] See, eg, *Salduz v Turkey* (App 36391/02) (2009) 49 EHRR 19; *Gafgen v Germany* (Grand Chamber) (App 22978/05) (2010) 52 EHRR 1; *Jalloh v Germany* (App 54810/00) (2007) 44 EHRR 32; and the cases considered below.

D.1 What are the Implied Rights?

There is extensive literature providing description and analysis of the content of the implied rights in great depth. This book does not attempt to replicate that depth of analysis, but instead adopts a cross-cutting analytical approach. In that sense, therefore, the *list* of implied rights is less important than how the analysis of those rights reveals the European Court's *approach* to implied rights generally. Nevertheless, it may be helpful to outline briefly the recognised implied rights at the beginning of this part.

It should be emphasised that the implicit nature of these rights means that different authors (and, indeed, different judgments of the European Court) will characterise the rights in different ways. In some cases, the implied rights may be recognised as independent rights; in others they will be characterised as forming part of another implied right or of an express right.[3] For present purposes, we need a brief working account of the implied rights. Thus, the scholarly work on the criminal aspects of Article 6 has identified implied rights including:

- the right to an adversarial hearing;[4]
- the right to be present at, and participate in, the hearing;[5]
- the equality of arms;[6]
- the right to silence and privilege against self-incrimination;[7]

[3] See, further, Emmerson, Ashworth and Macdonald, *Human Rights and Criminal Justice* (n 1 above) 101–4; *Golder v United Kingdom* (App 4451/70) (1979–80) 1 EHRR 524, Separate Opinion of Judge Fitzmaurice.

[4] See, eg, Pieter van Dijk and GJH van Hoof, *Theory and Practice of the European Convention on Human Rights*, 4th edn (Intersentia, 2006) 584; D Harris, M O'Boyle and C Warbrick, *Law of the European Convention on Human Rights*, 2nd edn (Oxford University Press, 2009) 254; Stefan Trechsel, *Human Rights in Criminal Proceedings* (Oxford University Press, 2006) 89; Sarah J Summers, *Fair Trials: the European Criminal Procedural Tradition and the European Court of Human Rights* (Hart Publishing, 2007) 112–23; R Clayton and H Tomlinson (eds), *The Law of Human Rights*, 2nd edn (Oxford University Press, 2009) 860; *Brandstetter v Austria* (App 11170/84) (1993) 15 EHRR 378; *Pirali Orujov v Azerbaijan* (App 8460/07) (3 February 2011).

[5] See, eg, Harris, O'Boyle and Warbrick, *Law of the European Convention on Human Rights* (n 4 above) 247, 250; Clayton and Tomlinson, *The Law of Human Rights* (n 4 above) 860; Summers, *Fair Trials* (n 4 above) 116–23; van Dijk and van Hoof, *Theory and Practice of the European Convention on Human Rights* (n 4 above) 586, 589–91; Trechsel, *Human Rights in Criminal Proceedings* (n 4 above) 252–61; *SC v United Kingdom* (App 60958/00) (2005) 40 EHRR 10, paras 28–37; *Jelcovas v Lithuania* (App 16913/04) (19 July 2011) para 106.

[6] See, eg, Clayton and Tomlinson, *The Law of Human Rights* (n 4 above) 860; Harris, O'Boyle and Warbrick, *Law of the European Convention on Human Rights* (n 4 above) 251, excerpting a passage from *Kress v France* (App 39594/98) (7 June 2001) para 72; van Dijk and van Hoof, *Theory and Practice of the European Convention on Human Rights* (n 4 above) 581–87, excerpting a passage from *Edwards v United Kingdom* (App 13071/87) (1993) 15 EHRR 417, para 36; Olivier Jacot-Guillarmod, 'Rights related to Good Administration of Justice' in R Macdonald, F Matscher and H Petzold (eds), *The European System for the Protection of Human Rights* (Martinus Nijhoff, 1993) 392–93; Trechsel, *Human Rights in Criminal Proceedings* (n 4 above) 96; *Plotnicova v Moldova* (App 38623/05) (15 May 2012) para 47.

[7] See, eg, Clayton and Tomlinson, *The Law of Human Rights* (n 4 above) 860; van Dijk and van Hoof, *Theory and Practice of the European Convention on Human Rights* (n 4 above) 592; Harris, O'Boyle and Warbrick, *Law of the European Convention on Human Rights* (n 4 above) 259; Trechsel, *Human Rights*

- the right to legal assistance during the pre-trial phase;[8]
- the right in some or all circumstances not to have evidence used where that evidence is obtained by torture or inhuman or degrading treatment, incitement, or entrapment;[9] and
- the right to reasons.[10]

As will be seen, the European Court itself has founded these implied rights on a variety of justifications. The Court has not provided an overarching account of the implied rights, how they relate to the express rights, how they are to be applied and developed, and how to assess when they have been infringed. Instead, the Court's jurisprudence has been marked by an incremental, piecemeal approach that lacks any underlying theory or explanation.

The lists of implied rights identified above, and in the literature, provide a framework with which to analyse the European Court's case law on the implied rights. It is important to bear in mind, however, that the Court does not always draw crisp distinctions between different implied rights, or between the express rights and the implied rights. This nebulous ambiguity should be considered when analysing the implied rights. To some extent, perhaps, ambiguity of this kind is a product of dealing with implied rights rather than express rights. It is, however, indicative of an incoherence in the way that the Court approaches implied rights generally and their relationship with the broader Article 6 structure.

A brief example of this ambiguity is evident in those cases in which the European Court has considered criminal proceedings based, in whole or in part,

in Criminal Proceedings (n 4 above) 340–59; T Ward and P Gardner, 'The Privilege Against Self-incrimination: In Search of Legal Certainty' [2003] *EHRLR* 388; Andrew Ashworth, 'Self-incrimination in European Human Rights Law: a Pregnant Pragmatism?' (2008) 30 *Cardozo Law Review* 751; John Jackson, 'Re-conceptualizing the Right of Silence as an Effective Fair Trial Standard' (2009) 58 *International and Comparative Law Quarterly* 835; Summers, *Fair Trials* (n 4 above) 130–31; *Bykov v Russia* (App 4378/02) (10 March 2009) para 92; *Gafgen v Germany* (Grand Chamber) (n 2 above) para 168.

[8] See, eg, Trechsel, *Human Rights in Criminal Proceedings* (n 4 above) 278–85. See also *Salduz v Turkey* (n 2 above); TAHM van de Laar and RL de Graaff, '*Salduz* and *Miranda*: Is the US Supreme Court Pointing the Way?' [2011] *EHRLR* 304; van Dijk and van Hoof, *Theory and Practice of the European Convention on Human Rights* (n 4 above) 59.

[9] See, eg, Harris, O'Boyle and Warbrick, *Law of the European Convention on Human Rights* (n 4 above) 264; van Dijk and van Hoof, *Theory and Practice of the European Convention on Human Rights* (n 4 above) 586; Trechsel, *Human Rights in Criminal Proceedings* (n 4 above) 111–13; Clayton and Tomlinson, *The Law of Human Rights* (n 4 above) 866–68; *Jalloh v Germany* (n 2 above); *Khan v United Kingdom* (App 35394/97) (2001) 31 EHRR 45; *Gafgen v Germany* (App 22978/05) (2009) 48 EHRR 13; *Bykov v Russia* (n 7 above); *Gafgen v Germany* (Grand Chamber) (n 2 above), but cf *Alchagin v Russia* (App 20212/05) (17January 2012) paras 62–74.

[10] See, eg, Clayton and Tomlinson, *The Law of Human Rights* (n 4 above) 860; van Dijk and van Hoof, *Theory and Practice of the European Convention on Human Rights* (n 4 above) 595–96; Harris, O'Boyle and Warbrick, *Law of the European Convention on Human Rights* (n 4 above) 268–69; Trechsel, *Human Rights in Criminal Proceedings* (n 4 above) 102–10; Clare Ovey and Robin White, *Jacobs and White: The European Convention on Human Rights*, 4th edn (Oxford University Press, 2006) 179; *Taxquet v Belgium* (Grand Chamber) (App 926/05) (2012) 54 EHRR 26; Paul Roberts, 'Does Article 6 of the European Convention on Human Rights Require Reasoned Verdicts in Criminal Trials?' (2011) *Human Rights Law Review* 1. See also B.5.1.

on evidence obtained through entrapment-style investigations or through surveillance. In these cases, there is some uncertainty over whether there are stand-alone entrapment and surveillance guarantees, or whether other guarantees simply apply to the particular factual scenario of entrapment and surveillance. In this way, part D explores a specific variation of the macro-arguments made in part C's analysis of the ambiguities over the internal structure of Article 6. An example of the European Court recognising a specific stand-alone right is evident in *Ramanauskas*. In that case, the Court emphasised that there was a specific and stand-alone guarantee relating to police incitement:

> 69. Article 6 of the Convention will be complied with *only if* the applicant was effectively able to raise the issue of incitement during his trial, whether by means of an objection or otherwise. It is therefore *not sufficient* for these purposes, contrary to what the Government maintained, that *general safeguards* should have been observed, such as equality of arms or the rights of the defence.[11]

In this passage, the European Court appears to recognise a guarantee that exists independently of the other Article 6 guarantees. Elsewhere, however, the European Court's approach appears to reduce the entrapment and surveillance guarantees to a simple fairness guarantee or to a subcategory of other guarantees. In *Khan*, for example, the European Court emphasised that with respect to unlawfully-obtained recordings, the 'central question . . . is whether the proceedings as a whole were fair'.[12] In *Edwards and Lewis*, in turn, the European Court analysed an entrapment issue with reference to the adversarial proceedings guarantee and the equality of arms guarantee.[13] This ambiguity in the European Court's case law should be borne in mind throughout the discussion of the implied rights.[14]

D.2 The Early Implied Rights Jurisprudence was Poorly Explained

Funke v France may be regarded as the first of the silence and self-incrimination guarantees cases, and an early example of the implied rights cases.[15] As an influen-

[11] *Ramanauskas v Lithuania* (App 74420/02) [2008] Crim LR 639 para 69 (emphasis added).

[12] *Khan v United Kingdom* (n 9 above) para 38.

[13] *Edwards and Lewis v United Kingdom* (App 39647/98) (2005) 40 EHRR 24, para 59.

[14] Further discussion of the proceedings as a whole test is at E.2.

[15] *Funke v France* (App 10828/84) (1993) 16 EHRR 297. See A Choo, *Compelling the Provision of Information: the Privilege Against Self-incrimination as a Human Right*, University of Warwick Legal Studies Research Paper Series 2010-20; Ashworth, 'Self-incrimination in European Human Rights Law' (n 7 above) 752–53. It may be noted that two earlier Commission decisions hinted at an implied silence and self-incrimination guarantee. In *I v Switzerland* (Commission) (App 13972/88) (14 May 1992), the dissent of Mr Loucaides referred to the need for safeguards to protect against self-incrimination and protect the right to silence; in *K v Austria* (Commission) (App 16002/90) (13 October 1992) the Commission appeared to recognise the privilege against self-incrimination in Art 10. On the latter, see also Trechsel, *Human Rights in Criminal Proceedings* (n 4 above) 342–43. On *Funke*, see also Harris, O'Boyle and Warbrick, *Law of the European Convention on Human Rights* (n 4 above) 260; van Dijk and van Hoof, *Theory and Practice of the European Convention on Human Rights* (n 4 above) 592–93.

tial case, it is worthy of close analysis, notwithstanding criticisms subsequently made of it.[16] In *Funke*, the applicant argued for the recognition of the implied privilege against self-incrimination on the basis that it was

> a general principle enshrined both in the legal orders of the Contracting States and in the European Convention and the International Covenant on Civil and Political Rights.[17]

The French government did not resist these arguments on principle, but instead argued that, on the facts, there had been no violation.[18] The European Commission of Human Rights agreed, holding that there had been no violation of Article 6; the Commission did not consider the privilege against self-incrimination on any theoretical level.[19] The European Court's analysis in *Funke* is curious. The Court recounted the arguments of the applicant and the government, and the decision of the Commission, before reaching its conclusion:

> The special features of customs law . . . cannot justify such an infringement of the right of anyone 'charged with a criminal offence', within the autonomous meaning of this expression in Article 6, to remain silent and not to contribute to incriminating himself. There has accordingly been a breach of [Article 6(1)].[20]

The European Court accepts, without explanation or reasoning of any kind, that the right to silence and the privilege against self-incrimination are rights of anyone charged with a criminal offence. At no point does the Court provide an indication of the grounds on which it reaches this conclusion, nor does it draw on doctrine or previous decisions in so doing: 'nothing was said about the scope of the privilege, or about its origins and rationale'.[21]

For present purposes, this is interesting because the European Court's jurisprudence about the implied privilege against self-incrimination emerged in a way that lacked theoretical underpinnings and also lacked any indication of the parameters within which such implications could be drawn. Moreover, if it is assumed that the Court reached its conclusion on the basis of the applicant's arguments, then the implication was drawn on the basis that the privilege against self-incrimination was:

[16] See, eg, Ward and Gardner, 'The Privilege Against Self-incrimination' (n 7 above) 390–91; Jackson, 'Re-conceptualizing the Right of Silence' (n 7 above); Ashworth, 'Self-incrimination in European Human Rights Law' (n 7 above) 752–53; Trechsel, *Human Rights in Criminal Proceedings* (n 4 above) 353–54.

[17] *Funke v France* (n 15 above) para 41. We might note that reference to the internal legal orders of contracting states had been made in various cases not related to the privilege against self-incrimination. See, eg, cases about voting rights and elections such as *Mathieu-Mohin and Clerfayt v Belgium* (App 9267/81) (2 March 1987); since then, see *Kudla v Poland* (App 30210/96) (2002) 35 EHRR 11; *SH and others v Austria* (App 57813/00) (1 April 2010).

[18] *Funke v France* (n 15 above) para 42.

[19] *Funke v France* (Commission) (App 10828/84) (8 October 1991) paras 47–70] (translated).

[20] *Funke v France* (n 15 above) para 44.

[21] Ashworth, 'Self-incrimination in European Human Rights Law' (n 7 above) 753. See also, on *Golder v United Kingdom* (n 3 above) and related cases, JG Merrills, *The Development of International Law by the European Court of Human Rights*, 2nd edn (Manchester University Press, 1995) 84–90.

> a general principle enshrined both in the legal orders of the Contracting States and in the European Convention and the International Covenant on Civil and Political Rights.[22]

Such an argument would open up a plethora of possible rights to be implied into the Convention; as will be seen below, the Court has only ever adopted this argument in a modified form. For now, one may note the considerable uncertainty underlying the Court's reasoning in *Funke*, and emphasise that this poorly-explained and poorly-justified jurisprudence cannot provide guidance as to the nature of the law. This lack of guidance is in respect of both the silence and self-incrimination guarantees but also the implied rights and Article 6 more generally.

D.3 At Least Eight Justifications for Implied Rights Can be Identified in the European Court's Case Law

The European Court has adopted at least eight different bases on which rights could be implied into Article 6. Identifying and analysing these justifications is important, both for what it tells us about the way the European Court approaches Article 6, but also for providing some indication of potential future expansions of the scope of the Article 6 implied rights. More broadly, given the extent to which the Article 6 case law is shaped by implied rights cases, this analysis also aids understanding of the Article 6 case law generally. The range of justifications also indicates something of the fluidity with which the European Court approaches its interpretative task.

It should be emphasised that the European Court has not catalogued these justifications itself. Nor has the European Court attempted to explain how the justifications interact and combine, or whether or not there is any sort of hierarchy of justifications. The European Court's apparent reluctance to articulate any sort of overarching view of how it approaches the recognition and interpretation of implied rights only adds to the incoherence and inconsistency that marks its approach to interpretation more generally. The opacity of the Court's reasoning creates uncertainty over not only the content of Article 6, but also over the likelihood that a 'new' implied right might be recognised.

D.3.1 'Generally Recognised International Standards at the Heart of a Fair Procedure'

While subsequent European Court decisions have not adopted the arguments made by the applicant in *Funke*, the European Court has adopted a modified ver-

[22] *Funke v France* (n 15 above) para 41. We might note that reference to the internal legal orders of contracting states had been made in various cases not related to the privilege against self-incrimination. See, eg, cases about voting rights and elections such as *Mathieu-Mohin and Clerfayt v Belgium* (n 17 above); since then, see *Kudla v Poland* (n 17 above); *SH and others v Austria* (n 17 above).

sion of that reasoning. Indeed, in *John Murray v United Kingdom*, the European Court referred to *Funke* and stated:

> Although not specifically mentioned in Article 6 of the Convention, there can be no doubt that the right to remain silent under police questioning and the privilege against self-incrimination *are generally recognised international standards* which lie at *the heart of the notion of a fair procedure* under Article 6.[23]

Here, then, the European Court indicates that it is willing to recognise an implied right where, among other things, the right constitutes a generally recognised international standard at the heart of the notion of a fair procedure. This passage, or passages like it, appear in many subsequent cases.[24]

It is worth disaggregating the component parts of this reasoning. First, it places importance on 'generally recognised international standards'. While the parties in *John Murray* referred to certain international instruments,[25] the judgment does not specify which principles or customs or documents the Court relies on for the purposes of establishing these international standards.[26] Nor does the judgment indicate, for example, what level of international conformity or practice would be required before a standard becomes truly 'international'.[27] These gaps matter

[23] *John Murray v United Kingdom* (App 18731/91) (1996) 22 EHRR 29, para 45 (emphasis added). For more on *John Murray*, see also Harris, O'Boyle and Warbrick, *Law of the European Convention on Human Rights* (n 4 above) 261–62; van Dijk and van Hoof, *Theory and Practice of the European Convention on Human Rights* (n 4 above) 594; Trechsel, *Human Rights in Criminal Proceedings* (n 4 above) 345–46, 356–58; Ashworth, 'Self-incrimination in European Human Rights Law' (n 7 above) 753–55.

[24] See, eg, *Saunders v United Kingdom* (App 19187/91) (1997) 23 EHRR 313, para 68; *Serves v France* (App 20225/92) (1999) 28 EHRR 265, para 46; *Heaney and McGuinness v Ireland* (App 34720/97) (2001) 33 EHRR 12, para 40; *Quinn v Ireland* (App 36887/97) (21 December 2000) para 40; *Luca v Italy* (App 33354/96) (2003) 36 EHRR 46, para 33; *JB v Switzerland* (App 31827/96) [2001] Crim LR 748, para 64; *Allan v United Kingdom* (App 48539/99) (2003) 36 EHRR 12, para 44; *Weh v Austria* (App 38544/97) (2005) 40 EHRR 37, para 39; *Shannon v United Kingdom* (App 6563/03) (2006) 42 EHRR 31, para 32; *Jalloh v Germany* (n 2 above) para 100; *Macko and Kozubal v Slovakia* (App 64054/00) (19 June 2007) para 48; *O'Halloran and Francis v United Kingdom* (App 15809/02) (2008) 46 EHRR 21, para 46; *Yaremenko v Ukraine* (App 32092/02) (12 June 2008) para 77; *Gafgen v Germany* (n 9 above) para 94; *Getiren v Turkey* (App 10301/03) (22 July 2008) para 123; *Panovits v Cyprus* (App 4268/04) (11 December 2008) para 65; *Shabelnik v Ukraine* (App 16404/03) (19 February 2009) para 55; *Bykov v Russia* (n 7 above) para 92; *Marttinen v Finland* (App 19235/03) (21 April 2009) para 60; *Ozcan Colak v Turkey* (App 30235/03) (6 October 2009) para 44; *Oleg Kolesnik v Ukraine* (App 17551/02) (2012) 54 EHRR 37, para 36; *Aleksandr Zaichenko v Russia* (App 39660/02) (18 February 2010), para 38; *Krumpholz v Austria* (App 13201/05) (18 March 2010) para 31; *Hakan Duman v Turkey* (App 28439/03) (23 March 2010) para 47; *Pavlenko v Russia* (App 42371/02) (1 April 2010) para 100; *Baran and Hun v Turkey* (App 30685/05) (20 May 2010) para 68; *Gafgen v Germany* (Grand Chamber) (n 2 above) para 168; *Desde v Turkey* (App 23909/03) (1 February 2011) para 127; *Nechiporuk and Yonalko v Ukraine* (App 42310/04) (21 April 2011) para 258; *Balitskiy v Ukraine* (App 12793/03) (3 November 2011) para 38.

[25] See, eg, *John Murray v United Kingdom* (n 23 above) para 42.

[26] On the European Court's general tendency to assert the state of the law in this area without providing details, see Monika Ambrus, 'Comparative Law Method in the Jurisprudence of the European Court of Human Rights in the Light of the Rule of Law' (2009) 2(3) *Erasmus Law Review* 354, 369.

[27] For example, the test could be analogous to that for customary international law (see, eg, *North Sea Continental Shelf Cases (Germany v Denmark; Germany v Netherlands)* [1969] ICJR 3), or to the US Supreme Court's test for assessing international trends (consider, eg, *Roper v Simmons* 543 US 551 (2005)); cf E Brems, *Human Rights: Universality and Diversity* (Martinus Nijhoff, 2001) 416–20.

because they shape our understanding of when an international standard may become a guaranteed right under Article 6, and because the Court has not provided any mechanism to determine which of the numerous generally recognised international standards warrant the full protection of Article 6.[28]

Second, perhaps it could be said that illumination is added by the requirement that these standards be 'at the heart of the notion of a fair procedure under Article 6'. It is unclear, however, whether 'a generally accepted international standard' would be protected if it was *not* 'at the heart of the notion': are the criteria each sufficient to ground an implied right, or are both necessary? It is also unclear what the European Court means by 'the heart of the notion', and whether, by implication, there are Article 6 standards and rights that are *not* at the heart of the notion of a fair procedure under Article 6. If the 'heart of the notion' is merely a rhetorical flourish, it renders the 'international standard' test unnecessarily opaque. If, on the other hand, it is a meaningful standard, then the interests of predictability and coherence demand that the European Court explain precisely which standards and rights are at the heart of the notion of a fair procedure, and which are not.[29]

Third, there is the sentence that follows the excerpted passage above:

> By providing the accused with protection against improper compulsion by the authorities these immunities *contribute to avoiding miscarriages of justice and to securing the aims of Article 6*.[30]

It is unclear to what extent this sentence provides an additional criterion that will be decisive as to whether or not a right is implied. Further, as has been considered at length in part A, the Court never provides meaningful guidance on what the aims of Article 6 *are*, whether those aims include avoiding miscarriages of justice, or how the undefined aims are best secured.[31]

In sum, recognising a right as implicit in Article 6 because of its position as an internationally-recognised right means that the implied right rests on shaky foundations.[32] Without coherent and logical explanation of the foundations of the guarantees, the Court does not meet the onus of justification. First, it obscures the nature of the silence and self-incrimination guarantees and the circumstances in which they will be infringed. This makes it difficult to understand or predict how the silence and self-incrimination guarantees would apply to a particular case. Second, it obscures the grounds on which *other* implied rights could be recognised, developed and deployed (or rebutted). This makes it difficult to understand the scope of Article 6's non-express guarantees. In the remainder of this section I consider other justifications for implied rights.

[28] See also A.5.

[29] For discussion of 'the very essence', see E.6.

[30] *John Murray v United Kingdom* (n 23 above) para 45 (emphasis added).

[31] Trechsel has different objections to this passage: Trechsel, *Human Rights in Criminal Proceedings* (n 4 above) 347.

[32] For more on the ways in which the European Court's use of comparative legal materials is problematic from a rule of law perspective, see Ambrus, 'Comparative Law Method in the Jurisprudence of the European Court of Human Rights' (n 26 above).

D.3.2 'Domestic State Practice'

The state practice of the contracting states – and of other jurisdictions – has been used by the European Court to help explain the recognition of the silence and self-incrimination guarantees. Ever since *Saunders*,[33] the European Court has stated that the silence and self-incrimination guarantees are 'primarily concerned' with 'respecting the will of an accused person'.[34] The Court has indicated that its focus on 'the will of an accused person' was grounded in 'the legal systems of the Contracting Parties to the Convention and elsewhere'.[35] It is unclear why, for this interpretative task, the European Court should use the domestic state practice of contracting parties as a tool to interpret implied guarantees that, it said, 'lie at the heart of the notion of a fair procedure under Article 6'.[36] If domestic law is to be an interpretative tool in such situations, the interests of clarity and consistency require the European Court to explain the circumstances in which it can be so used: must domestic state practice be the same in *all* contracting states? In a *majority*? In an *increasing* number?[37]

Moreover, the *Saunders* Court did not identify any particular domestic legal provisions or statutes, nor does it identify the jurisdictions to which it refers.[38] If the Court is to rely on domestic law to interpret the Convention in this way, the interests of clarity demand it explain how it uses domestic law, when domestic law may be so used, and which law it relies upon in so doing.

[33] See, by way of example, *Heaney and McGuinness v Ireland* (n 24 above) para 40; *Quinn v Ireland* (n 24 above) para 40; *Weh v Austria* (n 24 above) para 40; *Macko and Kozubal v Slovakia* (n 24 above) para 48; *Bykov v Russia* (n 7 above) para 92. On *Saunders* (n 24 above), see Trechsel, *Human Rights in Criminal Proceedings* (n 4 above) 342; Lord Hoffman, 'The Universality of Human Rights' (Judicial Studies Board Annual Lecture, 19 March 2009) paras 27–29.

[34] *Saunders v United Kingdom* (n 24 above) paras 68–69.

[35] ibid paras 68–69. See also Trechsel, *Human Rights in Criminal Proceedings* (n 4 above) 347; van Dijk and van Hoof, *Theory and Practice of the European Convention on Human Rights* (n 4 above) 593–94.

[36] *Saunders v United Kingdom* (n 24 above) paras 68–69. This is particularly so when one recalls other aspects of the European Court's Art 6 jurisprudence, such as its 'autonomous meaning' case law, in which state practice is explicitly relegated to secondary importance: see, eg, *Engel v Netherlands* (App 5100/71) (1979–80) 1 EHRR 647.

[37] See Merrills, *The Development of International Law by the European Court of Human Rights* (n 21 above) 81–84; Jonas Christoffersen, *Fair Balance: Proportionality, Subsidiarity and Primarity in the ECHR* (Martinus Nijhoff, 2009) 57–66; E Brems, 'The Margin of Appreciation Doctrine in the Case-Law of the ECtHR' (1996) 56 *Zeitschrift für Ausländisches Öffentliches Recht und Völkerrecht* 240, 276–88; L Helfer, 'Consensus, Coherence and the ECHR' (1993) 26 *Cornell Int'l LJ* 133; Andrew Legg, *The Margin of Appreciation in International Human Rights Law* (Oxford University Press, 2012) 124–25; cf *Atkins v Virginia* 536 US 304 (2002).

[38] For more on the ways in which the European Court's use of comparative legal materials is problematic from a rule of law perspective, see Ambrus, 'Comparative Law Method in the Jurisprudence of the European Court of Human Rights' (n 26 above) esp 369.

D.3.3 *'Article 6 Read as a Whole'*

The European Court has also stated that a right could be implied on the basis of 'Article 6, read as a whole'. Thus, in *Stanford v United Kingdom*, where the applicant complained of a violation of Article 6(1) because 'he was unable to hear the proceedings', the Court held that 'Article 6, read as a whole, guarantees the right of an accused to participate effectively in a criminal trial'.[39] Virtually identical language appears in cases such as *Evrenos Onen v Turkey* and *Uzunget and others v Turkey*.[40] Thus, the European Court is willing to imply the relevant right on the basis of reading Article 6 as a whole. Crucially, the Court does not identify any characteristics or qualities or attributes of 'Article 6 as a whole' on which it relies. Even if one accepts that this is a sensible and logical approach to interpretation, it remains unclear how such an amorphous justification might contribute to defining the *limits* or *content* of an implied right.

There is an additional uncertainty here. It is sometimes unclear in these cases if it is the European Court's view that Article 6 may be read as a whole and interpreted in such a way that it provides an implied stand-alone guarantee to participate in the hearing, *or* whether it is the European Court's view that in assessing whether a proceeding was fair as a whole, one of the relevant factors will be the extent to which the applicant was able to participate in the hearing. Much like the points made in part C about the relevance of internal structure to framing the scope of the Court's inquiry, this point also allows the Court a considerable degree of irrational flexibility.[41]

D.3.4 *'The Object and Purpose of Article 6 Read as a Whole'*

In a slight variation to the reasoning identified above, there are other cases in which the European Court recognises an implied right on the basis that it is guaranteed by the *object and purpose* of Article 6 read as a whole. Thus, in *Colozza*, the Court stated that, although not expressly mentioned in Article 6(1), 'the object and purpose of the Article taken as a whole show that a person "charged with a criminal offence" is entitled to take part in the hearing'.[42] Similar passages using the same justification, and often drawing on *Colozza*, appear in a significant num-

[39] *Stanford v United Kingdom* (App 16757/90) (23 February 1994) para 26. On *Stanford*, see R Kolb, 'The Jurisprudence of the ECHR on Detention and Fair Trial in Criminal Matters from 1992–1998' (2000) 21 *Human Rights Law Journal* 348, 357; Trechsel, *Human Rights in Criminal Proceedings* (n 4 above) 335.

[40] *Evrenos Onen v Turkey* (App 29782/02) (15 February 2007) para 27; *Uzunget and others v Turkey* (App 21831/03) (13 October 2009) para 34, citing *T and V v United Kingdom* (App 24724/94; 24888/94) (2000) 30 EHRR 121, para 83.

[41] See E.2 for more on how the European Court assesses the 'proceedings as a whole'.

[42] *Colozza v Italy* (App 9024/80) (1985) 7 EHRR 516, para 27. For more on *Colozza*, see, eg, van Dijk and van Hoof, *Theory and Practice of the European Convention on Human Rights* (n 4 above) 589; Trechsel, *Human Rights in Criminal Proceedings* (n 4 above) 252–56; Harris, O'Boyle and Warbrick, *Law of the European Convention on Human Rights* (n 4 above) 248.

ber of cases.[43] As seen in part A.2, the Court never identifies what the object and purpose of Article 6 actually *are*, nor does it articulate the links between that object and purpose (whatever they may be) and the right being implied.

Moreover, when this approach is contrasted with the approach immediately above, a further concern arises: the Court risks fostering the appearance that it will imply rights on the basis of *Article 6* read as a whole when it is able to do so, but when that fails it will imply rights on the basis of the *object and purpose* of Article 6 read as a whole.

D.3.5 'Implications Based on Other Convention Provisions'

In *Doorson v Netherlands*, the European Court considered the rights of witnesses and victims. In so doing, the Court stated:

> It is true that Article 6 does not explicitly require the interests of witnesses in general, and those of victims called upon to testify in particular, to be taken into consideration. However, their life, liberty or security of person may be at stake, as may interests coming generally within the ambit of Article 8 of the Convention. Such interests of witnesses and victims are in principle protected by other, substantive provisions of the Convention, which imply that Contracting States should organise their criminal proceedings in such a way that those interests are not unjustifiably imperilled. Against this background, *principles of fair trial also require* that in appropriate cases the interests of the defence are balanced against those of witnesses or victims called upon to testify.[44]

This passage has been cited in subsequent cases such as *Van Mechelen* and *Marcello Viola*.[45] This book does not seek to make arguments about Article 8. Instead, my argument here is focused on three aspects of relevance to Article 6. First, the European Court does not indicate precisely which 'principles of *fair trial*', as opposed to principles of the Convention generally, might justify drawing this implication. Second, the passage indicates that the rights of witnesses under *other*

[43] See, eg, *Somogyi v Italy* (App 67972/01) (2008) 46 EHRR 5, para 65; *Sejdovic v Italy* (App 56581/00) (10 November 2004) para 29; *Sejdovic v Italy* (App 56581/00) (1 March 2006) para 81; *Hermi v Italy* (App 18114/02) (28 June 2005) para 33; *Hermi v Italy* (App 18114/02) (2008) 46 EHRR 46, para 59; *Marcello Viola v Italy* (App 45106/04) (5 October 2006) para 52; *Demebukov v Bulgaria* (App 68020/01) (28 February 2008) para 44; *Sibgatullin v Russia* (App 32165/02) (23 April 2009) para 33; *Seyithan Demir v Turkey* (App 25381/02) (28 July 2009) para 37; *Makarenko v Russia* (App 5962/03) (22 December 2009) para 132; *Zhuk v Ukraine* (App 45783/05) (21 October 2010) para 26; *Jelcovas v Lithuania* para 106; *Abdulgadirov v Azerbaijan* (App 24510/06) (20 June 2013) para 33.

[44] *Doorson v Netherlands* (App 20524/92) (1996) 22 EHRR 330, para 70 (emphasis added). For more on *Doorson*, see, eg, Trechsel, *Human Rights in Criminal Proceedings* (n 4 above) 314–15, 317–19; Harris, O'Boyle and Warbrick, *Law of the European Convention on Human Rights* (n 4 above) 324–25; van Dijk and van Hoof, *Theory and Practice of the European Convention on Human Rights* (n 4 above) 646; Steven Greer, 'Constitutionalising Adjudication under the European Convention on Human Rights' (2003) *Oxford Journal of Legal Studies* 405, 424; Greer, *The European Convention on Human Rights* (n 1 above) 254; E Brems, 'Conflicting Human Rights: an Exploration in the Context of the Right to a Fair Trial in the European Convention on Human Rights' (2005) 27 *Human Rights Quarterly* 294, 317.

[45] *Van Mechelen and others v Netherlands* (App 21363/93) (1998) 25 EHRR 647, para 53; *Marcello Viola v Italy* (n 43 above) para 51.

Articles of the Convention may be sufficient to trigger co-extensive or complementary rights *under Article 6* that are distinct from the original 'source' rights. Third, the European Court's explanation for this reasoning is limited to the following: 'Contracting States should organise their criminal proceedings in such a way that those interests are not unjustifiably imperilled'. As logically compelling as this analysis may be, it imposes on the contracting states a burden to organise their criminal proceedings in such a way that is, at best, in tension with the Court's ostensible reluctance to so impose on contracting states in other situations (for example, the Court's reluctance to require the contracting states to organise their rules of admissibility in any particular way).[46] It may well be the case that rights other than Article 6 rights will play a role in criminal proceedings; what the Court has *not* done is indicate why that warrants the recognition of implied Article 6 rights buttressing the Article 8 rights.

This third aspect is also reflected in those explanations of the silence and self-incrimination guarantees that focus on respecting 'the will of an accused'.[47] This rationale was touched upon in D.3.2 above, in the context of relying on domestic state practice. For present purposes, it may simply be noted that the silence and self-incrimination guarantees have also been justified on the basis of other Convention guarantees, notably Article 3 and also Article 8.[48] Such reasoning rests on the notion that conduct contrary to the silence and self-incrimination guarantees may often, or always, involve elements that are invasive of privacy or degrading.[49] As sound as this logic may appear on its face, the Court has not provided any explanation of the circumstances in which it will be willing to imply a right in one Article on the basis of the content of another Article, nor how such a network of implications might affect the functioning of the Convention as a whole.

D.3.6 *'The Notion of an Adversarial Procedure'*

The case of *Stanford* was considered in part D.3.3 above, in the context of 'Article 6, read as a whole'. Here we consider it from another angle. In considering Stanford's complaint, the European Court held that:

> Nor is it in dispute that Article 6, read as a whole, guarantees the right of an accused to participate effectively in a criminal trial. In general this includes, inter alia, not only his right to be present, but also to hear and follow the proceedings. Such *rights are implicit in the very notion of an adversarial procedure* and can also be derived from the guarantees contained in [Article 6(3)(c), (d) and (e)].[50]

[46] cf B.6.

[47] *Saunders v United Kingdom* (n 24 above) paras 68–69.

[48] See, eg, Trechsel, *Human Rights in Criminal Proceedings* (n 4 above) 348–49.

[49] See, eg, ibid 348–49.

[50] *Stanford v United Kingdom* (n 39 above) para 26 (emphasis added). See, generally, Trechsel, *Human Rights in Criminal Proceedings* (n 4 above) 252–53, Harris, O'Boyle and Warbrick, *Law of the European Convention on Human Rights* (n 4 above) 250–51.

The Court concluded that, on the facts of this case, there had been no breach of Article 6(1).[51] Nevertheless, *Stanford* provided a statement of the law that recognised implied rights to participate, to be present, to hear proceedings and to follow proceedings, and did so partly based on 'the very notion of an adversarial procedure'.

Interestingly, this means that one of the bases on which the rights were implied did not rely on the right being implicit in *Article 6*. Instead, the European Court stated that these rights were implicit *in the very notion of an adversarial procedure*. The Court does not indicate here, or anywhere else in *Stanford*, its view of the relationship between Article 6 and 'the very notion of an adversarial procedure'. It is also unclear how broad the concept of 'the very notion of an adversarial procedure' is, whether that concept is co-extensive with Article 6's fair trial guarantees, and whether it provides any guarantees not explicitly protected by the provisions with which it is cited in *Stanford*. Since *Stanford*, the Court has frequently used 'the very notion of an adversarial procedure' as the basis for implied rights. Indeed, the *Stanford* formulation has been adopted in a great many decisions.[52] In addition to those rights dealt with in *Stanford*, cases such as *Popov* and *Evrenos Onen* also state that 'the right to receive legal assistance' could be implied by the 'very notion of an adversarial procedure'.[53]

D.3.7 'The Rule of Law'

In *Golder*, the European Court relied on 'the rule of law' as the basis for recognising the implied right to a court in Article 6.[54] *Golder*, although a civil case, is of

[51] *Stanford v United Kingdom* (n 39 above) para 32.

[52] See, eg, *Lagerblom v Sweden* (App 26891/95) (14 January 2003) para 49; *Ziliberberg v Moldova* (App 61821/00) (1 February 2005) para 40; *IH and others v Austria* (App 42780/98) (20 April 2006) para 33; *Taner v Turkey* (App 38414/02) (15 February 2007) para 24; *Mevlut Kaya v Turkey* (App 1383/02) (12 April 2007) para 18; *Vozhigov v Russia* (App 5953/02) (26 April 2007) para 40; *Mitrevski v FYROM* (App 33046/02) (21 June 2007) para 35; *Barisik and Alp v Turkey* (App 29765/02) (27 November 2007) para 36; *Dagli v Turkey* (App 28888/02) (27 November 2007) para 29; *Nurhan Yilmaz v Turkey* (App 21164/03) (11 December 2007) para 18; *Abbasov v Azerbaijan* (App 24271/05) (17 January 2008) para 31; *Erseven and others v Turkey* (App 27225/02) (24 January 2008) para 22; *Piroglu and Karakaya v Turkey* (App 36370/02) (18 March 2008) para 36; *Nurhan Yilmaz v Turkey (No 2)* (App 16741/04) (8 April 2008) para 20; *Timergaliyev v Russia* (App 40631/02) (14 October 2008) para 51; *Russu v Moldova* (App 7413/05) (13 November 2008) para 26; *Guvec v Turkey* (App 70337/01) (20 January 2009) para 123; *Grigoryevskikh v Russia* (App 22/03) (9 April 2009) para 78; *Lazoroski v FYROM* (App 4922/04) (8 October 2009) para 71; *Maksimov v Azerbaijan* (App 38228/05) (8 October 2009) para 39; *Sergey Timofeyev v Russia* (App 12111/04) (2 September 2010) para 77; *Zhuk v Ukraine* (n 43 above) para 26; *Pirali Orujov v Azerbaijan* (n 4 above) para 43; *Mammad Mammadov v Azerbaijan* (App 38073/06) (11 October 2011) para 31. See also the similar formulation of 'the very notion of a fair trial' in, eg, *Sabayev v Russia* (App 11994/03) (8 April 2010) para 32.

[53] *Popov v Russia* (App 26853/04) (13 July 2006) para 170; *Evrenos Onen v Turkey* (n 40 above) para 27.

[54] *Golder v United Kingdom* (n 3 above). See also Merrills, *The Development of International Law by the European Court of Human Rights* (n 21 above) 128–29; van Dijk and van Hoof, *Theory and Practice of the European Convention on Human Rights* (n 4 above) 557–59; Harris, O'Boyle and Warbrick, *Law of the European Convention on Human Rights* (n 4 above) 235–36.

interest here insofar as it relates to the implied rights. The *Golder* Court considered the text of the Convention, including its Preamble, and stated:

> It may also be accepted . . . that the Preamble does not include the rule of law in the object and purpose of the Convention, but points to it as being one of the features of the common spiritual heritage of the member States of the Council of Europe. The Court however considers, like the Commission, that it would be a mistake to see in this reference a merely 'more or less rhetorical reference', devoid of relevance for those interpreting the Convention. One reason why the signatory Governments decided to 'take the first steps for the collective enforcement of certain of the Rights stated in the Universal Declaration' was their profound belief in the rule of law. It seems both natural and in conformity with the principle of good faith . . . to bear in mind this widely proclaimed consideration when interpreting the terms of [Article 6(1)] according to their context and in the light of the object and purpose of the Convention. This is all the more so since the Statute of the Council of Europe, an organisation of which each of the States Parties to the Convention is a Member . . . refers in two places to the rule of law . . . And in civil matters one can scarcely conceive of the rule of law without there being a possibility of having access to the courts.[55]

The *Golder* Court went on to protest that:

> This is not an extensive interpretation forcing new obligations on the Contracting States: it is based on the very terms of the first sentence of [Article 6(1)] read in its context and having regard to the object and purpose of the Convention, a lawmaking treaty . . . and to general principles of law.[56]

The *Golder* decision has been described as one 'of the most creative steps taken by the European Court in its interpretation of any article of the Convention'.[57] However, in this decision the European Court implied a right into Article 6 on the basis of 'the principle of the rule of law' without ever expressly defining or describing what that principle means or what its limits may be. This failure to define the rule of law in this context meant that the Court left vague the extent to which it might serve as the basis for other implied rights. Moreover, and perhaps more interestingly, it is implicit in the language of *Golder* that the Court would have reservations about an interpretation that could be described as 'an extensive interpretation forcing new obligations on the Contracting States'. It is unclear whether such an 'extensive interpretation' would be grounds for refusing to recognise an implied right, and equally unclear how onerous obligations would need to be in order to refuse to recognise such a right. In any event, despite the European Court's protests, it seems plain that this was an interpretation that 'forc[ed] new obligations on Contracting States'.

[55] *Golder v United Kingdom* (n 3 above) para 34.

[56] ibid para 36.

[57] Harris, O'Boyle and Warbrick, *Law of the European Convention on Human Rights* (n 4 above) 235; cf Merrills, *The Development of International Law by the European Court of Human Rights* (n 21 above) 85–86.

D.3.8 'Drawing Implications from Specific Provisions of Article 6'

In other instances, the European Court has drawn implied rights from specific provisions of Article 6. Thus, for example, in *Colozza*, the Court added the following reasoning in support of an implied right to be present at criminal proceedings:

> Moreover, [Article 6(3)(c), (d) and (e)] guarantee to 'everyone charged with a criminal offence' the right 'to defend himself in person', 'to examine or have examined witnesses' and 'to have the free assistance of an interpreter if he cannot understand or speak the language used in court', and it is difficult to see how he could exercise these rights without being present.[58]

As was seen above, *Stanford* included a similar passage.[59] Similarly, in the context of the right to silence and the privilege against self-incrimination, the European Court in *Saunders* stated that the privilege in particular 'is closely linked to the presumption of innocence contained in [Article 6(2)] of the Convention'.[60] *Saunders* also went on to refer to the right not to incriminate oneself as one of 'the basic principles of a fair procedure inherent in' Article 6(1).[61]

This means of reasoning, it might be thought, has some advantages over the others adopted by the European Court. In terms of transparency and predictability, this method at least offers a broad indication of how the implied right is anchored in the text of Article 6. Nevertheless, if an 'implied right' is 'closely linked' to a particular express provision of Article 6, it is somewhat unclear whether it is accurate to speak of the implied right as separate to, or distinct from, the express right. For example, does the right to participate and be present at a hearing have a life of its own beyond the precise terms of Article 6(3) on which the *Colozza* Court relied in the extract above? As was the case with part C's analysis of the internal structure of Article 6, this matters because it affects the scope of the inquiry that the European Court makes when considering a particular case or assessing an alleged violation: for example, is the relevant inquiry 'have Articles 6(3)(c)–(e) been violated?' or is it 'has the right to be present been violated?'. The former question affords the opportunity for a broader range of considerations to be taken into account when assessing an alleged violation, especially in light of some of the analytical methods that will be considered in part D.4 and part E. Thus, the interests of clarity demand that the Court more fully articulate the relationship between the implied rights and the express provisions on which it is grounding these implied rights.

[58] *Colozza v Italy* (n 42 above) para 27.

[59] *Stanford v United Kingdom* (n 39 above) para 26.

[60] *Saunders v United Kingdom* (n 24 above) para 68. This has been cited in, eg, *Heaney and McGuinness v Ireland* (n 24 above) para 40.

[61] *Saunders v United Kingdom* (n 24 above) para 69.

D.3.9 Examples of 'Dogs that Did Not Bark' Emphasise these Criticisms

As well as considering the circumstances in which the European Court is willing to recognise implied rights, it may be worthwhile to consider examples of situations in which the Court was unwilling to recognise implied rights: the dogs that did not bark.[62] For present purposes, the *substance* of what was not recognised is less important than *the reasons* for so doing. Three examples will be considered.

First, a number of European Court cases consider the right to reimbursement of legal expenses for a person charged with a criminal offence, but against whom proceedings are discontinued. In *Lutz*, the Court stated:

> The Court points out, first of all . . . that *neither [Article 6(2)] nor any other provision of the Convention gives a person 'charged with a criminal offence' a right* to reimbursement of his costs where proceedings taken against him are discontinued.[63]

In *Lutz*, therefore, the Court stated that no right to reimbursement existed *because* no express provision of Article 6 provided for such a right. I make no normative claims that such a right should or should not exist. Instead, my focus is on the reasoning adopted, and the tension created by the fact that these statements appear to amount to a rejection of rights that are not expressly stated in Article 6.

The second example of a 'dog that did not bark' is drawn from *Peers v Greece*. In *Peers*, the Court undertook a cursory examination of an Article 6(2) argument, and bluntly rejected the notion of an implied right. The applicant, a remand prisoner, argued that the failure 'to provide for a special regime for remand prisoners' amounted to a violation of Article 6(2)'s presumption of innocence.[64] The Court 'recalled':

> that the Convention contains no Article providing for separate treatment for convicted and accused persons in prisons. It cannot be said that [Article 6(2)] has been violated on the grounds adduced by the applicant. There has accordingly been no violation of [Article 6(2)] of the Convention.[65]

In this passage, the Court's view appears to be that unless the Convention contains an Article providing for a right, that right will simply not be protected. It is extremely difficult to reconcile the approach taken in this 2001 decision with, for example, the entirety of the Court's jurisprudence relating to the privilege against self-incrimination. In the absence of reasoning providing explanation of why the Court adopted this sort of approach in this case, and a different sort of approach in, for example, the privilege against self-incrimination cases, there risks being great inconsistency and incoherence in the case law of the Court. For potential

[62] See A Conan Doyle, 'Silver Blaze' in A Conan Doyle, *The Memoirs of Sherlock Holmes* (Penguin, 1950).

[63] *Lutz v Germany* (App 9912/82) (1988) 10 EHRR 182, para 59 (emphasis added). See also *Leutscher v Netherlands* (App 17314/90) (1997) 24 EHRR 181, para 29, citing *Lutz v Germany* para 59. *Lutz* cites *Minelli v Switzerland* (App 8660/79) (1983) 5 EHRR 554, paras 34–35.

[64] *Peers v Greece* (App 28524/95) (2001) 33 EHRR 51, para 76.

[65] ibid para 78.

applicants and their lawyers, particularly those eager to argue for new implied rights or for redefinition of existing implied rights, reasoning like that in *Peers* can provide only bafflement in the place of guidance.

The third example is one that was discussed earlier in part B in the context of that part's discussion of evidence. In *Schenk v Switzerland*, the Court made its now-familiar statement about admissibility of evidence:

> While Article 6 of the Convention guarantees the right to a fair trial, *it does not lay down any rules* on the admissibility of evidence as such, which is *therefore primarily a matter for regulation under national law.*[66]

In this passage, the Court appears to state that because the express terms of Article 6 do not lay down rules on evidence, that area of law is *therefore* not within the scope of the Court's power. Indeed, *therefore* it is primarily a matter for national law. The *Schenk* Court's reluctance to engage with an area of law for which Article 6 does not make express provision stands in stark contrast to all of its implied rights case law. Of course, *Schenk* was decided more than four years before *Funke.* But the logic in *Schenk* continues to be of considerable influence today, and the parallel streams of reasoning in *Schenk* and *Funke* do not sit well together.[67]

In considering these three examples, I do not make any argument that the European Court reached the normatively 'wrong' decision in any of these cases. Instead, my aim has been to underline the incoherence and inconsistency in the way that the Court approaches its interpretative task in cases concerning implied rights or would-be implied rights. These three examples demonstrate that the Court risks looking opportunistic or casual in its performance of this interpretative work. If the Court wishes to treat these areas of law differently to those areas in which it *is* willing to recognise implied rights, then it is incumbent on the Court to explain why, and identify the characteristics of the various areas of law that warrant different and inconsistent treatment.

D.3.10 A Conclusion to the Analysis of the Foundations of the Implied Rights

The sections above have considered a variety of justifications for the implied rights, as well as several examples of situations in which the European Court either elected not to recognise an implied right or reasoned in a way that was inconsistent with its implied rights jurisprudence. In some cases the Court drew on several of these justifications; in others it relied on one alone.[68] The above analysis demonstrates, however, that the overriding characteristic of the justifications, whether used together or disaggregated, is a lack of clear explanation. This mani-

[66] *Schenk v Switzerland* (App 10862/84) (1991) 13 EHRR 242, para 46 (emphasis added).

[67] See Merrills, *The Development of International Law by the European Court of Human Rights* (n 21 above) 85.

[68] cf the analysis in Summers, *Fair Trials* (n 4 above) 116–17.

fests itself as both incoherence in the way that the Court explains each justification, and as incoherence in the way the Court views these justifications as complementing or competing with one another.

At this point, it is worth drawing a connection between the analysis here and the analysis preceding it in part C. Importantly, the European Court's jurisprudence on the implied rights shares some of the 'internal structure' problems that were identified more generally in part C. Thus, it is not always clear if a particular implied right is grounded in Article 6 as a whole, one aspect of Article 6 specifically, or whether it forms part of the Article 6 protections without being tied to any aspect of the text specifically. There is thus a lack of clarity on the relationship between the implied rights and the internal structures of Article 6. Equally, as will be seen in the next section, the implied rights often shade into one another, rendering their precise boundaries opaque.

D.4 The Case Law Indicates Uncertainty Over the Boundaries of the Implied Rights

This section considers the European Court's efforts to define the scope of the various implied rights. In a sense, defining the scope of the rights is a jurisprudential challenge that affects both express and implied rights, and this will be considered in the context of violation and infringement in part E. Here, however, I examine a number of ways in which the European Court has grappled with defining the scope and limits of the implied rights specifically.

As has been foreshadowed above, the European Court's jurisprudence does not always make it easy to draw lines between different implied rights, or make it clear how one implied right relates to another, or to the express rights.[69] In a sense, this is a very specific application of the problems relating to internal structure that were dealt with in part C.

Among the authors, for example, there is a diversity of viewpoints. Thus, some authors suggest that the implied rights could be described as merely component elements of the Article 6(1) 'fair hearing' guarantee. Indeed, Clayton and Tomlinson describe the implied rights as 'principles [that] have been developed by the Commission and the Court' that are elements of 'the content of the right to a fair hearing'.[70] These 'principles' are part of the analysis of the proceedings *as a whole* under the 'fair hearing' guarantee, rather than as stand-alone rights as such.[71] For Emmerson, Ashworth, and Macdonald, the implied rights are closely linked to the way that the European Court approaches the internal structure of Article 6. Thus, the fact that Article 6(2) and Article 6(3) constitute a non-exhaustive list of the components of a fair trial is seen as logically requiring that

[69] See, eg, W Wu, 'Interrogational Fairness under the European Convention on Human Rights' (2011) 39 *International Journal of Law, Crime and Justice* 37, 44–45.

[70] Clayton and Tomlinson, *The Law of Human Rights* (n 4 above) 860.

[71] ibid 860; Summers, *Fair Trials* (n 4 above) 105. We return to the proceedings as a whole at E.2.

other rights may be implied from the Article 6(1) guarantee.[72] These rights, however, are portrayed as stand-alone rights capable of being protected, and violated, independently of any other component of Article 6.[73] Similarly, Harris, O'Boyle and Warbrick note that Article 6's 'fair hearing' guarantee has 'an open-ended, residual quality' that allows 'for adding other particular rights not listed in Article 6 that are considered essential to a "fair hearing"'.[74] Here, therefore, emerges the first fault-line in seeking to understand the internal structure of Article 6 as it applies to the implied rights: the question is whether the implied rights are rights *extrapolated from and based on* Article 6(1) or simply *form part of* Article 6(1). The significance of this lies in the way that the answer to the question frames the scope of the inquiry within which the European Court analyses violations of the implied rights, in ways which are analysed in part E. Analysing the breach of an independent implied right may require a very different interpretative exercise to analysing the breach of the 'fair hearing' guarantee, of which the implied guarantee forms part.

There are two other, related, classes of uncertainty when it comes to the internal structure of Article 6 and the implied rights. The first relates primarily to the relationship between the implied rights and the express rights. The second relates primarily to the relationship between the different implied rights.

As to the first class of uncertainty, it was noted above that the implied rights are sometimes justified on the basis of a particular sub-article of Article 6. The uncertainty arises because sometimes the same implied right is treated as being linked to different express provisions within Article 6. If the silence and self-incrimination guarantees are taken as an example, it is evident that the Court has treated these guarantees as being linked to, and being capable of violating, Article 6 *simpliciter*, Article 6(1), and Article 6(2). Thus, for example, *Funke* simply described the silence and self-incrimination guarantees as relating to 'Article 6'.[75] By contrast, many cases refer to Article 6(1) specifically when identifying which provision of Article 6 had been violated in cases concerning the silence and self-incrimination guarantees. Thus, for example, in *Condron*, the European Court found a violation of Article 6(1): 'the applicants did not receive a fair hearing within the meaning of [Article 6(1)] of the Convention'.[76]

There are also instances, such as in *Saunders*, where the European Court focuses its analysis on Article 6(1) for the purposes of determining whether there has been a violation, but acknowledges that the silence and self-incrimination guarantees are 'closely linked to the presumption of innocence contained in Article 6(2) of

[72] Emmerson, Ashworth and Macdonald, *Human Rights and Criminal Justice* (n 1 above) 101–2.

[73] See ibid 88–91.

[74] Harris, O'Boyle and Warbrick, *Law of the European Convention on Human Rights* (n 4 above) 246. See also Trechsel, *Human Rights in Criminal Proceedings* (n 4 above) 84–86.

[75] *Funke v France* (n 15 above) paras 41–44.

[76] *Condron v United Kingdom* (App 35718/97) (2001) 31 EHRR 1, para 66. See also, eg, *Saunders v United Kingdom* (n 24 above) paras 76–81; *Averill v United Kingdom* (App 36408/97) (2001) 31 EHRR 36, para 52; *JB v Switzerland* (n 24 above) para 71.

the Convention'.[77] In turn, in a case such as *Heaney and McGuinness*, the Court identifies the violation as being of both Article 6(1) *and* Article 6(2):

> [T]here has been a violation of the applicants' right to silence and their right not to incriminate themselves guaranteed by [Article 6(1)] of the Convention. Moreover, given the close link, in this context, between those rights guaranteed by [Article 6(1)] of the Convention and the presumption of innocence guaranteed by [Article 6(2)] . . . the Court also concludes that there has been a violation of the latter provision.[78]

Importantly, the Court's justification for this approach is less due to the facts of the case and more due to the nature of the silence and self-incrimination guarantees.

Inconsistently, the European Court has elsewhere indicated that these matters are to be considered exclusively under Article 6(1). Indeed, in *Rieg v Austria*, the 'applicant complained about a violation of her right to remain silent and the privilege against self incrimination and the presumption of innocence', relying on Article 6(1) and Article 6(2).[79] The Court sourced the privilege against self-incrimination in Article 6(1) 'alone' and not in Article 6(2).[80] Thus in *Rieg*, the European Court refused to recognise an Article 6(2) basis for the silence and self-incrimination guarantees. It is hard to reconcile this interpretative choice with the fact that in *Weh*, ruling on *exactly the same Austrian law* less than *one year* earlier, the Court had expressly acknowledged that the guarantees are 'closely linked to the presumption of innocence contained in Article 6(2) of the Convention'.[81] The applicant in *Weh* did not argue for an Article 6(2) violation, but the European Court nonetheless recognised the role of Article 6(2) in providing the basis for the silence and self-incrimination guarantees.[82] Perversely, the applicant in *Rieg* did argue for an Article 6(2) violation, but the European Court refused to recognise the relevance of Article 6(2) in any way.

This analysis only deals with the silence and self-incrimination guarantees. But even from a brief consideration of this particular implied right, it is apparent that the Court is inconsistent and incoherent in explaining how the silence and self-incrimination guarantees relate to the express terms of Article 6. This incoherence makes it difficult to predict how the Court will act (how could the applicant in *Rieg*, for example, *possibly* imagine that the Article 6(2) argument would be

[77] *Saunders v United Kingdom* (n 24 above) para 68. See Trechsel, *Human Rights in Criminal Proceedings* (n 4 above) 342; van Dijk and van Hoof, *Theory and Practice of the European Convention on Human Rights* (n 4 above) 593; Lord Hoffman, 'The Universality of Human Rights' (n 33 above) paras 27–29; Andrew C Stumer, *The Presumption of Innocence* (Hart Publishing, 2010) 88–151; cf Ward and Gardner, 'The Privilege Against Self-incrimination' (n 7 above) 391–94.

[78] *Heaney and McGuinness v Ireland* (n 24 above) para 59.

[79] *Rieg v Austria* (App 63207/00) (24 March 2005) para 23.

[80] ibid paras 29–32.

[81] *Weh v Austria* (n 24 above) para 39. Both cases concerned the Austrian Motor Vehicles Act (Kraftfahrzeuggesetz). The *Rieg* Court expressly acknowledged that the *Rieg* application 'raises the same issue as *Weh v Austria*': *Rieg v Austria* (n 79 above) para 29. On *Weh*, see Choo, *Compelling the Provision of Information* (n 15 above).

[82] The applicant in *Weh* framed the argument with reference only to Article 6(1): *Weh v Austria* (n 24 above) para 32.

rejected out of hand when the *Weh* Court had expressly acknowledged the link between the silence and self-incrimination guarantees and Article 6(2)?). Moreover, this incoherence has significant consequences for any consideration of how the European Court approaches questions of violation and infringement, and it echoes the criticisms made in part C.

As to the second class of uncertainty, this relates to the relationship between the different implied rights. Here, one may point to instances where the dividing lines between different implied rights are somewhat murky. It is acknowledged here that, by their very nature, implied rights may often be less clearly defined than express provisions. My argument is not to the contrary. The argument, instead, is simply to identify a number of ways in which the European Court's explanation of the implied rights is vague and incoherent, such that it gives rise to rule of law concerns.

There is murkiness, for example, in the boundary between the right to equality of arms and the right to an adversarial procedure.[83] On multiple occasions, the Court has emphasised its view that these rights are distinct, separate, elements of Article 6.[84] It is clear, however, that the European Court is willing to conflate aspects of the two rights in its analysis.[85] Similarly, there is also some murkiness over the boundaries between 'the very notion of an adversarial procedure',[86] the right to be present and participate in a hearing,[87] the implied aspects of the right to receive legal assistance,[88] and the 'fundamental' implied right that criminal proceedings should be adversarial.[89] For present purposes, it is simply worth noting that the Court's reasoning in this area creates potential ambiguity over the relationship between the various implied rights. If one of the rights is merely a subcategory of the other, then the Court ought to outline that relationship clearly; if the rights warrant conceptual independence then the Court should clarify the basis for its reasoning, especially with regard to the foundations for the right to be present and participate.

Thus, this section has outlined several ambiguities about how the Court views Article 6 generally, and the implied rights specifically. When considered together with the analysis in part C, we begin to build an overall picture in which the boundaries of Article 6 rights are poorly defined and fluid. In part E, I turn to what forms of analysis are used by the Court within those poorly defined and fluid boundaries.

[83] cp Summers, *Fair Trials* (n 4 above) 110–12.

[84] See, eg, *Brandstetter v Austria* (n 4 above) para 66; *Ruiz-Mateos v Spain* (App 12952/87) (1993) 16 EHRR 505, para 62; *Salov v Ukraine* (App 65518/01) (2007) 45 EHRR 51, para 87; *Belziuk v Poland* (App 23103/93) (2000) 30 EHRR 614, para 37; cp Summers, *Fair Trials* (n 4 above) 104–5.

[85] See, eg, *Edwards and Lewis v United Kingdom* (n 13 above) para 59, see also para 54.

[86] See D.3.6.

[87] See, eg, *Stanford v United Kingdom* (n 39 above) para 26, and the authorities in D.3.6 above.

[88] See *Popov v Russia* (n 53 above) para 170; *Evrenos Onen v Turkey* (n 40 above) para 27.

[89] *Brandstetter v Austria* (n 4 above) para 66.

D.5 Building the Foundations for a New Approach to the Implied Rights

In concluding the analysis of the implied rights in this part, one may note that there are hints in the European Court's case law of rights that might, in future, be recognised as rights implicit in Article 6. Indeed, there have been indications in the case law of the possibility of implied rights such as:

- an implied right to be prosecuted under procedural rules established in advance;[90]
- an implied right to call expert witnesses where another expert witness completely changes their mind in the course of a hearing;[91]
- a qualified implied right for civilians to be tried in civilian courts;[92]
- an implied right to civilian clothing in the courtroom;[93]
- an implied guarantee to have a fair procedure applied to the determination of public interest immunity;[94] or
- an implied guarantee against the use of evidence obtained in breach of a Convention right.[95]

The difficulties with the Court's incoherent approach to the implied rights, outlined in this part, mean that it is difficult to determine whether, and if so when and how, these embryonic implied rights may crystallise into generally accepted implied rights. It is also worth acknowledging that many of these potential implied rights could also be categorised as simply being definitions of the broad 'fair trial' or 'fair hearing' guarantees, or as factors relevant to a 'proceedings as a whole' analysis. The latter form of analysis will be considered shortly in part E.2. For present purposes, the point is more modest: notwithstanding hints in the case law like those listed above, the Court's failure to rationalise and explain its implied rights jurisprudence in any coherent or consistent way makes it extremely difficult to predict the likely future direction of the Court's case law.

In light of the criticisms made in this part, how ought the Court approach the implied rights? When dealing with rights currently recognised as implicit in Article 6, the Court ought to explain more clearly the reasons *why* that right is implicit in Article 6 (where, for example, the cited reason is 'the object and purpose of Article 6', the Court ought to identify *which* objects and purposes it is relying on), and explain more precisely whether the Court regards the 'right' as an

[90] See, eg, *Coeme v Belgium* (App 32492/96) (22 June 2000) paras 102–104.

[91] *GB v France* (App 44069/98) (2002) 35 EHRR 36 paras 69–70.

[92] *Ergin v Turkey (No 6)* (App 47533/99) (2008) 47 EHRR 36, paras 36–47.

[93] *Samoila and Cionca v Romania* (App 33065/03) (4 March 2008) paras 82, 100.

[94] See, eg, *Jasper v United Kingdom* (App 27052/95) (2000) 30 EHRR 441, para 53; *Rowe and Davis v United Kingdom* (App 28901/95) (2000) 30 EHRR 1, para 62; and *Fitt v United Kingdom* (App 29777/96) (2000) 30 EHRR 480, para 50; see also E.2.3.

[95] *Jalloh v Germany* (n 2 above) paras 105–107.

independent guarantee or as a mere definitional gloss on an existing explicit or implicit right.[96] These forms of explanation would provide the Court's audience with considerably more guidance about its current jurisprudence, and about potential future directions for that jurisprudence, than the existing state of affairs.

[96] It should be noted that this latter choice may take on added significance if the normative arguments made in C.5 are adopted by the Court. The choice to regard a particular implied right as a stand-alone right would, I suggest, warrant the Court then looking *principally or even exclusively* at that implied right as the starting point for its analysis; if the implied right turned out to be merely definitional guidance for an existing explicit or implicit right, then the Court's analysis would be able to have reference to that explicit or implicit right. See C.5 for further discussion.

SECTION II

E

Assessing Infringements and Violations: the Puzzle of Article 6

This part looks at how the European Court assesses alleged violations of Article 6 rights. It forms the heart of this book.

Part E begins by identifying and explaining the origins of two characteristics of Article 6 that complicate the assessment of these alleged violations: its unqualified nature and its structure. It identifies what I describe as the puzzle of Article 6: given that Article 6 lacks an express guiding principle for assessing alleged violations of Article 6, how should the European Court assess such allegations? In the absence of such a meta-principle, how does Article 6 infringement analysis work in the Court's case law? Having explored the origins of this puzzle in the *travaux*, the main portion of this part then looks at a variety of different tools and devices that the European Court has used to assess alleged violations of Article 6. During the course of this part, a variety of arguments and criticisms will be made. But there are two macro-arguments that run through the part, echoing the two broad classes of argument outlined in the Introduction and elsewhere in this book.

First, for each of the array of tools and mechanisms used by the European Court to assess violations of Article 6, it will be shown that the European Court's case law reflects internal inconsistency as to how each specific tool and mechanism is identified, explained and applied. The individual arguments advanced with respect to each of these tools and mechanisms will be specifically related to the relevant method of assessment, but the overall picture will be one of incoherence.

Second, it will be argued that these tools and mechanisms are incoherently deployed by the European Court, with little explanation of why particular tools are used in particular situations and not in others. My argument is not that the European Court must adopt exactly the same analytical framework for all Article 6 rights in all circumstances. The argument is more focused: if the European Court is to adopt different analytical approaches for different cases, the interests of coherence and predictability demand that it offer explanations of some sort for why a particular analytical framework is applicable to one case but not to another. As it stands, I argue in this part, the European Court's case law is characterised by the sort of irrational flexibility that has already been seen elsewhere in the book.

Together, I will show that in assessing violations of Article 6, the European Court uses a set of analytical tools that are inconsistent with each other, and incoherent in themselves. Moreover, when the arguments made in previous parts are added to those made in part E, this level of incoherence generates considerable uncertainty in terms of the ways in which the European Court frames, explains, and assesses alleged Article 6 violations.

E.1 Article 6 is Different

Article 6 is different. In beginning any consideration of how the European Court analyses and deals with alleged violations of Article 6, it is important to emphasise those characteristics of Article 6 that make it different from many of the other Convention provisions. My argument is not that Article 6 is unique, and it is not that other Convention provisions lack unique features. The argument is narrower: simply put, there are several features of Article 6 that complicate the task of assessing potential violations. These features are critical to understanding the parameters within which the Court works when analysing Article 6, and to understanding why that work may be flawed.

E.1.2 Article 6 Does Not Have a Restrictions Clause

For those who draft human rights documents, and for those who use and think about human rights documents, a key question is this: under what circumstances, and for which rights, may a prima facie infringement of a right be justified?[1] Different human rights documents answer this question in different ways.[2] One option is a generally-applicable limitations clause specifying the circumstances in which it may be possible to justify an infringement of any of the protected rights. This course was adopted in, for example, section 1 of the Canadian Charter.[3]

A second option is to specify that particular justifications, or sets of justifications, are applicable to particular rights. Thus, in the case of the European Convention, for example, Article 8's protection of private and family life is qualified in this way:

> Article 8(2): There shall be no interference by a public authority with the exercise of this right except such as is in accordance with the law and is necessary in a democratic society in the interests of national security, public safety or the economic well-being of the country, for the prevention of disorder or crime, for the protection of health or morals, or for the protection of the rights and freedoms of others.

[1] As is evident in Alexy's work, there is considerable philosophical debate over the nature of limitations on rights. Here, and consistently throughout this book, our focus is less theoretical. See, eg, Robert Alexy, *A Theory of Constitutional Rights* (Oxford University Press, 2002) ch 6.

[2] See, eg, Julian Rivers, 'Proportionality and Variable Intensity of Review' (2006) 65 *Cambridge Law Journal* 174, 174–77.

[3] Constitution Act 1982 (Canada); Canadian Charter of Rights and Freedoms, s 1: 'The Canadian Charter of Rights and Freedoms guarantees the rights and freedoms set out in it subject only to such reasonable limits prescribed by law as can be demonstrably justified in a free and democratic society.'

And in the case of each of Articles 9 to 11, the European Convention provides a set of available justifications that overlap in part with each other and with Article 8, but also differ in part.[4]

A third option is to provide no express mechanism for resolving whether, if at all, an infringement might be justified. Thus, for example, the Sixth Amendment to the Constitution of the United States simply provides a series of guarantees and gives no express indication of any mechanism whereby restrictions on the rights contained therein might be justified. For now, the argument is not about how alleged infringements of these various provisions are justified *in practice* before the various relevant courts. The concern is simply with the structure of the guarantees; we will come to the reality of applying these guarantees later in this part.

In the European Convention, we see a combination of options two and three. The unqualified rights include, for example, those rights contained in Articles 2 to 7.[5] Under Article 15 of the Convention, the guarantees in Article 2,[6] Article 3, Article 4(1), and Article 7 cannot be derogated from. These guarantees, therefore, form a class of *unqualified and non-derogable* rights. In contrast, guarantees such as those in Article 5 and Article 6 are members of a class of *derogable and unqualified* rights.[7] It is possible to argue, as Ashworth does, that these classes of rights, together with the *qualified* rights, form a hierarchy of sorts.[8] For present purposes, this book does not need to make an argument about a hierarchy, but it adopts Ashworth's classification of the rights into these various groups.[9]

[4] For an analysis of how this 'somewhat disorderly' situation came about, see AW Brian Simpson, *Human Rights and the End of Empire* (Oxford University Press, 2001) 715.

[5] There is one qualification: for one of the Art 6 component rights, there is an express restrictions clause. Article 6(1) states that judgments 'shall be pronounced publicly but the press and public may be excluded from all or part of the trial in the interests of morals, public order or national security in a democratic society, where the interests of juveniles or the protection of the private life of the parties so require, or to the extent strictly necessary in the opinion of the court in special circumstances where publicity would prejudice the interests of justice'.' On this, see R Clayton and H Tomlinson (eds), *Fair Trial Rights*, 2nd edn (Oxford University Press, 2010) 62–66, 174–76; D Harris, M O'Boyle and C Warbrick, *Law of the European Convention on Human Rights*, 2nd edn (Oxford University Press, 2009) 271–78; Stefan Trechsel, *Human Rights in Criminal Proceedings* (Oxford University Press, 2006) 117–33; P van Dijk and GJH van Hoof, *Theory and Practice of the European Convention on Human Rights*, 4th edn (Intersentia, 2006) 596–602. References to Art 6 elsewhere in this part may refer to all of Art 6 apart from this guarantee with its stand-alone limitations provision.

[6] In the case of Art 2, Art 15 indicates that derogation is allowed 'in respect of deaths resulting from lawful acts of war'.

[7] On the nature of derogation, see, eg, Anna-Lena Svensson-McCarthy, *The International Law of Human Rights and States of Exception* (Martinus Nijhoff Publishers, 1998); Ben Emmerson, Andrew Ashworth and Alison Macdonald, *Human Rights and Criminal Justice*, 3rd edn (Sweet & Maxwell, 2012) 71–74; Harris, O'Boyle and Warbrick, *Law of the European Convention on Human Rights* (n 5 above) ch 16; A Mowbray, *Cases, Materials, and Commentary on the European Convention on Human Rights*, 3rd edn (Oxford University Press, 2012) ch 17.

[8] See Andrew Ashworth, 'Security, Terrorism and the Value of Human Rights' in B Goold and L Lazarus (eds), *Security and Human Rights*, 2nd edn (Hart Publishing, 2007); cf E Brems, 'The Margin of Appreciation Doctrine in the Case-Law of the ECtHR' (1996) 56 *Zeitschrift für Ausländisches Öffentliches Recht und Völkerrecht* 240, 264–69.

[9] The European Court itself has referred to a 'hierarchy of human rights',' but usually in the context of the right to life and only in passing. Typically the Court refers to the right to life being at the apex of this hierarchy: see *K-H W v Germany* (App 37201/97) (2003) 36 EHRR 59; *Tysiac v Poland* (App

The status of Article 6 as an derogable and unqualified right raises a number of normative questions: should the Article 6 guarantee(s) be interpreted as 'absolute',[10] with no infringement thereof being capable of justification? Should some infringements of Article 6 be justifiable? If so, what standard applies, and should it be similar to the standards used for the qualified rights? As will be seen, at various times the judgments of the European Court, and the work of scholars in this area, have offered differing views as to the appropriate answers to these questions. This part, then, is about the European Court's attempts to solve these questions; its attempts to solve the puzzle of Article 6. In a broader sense, this part is also about the deep incoherence running through the European Court's Article 6 case law.[11]

E.1.3 Article 6's Structure Creates Further Complexity

The second key characteristic worth identifying at this point relates to the complexity of Article 6's structure. Analytical difficulties arising from the structure of Article 6 have been discussed in part C. At this point I note two relevantly problematic aspects of Article 6's structure.

First, Article 6 appears to protect *two different* fair trials. In one sense, *all* of Article 6 is designed to protect what might be described as 'the right to a fair trial'. In this way, referring to 'fair trial rights' or 'the right to a fair trial' is shorthand for all of the various rights and guarantees, express and implied, that may be found in Article 6(1), Article 6(2), and the provisions of Article 6(3).[12] This is one of the 'fair trials'.

5410/03) (20 March 2007); *Kononov v Latvia* (App 36376/04) (17 May 2010). Compare the suggestion that the right to liberty is at the apex, para 1.15 of the Partly Dissenting Opinion of Judge Bushev in *Oao Neftyanaya Kompaniya Yukos v Russia* (App 14902/04) (20 September 2011). Legg offers a different framework for classifying rights, identifying 'absolute rights', 'strong rights', 'qualified rights' and 'weak rights': Andrew Legg, *The Margin of Appreciation in International Human Rights Law* (Oxford University Press, 2012) 204–16. On assessing qualifications to ostensibly unqualified rights in the German domestic context, see Alexy, *A Theory of Constitutional Rights* (n 1 above) 72–76.

[10] Article 6 is quite often described as 'absolute' in one way or another: see C Gearty, *Principles of Human Rights Adjudication* (Oxford University Press, 2004) 10; L Hoyano, 'What is Balanced on the Scales of Justice? In Search of the Essence of the Right to a Fair Trial' [2014] Crim LR 4; Kai Möller, *The Global Model of Constitutional Rights* (Hart Publishing, 2012) 13, 180; ADP Brady, *Proportionality and Deference under the UK HRA: An Institutionally Sensitive Approach* (Cambridge University Press, 2012) 171–73.

[11] For some analogous analysis regarding other Articles, see Janneke Gerards and Hanneke Senden, 'The Structure of Fundamental Rights and the European Court of Human Rights' (2009) 7 *International Journal of Constitutional Law* 619; H Battjes, 'In Search of a Fair Balance: the Absolute Character of the Prohibition of Refoulement under Article 3 ECHR Reassessed' (2009) 22 *Leiden Journal of International Law* 583; Mireille Delmas-Marty, 'The Richness of Underlying Legal Reasoning' in Mireille Delmas-Marty and Christine Chodkiewicz (eds), *The European Convention for the Protection of Human Rights: International Protection Versus National Restrictions* (Martinus Nijhoff, 1992).

[12] The heading to Art 6 was added to the text in 1998, when Protocol No 11 (ETS 155) entered into force. Among other things, Protocol No 11 prescribed various headings to be inserted into the European Convention's Articles.

If one looks at Article 6(1), however, the potential for *another* 'fair trial' is evident. The first sentence of Article 6(1) states:

> In the determination of his civil rights and obligations or of any criminal charge against him, everyone is entitled to a *fair and public hearing* within a reasonable time by an independent and impartial tribunal established by law.[13]

Thus Article 6(1) specifically guarantees 'a fair and public hearing'. This particular guarantee is one of several component parts of Article 6(1), which in turn is one of several component parts of Article 6.

Thus, it is possible to read Article 6 as containing two identifiable 'fair trial' rights or sets of rights. These rights may be similar, and may overlap, but it is important to note the potential for confusion and ambiguity.[14] This ambiguity is, perhaps, increased by the fact that Article 6 is one of the longer and more detailed provisions of the Convention. It is 13 times longer than Article 3, and is second only to Article 5 in its length and the number of subprovisions contained within it. In light of this, there may be a temptation to regard parts of Article 6 (such as Article 6(2) and (3)) as merely providing definitional assistance and elaboration on the meaning of Article 6(1).[15]

Indeed, it is possible to imagine a scenario in which the European Court treated Article 6(2) and Article 6(3)(a)–(e) as merely definitional. As seen in part C, however, this is not what the European Court has done. Or, more precisely, this is not what the Court has done in any consistent way: the Court has demonstrated a willingness to find violations of Article 6(2) and Article 6(3), whether in conjunction with Article 6(1) or independently. The rights in these Articles thus appear to have some independent existence and force. In other instances, as demonstrated in part C, Article 6(2) and Article 6(3) have been treated as being close to mere definitional provisions, a usage that does not sit well with the cases in which a violation is found of those provisions.

The second aspect of structural complexity relevant to the present discussion relates to the implied rights. The nature of implied rights means, as explained in part D, that their origins and definition can be especially vague. In terms of assessing infringements and violations, the case law reflects uncertainty over whether implied rights are 'absolute'.[16] With respect to justifiable infringements of implied

[13] Emphasis added.

[14] For a possible example of this confusion, see Olivier Jacot-Guillarmod, 'Rights related to Good Administration of Justice' in R Macdonald, F Matscher and H Petzold (eds), *The European System for the Protection of Human Rights* (Martinus Nijhoff, 1993) 381, where Jacot-Guillarmod misquotes a key passage from *Golder v United Kingdom* (App 4451/70) (1979–80) 1 EHRR 524, para 28. *Golder* refers to Art 6(1) but Jacot-Guillarmod's rendering of the quote has *Golder* referring to Art 6 more generally. For more on different approaches to 'fairness', see, eg, Sarah J Summers, *Fair Trials: the European Criminal Procedural Tradition and the European Court of Human Rights* (Hart Publishing, 2007) 97–128.

[15] A temptation manifestations of which have been seen above: see, eg, C.4.1.

[16] *John Murray v United Kingdom* (App 18731/91) (1996) 22 EHRR 29, paras 46–47; *Saunders v United Kingdom* (App 19187/91) (1997) 23 EHRR 313, paras 68–69, 74. See also R Kolb, 'The Jurisprudence of the ECHR on Detention and Fair Trial in Criminal Matters from 1992–1998' (2000) 21 *Human Rights Law Journal* 348, 356.

rights, the case law on the right to a court, for example, suggests that that right is subject to implied limitations.[17] The Court, however, has refused to rationally explain such limitations: it declined to 'elaborate a general theory of such limitations',[18] other than to suggest that they might be subject to a proportionality analysis.[19]

Thus far, two characteristics of Article 6 have been noted: a puzzle arises out of its unqualified nature, and it is structurally complex in a number of ways. Shortly, this part examine how these characteristics play out in the context of alleged violations of Article 6 generally, and how these factors interact with other characteristics of Article 6. Before doing so, however, I will examine whether the *travaux préparatoires* to the Convention provide any guidance on how these intertwined strands may be untangled.

E.1.4 The Travaux Préparatoires *Do Not Solve the Puzzle*

As explained in part A, under the Vienna Convention and the Court's case law, the *travaux* are a supplementary means of interpreting the European Convention.[20] At this point, we turn to the *travaux* to try to understand how the structure of the Convention, with its mixture of qualified and unqualified rights, and its drafting of Article 6, came about.

The drafters of the Convention did give some consideration to limitations clauses. At the outset, there was disagreement over the level of definitional detail that the Convention would provide for each of the protected rights (should the rights be 'listed' or 'defined'?).[21] Alongside this dispute, however, there was an initial sense that there should be a generally-applicable 'limitations clause designed to limit not so much the rights themselves as the powers of government'.[22] This debate was also intertwined with debate about the institutions to be created by any convention: there was, for example, extensive discussion of whether there should be a court.[23]

[17] *DeWeer v Belgium* (App 6903/75) (1979–80) 2 EHRR 439, para 49; *Peltier v France* (App 32872/96) (21 May 2002) para 35; *Gruais and Bosquet v France* (App 67881/01) (10 January 2006) para 26. See van Dijk and van Hoof, *Theory and Practice of the European Convention on Human Rights* (n 5 above) 557–78; Harris, O'Boyle and Warbrick, *Law of the European Convention on Human Rights* (n 5 above) 235–46; Clayton and Tomlinson, *Fair Trial Rights* (n 5 above)) 15–43, 140–55; Jonas Christoffersen, *Fair Balance: Proportionality, Subsidiarity and Primarity in the ECHR* (Martinus Nijhoff, 2009) 78–81.

[18] *DeWeer v Belgium* (n 17 above) para 49; see also B.2.

[19] *Peltier v France* (n 17 above) para 35; *Gruais and Bosquet v France* (n 17 above) para 26. For more on proportionality in this context, see below, and van Dijk and van Hoof, *Theory and Practice of the European Convention on Human Rights* (n 5 above) 573–75; Harris, O'Boyle and Warbrick, *Law of the European Convention on Human Rights* (n 5 above) 235–46.

[20] See A.1: Art 32 of the Vienna Convention allows for *travaux préparatoires* to be consulted as a supplementary means of interpretation.

[21] Simpson, *Human Rights and the End of Empire* (n 4 above) 658–59. See also Christoffersen, *Fair Balance* (n 17 above) 7–14.

[22] Simpson, *Human Rights and the End of Empire* (n 4 above) 658–59; Council of Europe, *Collected Edition of the Travaux Préparatoires* (Martinus Nijhoff, 1975) vol I, 168–70.

[23] See, eg, Simpson, *Human Rights and the End of Empire* (n 4 above) 712.

In a sitting on 5 September 1949, the Consultative Assembly considered a proposal that the Convention include a generally-applicable limitations clause (then identified as 'Article 6').[24] As Simpson notes, the clause 'was a modified version of Article 29(2)' of the Universal Declaration of Human Rights.[25] The Rapporteur, Teitgen, described a clause of this sort as being designed to provide states with the power to restrict rights for good cause, but not the power to restrict rights for selfish reasons or reasons against the 'public interest'.[26] Benvenuti of Italy later expressed the concern that, if 'Article 6' were enacted, 'every State which violates human rights . . . will always have an excuse'.[27] These concerns were shared by the United Kingdom; Simpson summarises the British argument that such a clause 'would be "a mockery and a fraud on the public", since it would allow governments to justify any form of oppression'.[28]

Concerns of this sort are indicative, perhaps, of the uncertainty over how the Convention would be likely to work in practice. And yet, as Simpson argues, the purpose of a draft clause like 'Article 6' was

> the exact reverse of what the [United Kingdom] Foreign Office thought; it was there to prevent governments from justifying any form of oppression.[29]

Despite the British concerns, a generally-applicable limitations clause became a feature of the early drafts.[30] As time went on, there were proposals to amend the list of public goals that might justify an infringement, and proposals to add specific limitations clauses to particular provisions.[31]

Then, in March 1950, the debate shifted. The drafters now considered two alternative proposals. What I will describe as 'Alternative One' included language based, to varying degrees, on a draft originally proposed by the United Kingdom,[32]

[24] Council of Europe, *Collected Edition of the Travaux Préparatoires* (n 22 above) vol I, 208. Another version of this clause appears at 230.

[25] Simpson, *Human Rights and the End of Empire* (n 4 above) 677.

[26] Council of Europe, *Collected Edition of the Travaux Préparatoires* (n 22 above) vol I, 278. See also 272 and Simpson, *Human Rights and the End of Empire* (n 4 above) 677.

[27] Council of Europe, *Collected Edition of the Travaux Préparatoires* (Martinus Nijhoff, 1975) vol II, 138.

[28] Simpson, *Human Rights and the End of Empire* (n 4 above) 688.

[29] ibid 688.

[30] For subsequent versions of such a clause, see Council of Europe, *Collected Edition of the Travaux Préparatoires* (Martinus Nijhoff, 1976) vol III, 224, 238. See also Simpson, *Human Rights and the End of Empire* (n 4 above) 658–60.

[31] Turkey proposed that 'Article 6' be amended such that limitations of rights would be allowed if they were for 'national unity and solidarity': Council of Europe, *Collected Edition of the Travaux Préparatoires* (n 30 above) vol III, 182–84. See also ibid 194; Council of Europe, *Collected Edition of the Travaux Préparatoires* (Martinus Nijhoff, 1977) vol IV, 24–26; Council of Europe, *Collected Edition of the Travaux Préparatoires* (n 30 above) vol III, 206, 266; Simpson, *Human Rights and the End of Empire* (n 4 above) 694.

[32] See Council of Europe, *Collected Edition of the Travaux Préparatoires* (n 30 above) vol III, 312–20. In the following passage, the terms 'alternative one' and 'alternative two' are used as shorthand for the two models. It may be noted that the *travaux* are not entirely consistent in referring to the two models; sometimes the *travaux* refer to one model as Alternative A and at other times refer to it as Alternative B. Contrast the above reference with, eg, Council of Europe, *Collected Edition of the Travaux Préparatoires* (n 31 above) vol IV, 16–18.

and was described as *defining* rather than *enumerating* or *listing* the rights.[33] It included specific limitations clauses for particular rights, and no generally-applicable limitations clause.[34] No specific limitations clause was inserted to cover fair trial rights.[35] It appears that Alternative One reflected British views that any Convention should 'make it quite clear what was the nature and extent of the obligations to be assumed by the States party'.[36] The fear was that agreeing to a mere list of rights, designed to be developed and elaborated upon by a court, would amount to signing 'a blank cheque'.[37] More generally, the British view was that arguments in favour of a list were 'profoundly alien to their legal culture'.[38]

'Alternative Two', however, retained a generally-applicable limitations clause as 'Article 6'.[39] It was said that this alternative *enumerated* or *listed* the rights rather than defining them.[40] Supporters of Alternative Two argued that debate about the precise wording of definitions may 'take a long time' and might delay the establishment of European institutions.[41] Rather than spending time debating precise definitions and specific limitation clauses, Alternative Two advocates argued that:

> [T]he rights and freedoms listed [in Alternative Two], including the general rules concerning their limitation, had for Western Europe a sufficiently precise meaning to allow the signatory States to be left the responsibility to lay down the conditions for the exercise of these rights and their protection in their own national laws.[42]

Views of this sort were expressed by, for example, representatives of Belgium, France, Ireland, and Italy; a French representative warned that the British definitions might be 'very dangerous' and 'extremely difficult' to formulate.[43] Throughout the middle months of 1950, various compromise proposals were discussed, and support slowly moved behind Alternative One.[44] This move was linked to compromises on other areas of contention, including concerns over institutional structure and the proposed convention's applicability to contracting

[33] See, eg, ibid 18.

[34] Council of Europe, *Collected Edition of the Travaux Préparatoires* (n 30 above) vol III, 280–88.

[35] See, eg, ibid 284.

[36] Council of Europe, *Collected Edition of the Travaux Préparatoires* (n 31 above) vol IV, 10.

[37] Simpson, *Human Rights and the End of Empire* (n 4 above) 663; Council of Europe, *Collected Edition of the Travaux Préparatoires* (n 31 above) vol IV, 82.

[38] Simpson, *Human Rights and the End of Empire* (n 4 above) 688. See also Council of Europe, *Collected Edition of the Travaux Préparatoires* (n 31 above) vol IV, 106; cf *Collected Edition of the Travaux Préparatoires* (n 31 above) vol IV, 108,110–12.

[39] See Council of Europe, *Collected Edition of the Travaux Préparatoires* (n 30 above) vol III, 320–24.

[40] See, eg, Council of Europe, *Collected Edition of the Travaux Préparatoires* (n 31 above) vol IV, 18. The differences between the two alternatives were summed up well by the United Kingdom representative in June 1950: see ibid 170.

[41] ibid 12.

[42] ibid 12–14.

[43] ibid 12–14, 108, 110; Council of Europe, *Collected Edition of the Travaux Préparatoires* (Martinus Nijhoff, 1979) vol V, 284–86.

[44] For examples of some of the relevant votes and the compromise proposals, see Council of Europe, *Collected Edition of the Travaux Préparatoires* (n 31 above) vol IV, 112, 178, 210, 286.

states' colonies.[45] With the benefit of hindsight, it may seem somewhat surprising that the final text of the Convention was thought to have been extremely detailed.

Thus, the Convention was left without a generally-applicable limitations clause, and with specific limitations clauses attaching to selected rights.[46] Several rights, including those contained in what became Article 6, lacked limitations clauses.[47] The *travaux* give no indication of whether the Convention's drafters viewed Article 6 as absolute, whether they had in mind some other limitations mechanism, or whether the matter was simply forgotten. The *travaux* do reflect that, as time went on, less attention was paid to the question of limitations. The British delegation may have originally proposed a scheme under which 'there would be specific limitations to each of the substantive rights, but no general limitations clause',[48] but the result of the negotiations was that the Convention was left without a general limitations clause, and with specific limitations only to *some of* the substantive rights.

While the *travaux* do not help solve the puzzle of Article 6, they do help contextualise the situation in which the puzzle came about: there was a series of political compromises, and an agenda on which there were multiple controversies to be dealt with by the drafters. The limitations issue was left to one side.

The *travaux* provide even less assistance on the structural complexities of Article 6, namely, how the drafters of the Convention regarded the relationship between the possible multiple 'fair trials' in Article 6. As the European Court said in its 1978 decision in *Konig v Germany (No 1)*, 'no very specific and exact ideas on the scope of [Article 6] emerge from the *travaux*'.[49]

That being said, Article 6's multiple, lengthy provisions are indicative of the approach to drafting adopted and advocated by the United Kingdom in the *travaux*. Indeed, the more detailed nature of Article 6 suggests the influence of the British approach: 'define the rights . . . and the limitations with the greatest possible precision'.[50] In this regard, Article 6 may be contrasted with, for example, earlier less detailed proposals for a fair trial guarantee;[51] the drafters elected to adopt a more detailed fair trial guarantee, with each of the component parts identified and articulated. Much as was the case with the analysis considered above, this insight does not help us resolve the question of 'multiple fair trials', but it does contextualise the language of the Convention.

The puzzle and complexity created by Article 6's drafting, therefore, cannot be solved by reference to the *travaux*.

[45] Simpson, *Human Rights and the End of Empire* (n 4 above) 712–13.

[46] Greer and Simpson both note that there is no obvious coherence to the limitations: Steven Greer, *The European Convention on Human Rights: Achievements, Problems and Prospects*, 2nd edn (Cambridge University Press, 2006) 197; Simpson, *Human Rights and the End of Empire* (n 4 above) 715.

[47] cf E.1.2 above.

[48] Simpson, *Human Rights and the End of Empire* (n 4 above) 704.

[49] *Konig v Germany (No 1)* (App 6232/73) (1979–80) 2 EHRR 170, Separate Opinion of Judge Matscher.

[50] Simpson, *Human Rights and the End of Empire* (n 4 above) 705, citing British ministerial brief.

[51] Council of Europe, *Collected Edition of the Travaux Préparatoires* (n 30 above) vol III, 222.

E.1.5 The European Court Uses a Variety of Analytical Tools to Assess Alleged Infringements of Article 6

In the remainder of this part, therefore, I consider the European Court's own attempts to solve the puzzle of Article 6 by examining a number of analytical tools used by the European Court, how these tools work, and how well they sit with one another. In turn, the tools considered are:

- the 'proceedings as a whole' test (E.2);
- 'counterbalancing' and 'defect curing' (E.3);
- the notion that some infringements render a trial irretrievably unfair (the 'never fair' jurisprudence) (E.4);
- the semi-structured balancing used in cases considering whether certain evidence was the 'sole or decisive' evidence against a defendant (E.5); and
- the extent to which the public interest can justify restrictions on Article 6 rights through balancing or proportionality analysis (E.6).

These analytical tools all represent attempts to solve the puzzle of Article 6. Throughout my analysis of these analytical tools run the two macro-arguments outlined above: first, that the European Court has not explained well how the different tools interrelate and when one should be used in preference to another. And second, that the tools themselves are often poorly explained and inconsistently applied.

E.2 The 'Proceedings as a Whole' Test is Used Inconsistently and Incoherently

This section considers the European Court's use of what I will describe as the 'proceedings as a whole' test. Frequently in Article 6 cases, the Court will insist that this test is the appropriate lens through which to analyse an alleged violation.[52] As will be demonstrated, its definition and boundaries have not been explained or made clear by the Court. One can, nonetheless, infer from the cases that the *theory* of the test is this: the existence of a violation of Article 6 will sometimes be contingent on the fairness of the proceedings as a whole. As such, the theory goes, examination of some alleged violations of Article 6 should not involve simply assessing the facts and legal standards most relevant for the precise violation alleged, or the precise subsection of Article 6 that is said to have been violated. Instead, where the 'proceedings as a whole' test is engaged, the appropriate course is to examine *all* of the factual circumstances constituting the 'proceedings

[52] Among recent cases, see, eg, *Hanzevacki v Croatia* (App 17182/07) (16 April 2009) para 20; *Orlov v Russia* (App 29652/04) (21 June 2011) para 99; *Asadbeyli and others v Azerbaijan* (App 3653/05) (11 December 2012) paras 130–139. See also the cases considered throughout this section.

as a whole' and to do so against a general test of *fairness*.[53] It must be emphasised that this is an inferred definition of the theory of the 'proceedings as a whole' test; as will become clear, the test works quite differently in reality.

At this stage, a point of clarification should be made. The 'fairness of the proceedings as a whole' test is *not* necessarily the same as the European Court's tendency, discussed in part C, to 'take together' two or more component parts of Article 6. Two component parts of Article 6 are sometimes taken together without assessing the alleged violations under the 'proceedings as a whole' test;[54] the 'proceedings as a whole' test is sometimes used in situations where multiple component parts are not 'taken together'.[55] Of course, the European Court can, and often does, use these two analytical tools together,[56] and later in this section the particular consequences that flow from this combination will be considered.[57]

I make several arguments with respect to the 'proceedings as a whole' test. First, in some cases the Court outlines the test, ostensibly applies it, but then *in substance does not perform* a 'proceedings as a whole' analysis. Second, in other cases the Court outlines the test, but then does not even *purport* to perform the 'proceedings as a whole' analysis. Third, the Court sometimes purports to apply the 'proceedings as a whole' test while also conducting inconsistent 'trial within a trial' analysis. Fourth, it will be argued that the flaws in the 'proceedings as a whole' test are exacerbated when combined with the European Court's 'taken together' approach. In making these specific arguments, a broader picture will also be formed as to how the 'fairness of the proceedings as a whole' test works in the Article 6 case law.

E.2.1 The European Court Frequently Does Not Consider the Proceedings as a Whole When It Purports to Apply the 'Proceedings as a Whole' Test

Frequently the European Court purports to be applying the 'proceedings as a whole' test but plainly considers something less than, or different to, the proceedings as a whole. This section explores examples of this tendency, and argues that in applying what it describes as the 'proceedings as a whole' test, the Court in practice frequently fails to live up to its rhetoric.

This tendency is evident in *Barbera, Messegue and Jabardo v Spain*, in which the applicants alleged 'a clear violation' of Article 6(1) 'in conjunction with' Article

[53] Summers argues that the European Court's focus on the fairness of the proceedings as a whole has 'overshadowed' 'concrete examples of the use of specific fairness': Summers, *Fair Trials* (n 14 above) 103.

[54] See, eg, *Prezec v Croatia* (App 48185/07) (15 October 2009) paras 20–32; *Penev v Bulgaria* (App 20494/04) (7 January 2010) paras 29–45.

[55] See, eg, *Jan Zawadzki v Poland* (App 648/02) (6 July 2010) paras 18–20; *Bykov v Russia* (App 4378/02) (10 March 2009) paras 89–90.

[56] See, eg, *Caka v Albania* (App 44023/02) (8 December 2009) para 77; *Rasmussen v Poland* (App 38886/05) (28 April 2009) para 56.

[57] See especially E.2.4.

6(2) and Article 6(3)(d).[58] In analysing these arguments, the European Court made the following statement:

> 68. As a general rule, it is for the national courts, and in particular the court of first instance, to assess the evidence before them as well as the relevance of the evidence . . . *The Court must, however, determine . . . whether the proceedings considered as a whole*, including the way in which prosecution and defence evidence was taken, *were fair* as required by [Article 6(1)].[59]

The Court then considered various arguments, and concluded (at paragraph 89) that 'the proceedings in question, taken as a whole, did not satisfy the requirements of a fair and public hearing': there was an Article 6(1) violation.[60] Having reached this conclusion, which the Court claimed was based on the proceedings as a whole, the judgment then turned to an alleged Article 6(2) violation. The applicants:

> 90. . . . also claimed to be victims of a failure to apply the presumption of innocence . . .
>
> 91. . . . In this case, it does not appear from the evidence that during the proceedings, and in particular the trial, the Audiencia Nacional or the presiding judge had taken decisions or attitudes reflecting such an opinion. The Court therefore does not find a violation of [Article 6(2)].[61]

It is worth emphasising the analytical steps taken by the European Court in this case: the Court had, on its own logic, reached a conclusion at paragraph 89 based on 'the 'proceedings as a whole' without considering the allegation of bias referred to in paragraph 90. Even if it was concluded that the allegation of bias was without merit, it is difficult to understand how the European Court could assess the fairness of 'the 'proceedings as a whole' without reference to an allegation of bias. Plainly, in the passage leading up to paragraph 89, the Court did *not* consider the 'proceedings as a whole'. As will be seen, this tendency – to notionally consider the proceedings as a whole while openly failing to do so – is repeated throughout the Court's 'proceedings as a whole' jurisprudence.

In *Pelissier and Sassi v France*, the applicants alleged two violations of Article 6: first, 'the use against the first applicant of a document whose admissibility was contested' and second, 'that they had been convicted of an offence different from the one charged'.[62] The applicants thus alleged violations of Article 6(1), Article 6(3)(a), and Article 6(3)(b).[63] The Court dealt first with the evidence argument. It described the relevant test thus:

[58] *Barbera, Messegue and Jabardo v Spain* (App 10588/83) (1989) 11 EHRR 360, para 67.

[59] ibid para 68 (emphasis added). This passage has been cited, directly or indirectly, in cases such as *Kostovski v Netherlands* (App 11454/85) (1990) 12 EHRR 434, para 39; *Windisch v Austria* (App 12489/86) (1991) 13 EHRR 281, para 25; and *Delta v France* (App 11444/85) (1993) 16 EHRR 574, para 35. See also H Petzold, 'The Convention and the Principle of Subsidiarity' in R Macdonald, F Matscher and H Petzold (eds), *The European System for the Protection of Human Rights* (Martinus Nijhoff, 1993) 54.

[60] *Barbera, Messegue and Jabardo v Spain* (n 58 above) para 89.

[61] ibid paras 90–91; cf Trechsel, *Human Rights in Criminal Proceedings* (n 5 above) 86–87.

[62] *Pelissier and Sassi v France* (App 25444/94) (2000) 30 EHRR 715, para 42.

[63] ibid para 42.

> 45. . . . *whether the proceedings considered as a whole,* including the way in which the evidence was taken, were fair as required by [Article 6(1)] . . .
>
> 46. The fairness of proceedings is assessed with regard to *the proceedings as a whole.*[64]

Thus, the European Court emphasised, twice in two paragraphs, that the analytical key was 'the 'proceedings as a whole'. It then conducted one paragraph of analysis on this point, reaching its conclusion in the course of that paragraph: 'the use . . . of the document in issue did not entail a violation of' Article 6(1).[65] Thus, the Court stated that the proceedings as a whole had been analysed, and that this analysis concluded that the proceedings as a whole were fair. Remarkably, however, it then moved on to assess the argument that the applicants 'had been convicted of an offence different from the one charged'. At first glance, one might assume these matters had been addressed during the Court's analysis of all aspects of the *proceedings as a whole.* They had not. The European Court went on to provide 15 paragraphs of analysis on this point, concluding there had been 'a violation of [Article 6(3)(a)] and [Article 6(3)(b)] of the Convention, taken together with [Article 6(1)], which provides for a fair trial'.[66] Bafflingly, then, the Court has plainly failed to assess the *proceedings as a whole* with respect to the first argument: a significant issue was ignored for the duration of that analysis.[67] Moreover, the Court has managed to state, within the space of 16 paragraphs, that the proceedings as a whole were fair, *but* that there were violations of three separate provisions of Article 6. It seems the Court described the first test incorrectly, and/or reached the second conclusion erroneously.

This trend continued in *Visser v Netherlands,* where the applicant complained about the use of anonymous witness evidence and alleged a violation of Article 6(1) and Article 6(3)(d).[68] The European Court emphasised that its role was 'to ascertain whether the proceedings as a whole, including the way in which evidence was taken, were fair'.[69] The Court then conducted its analysis, notionally of the proceedings as a whole, and reached this penultimate conclusion:

> 48. In these circumstances the Court is not satisfied that the interest of the witness in remaining anonymous could justify limiting the rights of the defence to the extent that they were limited.[70]

The Court then explained that it did not consider it necessary, in the course of its analysis of 'the 'proceedings as a whole,' to consider the possibility that counterbalancing measures might have had an impact on this penultimate conclusion:

[64] ibid paras 45–46 (emphasis added).

[65] ibid para 47.

[66] ibid para 63.

[67] See ibid paras 44–47.

[68] *Visser v Netherlands* (App 26668/95) (14 February 2002) para 34.

[69] ibid para 43, citing *Van Mechelen and others v Netherlands* (App 21363/93) (1998) 25 EHRR 647, para 50.

[70] *Visser v Netherlands* (n 68 above) para 48.

> 51. In the light of the above conclusion the Court does not find it necessary to examine further whether the procedures put in place by the judicial authorities could have sufficiently counterbalanced the difficulties faced by the defence as a result of the anonymity of the witness.[71]

The Court then concluded 'that the proceedings as a whole were not fair' and that there had thus been violations of Article 6(1) and Article 6(3)(d).[72] It seems odd that the Court could purport to assess the fairness of the proceedings as a whole without at least *considering* 'whether the procedures put in place by the judicial authorities could have sufficiently counterbalanced the difficulties faced by the defence'. A similar passage appeared in *Krasniki*.[73] In these cases, the Court purports to be considering the proceedings as a whole, and yet appears to voluntarily and expressly decline to consider certain aspects of the proceedings. This also raises the broader question of counterbalancing, which is dealt with in greater detail in part E.3 below.

In *Ocalan v Turkey*, the European Court found an independence and impartiality violation.[74] The Court then went on to consider a series of additional arguments alleging violations of Article 6(1), Article 6(2), and Article 6(3).[75] In assessing this series of alleged violations, the Grand Chamber referred to and adopted the reasons of the Chamber, including tests such as:

> 131 . . . The question, in each case, is whether the restriction, in the light of the *entirety of the proceedings*, has deprived the accused of a fair hearing . . .
>
> 133 . . . restrictions may be imposed on an accused's access to his lawyer if good cause exists. The relevant issue is whether, in the light of the *proceedings taken as a whole*, the restriction has deprived the accused of a fair hearing . . .
>
> 135 . . . in order to determine whether the aim of Article 6 – a fair trial – has been achieved, *regard must be had to the entirety of the domestic proceedings* conducted in the case.[76]

Throughout its analysis of these arguments, therefore, the *Ocalan* Court purports to be assessing the 'entirety' or 'whole' of the proceedings. Yet, throughout, it does so without referring to its own finding that the *tribunal was not independent and impartial*. How can any assessment of the fairness of the proceedings as a whole occur without reference to a lack of independence and impartiality? The European Court is, quite simply, not doing what it says it is doing when it applies a 'proceedings as a whole' analysis. The examples of this inexplicably incoherent method of reasoning are legion.[77] The critique of the decision in *Ocalan* is intensi-

[71] ibid para 51.
[72] ibid para 52.
[73] *Krasniki v Czech Republic* (App 51277/99) (28 February 2006) paras 85–86.
[74] *Ocalan v Turkey* (App 46221/99) (2005) 41 EHRR 45, para 118.
[75] ibid para 119.
[76] ibid paras 131–135 (emphasis added).
[77] See, eg, *Brennan v United Kingdom* (App 39846/98) (2002) 34 EHRR 18, paras 41, 45, 48, 58, 63; *Georgios Papageorgiou v Greece* (App 59506/00) (2004) 38 EHRR 30, paras 28–29, 35; *Jalloh v Germany* (App 54810/00) (2007) 44 EHRR 32, paras 108, 109, 110–122; *Popov v Russia* (App 26853/04) (13 July

fied when one takes into account the long line of doctrine and jurisprudence in which the Court itself has indicated that a hearing cannot be fair if the tribunal is not independent and impartial, something which will be returned to in part E.4 below.

In its decision in *Guvec v Turkey*, the Court adopted a truly peculiar approach to analysing a series of alleged Article 6 violations. The applicant alleged numerous breaches of Article 6(1), several breaches of Article 6(2), and several breaches of Article 6(3).[78] These allegations included an argument that the presence of a military judge on the bench of the domestic court constituted a violation of the independence and impartiality guarantees. In its analysis of the Article 6(1) arguments, the Court offered this breathtakingly poorly-explained paragraph:

> 122. The Court observes that in a number of applications against Turkey involving a complaint of an alleged lack of independence and impartiality on the part of State Security Courts, the Court has limited its examination to that aspect alone, not deeming it necessary to address any other complaints relating to the fairness of the impugned proceedings. *However, the Court deems it necessary to put this well rehearsed question aside in the instant case* because the particularly grave circumstances of the application present *more compelling* issues involving the effective participation of a minor in his trial and the right to legal assistance.[79]

To be clear here: the Court elected to ignore the independence and impartiality arguments not because it was unnecessary to consider them, but because there were more compelling issues to be considered. The Court did not even offer a finding on the independence and impartiality arguments. One may have sympathy for the European Court judges and the monotonous flow of Turkish independence-impartiality cases, but it is a very curious situation indeed if a court's usual approach to an important question of law can be cast aside with no explanation other than that there was a *more compelling* issue to consider instead. This might be troubling enough from the perspective of the rule of law, but then the Court concluded its analysis thus:

2006) paras 166–168, 169–74, 175, 178, 189; *Kollcaku v Italy* (App 25701/02) (8 February 2007) paras 54–56, 57, 66, 72; *Ferrantelli and Santangelo v Italy* (App 19874/92) (1997) 23 EHRR 288, paras 42–43, 44, 48, 53, 60 (see Trechsel, *Human Rights in Criminal Proceedings* (n 5 above) 65); *Caka v Albania* (n 56 above) paras 95, 100, 116; *Aleksandr Zaichenko v Russia* (App 39660/02) (18 February 2010) paras 46–60; *Krivoshapkin v Russia* (App 42224/02) (27 January 2011) paras 32–65; *Jan Zawadzki v Poland* (n 55 above) paras 12–20; *Moscicki v Poland* (App 52443/07) (14 June 2011) paras 47–50; *Sebalj v Croatia* (App 4429/09) (28 June 2011) paras 258–260, 265–267; *Huseyn and others v Azerbaijan* (App 35482/05) (26 July 2011) paras 214–234; *Romanova v Russia* (App 23215/02) (11 October 2011) paras 160–165; *Nevskaya v Russia* (App 24273/04) (11 October 2011) paras 43–47; *Sahin and Sahin v Turkey* (App 13279/05) (2012) 54 EHRR 20, paras 28–31; *Gabrielyan v Armenia* (App 8088/05) (10 April 2012) paras 70, 75, 87; *Korgul v Poland* (App 35916/08) (17 April 2012) paras 31–34; *Hajnal v Serbia* (App 36937/06) (19 June 2012) paras 107, 112, 132, 137; *Sorokins and Sorokina v Latvia* (App 45476/04) (28 May 2013) paras 110, 113, 114, 121; *Rudnichenko v Ukraine* (App 2775/07) (11 July 2013) paras 100, 109–10, 113, 119–20; *Khodorkovskiy and Lebedev v Russia* (App 11082/06) (25 July 2013) paras 599–600, 634, 645, 648, 698.

[78] *Guvec v Turkey* (App 70337/01) (20 January 2009) para 114.

[79] ibid para 122 (emphasis added).

> 132. The Court *has had regard to the entirety of the criminal proceedings against the applicant.* It considers that the shortcomings highlighted above, including in particular the de facto lack of legal assistance for most of the proceedings, exacerbated the consequences of the applicant's inability to participate effectively in his trial and infringed his right to due process.
>
> 133. There has, therefore, been a violation of [Article 6(1)] of the Convention in conjunction with [Article 6(3)(c)].[80]

First, it is extremely plain from paragraph 122 that the Court has *not* had regard to the entirety of the proceedings: it expressly disregarded a factor that it has elsewhere indicated to be crucial. But second, and more generally, what guidance does this decision offer? Is the moral of the story that any applicant's lawyers should attempt to avoid alleging boring familiar violations in favour of alleging compelling violations? This is not a decision that contributes to any coherent or consistent body of law, and it is certainly not judicial reasoning of a high calibre.

E.2.2 The Opaque Nature of the European Court's Reasoning Makes It Difficult to Determine Whether the 'Proceedings as a Whole' Test is Actually Being Used

The section above considered a number of cases in which the European Court outlined the 'proceedings as a whole' test, purported to apply it, but then its analysis elsewhere in the judgment indicated that the test may not actually have been applied. This section examines a variation on that theme: cases in which the Court outlined the 'proceedings as a whole' test, but then did not even purport to apply the test. In these cases, as will be seen, the proceedings as a whole test seems like a meaningless intermediary between the violation alleged and the conclusion reached on that violation.

Thus, in *AM v Italy*, the applicant alleged a violation of Article 6(1) and Article 6(3)(d) on the basis 'that the criminal proceedings against him had been unfair and that he had not been given an opportunity to examine or have examined' certain witnesses.[81] The European Court 'reiterated' that:

> 24. . . . The Court's task . . . is not to give a ruling as to whether statements of witnesses were properly admitted as evidence, but rather to ascertain whether the proceedings as a whole, including the way in which evidence was taken, were fair.[82]

But having made this broad proclamation of its role, and having outlined the crucial test as being the fairness of the proceedings as a whole, the European Court's conclusion did not actually answer the question it had set for itself. In fact, the Court did not mention the fairness of the proceedings as a whole anywhere else in its judgment. Its conclusion was as follows:

[80] ibid para 132–133 (emphasis added).
[81] *AM v Italy* (App 37019/97) (14 December 1999) para 20.
[82] ibid para 24.

> 28. Under these circumstances, the applicant cannot be regarded as having had a proper and adequate opportunity to challenge the witness statements that formed the basis of his conviction. He therefore did not have a fair trial and there has been a violation of [Article 6(1)] taken together with [Article 6(3)(d)].[83]

If the wording of the conclusion was read in the absence of paragraph 24, one could reasonably assume that the crucial factor to considering whether or not there had been a violation in this case was whether 'the applicant . . . had a proper and adequate opportunity to challenge the witness statements that formed the basis of his conviction'. It may readily be acknowledged that assessing the fairness of the proceedings as a whole could well *include* consideration of the extent to which an accused person could challenge a witness; that is not in dispute. The key point is this: if the Court identifies 'the fairness of the proceedings as a whole' as a determinative test of whether or not there has been a violation, the interests of clarity and consistency demand that it reach a conclusion as to whether *that test has been satisfied.* Instead, in *AM v Italy* and in the cases below, the Court failed to reach a conclusion on the test it has identified as crucial. Instead of reaching a conclusion on the fairness of the proceedings as a whole, it focused on the precise violation alleged. The reader is left in some uncertainty: is the fairness of the proceedings as a whole actually the decisive factor, or is the Court's much more narrow focus indicative of the truly important analysis for determining whether there has been a violation?

In *Luca v Italy*, the applicant relied on Article 6(1) and Article 6(3)(d) and argued 'that the criminal proceedings against him had been unfair and alleged that he had been convicted on the basis of statements made to the public prosecutor, without being given an opportunity to examine the maker of the statements . . . or to have him examined'.[84] In examining this argument, the European Court recalled that its role was 'to ascertain whether the proceedings as a whole, including the way in which evidence was taken, were fair'.[85] As in *AM*, the *Luca* Court did not refer to the proceedings as a whole anywhere else in the judgment. Instead, its analysis and its conclusions were much more narrowly focused. Its conclusion stated:

> 43. In the instant case, the Court notes that the domestic courts convicted the applicant solely on the basis of statements made by N. before the trial and that neither the applicant nor his lawyer was given an opportunity at any stage of the proceedings to question him.
>
> 44. In those circumstances, the Court is not satisfied that the applicant was given an adequate and proper opportunity to contest the statements on which his conviction was based.

[83] Ibid para 28.

[84] *Luca v Italy* (App 33354/96) (2003) 36 EHRR 46, para 31. See also E Brems, 'Conflicting Human Rights: an Exploration in the Context of the Right to a Fair Trial in the European Convention on Human Rights' (2005) 27 *Human Rights Quarterly* 294, 310–11.

[85] *Luca v Italy* (n 84 above) para 38.

> 45. The applicant was, therefore, denied a fair trial. Accordingly, there has been a violation of [Article 6(1)] and [Article 6(3)(d)].[86]

A very similar pattern of reasoning played out in *Solakov v FYROM*.[87] This book does not argue that the Court was in any way wrong to focus on the Article 6(3)(d) issue. But it does argue that if the Court promises to ascertain whether the proceedings as a whole were fair, then it should do that. If the European Court regards determining the Article 6(3)(d) issue as somehow wholly decisive of the broader 'proceedings as a whole' issue, then it should articulate that justification. If it is simply assessing the proceedings against the text of Article 6(3)(d), then that may well be desirable, but it should not be done while pretending to consider the proceedings as a whole. The interests of clarity and predictability would be better served by the Court discarding the intermediary 'proceedings as a whole' step. Instead, the Court could simply and clearly identify the key test as whether or not the applicant had an adequate and proper opportunity to contest the statements on which his conviction was based.

In *Allan v United Kingdom*, the applicant 'complained of the use at his trial of evidence gathered by the covert recording devices and of the admission of evidence from the prisoner H concerning conversations which they had together in their cell' and alleged a violation of Article 6.[88] The Court offered some 'general principles',' including this statement:

> The question which must be answered is whether the proceedings as a whole, including the way in which the evidence was obtained, were fair.[89]

And yet, despite identifying the 'question which must be answered' as the fairness of the proceedings as a whole, what seemed to be decisive for the Court's analysis was its detailed discussion of the silence and self-incrimination guarantees. That discussion concluded in this way:

> In those circumstances, the information gained by the use of H. in this way may be regarded as having been obtained in defiance of the will of the applicant and its use at trial impinged on the applicant's right to silence and privilege against self-incrimination. Accordingly, in this respect there has been a violation of [Article 6(1)].[90]

It is entirely fitting that a silence and self-incrimination case of this kind focuses on the silence and self-incrimination guarantees. But if the assessment of those guarantees is the decisive factor for the Court, then it should refrain from stating that the decisive factor will be some nebulous consideration of the proceedings as a whole. Claiming to assess the proceedings as a whole and then not even reaching a conclusion on that point renders the Court's reasoning opaque.

[86] ibid paras 43–45. See also Trechsel, *Human Rights in Criminal Proceedings* (n 5 above) 301–2.

[87] See *Solakov v FYROM* (App 47023/99) (31 October 2001) paras 57–67.

[88] *Allan v United Kingdom* (App 48539/99) (2003) 36 EHRR 12, para 37. See Trechsel, *Human Rights in Criminal Proceedings* (n 5 above) 350.

[89] *Allan v United Kingdom* (n 88 above) para 42.

[90] ibid paras 52–53.

In these various types of case, therefore, the European Court has identified the determinative test as being the fairness of the proceedings as a whole, before ignoring the proceedings as a whole to focus on the specific Article 6 guarantee alleged to have been violated in the case at hand. This may be understandable. It is also not necessarily inconsistent with the 'proceedings as a whole' test – the specific provision identified may have a crucial or decisive impact on the proceedings as a whole – but this is rarely explained by the Court and in any event does not foster clear and coherent reasoning. If 'the proceedings as a whole' is what matters, then the Court ought to reach a conclusion as to whether the proceedings as a whole have been fair; if a more specific inquiry is what matters, then the Court ought to clearly identify that inquiry and then apply it. The ability of the Court's case law to provide guidance in this area is questionable.

E.2.3 The European Court's 'Trial Within a Trial' Analysis is Inconsistent with its 'Proceedings as a Whole' Analysis and is Also Internally Incoherent

The flaws inherent in the European Court's 'proceedings as a whole' jurisprudence are particularly evident in a series of cases in which the European Court considered the issues of public interest immunity and the disclosure of evidence guarantees under Article 6. In this section, I first sketch out what will be called the European Court's 'trial within a trial' jurisprudence, and then go on to argue that not only does that jurisprudence sit uncomfortably with the Court's 'proceedings as a whole' jurisprudence, but that it is also incoherent on its own terms.

In February 2000, the Court decided a set of cases relating to public interest immunity.[91] These cases (*Jasper v United Kingdom, Rowe and Davis v United Kingdom* and *Fitt v United Kingdom*[92]) all included a curious method of assessing whether there had been a violation of Article 6 in public interest immunity cases. As will be seen, these decisions, and the subsequent jurisprudence of the European Court, established an analytical test that sought *not* to guarantee a fair hearing, but to guarantee a fair hearing within a hearing. It must be acknowledged that the jurisprudence around public interest immunity, and related issues such as closed material proceedings, is somewhat fraught. Nevertheless, what follows in this subsection is less a condemnation of the European Court for crafting an imperfect solution than it is a critique of the divergence in this area between how the Court *states* the law and how it *applies* that law. My analysis here focuses on extracts

[91] See, generally on public interest immunity, van Dijk and van Hoof, *Theory and Practice of the European Convention on Human Rights* (n 5 above) 588; Greer, *The European Convention on Human Rights* (n 46 above) 253; Emmerson, Ashworth and Macdonald, *Human Rights and Criminal Justice* (n 7 above) 534.

[92] *Jasper v United Kingdom* (App 27052/95) (2000) 30 EHRR 441; *Fitt v United Kingdom* (App 29777/96) (2000) 30 EHRR 480; *Rowe and Davis v United Kingdom* (App 28901/95) (2000) 30 EHRR 1. See Greer, *The European Convention on Human Rights* (n 46 above) 253; Steven Greer, 'Constitutionalising Adjudication under the European Convention on Human Rights' (2003) *Oxford Journal of Legal Studies* 405, 424.

from *Jasper*, but virtually identical language and reasoning was used in *Rowe and Davis* and *Fitt*, and in subsequent cases such as *PG and JH*.[93] Reference is made to those decisions in the footnotes as appropriate.

In *Jasper*, the applicant had been convicted of an offence related to cannabis importation. At the European Court, he alleged violations of Article 6(1), Article 6(3)(b) and Article 6(3)(d). The Court indicated that it would 'confine its examination to the question whether *the proceedings in their entirety* were fair'.[94] The reasoning that followed is worthy of close analysis. The Court first emphasised that Article 6 protected the right to an adversarial trial. This right included, among other things, a guarantee that 'prosecution authorities should disclose to the defence all material evidence in their possession for or against the accused'.[95] Next, the European Court explained the circumstances in which the disclosure guarantee might be capable of restriction:

> [T]he entitlement to disclosure of relevant evidence is not an absolute right. In any criminal proceedings there may be competing interests, such as national security or the need to protect witnesses at risk of reprisals or keep secret police methods of investigation of crime, which must be weighed against the rights of the accused. In some cases it may be necessary to withhold certain evidence from the defence so as to preserve the fundamental rights of another individual or to safeguard an important public interest. However, *only such measures restricting the rights of the defence which are strictly necessary are permissible* under Article 6(1).[96]

Moreover, the domestic authorities would need to ensure that 'any difficulties caused to the defence' by the restriction were 'counterbalanced'.[97] It should be noted that Article 6 does not set forth the test that any restrictions of this sort should be 'strictly necessary', and certainly makes no provision for a counterbalancing process: the Court here is grappling with the broader problems associated with Article 6's lack of an express meta-principle for analysing infringements.[98]

Having clearly stated that the permissibility of restrictions on defence rights would depend on whether those restrictions were strictly necessary, the European Court went on to state:

[93] *PG and JH v United Kingdom* (App 44787/98) (2008) 46 EHRR 51; cf *McKeown v United Kingdom* (App 6684/05) (2012) 54 EHRR 7, paras 43–55.

[94] *Jasper v United Kingdom* (n 92 above) para 50 (emphasis added). See, for equivalent passages, *Rowe and Davis v United Kingdom* (n 92 above) para 59; *Fitt v United Kingdom* (n 92 above) para 43; *Dowsett v United Kingdom* (App 39482/98) (2004) 38 EHRR 41, para 40. It is not clear why the European Court regards considering the 'proceedings as a whole' as in some way 'confining' its 'examination'.

[95] *Jasper v United Kingdom* (n 92 above) para 51. See *Rowe and Davis v United Kingdom* (n 92 above) para 60; *Fitt v United Kingdom* (n 92 above) para 44; *PG and JH v United Kingdom* (n 93 above) para 67.

[96] *Jasper v United Kingdom* (n 92 above) para 52 (emphasis added). See *Rowe and Davis v United Kingdom* (n 92 above) para 61; *Fitt v United Kingdom* (n 92 above) para 45; *PG and JH v United Kingdom* (n 93 above) para 68.

[97] *Jasper v United Kingdom* (n 92 above) para 52. See *Rowe and Davis v United Kingdom* (n 92 above) para 61; *Fitt v United Kingdom* (n 92 above) para 45; *PG and JH v United Kingdom* (n 93 above) para 68.

[98] We return to counterbalancing and defect curing at E.3.

> In cases where evidence has been withheld from the defence on public interest grounds, *it is not the role of this Court to decide whether or not such non-disclosure was strictly necessary* since, as a general rule, it is for the national courts to assess the evidence before them. In any event, in many cases, such as the present, where the evidence in question has never been revealed, it would not be possible for the Court to attempt to weigh the public interest in non-disclosure against that of the accused in having sight of the material.[99]

Remarkably, therefore, the Court expressly abdicated any responsibility for assessing whether a restriction on Article 6 rights was permissible. Importantly, the standard that was applied – 'strictly necessary' – was articulated by the Court rather than by the Convention, and the very same Court then refused to apply the standard it had articulated. Having gone through the exercise of articulating and then refusing to apply the relevant standard, the European Court then sought a way out of this endogenous predicament.

The Court's solution was to change the question. Instead of asking whether Article 6's guarantees had been violated by a restriction that was not strictly necessary, the Court shifted its focus:

> It must therefore scrutinise *the decision-making procedure* to ensure that, as far as possible, it complied with the requirements to provide adversarial proceedings and equality of arms and incorporated adequate safeguards to protect the interests of the accused.[100]

Thus, it is not the *hearing* or the *trial* that should comply with the requirements of Article 6. Instead, the decision-making procedure *within* the hearing or trial should comply with the requirements of Article 6. The result of this analysis, it becomes clear, is what will determine whether or not Article 6 has been complied with. The Court concluded:

> [T]hat, as far as possible, the *decision-making procedure* complied with the requirements of adversarial proceedings and equality of arms and incorporated adequate safeguards to protect the interests of the accused. *It follows* that there has been no violation of [Article 6(1)] in the present case.[101]

Thus, the Court abdicated its responsibility to determine whether or not the hearing that the applicant received was fair, in favour of determining whether or not *one procedural aspect* of that hearing could be regarded as meeting standards that were designed for testing the fairness of overall hearings.[102]

[99] *Jasper v United Kingdom* (n 92 above) para 53 (emphasis added). See *Rowe and Davis v United Kingdom* (n 92 above) para 62; *Fitt v United Kingdom* (n 92 above) para 46; *PG and JH v United Kingdom* (n 93 above) para 69. For more on the role of the Court, see part B.

[100] *Jasper v United Kingdom* (n 92 above) para 53 (emphasis added). See *Rowe and Davis v United Kingdom* (n 92 above) para 62; *Fitt v United Kingdom* (n 92 above) para 46; *PG and JH v United Kingdom* (n 93 above) para 68; *Natunen v Finland* (App 21022/04) (2009) 49 EHRR 32, para 41.

[101] *Jasper v United Kingdom* (n 92 above) para 58 (emphasis added). See *Rowe and Davis v United Kingdom* (n 92 above) paras 66–67 (finding a violation); *Fitt v United Kingdom* (n 92 above) para 50 (finding no violation); and *PG and JH v United Kingdom* (n 93 above) para 73 (no violation).

[102] A vigorous dissent from Judges Palm, Fischbach, Vajic, Thomassen, Tsatsa-Nikolovska and Traja followed, but even that dissent accepted 'the majority's statement of the law as set out at ... [51]–[53]'. Note that Judge Hedigan's dissent was perhaps more critical of the majority's legal reasoning.

In the *Jasper* line of cases, therefore, the European Court has effectively created a class of case to which Article 6's provisions do not apply; instead, the provisions only apply to a portion of the case.[103] It has done so with very little explanation or justification for any or all of the steps in its reasoning, making it difficult to predict whether there are other areas of Article 6 jurisprudence that might be susceptible to this sort of analysis. Moreover, perhaps most remarkably, the Court adopted this analytical course after claiming that it would focus on 'whether the proceedings in their entirety were fair'.[104] Yet, of course, it did no such thing. As its conclusion makes clear, its focus was on whether '*the decision-making procedure* complied with the requirements of adversarial proceedings and equality of arms and incorporated adequate safeguards to protect the interests of the accused'.[105] If one was charitable to the Court, perhaps it could be said that in cases like this the decision-making procedure was *the decisive factor* for the proceedings as a whole – but in that case, why bother with the intermediary and inaccurate analytical step? In *Jasper*, and in a series of cases after it, the Court conducted analysis that was inconsistent with the 'proceedings as a whole' test it purported to apply, and that was internally incoherent. The distance between the law as stated, and the law as applied, is concerning.

E.2.4 The Ambiguity in the 'Proceedings as a Whole' Test is Only Exacerbated When Combined with the European Court's 'Taken Together' Approach

We have seen, throughout the sections above, that there is considerable ambiguity and incoherence in the way that the European Court uses the 'proceedings as a whole' test. This ambiguity risks creating a perception that the Court could choose which way it applies the 'proceedings as a whole' test in order to reach a particular result in a particular case. That ambiguity is exacerbated when the 'proceedings as a whole' test is combined with the 'taken together' approach outlined in part C.4.3.

When it applies the 'taken together' approach, the European Court is conflating two or more legal tests, and is doing so without specifying clearly how that conflation may shape or affect its analysis of the alleged violations. When it joins that 'taken together' approach with the 'fairness of the proceedings as a whole',' suddenly the Court has notionally provided itself with a legal test that might be applicable to the provisions that are taken together (namely, were the proceedings as a whole fair?) but it has also notionally conflated all the possibly relevant facts. The assessment of a precise violation based on particular facts is impossible if one

[103] cf Greer's analysis of the 'trial within' approach: Greer, *The European Convention on Human Rights* (n 46 above) 253.

[104] *Jasper v United Kingdom* (n 92 above) para 50.

[105] ibid para 58 (emphasis added). See *Rowe and Davis v United Kingdom* (n 92 above) paras 66–67 (finding a violation) and *Fitt v United Kingdom* (n 92 above) para 50 (finding no violation).

remains loyal to these two tests, and the result is reasoning that is opaque, unfocused, and poorly explained. It is a clear example of irrational flexibility. The 'taken together' cog and the 'proceedings as a whole' cog turn each other so as to generate considerable uncertainty and unpredictability in terms of the scope of the infringement inquiry and the content of the test applied within that inquiry.

An example of this may be seen in *Bernard v France*, where the applicant argued that 'comments made by the two psychiatric experts at his trial . . . had infringed his right to a fair trial and the principle of the presumption of innocence'.[106] The European Court outlined the test in this way:

> The Court reiterates in the first place that 'the presumption of innocence enshrined in [Article 6(2] is one of the elements of the fair criminal trial that is required by [Article 6(1)]'. It will accordingly consider the applicant's complaints from the standpoint of these two provisions taken together. *In so doing, it must consider the criminal proceedings as a whole . . . The Court's task is to ascertain whether the proceedings considered as a whole, including the way in which the evidence was taken, were fair.*[107]

In this passage, therefore, the 'taken together' and 'proceedings as a whole' tests quickly combine to turn an Article 6(2) argument into an argument about the fairness of the proceedings as a whole. Despite the ostensibly seductive logic deployed by the Court in this passage, it remains somewhat unclear why an applicant who wishes to establish a violation of the presumption of innocence must establish that the 'proceedings as a whole' were 'unfair'. Why not simply establish that the presumption has been violated? It also leads one to wonder whether applicants with Article 6(2) complaints might be well advised to avoid also alleging Article 6(1) complaints, lest the European Court conflate away the applicant's arguments.

A more recent, but equally compelling, example is provided by the Grand Chamber's decision in *Al-Khawaja and Tahery*. In concluding its analysis of the 'sole or decisive rule' in that case,[108] the Court stated that it 'has always interpreted Article 6(3) in the context of an overall examination of the fairness of the proceedings' and that Article 6(3)(c) 'was one element, amongst others, of the concept of a fair trial in criminal proceedings contained in Article 6(1)'.[109] Having invoked the 'taken together' approach in this way, the *Al-Khawaja and Tahery* Court went on to describe:

[106] *Bernard v France* (App 22885/93) (2000) 30 EHRR 808, para 31.

[107] ibid para 37 (emphasis added). Compare similar examples in recent cases such as *Caka v Albania* (n 56 above) para 77; *Rasmussen v Poland* (n 56 above) para 56; *Huseyn and others v Azerbaijan* (n 77 above) para 58; *Bandaletov v Ukraine* (App 23180/06) (31 October 2013) para 54.

[108] We will return to this test in more detail at E.5.

[109] *Al-Khawaja and Tahery v United Kingdom* (Grand Chamber) (App 26766/05) (2012) 54 EHRR 23, paras 143, 145. This is taken even further in recent cases which use language such as 'the guarantees in [Art 6(3)(d)] are specific aspects of the right to a fair hearing set forth in [Art 6(1)] which must be taken into account in any assessment of the fairness of proceedings': *Pichugin v Russia* (App 38623/03) (23 October 2012) para 194 (cited without comment in Anand Doobay, 'The Right to a Fair Trial in Light of the Recent ECtHR and CJEU Case-law' (2013) (Online) *Academy of European Law ERA Forum* 1.1). See also *Stefancic v Slovenia* (App 18027/05) (25 October 2012) para 36; *Hummer v Germany* (App 26171/07) (19 July 2012) para 37.

> the traditional way in which the Court approaches the issue of the overall fairness of the proceedings, namely to weigh in the balance the competing interests of the defence, the victim, and witnesses, and the public interest in the effective administration of justice.[110]

The European Court thus links together the 'taken together' approach and the 'proceedings as a whole' approach in a way that allows it to conduct the sort of open-ended balancing and counterbalancing that will be considered below. Moreover, it does so on the basis of a conflated misrepresentation about its previous case law: to say that it 'has always interpreted Article 6(3) in the context of an overall examination of the fairness of the proceedings' is demonstrably false. Indeed, as seen in part C, and as is pointed out by the Joint Partly Dissenting and Partly Concurring Opinion of Judges Sajo and Karakas in *Al-Khawaja and Tahery*:

> in applying the holistic approach (now presented as 'an overall examination') in order to determine the fairness of the trial, this Court has never stated that fairness can still be achieved if one of the fundamental rights is deprived of its essence. With regard to the right to cross-examine witnesses and the related but broader equality-of-arms principle, the Court has systematically and consistently drawn a bright line, which it has never abandoned, in the form of the sole or decisive rule. Today this last line of protection of the right to defence is being abandoned in the name of an overall examination of fairness.[111]

Thus, the majority judgment in *Al-Khawaja and Tahery* provides an unwittingly articulate demonstration of the flaws in the Court's 'proceedings as a whole' jurisprudence.

E.2.5 The 'Proceedings as a Whole' Test Risks Radically Undermining the Text of Article 6

The sections above have identified a variety of flaws in the way the European Court applies the 'proceedings as a whole' test. In this section, I argue that even if these flaws could be ignored, the 'proceedings as a whole' test is fundamentally ambiguous and vague.

As is evident in the many cases discussed above, the European Court never defines the 'fairness of the proceedings as a whole'. In some cases the Court hints that the test may be linked specifically to Article 6(1)'s guarantee of a 'fair and public hearing',[112] but in many others the test seems much more nebulous and capable of being applied in the context of various other Article 6 guarantees. In so many of the cases discussed above, the Court simply asserts that the proceedings as a whole were fair or unfair without any structured or replicable reasoning process.[113]

[110] *Al-Khawaja and Tahery v United Kingdom* (Grand Chamber) (n 109 above) para 146.

[111] ibid Joint Partly Dissenting and Partly Concurring Opinion of Judges Sajo and Karakas.

[112] See, eg, *Barbera, Messegue and Jabardo v Spain* (n 58 above) para 89.

[113] See ibid paras 70–90 and Bill O'Brian, *Confrontation: the Defiance of the English Courts,*' University of Warwick School of Law Legal Studies Research Papers 2010–09 Paper 1, 23–24.

There is also a broader concern. It is difficult to conceive how the European Court could combine the 'fairness of the proceedings as a whole' test with any view of Article 6 as containing a series of separate, discreet guarantees: why not disregard the specific guarantees of Article 6(1) to (3) and instead just ask whether the proceedings as a whole were fair? If the 'proceedings as a whole' test is a useful tool capable of being applied to any Article 6 case, then Article 6 collapses into a simple two-word 'fair trial' guarantee and the actual text of Article 6(1), Article 6(2) and Article 6(3) becomes redundant. In this way, there are echoes of, and links to, part C. If, however, the test is only appropriate for certain types of Article 6 case, then the interests of predictability and transparency demand that the European Court explain why and how the test should apply to different types of case. And if the problems with the 'proceedings as a whole' test mean that normatively it should be put to one side, then it is incumbent on the European Court to adopt another, clearer, tool of analysis.

The 'proceedings as a whole' test is also linked to other analytical tools that the European Court uses when assessing alleged violations of Article 6. Later in this part, I consider the related ideas of counterbalancing and defect-curing, both of which are closely linked to the European Court's use of the 'proceedings as a whole' test. Indeed, as touched upon with respect to *Al-Khawaja and Tahery* above, this book demonstrates the extent to which the 'proceedings as a whole' test and the European Court's analysis of the internal structure of Article 6 provide the basis for free-wheeling balancing and counterbalancing analysis in the Article 6 context.

If the European Court wishes to convert Article 6 into a simple, two-word 'fair trial' guarantee, in which every alleged violation boils down to whether the proceedings as a whole were fair, then it should say so. If it were to do so, it would need to stop finding separate violations of Article 6(2) and Article 6(3): under a two-word guarantee theory of interpretation, those sub-articles are there only for definitional assistance and not to provide guarantees. As matters stand, the 'proceedings as a whole' test risks undermining the text and structure of Article 6 in a way that diminishes the capacity of the Court's case law to provide any form of guidance.

E.3 Counterbalancing and Defect-Curing are Attempts to Provide a Modest Amount of Structure to the European Court's Balancing

This section considers two tools that the European Court uses to assess alleged violations of Article 6. In contrast to the unstructured analysis considered in the previous section, these two tools constitute attempts to conduct a semi-structured form of analysis. The first is the notion of 'counterbalancing', by which a potential violation is described as having been offset by other factors in the same proceedings. The second is the notion of 'curing defects in proceedings', by which a would-be violation is identified but is said to have been 'cured' by subsequent events (often, by an appeal). The two tools are similar: both involve a vaguely-structured balancing process in which one factor (the alleged violation) is balanced against another identified factor (respectively, the counterbalancing element or the curing element). The Court seems to view them as distinct, albeit sometimes overlapping, tools and so the analysis that follows in this section will be shaped by that view.

In this section, it will be argued that the two methods may be regarded as an attempt to provide a modest amount of structure to the European Court's Article 6 balancing process, but that the methods are flawed. It will be argued that whatever vague sense of structure results from the Court's approach, that sense is, in fact, deceptive. As I will show, the methods are internally incoherent, but there are also broader external inconsistencies between the ways that the Court uses these methods and the ways it is willing to use other methods of assessing alleged violations of Article 6.[114] Counterbalancing will be examined first; curing defects will follow.

E.3.1 The European Court Provides Only Limited Guidance on How It Intends Counterbalancing to Work

In discussing counterbalancing, it is important to note at the outset that the European Court does not set out a clear explanation of how it sees counterbalancing working, the circumstances in which counterbalancing may be conducted as part of Article 6 analysis, or the details of how such counterbalancing should be structured. It should also be noted that while the Court often refers to counterbalancing using that name, sometimes it refers to the same concept using different language. This section considers the extent to which the Court provides any guidance on how its idea of counterbalancing is intended to work. While there are cases such as *Luca v Italy*, *A v United Kingdom*, and *Al-Khawaja and Tahery* in which the European Court attempts to provide a more structured analysis of counterbalancing than usual,[115] it is argued that overall the Court provides very little guidance indeed, and that in some cases references to counterbalancing may simply be a circumlocution.

The earliest use of 'counterbalancing' in the context of Article 6 appears to have been in the Court's 1989 decision in *Kostovski v Netherlands.* In that case, the applicant alleged a violation of Article 6 because of the 'use as evidence . . . of reports of statements by two anonymous persons' who were not then heard at

[114] cp Hoyano's view that, in the European Court's case law, 'counterbalancing measures have been closely scrutinised to ensure that, pragmatically, there had been adequate compensation for the disadvantage to which the measure has put that party': Hoyano, 'What is Balanced on the Scales of Justice?' (n 10 above) 11.

[115] See *Luca v Italy* (n 84 above) paras 39–40; *A v United Kingdom* (App 3455/05) (2009) 49 EHRR 29, paras 217–20; *Al-Khawaja and Tahery v United Kingdom* (Grand Chamber) (n 109 above) paras 152–165; but cf criticism of counterbalancing in *Al-Khawaja*: Hoyano, 'What is Balanced on the Scales of Justice?' (n 10 above) 21–22.

trial.[116] The reference to counterbalancing came towards the end of the Court's Article 6 analysis:

> In these circumstances it cannot be said that the handicaps under which the defence laboured were counterbalanced by the procedures followed by the judicial authorities.[117]

The Court did not explain what it meant by counterbalancing, nor did it explain the requisite standard or level that would need to be reached in order for 'handicaps' to be satisfactorily counterbalanced. It merely referred to counterbalancing measures in this offhand way during the course of its analysis. Nevertheless, this passage formed the basis for much subsequent consideration by the Court.

By the time of its 1996 decision in *Doorson*, which directly cited *Kostovski*, the passing reference to counterbalancing had become a firmer test:

> no violation of [Article 6(1)] taken together with [Article 6(3)(d)] . . . can be found if it is established that the handicaps under which the defence laboured were sufficiently counterbalanced by the procedures followed by the judicial authorities.[118]

Thus, for the *Doorson* Court, identifying potential counterbalancing factors was a crucial part of its assessment of whether or not the use of anonymous witnesses constituted a violation of Article 6. The process of counterbalancing was part of the attempt by the Court in *Doorson* to protect 'the interests of witnesses . . . and . . . victims'.[119] Significantly, however, the *Doorson* Court did not explain how the counterbalancing test would work, other than to say that counterbalancing measures:

> must be considered sufficient to have enabled the defence to challenge the evidence of the anonymous witnesses and attempt to cast doubt on the reliability of their statements.[120]

This passage appears to suggest that counterbalancing measures will be sufficient if they give the applicant a set of rights that are similar to those that have been 'taken away', even if they do not offer the full protection provided by the guarantees that have been violated. This form of reasoning suggests, therefore, that a violation of a particular Article 6 guarantee may be offset by providing a diluted but similar version of the same Article 6 guarantee. This is, perhaps, implicit in any notion of counterbalancing. But the *Doorson* Court performed this analysis

[116] *Kostovski v Netherlands* (n 59 above) para 38.

[117] ibid para 43; Trechsel, *Human Rights in Criminal Proceedings* (n 5 above) 319.

[118] *Doorson v Netherlands* (App 20524/92) (1996) 22 EHRR 330, para 72, citing *Kostovski v Netherlands* (n 59 above) para 43. On *Doorson*, see Brems, 'Conflicting Human Rights', (n 84 above) 317; Trechsel, *Human Rights in Criminal Proceedings* (n 5 above) 314–19; Harris, O'Boyle and Warbrick, *Law of the European Convention on Human Rights* (n 5 above) 324–25; van Dijk and van Hoof, *Theory and Practice of the European Convention on Human Rights* (n 5 above) 646; Greer, 'Constitutionalising Adjudication under the European Convention on Human Rights' (n 92 above) 424; Greer, *The European Convention on Human Rights: achievements, problems and prospects* (n 46) 254.

[119] *Doorson v Netherlands* (n 118 above) para 70.

[120] ibid para 75. See also, eg, *SN v Sweden* (App 34209/96) (2004) 39 EHRR 13, paras 52–53; *A v United Kingdom* (n 115 above) para 205.

without providing a mechanism that explained how to weigh the significance of the complainants' and witnesses' interest in specific or general cases against the Article 6 guarantee, and without explaining why the complainants' and witnesses' interest in *this sort of case specifically* could justify restrictions on Article 6 rights. In the absence of such guiding principles, it becomes difficult to determine when to 'open the door' to counterbalancing measures.

In *Dowsett v United Kingdom*, the applicant argued that there had been a violation of Article 6(1) and Article 6(3)(b) on the basis that there had been 'non-disclosure of evidence which was acknowledged to be relevant and material'.[121] The Court stated that disclosure was 'not an absolute right':

> In any criminal proceedings there may be competing interests, such as national security or the need to protect witnesses at risk of reprisals or to keep secret police methods of investigating crime, which must be weighed against the rights of the accused.[122]

The Court added:

> in order to ensure that the accused receives a fair trial, any difficulties caused to the defence by a limitation on its rights must be sufficiently counterbalanced by the procedures followed by the judicial authorities.[123]

It was not clear whether the *Dowsett* Court actually identified any possible counterbalancing measures in this case. Its conclusion on this point merely stated that:

> An application to the Court of Appeal in those circumstances could not be regarded as an adequate safeguard for the defence.[124]

Although it did identify weaknesses in the appellate procedure, the Court did not identify a test against which the 'adequacy' of the counterbalancing safeguard could reliably be measured. Merely describing the procedure available in a given case and then stating whether or not that procedure was 'adequate' does not provide a predictable or replicable test.

Similarly, in *Edwards and Lewis*, the Court considered counterbalancing in the context of an alleged entrapment scenario. Citing the public interest immunity cases, the Court stated:

> The entitlement to disclosure of relevant evidence is not, however, an absolute right . . . in order to ensure that the accused receives a fair trial, any difficulties caused to the defence by a limitation on its rights *must be sufficiently counterbalanced by the procedures followed by the judicial authorities.*[125]

The Court did not expressly conduct any analysis of the counterbalancing safeguards in this case, but did conclude:

[121] *Dowsett v United Kingdom* (n 94 above) para 35.

[122] ibid paras 41–42, citing *Doorson v Netherlands* (n 118 above) para 70.

[123] *Dowsett v United Kingdom* (n 94 above) para 42, citing *Doorson v Netherlands* (n 118 above) para 72; *Van Mechelen and others v Netherlands* (n 69 above) para 54.

[124] *Dowsett v United Kingdom* (n 94 above) para 49.

[125] *Edwards and Lewis v United Kingdom* (App 39647/98) (2005) 40 EHRR 24, para 53 (Fourth Section judgment) (emphasis added); Trechsel, *Human Rights in Criminal Proceedings* (n 5 above) 113.

> the Court does not consider that the procedure employed to determine the issues of disclosure of evidence and entrapment complied with the requirements to provide adversarial proceedings and equality of arms and incorporated adequate safeguards to protect the interests of the accused. It follows that there has been a violation of [Article 6(1)].[126]

Instead of providing an analytical test, the Court simply identified how the procedure worked, identified some shortcomings with respect to the relevant Article 6 tests, and then declared that those shortcomings meant that the counterbalancing measures were inadequate. But in any case in which counterbalancing has come into play, *by definition there will be shortcomings with respect to the Article 6 guarantee*: if there were not, there would be nothing to be counterbalanced. What any doctrine of counterbalancing would need in order to provide adequate guidance, and what the Court's jurisprudence lacks, is a sense of how to determine whether a counterbalancing measure has adequately eliminated *enough* of the shortcoming such that there has not been a violation, and how to determine what weight should be accorded to any public interest in reaching that decision.[127]

Another example in support of this argument may be found in *Van Mechelen v Netherlands*. In that case, the Court countenanced the possibility of counterbalancing measures as helping to ameliorate the problems caused by anonymous prosecution witnesses:

> 54. However, if the anonymity of prosecution witnesses is maintained, the defence will be faced with difficulties which criminal proceedings should not normally involve. Accordingly, the Court has recognised that in such cases [Article 6(1)] taken together with [Article 6(3)(d)] . . . requires that the handicaps under which the defence labours *be sufficiently counterbalanced* by the procedures followed by the judicial authorities.[128]

In *Van Mechelen*, the Court did not consider the potentially-counterbalancing factors as sufficient:

> 62. It is true . . . that the anonymous police officers were interrogated before an investigating judge, who had himself ascertained their identity and had, in a very detailed official report of his findings, stated his opinion on their reliability and credibility as well as their reasons for remaining anonymous.
>
> However these measures cannot be considered a proper substitute for the possibility of the defence to question the witnesses in their presence and make their own judgment as to their demeanour and reliability. It thus cannot be said that the handicaps under which the defence laboured were counterbalanced by the above procedures.[129]

[126] *Edwards and Lewis v United Kingdom* (n 125 above) para 59 (Fourth Section judgment).

[127] The question of when a counterbalancing measure will be 'enough' is complicated by suggestions in the European Court's case law that it may be sufficient to counterbalance 'part' of the disadvantage suffered by the defence: *Stefancic v Slovenia* (n 109 above) para 47.

[128] *Van Mechelen and others v Netherlands* (n 69 above) para 54 (emphasis added). This passage is drawn upon in, eg, *Rasmussen v Poland* (n 56 above) para 42. See Brems, 'Conflicting Human Rights' (n 84 above) 318.

[129] *Van Mechelen and others v Netherlands* (n 69 above) para 62.

This analysis is somewhat curious. In identifying the quality it seeks in a counterbalancing measure – that it be 'a proper substitute for the possibility of the defence to question the witnesses in their presence and make their own judgment' – the European Court appears to be stating that only compliance with the Article 6 guarantees is capable of 'neutralising' a violation. And yet, if there has been compliance with the Article 6 guarantee, there is nothing to neutralise.

In a particularly scathing Separate Opinion in *Kostecki v Poland*, Judge De Gaetano considered the majority's counterbalancing analysis:

> One may well ask in the instant case, what are the 'counterbalancing factors' to be considered or to be taken into account? None have been indicated in the judgment. Possibly none exist.[130]

If, however, one attempts to describe the European Court's counterbalancing jurisprudence in these cases, those decisions tend to amount to reasoning along the following pattern:

- the applicant alleges a violation of guarantee *x* and substantiates that allegation;
- the relevant government identifies measures possibly capable of being regarded as counterbalancing measures; and
- the European Court identifies ways in which the counterbalancing measures do not completely remove the violation of guarantee *x*, or ways in which implementing the counterbalancing measures is not the same as complying with guarantee *x*.

The appearance in the cases in this subsection, therefore, is that the notion of counterbalancing measures is simply a circumlocution that adds a gloss to the plain question of whether or not a particular guarantee has been violated. In reality, it seems, weighing up counterbalancing factors is simply a slightly more complicated version of a broad-brush 'proceedings as a whole' test. And while there may be reason to applaud attempts at providing structure to the Article 6 balancing exercise, the risk with the Court's counterbalancing cases is that it provides the appearance of structure without adding anything to the analytical tools available to the Court.

E.3.2 In Some Instances, Counterbalancing Can Involve 'Giving' Applicants Rights which the Applicants Already Held

This subsection deals with a possible corollary of the argument made in the previous section. In cases where the European Court recognises that a potential violation has been neutralised, or counterbalanced away, the substance of the judgments often involves simply highlighting other rights to which the applicant was *already entitled* under Article 6. At the risk of oversimplifying, in these cases, the Court's counterbalancing logic seems to be that while an applicant may have

[130] *Kostecki v Poland* (App 14932/09) (4 June 2013) para 4 of Separate Opinion.

lost her right to *x* under Article 6, she has not lost her right to *y*, and therefore the violation of *x* may be forgiven. It will be argued that this form of reasoning raises questions about the extent to which the Court's references to counterbalancing mask an incoherent case law.

In *Jasper* and the public interest immunity cases, the Court outlined a theory of counterbalancing that would be triggered in cases where it was considered necessary to withhold certain evidence from the defence:

> 52. . . . In some cases it may be necessary to withhold certain evidence from the defence so as to preserve the fundamental rights of another individual or to safeguard an important public interest. However, only such measures restricting the rights of the defence which are strictly necessary are permissible under [Article 6(1)]. Moreover, in order to ensure that the accused receives a fair trial, any difficulties caused to the defence by a limitation on its rights *must be sufficiently counterbalanced* by the procedures followed by the judicial authorities.[131]

The Court's counterbalancing analysis in *Jasper* is complicated in two significant ways. The first is this: as is dealt with earlier in this part, the *Jasper* Court makes considerable play of the fact that in a public interest immunity case, the role of the Court is to assess the fairness not of the trial as such, but of the 'decision-making procedure' used to decide the public interest immunity issue.[132] What the *Jasper* Court does not make clear is whether the 'counterbalancing' should be done within this decision-making procedure, or within the hearing more generally. The second complication is that the *Jasper* Court does not expressly identify which measures it regarded as the counterbalancing measures. It seems likely that this is the passage considering counterbalances:

> 55. The Court is satisfied that the defence were kept informed *and permitted to make submissions and participate* in the above decision-making process as far as was possible without revealing to them the material which the prosecution sought to keep secret on public interest grounds. Whilst it is true that in a number of different contexts the United Kingdom has introduced, or is introducing, a 'special counsel', the Court does not accept that such a procedure was necessary in the present case . . .
>
> 56. The fact that the need for disclosure was at all times *under assessment by the trial judge* provided a further, important, safeguard in that it was his duty to monitor throughout the trial the fairness or otherwise of the evidence being withheld. *It has not been suggested that the judge was not independent and impartial* within the meaning of [Article 6(1)]. He was fully versed in all the evidence and issues in the case and in a position to monitor the relevance to the defence of the withheld information both before and during the trial . . . The jurisprudence of the English Court of Appeal shows that the assessment which the trial judge must make fulfils the conditions which, according to

[131] *Jasper v United Kingdom* (n 92 above) para 52 (emphasis added). See, for similar passages, *Rowe and Davis v United Kingdom* (n 92 above) para 61; *Fitt v United Kingdom* (n 92 above) para 45. See also Andrew Ashworth, *Human Rights, Serious Crime and Criminal Procedure* (Sweet & Maxwell, 2002) 129–30.

[132] See, eg, *Jasper v United Kingdom* (n 92 above) para 53. There is more discussion of this point at E.2.3.

> the Court's case-law, are essential for ensuring a fair trial in instances of non-disclosure of prosecution material. *The domestic trial court in the present case thus applied standards which were in conformity with the relevant principles* of a fair trial embodied in [Article 6(1)]. Furthermore, during the *appeal proceedings* the Court of Appeal also considered whether or not the evidence should have been disclosed, providing an additional level of protection for the applicant's rights.[133]

Thus, it seems that the European Court relied on counterbalancing factors such as that 'the defence were kept informed and permitted to make submissions and participate in the above decision-making process as far as was possible' and that it had not been 'suggested that the judge was not independent and impartial'. But these factors are *already the subject of Article 6 guarantees.* That is, an accused person is *already entitled* to these things, and the European Court appears to be justifying one restriction on Article 6 by reassuring the accused person that Article 6 would not be restricted in other ways as well. Admittedly, the Court does identify a number of overlapping guarantees that have been complied with, and it may have seen significance in the combination of these overlapping guarantees. But the notion that a restriction on Article 6 can be 'counterbalanced' by the absence of *other* restrictions on Article 6 is quite perverse.

In *Grayson and Barnham*, two applicants each argued 'that, in confiscation proceedings following his conviction for drugs offences, the fact that the legal burden of proof was on him to show that he did not have realisable assets equivalent to the benefit figure offended the basic principles of a fair procedure, in breach of Article 6'.[134] The applicant's focus was on Article 6(1) rather than Article 6(2), but there was nonetheless much discussion of the presumption of innocence. In the course of its analysis, the Court cited *Salabiaku* in stating that presumptions of fact or law:

> are not prohibited in principle, as long as States remain within reasonable limits, taking into account the importance of what is at stake and maintaining the rights of the defence.[135]

In assessing the extent to which the presumption in this case violated the applicant's Article 6 right to a fair trial, the Court referred several times to the counterbalancing 'safeguards' present in the confiscation procedure:

> 45. Throughout these proceedings, the rights of the defence were protected by the safeguards built into the system. Thus, in each case the assessment was carried out by a court with *a judicial procedure including a public hearing, advance disclosure of the prosecution case and the opportunity for the applicant to adduce documentary and oral evidence.* Each applicant was represented by *counsel* of his choice. The *burden was on the prosecution* to establish that the applicant had held the assets in question during the relevant period. Although the court was required by law to assume that the assets derived from drug trafficking, this assumption could have been rebutted if the appli-

[133] ibid paras 55–56 (emphasis added). See also *Fitt v United Kingdom* (n 92 above) paras 48–50.

[134] *Grayson and Barnham v United Kingdom* (App 19955/05) (2009) 48 EHRR 30, para 3.

[135] ibid para 40, citing *Salabiaku v France* (App 10519/83) (1991) 13 EHRR 379, para 28.

> cant had shown that he had acquired the property through legitimate means. Furthermore, the judge had a discretion not to apply the assumption if he considered that applying it would give rise to a serious risk of injustice . . .
>
> 48. Each of the present applicants chose to give oral evidence relating to his realisable assets. Again, they had the advantage of the safeguards referred to in paragraph 45 above. They were *legally represented* and had been informed, through the judges' detailed rulings, exactly how the benefit figure had been calculated. Each applicant was given the opportunity to explain his financial situation and describe what had happened to the assets which the judge had taken into account in setting the benefit figure.[136]

The European Court found no violation of Article 6(1) for either applicant.[137] Virtually all of these counterbalancing safeguards are *required* by Article 6. The Court is thus reasoning that, because a particular procedure did not violate Article 6 in certain respects, that makes a violation in another respect less likely or less serious. My argument is not that the Court reached an incorrect decision on the substance of the right. The argument is, instead, to highlight the extent to which the Court appears to accept that compliance with some parts of Article 6 may be relevant to whether or not another part of Article 6 has been violated. In a sense, as was foreshadowed at the outset of this section, this reflects the fact that the Court's analysis of counterbalancing and safeguards often amounts to a slightly more structured version of its 'proceedings as a whole' jurisprudence.

This sense was reinforced by the Grand Chamber's decision in *Al-Khawaja and Tahery*. In that case, the Court effectively defined 'sufficiently counterbalanced' as being synonymous with the fairness of the proceedings as a whole. In one paragraph, the Grand Chamber set up the relevant test as being one in which counterbalancing plays a part:

> [I]n cases concerning the withholding of evidence from the defence in order to protect police sources, the Court has left it to the domestic courts to decide whether the rights of the defence should cede to the public interest and has confined itself to verifying whether the procedures followed by the judicial authorities *sufficiently counterbalance the limitations on the defence with appropriate safeguards* . . . Similarly, in the case of Salduz . . . the Court reiterated that the right to legal assistance . . . was one element, amongst others, of the concept of a fair trial in criminal proceedings contained in Article 6(1).
>
> The Court is of the view that the sole or decisive rule should also be applied in a similar manner. It would not be correct, when reviewing questions of fairness, to apply this rule in an inflexible manner.[138]

It then goes on to explain how the flexible counterbalancing test would work, making express reference to the 'proceedings as a whole' test:

[136] *Grayson and Barnham v United Kingdom* (n 134 above) paras 45, 48 (emphasis added).

[137] ibid para 50.

[138] *Al-Khawaja and Tahery v United Kingdom* (Grand Chamber) (n 109 above) paras 145–146 (emphasis added). See also *Salikhov v Russia* (App 23880/05) (3 May 2012) para 118.

> the traditional way in which the Court approaches the issue of the overall fairness of the proceedings, namely to weigh in the balance the competing interests of the defence, the victim, and witnesses, and the public interest in the effective administration of justice.[139]

Thus, the counterbalancing reasoning infrastructure seems simply to amount to a circumlocution delaying the inevitable arrival of the 'proceedings as a whole' test.

Similarly flawed analysis is evident in *AL v Finland*, in which the applicant had been accused and convicted of sexually abusing a child relative. At the European Court, the applicant alleged a violation of Article 6(3)(d) 'in that he was denied the opportunity to put questions to [the complainant], although her account, recorded on videotape, had been treated as decisive evidence against him'.[140] In considering this argument, the Court noted:

> Criminal proceedings concerning sexual offences are often perceived as an ordeal by the victim, in particular when the latter is unwillingly confronted with the defendant. These features are even more prominent in a case involving a minor . . . Therefore, the Court accepts that in criminal proceedings concerning sexual abuse, certain measures may be taken for the purpose of protecting the victim, provided that such measures can be reconciled with an adequate and effective exercise of the rights of the defence. *In securing the rights of the defence, the judicial authorities may be required to take measures which counterbalance the handicaps under which the defence labours.*[141]

The Court did not expressly outline what measures might constitute counterbalances in this case. The closest it came was this passage, noting opportunities the applicant had *not* had:

> the applicant was not afforded an opportunity to put questions to R. at any stage of the proceedings. His request to hear [the complainant] before the Court of Appeal was refused. His further request to hear [the complainant] before a court, or by some other means, was to no avail, as the Supreme Court refused leave to appeal.[142]

All these safeguards are guaranteed by Article 6. Ultimately, in this case, the Court found a violation of Article 6.[143] But in reaching that conclusion, the European Court gave no indication of what counterbalancing safeguards (other than those *already embodied in Article 6*) might have ameliorated the effect of what would otherwise constitute a violation of Article 6.[144] In this way, the 'counterbalancing' analysis amounted to asking simply whether or not Article 6 had been complied with.

The cases above further fill out the picture of how the European Court uses counterbalancing in its analysis of alleged infringements. In this section and the last section, we have seen two different ways in which it seems that 'counterbal-

[139] *Al-Khawaja and Tahery v United Kingdom* (Grand Chamber) (n 109 above) para 146.
[140] *AL v Finland* (App 23220/04) (27 January 2009) para 23.
[141] ibid para 39 (emphasis added).
[142] ibid para 42.
[143] ibid para 45.
[144] See also Greer, *The European Convention on Human Rights* (n 46 above) 254.

ancing' simply collapsed into an analysis of whether or not the proceedings as a whole had been fair, or simply whether there had been a fair trial. In these cases, there is reason to think that the nomenclature of counterbalancing is simply a circumlocution masking a basic 'proceedings as a whole' analysis.

E.3.3 In Other Instances, Counterbalancing Appears to Involve the European Court Requiring the Provision of Specific Extra Rights in an Arbitrary Way

As was seen above, there are many cases in which the European Court does not specify counterbalancing measures beyond the guarantees secured by the text of Article 6. In a number of cases, however, the Court does more explicitly identify the counterbalancing measures that it requires.

In *Riepan v Austria*, the applicant was a prisoner charged with having threatened a prison official; the relevant Austrian court decided to hold the hearing within a closed area of the prison.[145] The applicant argued that he was thus 'deprived of a public hearing'.[146] The Court stated:

> [T]he holding of a trial outside a regular courtroom, in particular in a place like a prison, to which the general public in principle has no access, presents a serious obstacle to its public character. In such a case, *the State is under an obligation to take compensatory measures* in order to ensure that the public and the media are duly informed about the place of the hearing and are granted effective access.[147]

The European Court then examined possible counterbalancing 'compensatory measures':

> 30. The Court will therefore examine whether such measures were taken in the present case. As to the question whether the public could obtain information about the date and place of the hearing, the Court notes that the hearing was included in a weekly hearing list held by the Steyr Regional Court, which apparently contained an indication that the hearing would be held at Garsten Prison . . . However, apart from this routine announcement, no particular measures were taken, such as a separate announcement on the Regional Court's notice-board accompanied, if need be, by information about how to reach Garsten Prison, with a clear indication of the access conditions. Moreover, the other circumstances in which the hearing was held were hardly designed to encourage public attendance: it was held early in the morning [8.30 am] in a room which, although not too small to accommodate an audience, does not appear to have been equipped as a regular courtroom.
>
> 31. In sum, the Court finds that the Steyr Regional Court failed to adopt adequate compensatory measures to counterbalance the detrimental effect which the holding of the applicant's trial in the closed area of Garsten Prison had on its public character.

[145] *Riepan v Austria* (App 35115/97) (14 November 2000) paras 9–18.
[146] ibid para 23.
[147] ibid para 29 (emphasis added).

> Consequently, the hearing . . . did not comply with the requirement of publicity laid down in [Article 6(1)].[148]

In this case, then, the Court's description of possible counterbalancing measures focuses on providing guarantees *above and beyond* what it views Article 6 requiring in a normal case. In this way *Riepan* differs from the many cases identified above. Here, the Court required special instructions on how to get to the venue, that the hearing be held in a courtroom 'equipped as a regular courtroom',' and that it not be held too early in the morning. These counterbalancing measures may be perfectly sensible, but in the absence of explanation of how the Court arrived at them, it is extremely difficult to predict how future cases are likely to be resolved, and for officials in contracting states to have their behaviour guided by this sort of decision. The Court does not explain, for example, the way in which Article 6 requires that a courtroom should be 'equipped', or why 8.30 am is too early in the morning for the purposes of Article 6's guarantees.

In *T and V v United Kingdom*, the European Court considered particular safeguards that had been put in place for two children on trial for murder and abduction. These counterbalancing safeguards included the applicants having had the trial procedure explained to them, visiting the courtroom before the proceedings, and shortening the hearings.[149] Nevertheless, the Court considered that the proceedings would have been 'incomprehensible and intimidating' for the applicants at times, and that the applicants' 'skilled and experienced lawyers' were not sufficient to safeguard their Article 6 rights.[150] Indeed

> although the applicant's legal representatives were seated, as the Government put it, 'within whispering distance', it is highly unlikely that the applicant would have felt sufficiently uninhibited, in the tense courtroom and under public scrutiny, to have consulted with them during the trial or, indeed, that, given his immaturity and his disturbed emotional state, he would have been capable outside the courtroom of cooperating with his lawyers and giving them information for the purposes of his defence.[151]

It may be worth noting that the European Court did not specify any counterbalancing measures that *could* have been taken in order to protect the applicants' right to participate effectively in the trial under Article 6, or a test with which to identify such measures. The absence of such an indication may be contrasted with the case of *SC v United Kingdom*, decided four and a half years after *T and V*.

In *SC*, the applicant was also a child who had been charged with various criminal offences. Having been convicted in the Crown Court of one such offence, and having been unsuccessful on appeal, the applicant argued before the European Court that he 'was so intellectually backward' that he:

[148] ibid paras 30–31 (the reference to the time of the hearing is drawn from para 14). See Trechsel, *Human Rights in Criminal Proceedings* (n 5 above) 127.

[149] *T and V v United Kingdom* (App 24724/94; 24888/94) (2000) 30 EHRR 121, para 86.

[150] ibid paras 86–88.

[151] ibid para 88.

> should not have been tried by a judge and jury, in a court open to the public to which the press was given free access. Instead, the applicant [argued that he] should have been tried in the privacy of a specialist Youth Court with proper sentencing powers.[152]

The European Court acknowledged that some steps had been taken in the Crown Court to accommodate the applicant's position and to 'ensure that the procedure was as informal as possible': the lawyers 'did not wear wigs and gowns and the applicant was allowed to sit next to his social worker'.[153] Nevertheless, the European Court concluded that these measures were not enough. More counterbalancing measures were required in a case of this sort:

> [I]t is essential that [the applicant] be tried in a specialist tribunal which is able to give full consideration to, and make proper allowance for, the handicaps under which he labours, and adapt its procedure accordingly.[154]

In this case, therefore, the Court required that the only way to try someone in the position of the applicant would be to do so in a specialist tribunal. This conclusion is, perhaps, a more explicit version of what the Court said in *T and V v United Kingdom*, insofar as it expressly identifies what steps could be taken to allow the applicant's trial to comply with Article 6. The *T and V* Court saw it as sufficient to identify the flaws in the process; the *SC* Court took matters a step further and also identified the way in which those flaws would be capable of being counterbalanced.

It must be noted that there are rare examples of the European Court spelling out its approach to counterbalancing more clearly and precisely. Indeed, the Grand Chamber in *Taxquet* held that, in proceedings involving a jury:

> Article 6 requires an assessment of whether sufficient safeguards were in place to avoid any risk of arbitrariness and to enable the accused to understand the reasons for his conviction. Such procedural safeguards may include, for example, directions or guidance provided by the presiding judge to the jurors on the legal issues arising or the evidence adduced, and precise, unequivocal questions put to the jury by the judge, forming a framework on which the verdict is based or sufficiently offsetting the fact that no reasons are given for the jury's answers. Lastly, regard must be had to any avenues of appeal open to the accused.[155]

Similarly, the analysis in *Luca v Italy* of ways in which an Article 6(3)(d) infringement could be counterbalanced, and the analysis in the Grand Chamber's *Al-Khawaja and Tahery* decision of ways in which a trial judge's directions to a jury might be capable of acting as a counterbalance, all demonstrate ways in which the European Court can be somewhat more precise in its counterbalancing

[152] *SC v United Kingdom* (App 60958/00) (2005) 40 EHRR 10, para 26.

[153] ibid para 30.

[154] ibid para 35.

[155] *Taxquet v Belgium* (Grand Chamber) (App 926/05) (2012) 54 EHRR 26, para 92. See Paul Roberts, 'Does Article 6 of the European Convention on Human Rights Require Reasoned Verdicts in Criminal Trials?' (2011) *Human Rights Law Review* 1; N Bratza, 'The Relationship between the UK Courts and Strasbourg' [2011] *EHRLR* 505; Mark Coen, '"With Cat-like Tread": Jury Trial and the European Court of Human Rights' (2014) *Human Rights Law Review* (Advance Access) 1, 16–21.

analysis.[156] Unfortunately, as the analysis above has demonstrated, judgments of this sort are unusual in the Court's jurisprudence.

Cases like *Riepan* and *SC*, therefore, are examples demonstrating that the Court is occasionally willing to identify explicitly what counterbalancing factors are required by its counterbalancing analysis. But the way in which this guidance is provided by the European Court gives very little indication of how the precise combination of counterbalancing factors had been arrived at (why, in *Riepan*'s case, was 8.30 am too early in the morning?). The counterbalancing jurisprudence of the Court leaves much to be desired.

E.3.4 The 'Defect-Curing' Technique is Another Form of Semi-Structured Balancing

This section examines the European Court's jurisprudence about curing defects in proceedings. In general terms, the curing defects jurisprudence usually holds that 'defects' at the trial stage of criminal proceedings may be 'cured' by appellate proceedings in some or all circumstances, and that potential infringements may thereby be saved from becoming violations in the eyes of the Court. To some extent, it could be said that the notion of curing defects is simply a somewhat more structured version of the unstructured violation analysis that characterises much of the Article 6 case law, and much of the European Court's 'proceedings as a whole' jurisprudence. Indeed, it involves balancing one potentially-violating identified factor against other identified complying factors and weighing up the extent to which the latter has ameliorated the former. In this section, I argue that the Court does not properly explain why this analytical technique is appropriate in some cases and not in others, or how the technique is to work in those cases in which it is applicable.

While the focus of this section is, as with the rest of the book, on the European Court's jurisprudence on *criminal* fair trial rights, it may be noted that there is overlap here with the Court's *civil* fair trial rights jurisprudence. Indeed, while they are beyond the scope of this book, it is worth nothing that issues analogous to those considered in this section are often raised in the context of planning law and administrative law.[157]

It may be that the origins of the defect-curing jurisprudence are in some way thematically linked to the Convention's 'exhaustion of domestic remedies' admis-

[156] See *Luca v Italy* (n 84 above) paras 39–40; *Al-Khawaja and Tahery v United Kingdom* (Grand Chamber) (n 109 above) paras 152–165. See also the Grand Chamber's Art 5 analysis in *A v United Kingdom* (n 115 above) paras 217–20; *Pesukic v Switzerland* (App 25088/07) (6 December 2012) paras 49–53.

[157] See, eg, PP Craig, *Administrative Law*, 7th edn (Sweet & Maxwell, 2012) 420–31; Timothy Endicott, *Administrative Law*, 2nd edn (Oxford University Press, 2011) 171–74; P Cane, *Administrative Law*, 5th edn (Oxford University Press, 2011) 96–102; W Wade and CF Forsyth, *Administrative Law*, 10th edn (Oxford University Press, 2009) 386–88; *Tsfayo v United Kingdom* (App 60860/00) (14 November 2006); *R (Alconbury) v Secretary of State for the Environment, Transport and the Regions* [2003] 2 AC 295.

sibility requirement.[158] Importantly, however, defect-curing as it is analysed here primarily takes place not in the context of decisions about the *admissibility* of the complaint, but rather takes place in the context of assessing whether there has been *a violation* of Article 6.

In any event, whatever the origins of the defect-curing technique, the Court has often made statements along the lines of that made in *Kyprianou v Cyprus*:

> The possibility certainly exists that a higher or the highest court might, in some circumstances, make reparation for defects that took place in the first-instance proceedings.[159]

As will be seen in the following subsections, however, the apparent simplicity of statements of this sort belies a hidden complexity. That complexity takes two forms: first, uncertainty over what the Court will require in order for an appellate process to successfully cure a defect. Second, uncertainty over when it is appropriate to utilise the tool of defect curing *at all*.

E.3.5 There is Uncertainty Over What is Required in Order for an Ameliorating Act to 'Cure' a Defect

This section examines what characteristics the European Court requires of an appellate court in order for it to be capable of curing defects. There are two threads that run through this case law: the powers of review possessed by the 'curing' court and the extent to which a curing court's appellate processes provide protection for certain Article 6 guarantees. It is worth recalling here that the Court does not always require that appellate proceedings comply with every one of the Article 6 guarantees.[160] But, as will be seen, in cases where an appellate court is said to have 'cured' a defect in earlier proceedings, the Court will sometimes require that particular Article 6 guarantees be respected in the appellate proceedings.

In *Weber v Switzerland*, the applicant argued that there had been a breach of Article 6(1) insofar as the initial judgment in his case (given by the President of the Cassation Division), and the subsequent judgment in the first of two appeals, had been given without any public hearing.[161] The second appeal's proceedings, in

[158] See, eg, *Guzzardi v Italy* (App 7367/76) (1981) 3 EHRR 333, para 72; *De Wilde and others v Belgium* (App 2832/66) (1979–80) 1 EHRR 373, para 50; *DeCubber v Belgium* (App 9186/80) (1985) 7 EHRR 236, para 33. See van Dijk and van Hoof, *Theory and Practice of the European Convention on Human Rights* (n 5 above) 617–18; Trechsel, *Human Rights in Criminal Proceedings* (n 5 above) 69; Summers, *Fair Trials* (n 14 above) 118–20; R Clayton and H Tomlinson (eds), *The Law of Human Rights*, 2nd edn (Oxford University Press, 2009) 2072–75.

[159] *Kyprianou v Cyprus* (App 73797/01) (2007) 44 EHRR 27, para 134. See Trechsel, *Human Rights in Criminal Proceedings* (n 5 above) 66.

[160] See, eg, discussion of the right to be present at an appeal: Clayton and Tomlinson, *Fair Trial Rights* (n 5 above) 157–58; Trechsel, *Human Rights in Criminal Proceedings* (n 5 above) 257–61; Harris, O'Boyle and Warbrick, *Law of the European Convention on Human Rights* (n 5 above) 250; van Dijk and van Hoof, *Theory and Practice of the European Convention on Human Rights* (n 5 above) 589–91.

[161] *Weber v Switzerland* (App 11034/84) (1990) 12 EHRR 355, para 28.

the Federal Court, *had* involved a public hearing. After dealing with preliminary issues, the European Court's analysis was brief:

> The applicant was consequently entitled in principle to a public hearing in the determination of the 'criminal charge' against him. The President of the Criminal Cassation Division, however, did not hold a hearing at all but gave his decision after a summary investigation entirely in written form, as provided for in . . . the Vaud Code of Criminal Procedure. The Criminal Cassation Division too dismissed the applicant's appeal without hearing argument, as it was empowered to do by . . . the same Code. The fact that the proceedings in the Federal Court were public *did not suffice to cure the two defects just noted.* Having before it a public-law appeal, the Federal Court could only satisfy itself that there had been no arbitrariness and not determine all the disputed questions of fact and law . . . There has therefore been a breach of [Article 6(1)].[162]

In this passage, therefore, the European Court regards the public hearing at the final stage as not 'curing' the earlier defects. Crucially, however, it appears that this was because the Federal Court was unable to determine 'all the disputed questions of fact and law'. The constraints on the Federal Court's powers made it unable to cure a defect for the purposes of the European Court's analysis. Similarly, in *Condron*, the inability of the appellate court to review the jury's reasons meant that it lacked sufficient powers of review and hence could not cure defects.[163]

Another of the characteristics that must be possessed by an appellate court in order for it to have 'curing powers' was evident in *T v Austria.* In that case the applicant argued that:

> [H]is rights under [Article 6(3)(a)] and [Article 6(3)(b)] were violated in that the District Court, before imposing a fine for abuse of process on him, did not inform him of the suspicion that he had made false or incomplete statements in his legal aid request.[164]

The European Court considered whether subsequent appellate proceedings might have cured these problems, but stated:

> [T]he appeal was not capable of remedying the shortcomings of the first instance proceedings, because the Regional Court confirmed the District Court's decision . . . without a hearing and rejected the submissions made by the applicant in his defence as constituting new facts which were inadmissible on appeal.[165]

In *T*, therefore, the European Court was clear in demanding that any appellate process must itself comply with certain Article 6 guarantees, such as having a hearing, if it is to properly cure defects in an earlier stage of the proceedings. One may recall that there is not necessarily an automatic right to a hearing in appellate

[162] ibid paras 39–40 (emphasis added). On *Weber*, see Trechsel, *Human Rights in Criminal Proceedings* (n 5 above) 20–21; van Dijk and van Hoof, *Theory and Practice of the European Convention on Human Rights* (n 5 above) 552.

[163] *Condron v United Kingdom* (App 35718/97) (2001) 31 EHRR 1, para 63.

[164] *T v Austria* (App 27783/95) (14 November 2000) para 68.

[165] ibid para 71.

proceedings.[166] But in this case, the European Court suggests that an appellate process lacking certain Article 6 rights cannot cure a flawed trial process for the purposes of the Court's jurisprudence.[167]

This way of approaching curing defects was also considered in *Riepan*, decided on the same day as *T*. In that case, the European Court stated:

> In a number of cases [the Court] has found that the fact that proceedings before an appellate court are held in public cannot remedy the lack of a public hearing at the lower instances where the scope of the appeal proceedings is limited, in particular where the appellate court cannot review the merits of the case, including a review of the facts and an assessment of the proportionality between the fault and the sanction.[168]

In cases like *Riepan*, the Court also clarifies another aspect of its curing jurisprudence. In assessing whether the appellate court had cured defects earlier in the criminal process, the Court stated that:

> [A]n examination of the facts of the present case reveals that the review carried out by the Linz Court of Appeal did not have the requisite scope. It is true that the appellate court could review the case as regards questions of law and fact and could reassess the sentence. However, apart from questioning the applicant, the court did not take any evidence, and in particular did not rehear the witnesses. It is of little importance that the applicant did not request a rehearing of the witnesses . . . Accordingly, the Court finds that the lack of a public hearing before the Steyr Regional Court was not remedied by the public hearing before the Linz Court of Appeal.[169]

Here, then, the European Court requires not only that the appellate court have the *ability* to 'review the case as regards questions of law and fact' and to 'reassess the sentence',' but also that the appellate court *actually conduct* a rigorous review, even if the applicant does not make such a request. This approach is also evident in cases including *Kyprianou v Cyprus*.[170]

In *Condron v United Kingdom*, however, the Court appeared to adopt a different view of what an appellate court would need to do in order to cure defects. In that case, the Court placed significance on the fact that the appellate court's analytical task was different to the analytical task of the European Court itself:

> The Court must also have regard to the fact that the Court of Appeal was concerned with the safety of the applicants' conviction, not whether they had in the circumstances received a fair trial. In the Court's opinion, the question whether or not the rights of the defence guaranteed to an accused under Article 6 of the Convention were secured in

[166] See, eg, *Jan-Ake Andersson v Sweden* (App 11274/84) (1993) 15 EHRR 218, para 27; *Helmers v Sweden* (App 11826/85) (1993) 15 EHRR 285, para 36; *Muttilainen v Finland* (App 18358/02 (22 May 2007) para 23; *RH v Finland* (App 34165/05) (2 June 2009) para 29. See also Clayton and Tomlinson, *Fair Trial Rights* (n 5 above) 175; van Dijk and van Hoof, *Theory and Practice of the European Convention on Human Rights* (n 5 above) 598–99; *Huseyn and others v Azerbaijan* (n 77 above) para 214.

[167] See also *Sakhnovskiy v Russia* (App 21272/03) (5 February 2009) paras 23–53; *Sakhnovskiy v Russia* (App 21272/03) (2 November 2010) paras 99–109.

[168] *Riepan v Austria* (n 145 above) para 37.

[169] ibid para 41.

[170] *Kyprianou v Cyprus* (n 159 above) paras 134–135.

> any given case cannot be assimilated to a finding that his conviction was safe in the absence of any enquiry into the issue of fairness.[171]

In this passage, therefore, the Court indicates that, in order to cure a defect, an appellate court must not only have broad review powers, but that those review powers must be at least partly directed towards establishing whether or not there was a fair trial at the initial hearing. Thus the *Condron* Court appears to require that, in order for a defect to be cured, the appellate court must conduct an analysis similar to that conducted by the European Court. Unlike some of the cases above, in which it appeared that the Court would find a defect to be cured if the appellate court's process had the *effect* of ameliorating a potential violation of Article 6 in the trial process, this case requires that the appellate court identify the defect *in Article 6 terms* in order for the defect to be cured. That is, under *Condron*, it is not enough that the European Court can look at a particular appellate procedure and recognise that that procedure, in substance, ameliorated a flaw in the earlier stage of proceedings. The European Court must be able to identify how the appellate court conducted a fair trial analysis under Article 6.

If these cases are read together, then, the European Court's position appears to be this: it may be enough for the 'curing' court simply to be able to determine all the disputed questions of fact and law. Or, the Court may also require that the curing court operated with certain of the Article 6 rights in its own proceedings (the right to a hearing, for example). Or, the Court may require that the curing court not only had the ability to do these things in these circumstances, but that it did so.[172] Finally, the Court may require not only that the curing court had all of these characteristics, but also that it turned its mind to the question of an Article 6 analysis rather than simply to analysis of the safeness of a conviction. These positions are by no means irreconcilable, but the Court has not reconciled them, and there is evident uncertainty as to what is required of an appellate court before it may cure a particular type of defect. For any applicant, government, or domestic appellate court, the Court's judgments lack any sense of systematic guidance as to why certain Article 6 guarantees are crucial to an appellate court's ability to cure defects and how intense any review should be.

E.3.6 There is Uncertainty Over When the Defect-Curing Technique May be Utilised

Within the European Court's defect-curing case law, and even within individual cases dealing with defect-curing, there is significant uncertainty over when it is

[171] *Condron v United Kingdom* (n 163 above) para 65. On the relationship between fairness of trials and safeness of convictions, see Ian Dennis, 'Fair Trials and Safe Convictions' (2003) 56 *Current Legal Problems* 211.

[172] It seems that the case law indicates that the result of that review need not be favourable to the applicant; the important thing is that the review be conducted, eg, *Dallos v Hungary* (App 29082/95) (2003) 37 EHRR 22, paras 50–53. On what is described here as defect curing, see also Hoyano, 'What is Balanced on the Scales of Justice?' (n 10 above) 26–27.

appropriate for the European Court to engage in defect-curing analysis. In this section I point to several examples of this uncertainty.

A useful example of inconsistency *within* a case is provided by *DeCubber v Belgium*. In that judgment, the Court offered a forceful statement explaining why it would be rare that subsequent appellate proceedings could cure flawed trial proceedings. The Court began by noting that the existence in a particular contracting state of appellate courts that complied with Article 6's guarantees did not mean 'that the lower courts do not [also] have to provide the required guarantees'.[173] The government had argued, on the basis of *LeCompte, Albert and LeCompte* and *Sutter*, that guarantees in trial proceedings could be reduced if full-guarantee appellate proceedings were available.[174] The European Court rejected this argument, noting that those cases had not involved criminal proceedings, and stated:

> The reasoning adopted in the three above-mentioned judgments, to which should be added the *Campbell and Fell* judgment . . . cannot justify reducing the requirements of [Article 6(1)] in its traditional and natural sphere of application. A restrictive interpretation of this kind would not be consonant with the object and purpose of [Article 6(1)].[175]

Thus, the European Court made a forceful statement that the Article 6 guarantees could not be watered down at the trial stage of criminal proceedings, even if there was an appellate court available; this statement has been drawn on in subsequent cases.[176] But in the next paragraph of *DeCubber*, the European Court appeared to contradict these sentiments. Indeed, in paragraph 33, the European Court offered a tentative explanation of how flaws in proceedings might be 'cured' by appellate processes:

> The possibility certainly exists that a higher or the highest court might, in some circumstances, make reparation for an initial violation of one of the Convention's provisions: this is precisely the reason for the existence of the rule of exhaustion of domestic remedies . . . The particular defect in question [in this case] did not bear solely upon the conduct of the first-instance proceedings: its source being the very composition of the Oudenaarde criminal court, the defect involved matters of internal organisation and the Court of Appeal did not cure that defect since it did not quash on that ground the judgment . . . in its entirety.[177]

It is difficult to reconcile these passages. In the first passage, the European Court stood firmly against reducing the protection afforded by Article 6 to criminal trial

[173] *DeCubber v Belgium* (n 158 above) para 32.

[174] ibid paras 31–32. See, eg, van Dijk and van Hoof, *Theory and Practice of the European Convention on Human Rights* (n 5 above) 567.

[175] *DeCubber v Belgium* (n 158 above) para 32. This passage was cited by the European Court as an explanation for its approach in *Findlay v United Kingdom* (App 22107/93) (1997) 24 EHRR 221, para 79.

[176] *Findlay v United Kingdom* (n 175 above) para 79.

[177] *DeCubber v Belgium* (n 158 above) para 33. See also *Idalov v Russia* (App 5826/03) (22 May 2012) paras 179–182.

proceedings. In the next passage, the Court expressly countenanced the reduction of rights protection in criminal trial proceedings provided that an appellate court subsequently quashes the trial judgment. The *De Cubber* Court seems unable to decide whether or not appellate processes can 'justify reducing the requirements of [Article 6(1)] in its traditional and natural sphere of application'.[178] Judgments marked by this sort of uncertainty provide little guidance.

A further example of inconsistency within an individual case is provided by *Riepan v Austria*. In the course of its analysis, the *Riepan* Court attempted to draw an analogy between its view of the independence and impartiality guarantees and its view of the publicity guarantee:

> [T]he Court has, in the context of the requirement of a tribunal's independence and impartiality, rejected the possibility that a defect at first instance could be remedied at a later stage, finding that the accused was entitled to a first-instance tribunal that fully met the requirements of [Article 6(1)]. The Court considers that a normal criminal trial requires *the same kind* of fundamental guarantee in the form of publicity . . . Given the possible detrimental effects that the lack of a public hearing before the trial court could have on the fairness of the proceedings, the absence of publicity *could not in any event be remedied by anything other than a complete re-hearing before the appellate court.*[179]

But it is somewhat unclear what, precisely, the Court's analogy is. The European Court appears to state that independence and impartiality violations can never be cured, and that publicity violations should be treated in the same way. The European Court then goes on to outline a way in which publicity violations *could* be cured. This is confusing, and suggests a broader uncertainty about how and when defect-curing is an appropriate approach to violations of Article 6 guarantees.

If the two cases above involved examples of internal incoherence, we now turn to two cases that demonstrate inconsistency *between* cases. The cases were decided less than a month apart, but adopt different approaches to the question of defect-curing. In *Macin v Turkey (No 2)*, the applicant was tried before a tribunal that, during the early stages, included a military judge. The military judge was replaced by a civilian judge during the course of proceedings. The question was whether the replacement of the military judge during the proceedings vitiated the otherwise potentially-infringing nature of that judge's presence for independence and impartiality purposes. In its analysis, the European Court noted that there had been five hearings before the replacement and seventeen afterwards. The European Court concluded that 'replacing the military judge has dispelled the doubts of the [applicant] about the independence and impartiality of the court which sentenced him'.[180] That is, measures taken subsequent to the potentially-violating incident were sufficient to 'cure' that defect such that there was no violation.

[178] *DeCubber v Belgium* (n 158 above) para 32.

[179] *Riepan v Austria* (n 145 above) para 40 (emphasis added). This passage is drawn upon and cited in *Krestovskiy v Russia* (App 14040/03) (28 October 2010) para 34.

[180] *Macin v Turkey (No 2)* (App 38282/02) (24 October 2006) para 30 (translated).

Curiously, almost the opposite result was reached in similar circumstances in *Kavak v Turkey*, decided less than three weeks after *Macin v Turkey (No 2)*. After conducting analysis of the applicant's argument that there had been a violation of Article 6 because a military judge had participated in an early stage of the proceedings, the European Court stated:

> 48. However, the Court recalls that in *Ocalan*, the Grand Chamber found that 'when a military judge is involved in one or more procedural steps that remain valid in subsequent criminal proceedings concerned, the accused could reasonably have doubts as to the legality of the whole procedure'. Thus, the fact that a military judge has participated in a trial against a civilian in a pleading an inherent part of the proceedings, deprives the whole procedure of the appearance of having been led by a independent and impartial tribunal.
>
> 49. Accordingly, there has been a violation of Article 6(1).[181]

In these two decisions there are two fundamentally different approaches not only to the independence and impartiality guarantees but also to the extent to which a violation of Article 6 may be 'cured' of its defects by subsequent action. It might be noted that *Ocalan* was not referred to in the *Macin* decision. The European Court does not acknowledge the discrepancy between *Kavak* and *Macin (No 2)*, let alone attempt to explain or rationalise it.[182]

The European Court's approach to defect-curing is thus marked by uncertainty and incoherence, in a way that is indicative of a broader lack of guidance as to how violations of Article 6 are to be assessed.

E.3.7 Concluding this Section

Both counterbalancing and defect-curing ostensibly involve the European Court using some structure in its assessment of alleged violations. By identifying and characterising the factors to be balanced as 'counterbalancing measures' or 'defects' or 'curing procedures', the European Court appears to provide more clearly structured reasoning than that in its 'proceedings as a whole' jurisprudence. This clarity, however, is undermined significantly by the internal incoherence of the methods, and by broader external inconsistencies between the ways that the Court uses these methods and the ways it is willing to use other methods of assessing alleged violations of Article 6. Moreover, ultimately, as has been seen, both counterbalancing and defect-curing seem to amount to versions of the Court's 'proceedings as a whole' doctrine. If the Court adopted an approach in which it focused on individual violations assessed with respect to the facts relevant to the alleged violation, then it might be difficult to argue that it was relevant that there were counterbalancing factors, or that there were appellate proceedings of one sort or another. With the 'proceedings as a whole' doctrine enlivened,

[181] *Kavak v Turkey* (App 69790/01) (9 November 2006) paras 48–49 (translated).
[182] Judge Türmen of Turkey, it may be noted, participated in both decisions.

however, the European Court may choose to take into account those things in the course of assessing a specific alleged violation.

E.4 The European Court's 'Never Fair' Case Law is Inconsistent with Its Other Case Law, and Internally Incoherent

The sections above examined ways in which the European Court has attempted to incorporate semi-structured balancing techniques into its analysis of potential violations of Article 6. This section considers situations in which the Court has elected *not* to conduct that sort of semi-structured balancing. The argument being constructed here is that the Court demonstrates great incoherence in the way that it uses its analytical tools. With very little explanation, it will disregard its counter-balancing and defect-curing jurisprudence and instead choose to analyse a potential violation through what will be described as the 'never fair' method. But even then, *that* method will not be applied regularly and methodically. The picture being painted here is one of inconsistencies piled upon inconsistencies. Of course, it is possible to imagine an analytical meta-framework in which the Court carefully chose different analytical tools for different sorts of violations, and explained why each tool was applicable or inapplicable to a given situation. But this is not what the Court does. On one level, it simply fails to explain the rationale for its pick-and-choose approach to analysing violations. On another, the methods that it purports to use are, themselves, used incoherently.

There are several arguments made in this section. First, it is established that the Court uses the 'never fair' formulation, and does so in a way that does not square with its attempts at counterbalancing and defect-curing. Second, it is established that the Court's use of the 'never fair' formulation is inconsistent on its own terms. Third, it will be argued that one possible explanation for some inconsistencies in the use of the 'never fair' formulation may lay in the way the Court orders remedies for Article 6 violations.

E.4.1 The European Court Uses the 'Never Fair' Formulation in a Way that is Inconsistent with Its Attempts at Semi-structured Balancing

This subsection gives a descriptive account of the European Court's 'never fair' analysis, and identifies tensions between that analysis and the analytical tools critiqued above. A typical statement of what I will describe as the 'never fair' analysis is seen in *Ciraklar v Turkey*. In that case, the Court found a violation of Article 6(1) on independence and impartiality grounds.[183] It then began to consider an argument arising out of Article 6(3)(d), but concluded as follows:

[183] *Ciraklar v Turkey* (App 19601/92) (28 October 1998) paras 40–41.

> The Commission was of the view that 'a court whose lack of independence and impartiality has been established cannot, in any circumstances, guarantee a fair trial to the persons subject to its jurisdiction'. Having regard to its finding that Mr Ciraklar's right to a fair hearing by an independent and impartial tribunal has been infringed, the Court considers that it is unnecessary to examine this complaint.[184]

In a long line of cases, the European Court has stated that a violation of the independence and impartiality guarantees will mean that the trial as a whole can never be fair. A frequently-expressed and important corollary of this position is expressed in the Court's statements that, once an independence or impartiality violation has been found, it will regard it as unnecessary to consider any other Article 6 arguments.[185] Thus, in *Ergin v Turkey (No 6)*, the Court found a violation on independence and impartiality grounds.[186] The Court then went on to state, with reference to an additional Article 6 argument made by the applicant:

> The Court observes that it has already held in similar cases that a court whose lack of independence and impartiality has been established cannot, in any event, guarantee a fair trial to the persons subject to its jurisdiction. *Having regard to its finding that the applicant's right to a hearing by an independent and impartial tribunal has been infringed, the Court considers that there is no cause to examine the other complaint* relating to Article 6 of the Convention.[187]

Versions of the 'never fair' approach appear extremely frequently in independence and impartiality cases.[188] While these cases concern the independence and impartiality guarantees, analogies may be drawn with, for example, those cases in which the Court has stated that the use of evidence obtained by torture or incitement may mean that a trial can never be fair,[189] or the requirement that access to

[184] ibid paras 44–45. Curiously, the passage cited from the Commission does not seem to appear in the Commission's decision: *Ciraklar v Turkey* (Commission) (App 19601/92) (19 January 1995).

[185] Indeed, this statement standing alone would also amount to an implicit statement that a hearing in which there had been an independence or impartiality violation could never be fair.

[186] *Ergin v Turkey (No 6)* (App 47533/99) (2008) 47 EHRR 36, para 54.

[187] ibid paras 55–56 (emphasis added) citing *Ciraklar v Turkey* (n 183 above) paras 44–45.

[188] See, eg, *Caplik v Turkey* (App 57019/00) (15 July 2005) para 33; *Demicoli v Malta* (App 13057/87) (1992) 14 EHRR 47, paras 40–43; *Findlay v United Kingdom* (n 175 above) para 80; *Incal v Turkey* (App 22678/93) (2000) 29 EHRR 449, paras 73–74; *Buyukdag v Turkey* (App 28340/95) (21 December 2000) paras 73–76; *Gerger v Turkey* (App 24919/94) (8 July 1999) paras 62–65; *Morris v United Kingdom* (App 38784/97) (2002) 34 EHRR 52, paras 77–79; *YB and others v Turkey* (App 48173/99) (28 October 2004) para 38; *Orhan Aslan v Turkey* (App 48063/99) (20 October 2005) paras 57–61; *Celik v Turkey* (App 61650/00) (15 July 2005) paras 28–33; *Duran Sekin v Turkey* (App 41968/98) (2 February 2006) paras 34–39; *Tokay and Ulus v Turkey* (App 48060/99) (23 March 2006) paras 34–39; *Akkas v Turkey* (App 52665/99) (23 October 2003) paras 22–23; *Ozertikoglu v Turkey* (App 48438/99) (22 January 2004) paras 24–25; *Serdar Ozcan v Turkey* (App 55427/00) (8 April 2004) paras 24–25; *Isik v Turkey* (App 50102/99) (5 June 2003) paras 37–39; *Unal v Turkey* (App 48616/99) (10 November 2004) paras 27–28; *Vera Fernandez-Huidobro v Spain* (App 74181/01) (6 January 2010) para 12 of Dissent of Judge Casadevall; *Nechiporuk and Yonalko v Ukraine* (App 42310/04) (21 April 2011) paras 259–261. It may be noted that, curiously, some of these passages appear to attempt to confine this approach to cases involving Turkey.

[189] See *Jalloh v Germany* (n 77 above); *Gafgen v Germany* (Grand Chamber) (App 22978/05) (2010) 52 EHRR 1; *Gorgievski v FYROM* (App 18002/02) (16 July 2009) para 49. See also *Hakan Duman v Turkey* (App 28439/03) (23 March 2010) paras 52–53; *Dan v Moldova* (App 8999/07) (5 July 2011) paras 33–35; *Vanfuli v Russia* (App 24885/05) (3 November 2011) para 104; *El Haski v Belgium* (App

a lawyer should generally be provided as from the first interrogation by the police of a suspect.[190]

In the cases identified above, the Court does not explain why independence and impartiality violations are subject to this analytical regime, whereas infringements of other Article 6 guarantees are often capable of being 'cured' or 'counterbalanced'. Why, for example, would an infringement of the right to disclosure of documents not mean that the trial could never be fair? [191] Why, indeed, does an insufficiently public trial not render that trial automatically unfair?[192] And why do violations of Article 6(3)(a) and Article 6(3)(b) not render a trial unfair, but instead trigger a defect-curing analysis?[193] Instead, in those cases (and many others discussed in previous sections), the Court employs a counterbalancing analysis or a defect-curing analysis. To put the rhetorical questions another way, if the Court is committed to semi-structured balancing of the sort identified above, why could independence or impartiality violations not be subject to a counterbalancing or defect-curing analysis? Importantly, this is *not* an argument that the Court could not elect to treat violations of some guarantees differently to violations of other guarantees. It *is* an argument about clarity and coherence: if the Court wishes to establish a hierarchy of Article 6 rights, in which violations of some guarantees are more serious than others, or are treated differently from others, then it ought to explain and justify that hierarchy or differentiation. It has not done so.

E.4.2 The 'Never Fair' Formulation Does Not Sit Well with the European Court's Analysis of the Proceedings as a Whole

In this section the analysis of 'never fair' is linked with the analysis above related to the 'proceedings as a whole' test. In the analysis above, there were noted several cases in which the European Court purported to be reaching a conclusion based on the fairness of the proceedings as a whole, but then went on to consider other Article 6 factors separately and discretely. That form of analysis, it was argued, suggested that the Court was not *actually* considering the fairness of the proceedings as a whole. Here I note two ways in which this point plays out in the context of the Court's 'never fair' analysis.

649/08) (2013) 56 EHRR 31, para 85; *Grinenko v Ukraine* (App 33627/06) (15 November 2012) para 91; *Martin v Estonia* (App 35985/09) (30 May 2013) para 97; *Kaciu and Kotorri v Albania* (App 33192/07) (25 June 2013) paras 124–128; *Potcoava v Romania* (App 27945/07) (17 December 2013) para 31; cf *Gladyshev v Russia* (App 2807/04) (30 July 2009) para 75; *Alchagin v Russia* (App 20212/05) (17 January 2012) paras 69–74.

[190] *Salduz v Turkey* (App 36391/02) (2009) 49 EHRR 19, para 55.

[191] cf *Dowsett v United Kingdom* (n 94 above) para 42; *Doorson v Netherlands* (n 118 above) para 72; *Van Mechelen and others v Netherlands* (n 69 above) para 54.

[192] cf *Riepan v Austria* (n 145 above) paras 30–31.

[193] *T v Austria* (n 164 above) para 71.

First, there are cases in which the Court purports to be assessing the fairness of the proceedings as a whole, but that analysis is cut short by the use of a 'never fair' analysis. Thus, for example, in *Gafgen* the Grand Chamber stated that:

> The question which must be answered is *whether the proceedings as a whole, including the way in which the evidence was obtained, were fair.* This involves an examination of the unlawfulness in question and, where the violation of another Convention right is concerned, the nature of the violation found.[194]

But while the Court placed emphasis on the fairness of the proceedings as a whole, the application of that test came down to one factor:

> 166. . . . the Court has found in respect of confessions, as such, that the admission of statements obtained as a result of torture as evidence to establish the relevant facts in criminal proceedings rendered the proceedings as a whole unfair. This finding applied irrespective of the probative value of the statements and irrespective of whether their use was decisive in securing the defendant's conviction.[195]

In this passage, the European Court presents the discussion of evidence obtained by torture within the context of the 'proceedings as a whole' analysis. Yet it seems that the effect of the Court's analysis is that, regardless of what happened in the rest of the proceedings as a whole – regardless of any potentially exacerbating or ameliorating features of the proceedings as a whole – the proceedings *will not be capable of being fair.* In such circumstances, the key test seems to be whether evidence obtained in breach of Article 3 has been used rather than whether the proceedings as a whole were unfair. To be clear, this is emphatically *not* an argument that evidence obtained by torture renders a trial anything other than unfair; it *is* an argument about the clarity with which the European Court explains its reasons.

Second, there are a number of cases in which the Court reaches a conclusion that proceedings could never be fair but then, in the context of a separately alleged Article 6 violation, goes on notionally to consider the fairness of the proceedings as a whole. In *Haci Ozen v Turkey*, for example, the Court first considered an independence and impartiality argument, and found a violation on that basis.[196] Having found that violation, the Court then turned to consider a more general fairness argument.[197] The consideration of this additional argument began by noting that, usually, an independence or impartiality violation would mean the trial could never be fair:

[194] *Gafgen v Germany* (Grand Chamber) (n 189 above) para 163 (emphasis added). See M Spurrier, 'Gafgen v Germany: Fruit of the Poisonous Tree' [2010] *EHRLR* 513; Steven Greer, 'Should Police Threats to Torture Suspects Always be Severely Punished? Reflections on the Gafgen Case' (2011) 11(1) *Human Rights Law Review* 67; H Sauer and M Trilsch, 'Gafgen v Germany (Case Comment)' (2011) 105 *American Journal of International Law* 313; S Ast, 'The Gafgen Judgment of the ECtHR: On the Consequences of the Threat of Torture for Criminal Proceedings' (2010) 11(12) *German Law Journal* 1393.

[195] *Gafgen v Germany* (Grand Chamber) (n 189 above) para 166. See also *Stanimirovic v Serbia* (App 26088/06) (18 October 2011) paras 50–51; *Kaciu and Kotorri v Albania* (n 189 above) para 117.

[196] *Haci Ozen v Turkey* (App 46286/99) (12 April 2007) paras 93–94.

[197] ibid paras 95–105.

> The Court . . . has already held in previous cases that a court whose lack of independence and impartiality has been established cannot in any circumstances guarantee a fair trial to the persons under its jurisdiction and that, accordingly, it is not necessary to examine complaints regarding the fairness of the proceedings before that court.[198]

On the facts of this case, the Court stated, it was nonetheless necessary to consider the additional arguments.[199] In the course of assessing those additional arguments, the Court described the relevant analytical framework in familiar terms:

> The question which must be answered is whether the proceedings as a whole, including the way in which the evidence was obtained, were fair.[200]

In the course of this subsequent analysis, in which it purported to consider 'the proceedings as a whole', the Court did not mention the independence or impartiality issue once. Thus, the Court was purporting to analyse the proceedings as a whole while completely leaving out a factor that, on its own analysis, was sufficient *in itself* to render the trial irretrievably unfair.[201] Indeed, there are a number of cases in which the Court reaches a conclusion on alleged independence and impartial violations and then, separately, purports to consider the fairness of the proceedings as a whole without making any reference to its earlier conclusion on independence and impartiality.[202] For this reason, looking at the 'never fair' case law helps to illustrate and emphasise the flawed nature of the way the Court conducts its 'proceedings as a whole' analysis.

E.4.3 The European Court is Inconsistent in Its Use of the 'Never Fair' Formulation

The subsections above have identified, described, and criticised the way the European Court uses the 'never fair' formulation, principally for independence and impartiality violations. The subsections above focused on the 'external' inconsistencies and incoherencies between how the European Court uses 'never fair' on the one hand, and how it uses defect curing, counterbalancing, and the 'proceedings as a whole' test, on the other hand. This subsection turns briefly to the 'internal' inconsistencies and incoherencies between how the Court uses 'never fair' in some cases but not in others. I focus on three case examples in which the Court acknowledged the possibility that independence or impartiality violations might be capable of being counterbalanced or cured and, in so doing,

[198] ibid para 97.

[199] ibid para 98.

[200] ibid para 100.

[201] The European Court concluded that the use of the statements had 'rendered [the applicant's] trial as a whole unfair' and that there had thus been a violation of Art 6(1) and Art 6(3)(c): ibid paras 104–105.

[202] See, eg, *Sadak and others v Turkey* (App 29900/96) (2003) 36 EHRR 26, paras 31–43, [59–69; *Hulki Gunes v Turkey* (App 28490/95) (2006) 42 EHRR 27, paras 80–96; *Ocalan v Turkey* (n 74 above) paras 118–148.

acknowledged the possibility that an independence or impartiality violation might not always render a trial irretrievably unfair.[203]

In *Belilos v Switzerland*, the Court held that 'the applicant could legitimately have doubts as to the independence and organisational impartiality of the Police Board, which accordingly did not satisfy the requirements of [Article 6(1)] in this respect'.[204] In many of the cases discussed above, this would have been sufficient for the Court to conclude that the trial could never be fair. Here, however, the Court went on to state that it 'must satisfy itself that the available forms of appeal made it possible to remedy the deficiencies noted in the proceedings at first instance'.[205] The *Belilos* Court ultimately found a violation of Article 6(1), but *only* because the cantonal and federal appellate proceedings in Switzerland did not provide sufficient safeguards to ameliorate the independence and impartiality violations.[206] For example, in the case of the cantonal court, the Court stated:

> [The Criminal Cassation Division of the Vaud Cantonal Court] also acknowledged that the proceedings before it included neither oral argument nor the taking of evidence by, for example, hearing witnesses . . . These various factors lead to the conclusion that the jurisdiction of the Criminal Cassation Division of the Vaud Cantonal Court was not in the instant case sufficient for the purposes of [Article 6(1)].[207]

Thus, while the *Belilos* Court found a violation, it was plain that there would have been no violation had the Swiss appellate proceedings had additional counterbalancing or defect-curing safeguards.

The second case is *De Haan v Netherlands*, in which the Court considered an independence and impartiality complaint. The Court found that the applicant's 'fears' as to independence and impartiality 'were objectively justified'.[208] Once again, this would have been sufficient to render the trial unfair in many of the cases discussed above. In *De Haan*, however, the Court moved to a further stage of analysis:

> Nonetheless no violation of [Article 6(1)] could be found if the decision of the Appeals Tribunal was subject to subsequent control by a judicial body that had full jurisdiction and did provide the guarantees of Article 6 . . .
>
> However, the possibility exists that a higher or the highest tribunal may, in some circumstances, make reparation for an initial violation of one of the Convention's provisions. The Central Appeals Tribunal had the power to quash the decision appealed against on the ground that the composition of the Appeals Tribunal had not been such as to guarantee its impartiality and to refer the case back to the Appeals Tribunal for

[203] cf Greer, *The European Convention on Human Rights* (n 46 above) 252.

[204] *Belilos v Switzerland* (App 10328/83) (1988) 10 EHRR 466, para 67.

[205] ibid para 68 citing *Ozturk v Germany* (App 8544/79) (21 February 1984) para 56. The relevant passage of *Ozturk* related to curing potential violations of Art 6(3)(e) rather than potential violations of the independence and impartiality guarantees.

[206] *Belilos v Switzerland* (n 204 above) paras 69–73.

[207] ibid para 70. See a similar passage in *Romenskiy v Russia* (App 22875/02) (13 June 2013) paras 18–31 and esp 29; see also Trechsel, *Human Rights in Criminal Proceedings* (n 5 above) 47–48, 56–57.

[208] *De Haan v Netherlands* (App 22839/93) (1998) 26 EHRR 417, para 51.

> rehearing if necessary. However, it declined to do so and, as a consequence, *did not cure the failing* in question.
>
> In conclusion, there has been a violation of [Article 6(1)].[209]

The *De Haan* Court thus explicitly acknowledges that a hearing may be cured of an independence or impartiality violation. The violation here was not cured on these facts, but the possibility was there. This stands in stark contrast to *Ciraklar*, *Ergin (No 6)* and the long list of cases outlined above, in which an independence or impartiality violation meant the proceedings could *never* be fair.

In *Kyprianou*, the Grand Chamber considered an argument that there had been 'a breach of the principle of impartiality' in the domestic trial court, and that the breach had not been rectified by the domestic appellate court. The Court concluded its analysis of this argument in this way:

> [T]he Court shares the Chamber's view that the Supreme Court *did not remedy the defect* in question. The possibility certainly exists that a higher or the highest court might, in some circumstances, make reparation for defects that took place in the first-instance proceedings. In the present case, although the parties disagree as to the precise scope of the powers of the Supreme Court, it is clear that it had the power to quash the decision on the ground that the Limassol Assize Court had not been impartial. However, it declined to do so and upheld the conviction and sentence. As a consequence, it did not cure the failing in question.
>
> In the light of the foregoing and having examined the facts of the case under both the objective and subjective tests enshrined in its case-law, the Court finds that the Limassol Assize Court was not impartial within the meaning of [Article 6(1)].[210]

Very similar suggestions were made in cases such as *Chmelir*, *Ozerov* and *Krivoshapkin*.[211] It is in no way clear that the Court would be able to reconcile these suggestions (that an impartiality violation might be able to be cured by the appellate process) with its often-expressed view that a non-impartial trial can never be fair.

In these examples, therefore, the European Court countenances the possibility that an independence or impartiality violation might be cured or counterbalanced. In each of these cases, the Court reached a tentative conclusion that the independence or impartiality violation had been established, before going on to assess potential counterbalancing or curing factors. It is conceivable that the Court could design an interpretative framework within which some, but not all,

[209] ibid paras 52–54 (emphasis added). See also Trechsel, *Human Rights in Criminal Proceedings* (n 5 above) 75–76.

[210] *Kyprianou v Cyprus* (n 159 above) paras 134–135 (emphasis added) citing *DeCubber v Belgium* (n 158 above) para 33; *Findlay v United Kingdom* (n 175 above) paras 78–79; *De Haan v Netherlands* (n 208 above) paras 52–55; *Guzzardi v Italy* (n 158 above) para 72; *Van Oosterwijck v Belgium* (App 7654/76) (1981) 3 EHRR 557, para 34; *Adolf v Austria* (App 8269/78) (1982) 4 EHRR 313, paras 38–41; *Airey v Ireland* (App 6289/73) (1979–80) 2 EHRR 305, para 18; *De Wilde and others v Belgium* (n 158 above) para 50.

[211] *Chmelir v Czech Republic* (App 64935/01) (2007) 44 EHRR 20, para 68; *Ozerov v Russia* (App 64962/01) (18 May 2010) paras 35, 55–58; *Krivoshapkin v Russia* (n 77 above) paras 37–40, esp para 40.

independence and impartiality violations could be cured or balanced away. It is equally conceivable that the Court could design a framework within which it could not be said that there had been an independence or impartiality violation unless the Court had also checked that violation against potential counterbalancing or curing factors. What is important here is that the Court has given no sign of implementing such a system. Instead, one is left with a distinct impression that the Court adopts an incoherent approach to independence and impartiality violations, and to the circumstances in which it is appropriate to cure defects or counterbalance shortcomings.

E.4.4 Some Inconsistency May be Explained by the Availability of Remedies for Article 6 Violations

In this section, I suggest that one explanation for the European Court's inconsistent approach to its 'never fair' analysis may lie in the way that the European Court has approached remedies available for violations of Article 6.

It is necessary to provide some initial context for this argument. When it comes to remedial measures for violations of the independence and impartiality guarantees, the general trend in the Court's case law has been to embrace the view that 'in principle *the most appropriate remedy would be to retry the applicant* in due course by an independent and impartial tribunal'.[212] In other cases, such as *Ciraklar*, the mere finding of a violation has been found to be a sufficient remedy.[213] It is readily acknowledged that the Court has made statements indicating that it will be flexible in terms of appropriate remedial measures.[214] The point, however, is that there is a clear body of law in favour of retrials and reopening of hearings being the appropriate remedy for independence and impartiality violations. This has the crucial result that, in many cases, there is no compensation awarded on account of the independence and impartiality violation specifically.[215]

How does this approach to remedies interact with the Court's inconsistent and incoherent approach to 'never fair' analysis? As was seen above, in many of the

[212] *Gencel v Turkey* (App 53431/99) (23 October 2003) para 27 (translated) (emphasis added). See also, eg, *Tahir Duran v Turkey* (App 40997/98) (29 January 2004) para 23, citing *Gencel v Turkey* (above) para 27; *Halis v Turkey* (App 30007/96) (11 January 2005) para 49; *YB and others v Turkey* (n 188 above) para 57; *Baran v Turkey* (App 48988/99) (10 November 2004) para 48; *Salduz v Turkey* (n 190 above) para 72; *Gocmen v Turkey* (App 72000/01) (17 October 2006) para 87; *Paraskeva Todorova v Bulgaria* (App 37193/07) (25 March 2010) para 52; *Satik v Turkey (No 2)* (App 60999/00) (8 July 2008) para 74; *Haci Ozen v Turkey* (n 196 above) para 111; *Sejdovic v Italy* (App 56581/00) (1 March 2006) paras 125–128; *Sannino v Italy* (App 30961/03) (2009) 48 EHRR 25, paras 69–71. For more on remedies generally, see I Nifosi-Sutton, 'The Power of the ECHR to Order Specific Non-monetary Relief: a Critical Appraisal from a Right to Health Perspective' (2010) 23 *Harvard HR Journal* 51.

[213] *Ciraklar v Turkey* (n 183 above) para 49.

[214] See, eg, *Scoppola v Italy (No 2)* (App 10249/03) (17 September 2009) paras 150–151; *Assanidze v Georgia* (App 71503/01) (2004) 39 EHRR 32, para 202; *Ocalan v Turkey* (n 74 above) paras 210–12; *Henryk Urban and Ryszard Urban v Poland* (App 23614/08) (30 November 2010) para 64.

[215] Which is not to say that an award is not possible for legal costs and expenses at the domestic level: see, eg, *Grieves v United Kingdom* (App 57067/00) (2004) 39 EHRR 2, paras 94–98.

'never fair' cases, a conclusion that there has been an independence or impartiality violation is sufficient to cut off any further consideration of Article 6 arguments, even where those arguments relate to possible additional violations.[216] When combined with the Court's approach to remedies for independence and impartiality violations, this can mean that applicants who are successful on an independence or impartiality argument may receive a retrial, but not compensation, as a remedy for their Article 6 violation. On the other hand, if the Court conducts its analysis of the independence or impartiality violation in such a way that further Article 6 arguments *may* be considered, then the applicant may have an increased chance of obtaining damages or compensation. The way in which the Court frames its independence or impartiality analysis, therefore, may be crucial to the question of what damages (if any) the applicant will receive. One can see how this plays out by considering two examples.

In *Sahiner*, the European Court first found a reasonable time violation.[217] It then went on to find an independence and impartiality violation.[218] On the point of remedies, the Court stated:

> 51. The Court considers that the finding of a violation in respect of the trial by a tribunal which lacked independence and impartiality constitutes in itself sufficient compensation for any non-pecuniary damage suffered by the applicant. It reiterates that it can award reparation only in respect of its finding that there has been a violation of the Convention as regards the unreasonable length of the criminal proceedings and make its calculation accordingly.
>
> 52. The Court considers that the applicant must have suffered a certain amount of distress, having regard to the total length of the proceedings against him. Deciding on an equitable basis, it awards him the sum of FRF 100,000.[219]

If the Court had analysed the independence and impartiality violation differently – if, for example, it had analysed that violation *before* analysing the reasonable time violation – then arguably under a 'never fair' approach there would have been no need even to *consider* the reasonable time violation.[220] In such a circumstance there may also have been no award of damages.

In *Sadak*, the Court first found an independence and impartiality violation.[221] It then went on to acknowledge that:

> [I]t has already held in previous cases that a court whose lack of independence and impartiality has been established cannot, in any circumstances, guarantee a fair trial to

[216] See, eg, *Ergin v Turkey (No 6)* (n 186 above) paras 55–56; *Funke v France* (App 10828/84) (1993) 16 EHRR 297, paras 38–46; *Kadubec v Slovakia* (App 27061/95) (2001) 33 EHRR 41, paras 54–64; *Gerger v Turkey* (n 188 above) paras 53–65.

[217] *Sahiner v Turkey* (App 29279/95) (25 September 2001) para 30.

[218] ibid para 47.

[219] ibid paras 51–52.

[220] As in *Funke v France* (n 216 above) paras 38–46. For more on reasonable time violations, see Martin Kuijer, 'The Right to a Fair Trial and the Council of Europe's Efforts to Ensure Effective Remedies on a Domestic Level for Excessively Lengthy Proceedings' (2013) 13(4) *Human Rights Law Review* 777.

[221] *Sadak and Ors v Turkey* (n 202 above) para 40.

> the persons subject to its jurisdiction and that, accordingly, it is unnecessary to examine the complaints regarding the fairness of the proceedings before that court.[222]

Nevertheless, in light of 'the particular circumstances of the case', the Court continued to address the applicants' other Article 6 arguments.[223] The Court went on to find additional violations: a violation of Article 6(3)(a) and Article 6(3)(b) together with Article 6(1), and a violation of Article 6(3)(d) together with Article 6(1).[224] Bafflingly, after making those findings the Court decided that it did not need to go any further and consider *other* Article 6 arguments.[225] Why it was necessary to go beyond the independence and impartiality guarantee was unclear to start with; why it was then necessary to go only so far and no farther is entirely puzzling. In any event, the important thing is that the Court chose to frame its analysis in a way that allowed it to consider aspects of Article 6 other than simply the independence and impartiality guarantees. This, in turn, opened remedial doors that may not have been open if the Court had framed its analysis in the usual 'never fair' way. And, in turn, the Court said the following with respect to remedies:

> Whilst it cannot speculate as to the outcome of the trial had the position been otherwise, it does not find it unreasonable to regard the applicants as having suffered a loss of real opportunities . . . To that must be added non-pecuniary damage, which the findings of violations in this judgment do not sufficiently remedy. Making its assessment on an equitable basis as required by Article 41, the Court awards USD 25,000 to each of the four applicants in respect of all heads of damage taken together.[226]

Thus, as one of the 'heads of damage', the independence and impartiality violation contributed towards the non-pecuniary damages awarded to the applicants. Had the analysis been framed in the usual way and had the Court adopted its usual approach to independence and impartiality violations, the applicants would not have received damages.

In these case studies, and in similar cases like *Salov* and *Nestak*,[227] one sees how the incoherence in the Court's analysis manifests itself. The inconsistency has measurable impact in terms of the remedies awarded and capable of being awarded to applicants, and it risks creating the appearance that the European

[222] ibid para 41; cf Trechsel, *Human Rights in Criminal Proceedings* (n 5 above) 217.

[223] The European Court indicated that such consideration was necessary because whether or not there had been a fair trial would affect the Court's findings on Art 10, Art 11 and Art 14. This logic is questionable: by the European Court's own admission, the finding of an impartiality and independence violation should have answered the fair trial question decisively: cf *Sadak and others v Turkey* (n 202 above) para 42.

[224] ibid paras 59, 68. Perhaps unsurprisingly, the second of these violations was notionally based on the fairness of the proceedings as a whole, despite making no reference to the fact that the European Court had already found two violations of the right to a fair trial in these same proceedings: see, eg, para 63.

[225] ibid para 69.

[226] ibid para 77.

[227] *Salov v Ukraine* (App 65518/01) (2007) 45 EHRR 51, paras 78–98, 122; *Nestak v Slovakia* (App 65559/01) (2009) 48 EHRR 20, paras 83, 91, 101, 102, 106; see also *Rudnichenko v Ukraine* (n 77 above) paras 109–110, 119–120.

Court will craft its analytical framework on the basis of pragmatic awarding of damages rather than on the basis of principle.

E.4.5 The 'Never Fair' Jurisprudence Sits Awkwardly with the European Court's Other Approaches to Assessing Violations and is Internally Inconsistent

This section, therefore, has shown how the European Court's use of the 'never fair' analytical tool is flawed: it is inconsistent with other analytical tools used by the Court, and it is applied in a way that lacks detailed or thoughtful explanation of how this analytical method is thought to work.

There is no question that the Court *could* design and adopt a highly calibrated and nuanced analytical framework, in which it treated some violations as warranting a 'never fair' treatment and other violations as warranting a defect-curing or counterbalancing analysis, and offered reasoned explanation for the different approaches. Such a framework has not, however, been identified or articulated by the Court.

E.5 Assessing Whether Certain Evidence was the 'Sole or Decisive' Evidence Against a Defendant Involves a Particularly Opaque Form of Semi-structured Balancing

This section considers a form of semi-structured balancing that the European Court frequently employs in cases concerning the admission and use of evidence. Substantive analysis of how the Court's case law interacts with the domestic law of evidence is beyond the scope of this book.[228] This section's aim is more modest: it aims to chart a semi-structured balancing process used by the Court in assessing alleged violations of this sort. Principally, this section is concerned with how the Court approaches the situations where it is said that the fairness of a trial was compromised in some way by:

- evidence that was obtained in an unlawful way or a way that may not be consistent with the Convention; and/or

[228] See, eg, in the UK context, I Dennis, *The Law of Evidence*, 3rd edn (Sweet & Maxwell, 2007); P Murphy, *Murphy on Evidence*, 10th edn (Oxford University Press, 2008); Colin Tapper, *Cross and Tapper on Evidence*, 12th edn (Oxford University Press, 2010); Mark Coen, 'Hearsay, Bad Character and Trust in the Jury: Irish and English Contrasts' (2013) 17 *International Journal of Evidence and Proof* 250; S Wallace, 'The Empire Strikes Back: Hearsay Rules in Common Law Legal Systems and the Jurisprudence of the ECtHR' [2010] *EHRLR* 408; E Bjorge, 'Exceptionalism and Internationalism in the Supreme Court: *Horncastle* and *Cadder*' (2011) *Public Law* 475; O'Brian, *Confrontation: the Defiance of the English Courts* (n 113 above); CC Murphy, *Human Rights Law and the Challenges of Explicit Judicial Dialogue*, Jean Monnet Working Paper No 10/2012; Mike Redmayne, 'Confronting Confrontation' in P Roberts and J Hunter (eds), *Criminal Evidence and Human Rights* (Hart Publishing, 2012); *R v Horncastle* [2009] UKSC 14, [2010] 2 AC 373; *Al-Khawaja and Tahery v United Kingdom* (Grand Chamber) (n 109 above).

- evidence that was admitted into evidence in an unlawful way or in circumstances that may not be consistent with the Convention.

For the purposes of this section, I refer to these categories of evidence as 'the two categories'. This section argues that the Court's approaches to the two categories have varied considerably and that the result is an opaque semi-structured balancing process that raises a number of concerns in terms of coherence and predictability.

In many Article 6 criminal cases, an applicant alleges that he or she has been denied a fair trial because of the use of evidence from one of the two categories. For a long time, the European Court's response to such allegations involved an assessment of whether the applicant's conviction was based *solely or to a decisive extent* on the evidence from the two categories. If it was, the Court reasoned in a string of cases, there would be a violation of the Article 6(1) fair hearing guarantee, or of one of the relevant specific Article 6 guarantees. Among the earliest cases to use this form of reasoning were the Court's 1986 decision in *Unterpertinger* and its 1988 decision in *Schenk*.[229] In *Schenk*, for example, the Court stated that it:

> [A]ttaches weight to the fact that the recording of the telephone conversation was *not the only evidence on which the conviction was based.* The Rolle Criminal Court . . . carefully stated in several passages of its judgment that it relied on evidence other than the recording but which corroborated the reasons based on the recording for concluding that Mr. Schenk was guilty.[230]

The European Court went on to conclude that, assessing the fairness of the proceedings as a whole, the use of the relevant 'two categories' evidence in this case 'did not deprive the applicant of a fair trial and therefore did not contravene' Article 6(1).[231] Perhaps the most often-quoted articulation of this approach came in *Van Mechelen*: 'a conviction should not be based either solely or to a decisive extent on anonymous statements'.[232] Versions of this approach were quoted and applied in a long string of cases.[233] In effect, it appears to hold that fair trial concerns are raised when a conviction is based solely or to a decisive extent on evidence from the two categories.[234] In cases where there is other evidence, there will

[229] See *Unterpertinger v Austria* (App 9120/80) (1991) 13 EHRR 175, para 33; *Schenk v Switzerland* (App 10862/84) (1991) 13 EHRR 242, para 48. Searches did not reveal any earlier examples. See also O'Brian, *Confrontation: the Defiance of the English Courts* (n 113 above).

[230] *Schenk v Switzerland* (n 229 above) para 48 (emphasis added).

[231] ibid para 49; see also para 46.

[232] *Van Mechelen and others v Netherlands* (n 69 above) para 55; see also paras 63–66. *Van Mechelen* cited *Doorson v Netherlands* (n 118 above) para 76.

[233] For example, *Saidi v France* (App 14647/89) (1994) 17 EHRR 251, para 44; *Bernard v France* (n 106 above) paras 40–41; *AM v Italy* (n 81 above) paras 25–28; *Luca v Italy* (n 84 above) paras 40–45; *Solakov v FYROM* (n 87 above) para 57; *Visser v Netherlands* (n 68 above) paras 43–46; *Hulki Gunes v Turkey* (n 202 above) paras 86, 96; *Kollcaku v Italy* (n 77 above) para 70; *Panasenko v Portugal* (App 10418/03) (22 July 2008) paras 57–58; *Shabelnik v Ukraine* (App 16404/03) (19 February 2009) para 59.

[234] For an important consideration of the sole and decisive rule, which situates the rule in a slightly different way to that adopted in this book, see Hoyano, 'What is Balanced on the Scales of Justice?' (n 10 above).

be less of a concern.[235] Until recently, the Court had provided little articulation of what it means by 'solely or to a decisive extent', or of the rationale for such a rule.[236] While the decision in *Al-Khawaja and Tahery* recently provided some exploration of the rule,[237] it will be shown that that decision did not resolve certain key ambiguities.

But the approach of the European Court in cases like *Schenk* and *Van Mechelen* is only part of the story. Indeed, in two significant ways, the Court has complicated the position.

First, the European Court has given a number of indications that a conviction *may*, in fact, be based solely or to a decisive extent on evidence from the two categories, provided that the evidence in question is particularly strong and reliable. Thus, in *Khan* the Court stated:

> The Court next notes that the contested material in the present case *was in effect the only evidence against the applicant* and that the applicant's plea of guilty was tendered only on the basis of the judge's ruling that the evidence should be admitted. However, the relevance of the existence of evidence other than the contested matter depends on the circumstances of the case. In the present circumstances, *where the tape recording was acknowledged to be very strong evidence, and where there was no risk of it being unreliable, the need for supporting evidence is correspondingly weaker.* It is true that, in the case of *Schenk*, weight was attached by the Court to the fact that the tape recording at issue in that case was not the only evidence against the applicant. However, the Court notes in this regard that the recording in the *Schenk* case, although not the only evidence, was described by the Criminal Cassation Division of the Vaud Cantonal Court as having 'a perhaps decisive influence, or at the least a not inconsiderable one, on the outcome of the criminal proceedings'. Moreover, this element was not the determining factor in the Court's conclusion.[238]

The European Court went on to find that 'the secretly taped material did not conflict with the requirements of fairness guaranteed by' Article 6(1).[239] Even leaving aside the Court's torturous attempt to dismiss *Schenk*,[240] it may be noted that the

[235] Including, extraordinarily, in a case where a confession was obtained by inhuman and degrading treatment in violation of Art 3, but was only one piece of evidence and was counterbalanced by other factors: *Alchagin v Russia* (n 189 above) paras 69–74.

[236] cf Summers, *Fair Trials* (n 14 above) 139.

[237] *Al-Khawaja and Tahery v United Kingdom* (Grand Chamber) (n 109 above) paras 126–147.

[238] *Khan v United Kingdom* (App 35394/97) (2001) 31 EHRR 45, para 37 (emphasis added); Trechsel, *Human Rights in Criminal Proceedings* (n 5 above) 113.

[239] *Khan v United Kingdom* (n 238 above) para 40; cp the Partly Concurring, Partly Dissenting Opinion of Judge Loucaides: 'This is the first case which comes before the Court where the only evidence against an accused in a criminal case which also led to his conviction was evidence secured in a manner contrary to the provisions of Article 8 of the Convention'.

[240] There are two prongs to the *Khan* Court's attempt to dismiss *Schenk*. First, *Khan* argues that, regardless of what the *Schenk* judgment actually said, the case involved the use of a questionable piece of evidence where that evidence was the decisive basis for the conviction. *Khan*'s proof of this lies in the judgment of the Swiss domestic court ('perhaps decisive') in the *Schenk* case rather than the judgment of the European Court itself. In so doing, *Khan* ignores the text of the *Schenk* European Court judgment, which plainly states: 'It emerges clearly . . . that the criminal court took account of a combination of evidential elements before reaching its opinion': *Schenk v Switzerland* (n 229 above) para 48. This reasoning in *Khan* is clumsy at best. Secondly, *Khan* argues that the relevant discussion in *Schenk* 'was

reasoning used in *Khan* fundamentally undermines the rule articulated by *Van Mechelen* and outlined above. This undermining continued in cases citing *Khan*, such as *Allan*. By the time of *Allan*, decided two and a half years after *Khan*, the rule had become radically different to that outlined in *Van Mechelen*:

> While *no problem of fairness necessarily arises where the evidence obtained was unsupported by other material*, it may be noted that where the evidence is very strong and there is no risk of its being unreliable, the need for supporting evidence is correspondingly weaker.[241]

This approach has created a group of cases that runs parallel to those identified above as citing the *Schenk-Van Mechelen* rule: the *Khan-Allan* rule is quoted and applied in *Jalloh*, *Galstyan*, *Yaremento*, *Satik (No 2)*, *Panovits*, *Bykov*, *Gafgen*, and *AS v Finland*.[242] Over the last decade, therefore, the Court has been issuing decisions offering two very different versions of how best to analyse the fairness of a trial in which use has been made of evidence from the two categories. Of course, if the Court wants to have different rules for different types of evidence, or for different Article 6 rights, it may do so. But given that the two lines of cases sprang from the same roots, use extremely similar language, and attempt to solve similar problems, the interests of predictability and clarity demand that the Court explain why one rule is applicable to one class of case and the other rule is applicable to another class, and the logical reason why one of the two lines of case could not cover all situations. The current two-track approach risks the appearance that the Court might pick whichever line of cases best suits its view and reason backward from that.

Regrettably, whatever else it may have resolved, the decision in *Al-Khawaja and Tahery* did little to resolve this uncertainty.[243] The key conclusion of *Al-Khawaja and Tahery* relevant to this point was:

> [T]hat, where a hearsay statement is the sole or decisive evidence against a defendant, its admission as evidence will not automatically result in a breach of Article 6(1). At the

not the determining factor in the [*Schenk*] Court's conclusion'. Even if we accept that this is a legitimate interpretative tool for the *Khan* Court to deploy, it is not clear the *Schenk* judgment reflects *Khan*'s analysis on this point either: the relevant passage constituted fully *half* of the *Schenk* application of law to the facts, and was the last thing discussed before the Court reached its conclusion: ibid para 48. The reasoning in this passage of *Khan* is disingenuous.

[241] *Allan v United Kingdom* (n 88 above) para 43 (emphasis added) citing *Khan v United Kingdom* (n 238 above) para 37. In at least one admissibility decision, the European Court went so far as to suggest that, even where a conviction was based decisively on anonymous evidence, it could be counterbalanced: *Ellis and Simms v United Kingdom (Admissibility)* (App 46099/06) (10 April 2012) paras 81–89.

[242] *Jalloh v Germany* (n 77 above) para 96; *Galstyan v Armenia* (App 26986/03) (2010) 50 EHRR 25, para 77; *Yaremenko v Ukraine* (App 32092/02)) (12 June 2008) para 76; *Satik v Turkey (No 2)* (n 212 above) para 55; *Panovits v Cyprus* (App 4268/04) (11 December 2008) para 82; *Bykov v Russia* (n 55 above) para 90; *Gafgen v Germany* (Grand Chamber) (n 189 above) para 164; *AS v Finland* (App 40156/07) (28 September 2010) para 52.

[243] For a discussion of *Al-Khawaja and Tahery v United Kingdom* (Grand Chamber) (n 109 above) including possible political motivations for the decision, see C Gearty, 'Al-Khawaja and Tahery v United Kingdom', *UK Constitutional Law Group Blog* (9 January 2012), http://ukconstitutionallaw.org/2012/01/09/conor-gearty-al-khawaja-and-tahery-v-united-kingdom/.

> same time where a conviction is based solely or decisively on the evidence of absent witnesses, the Court must subject the proceedings to the most searching scrutiny . . . The question in each case is whether there are sufficient counterbalancing factors in place, including measures that permit a fair and proper assessment of the reliability of that evidence to take place. This would permit a conviction to be based on such evidence only if it is sufficiently reliable given its importance in the case.[244]

In short, this approach seems like a watered-down version of the *Schenk-Van Mechelen* rule, albeit a version in tension with the oft-cited passage from *Van Mechelen* excerpted above. Frustratingly, the *Al-Khawaja and Tahery* Court does not refer to, or acknowledge the existence of, the *Khan-Allan* rule. Even if the *Al-Khawaja and Tahery* approach could be seen as the adoption of a compromise path between the *Schenk-Van Mechelen* rule and the *Khan-Allan* rule, the *Al-Khawaja and Tahery* Court risks generating uncertainty by neglecting to acknowledge or discuss these cases in any depth. One is thus left with uncertainty as to whether *Al-Khawaja and Tahery* was an attempt to reconcile the rules, or acts as a third class of rule to operate alongside the earlier rules.

Second, in a thematically related line of argument, the European Court has complicated the position with respect to the silence and self-incrimination guarantees. This issue arises on the basis that the Court regards the silence and self-incrimination guarantees as non-absolute. The formulation reached in *John Murray*, and adopted in subsequent decisions, is two-fold. First, it states that:

> On the one hand, it is self-evident that it is incompatible with the immunities under consideration to base a conviction solely or mainly on the accused's silence or on a refusal to answer questions or to give evidence himself.[245]

Having outlined a circumstance in which silence may *not* be used against an accused, the Court then went on to outline a situation in which silence *could* be used:

> On the other hand, the Court deems it equally obvious that these immunities cannot and should not prevent that the accused's silence, in situations which clearly call for an explanation from him, be taken into account in assessing the persuasiveness of the evidence adduced by the prosecution.[246]

Two points should be made here. First, this dichotomy of 'two extremes'[247] is a false dichotomy. The Court's framework does not contemplate the possibility that

[244] *Al-Khawaja and Tahery v United Kingdom* (Grand Chamber) (n 109 above) para 147. See Hoyano, 'What is Balanced on the Scales of Justice?' (n 10 above); Redmayne, 'Confronting Confrontation' (n 228 above); and subsequent applications of this formulation in, eg, *Kostecki v Poland* (n 130 above) para 62; *Rosin v Estonia* (App 26540/08) (19 December 2013) para 54.

[245] *John Murray v United Kingdom* (n 16 above) para 47. See also Harris, O'Boyle and Warbrick, *Law of the European Convention on Human Rights* (n 5 above) 261–62; van Dijk and van Hoof, *Theory and Practice of the European Convention on Human Rights* (n 5 above) 594; Trechsel, *Human Rights in Criminal Proceedings* (n 5 above) 345–46, 356–68; Andrew Ashworth, 'Self-Incrimination in European Human Rights Law: a Pregnant Pragmatism?' (2008) 30 *Cardozo Law Review* 751, 753–55.

[246] *John Murray v United Kingdom* (n 16 above) para 47. Ashworth discusses this passage, for different purposes: Ashworth, 'Self-Incrimination in European Human Rights Law' (n 245 above) 755.

[247] *John Murray v United Kingdom* (n 16 above) para 47.

the accused might wish to remain silent in a situation which 'clearly call[s] for an explanation' *and* where taking that silence into account in assessing the prosecution evidence might be crucial to the conviction of the accused. What should domestic courts do in a situation where the accused's conduct 'clearly call[s] for an explanation', but where there is little or no other evidence against the accused? Outlining the framework in this way does not provide the boundaries of the guarantees; it merely renders those guarantees more opaque. Second, it should not go unnoticed that the Court's reasoning in this passage is based on what is 'obvious'. No further explanation is offered. The interests of predictability require more than this sort of simple assertion: as Alexy put it in a different context, relying on what is 'obvious' risks degenerating into 'rationally uncontrollable' answers and 'intuitionism'.[248] Moreover, there must be considerable doubt as to whether it is in any way 'obvious' that the right to silence or the privilege against self-incrimination mean that accused persons should sometimes be required to speak. Apart from anything else, this doubt is reflected in the uncertainty in the Court's own case law as to whether or not the silence and self-incrimination guarantees are absolute.[249]

Notwithstanding these flaws, the *John Murray* passage has been 'recalled' in cases such as *O'Halloran and Francis*, *Condron*, and *Al-Khawaja and Tahery*.[250] Importantly, the 'on the other hand' principle outlined in this passage opens the door to a balancing exercise in which the nature of the evidence is weighed against the strength of the case against the applicant. The structure of that balancing exercise goes undefined, other than to say that it should be 'determined in light of all the circumstances of the case'.[251] To the extent that *Al-Khawaja and Tahery* elaborated upon such a balancing exercise, it was simply to state that it would 'weigh in the balance the competing interests of the defence, the victim, and witnesses, and the public interest in the effective administration of justice'.[252]

The European Court's use of balancing in the context of the silence and self-incrimination guarantees is also evident in its statements that the guarantees did not prevent people from being asked a question where the answer to that question was 'a simple fact . . . which is not in itself incriminating'. This suggestion, outlined in cases including *Weh*, *Rieg*, and *O'Halloran*, has been criticised by Ashworth as 'unsatisfactory'.[253] Moreover, simply put, such an approach is inconsistent with the Court's rhetoric on the silence and self-incrimination guarantees.

[248] Alexy, *A Theory of Constitutional Rights* (n 1 above) 73.

[249] cf *Saunders v United Kingdom* (n 16 above) paras 68–69, 74; *John Murray v United Kingdom* (n 16 above) paras 46–47.

[250] *O'Halloran and Francis v United Kingdom* (App 15809/02) (2008) 46 EHRR 21, para 46; *Condron v United Kingdom* (n 163 above) para 56; *Al-Khawaja and Tahery v United Kingdom* (Grand Chamber) (n 109 above) para 138.

[251] A formulation perilously close to the 'proceedings as a whole' formulation that is addressed at E.2.

[252] *Al-Khawaja and Tahery v United Kingdom* (Grand Chamber) (n 109 above) para 146.

[253] Ashworth, 'Self-Incrimination in European Human Rights Law' (n 245 above) 771. See *Weh v Austria* (App 38544/97) (2005) 40 EHRR 37, para 54; ibid para 54; *Rieg v Austria* (App 63207/00) (24 March 2005) para 31.

It is difficult to reconcile the notion that simple questions can be asked in order to assist the prosecution with the rhetoric used by the Court:

> 39. . . . The right not to incriminate oneself in particular presupposes that the prosecution in a criminal case seek to prove their case against the accused without resort to evidence obtained through methods of coercion or oppression in defiance of the will of the accused. In this sense the right in question is closely linked to the presumption of innocence contained in [Article 6(2)].
>
> 40. The right not to incriminate oneself is primarily concerned with respecting the will of an accused person to remain silent.[254]

In allowing the use of 'simple facts', the Court plainly and unashamedly assists the 'prosecution in a criminal case' to 'prove their case against the accused' with 'resort to evidence obtained through methods of coercion or oppression in defiance of the will of the accused'. It involves *not* respecting the accused's will to remain silent. This is strikingly incoherent and inconsistent. A broadly similar narrowing of the guarantees' protection was evident in *Grayson and Barnham*:

> 49. . . . it was not unreasonable to expect the applicants to explain what had happened to all the money shown by the prosecution to have been in their possession . . . Such matters fell within the applicants' particular knowledge and the burden on each of them would not have been difficult to meet if their accounts of their financial affairs had been true.
>
> 50. There has, therefore, been no violation of [Article 6(1)].[255]

By 'expect[ing] the applicants to explain' and effectively compelling them to provide 'matters . . . within the applicants' particular knowledge', the Court facilitates precisely that which it purports to prevent: the prosecution being able to compel or require an accused person to aid their own prosecution. This incoherence is troubling. The Court ought either to adopt less dramatic rhetoric about the importance of the silence and self-incrimination guarantees and explain how a more limited guarantee is in keeping with Article 6; or it ought to adopt an approach to Article 6 that practices what it preaches. As it stands, an unexplained and unprincipled balancing process undermines the coherence of the Court's case law.

E.6 The European Court is Inconsistent in Approaching the Extent to Which the Public Interest May Justify a Restriction on Article 6

So far this part has looked at unstructured and semi-structured methods with which the European Court has sought to analyse alleged violations of Article 6,

[254] *Weh v Austria* (n 253 above) paras 39–40.
[255] *Grayson and Barnham v United Kingdom* (n 134 above) paras 49–50.

and has demonstrated inconsistency between those methods and within those methods. In this section I consider directly the extent to which the Court has regarded the public interest as capable of justifying restrictions on Article 6 rights. The role of the public interest in these cases is used to explore the Court's attempts to conduct structured balancing or proportionality analysis in Article 6 cases. It will be demonstrated in this section that at times the European Court has embraced such balancing enthusiastically in the Article 6 context, and at other times has forbidden it.[256] Of course, balancing and proportionality can be deployed in other contexts too (and this section touches on one such context) but it is analysis of public interest balancing that provides particularly useful insights into the Court's case law.[257] As Stumer put it in another context, the concern here is with 'attempts to limit Article 6 rights by reference to the community interest'.[258]

Thus this section examines the instances in which the European Court has directly or indirectly utilised proportionality as an analytical tool in Article 6 cases. It is worth explaining what I mean here by 'proportionality'. There are various competing definitions for proportionality as an analytical tool, and considerable scholarly discussion in the literature about when proportionality should be used and how any proportionality inquiry should be structured.[259] Thinking about proportionality generally, the literature identifies differences between, for example, 'rigorously applied' heavily-structured proportionality analysis, on the one hand, and more opaque 'broad-brush' balancing.[260] In the Article 6 context, however, the boundaries between these different forms are more slippery.[261] Indeed, as has been seen, the central puzzle of Article 6 is how to resolve alleged violations of Article 6 and, as part of that puzzle, there is uncertainty about the appropriateness of using proportionality or balancing *at all* in the Article 6

[256] Compare below, eg, the discussion at E.6.1 with the discussion at E.6.3 and E.6.4.

[257] See E.6.2 for the other context.

[258] Andrew C Stumer, *The Presumption of Innocence* (Hart Publishing, 2010) 110.

[259] See, eg, Rivers, 'Proportionality and Variable Intensity of Review' (n 2 above); Alexy, *A Theory of Constitutional Rights* (n 1 above); Greer, *The European Convention on Human Rights* (n 46 above); Möller, *The Global Model of Constitutional Rights* (n 10 above) 178–205, and esp 180–81; Brady, *Proportionality and Deference under the UK HRA* (n 10 above); T Hickman, 'Proportionality: Comparative Law Lessons' (2007) *Judicial Review* 31; Mark Elliott, *Proportionality and Deference: the Importance of a Structured Approach*, Cambridge Legal Studies Research Paper Series Paper No 32/2013/; A Mowbray, 'A Study of the Principle of Fair Balance in the Jurisprudence of the ECtHR' (2010) 10 *Human Rights Law Review* 289; Jeremy McBride, 'Proportionality and the European Convention on Human Rights' in Evelyn Ellis (ed), *The Principle of Proportionality in the Laws of Europe* (Hart Publishing, 1999); L Lazarus, B Goold and G Swiney, *Public Protection, Proportionality, and the Search for Balance*, Ministry of Justice Research Series 10/07 (2007); G Letsas, 'Rescuing Proportionality' in Rowan Cruft and Massimo Renzo (eds), *Philosophical Foundations of Human Rights* (Oxford University Press, 2013); E Thomas Sullivan and Richard S Frase, *Proportionality Principles in American Law* (Oxford University Press, 2008); Christoffersen, *Fair Balance* (n 17 above) 33–35, 69–76; Jeremy Waldron, 'Security and Liberty: the Image of Balance' (2003) (11)2 *Journal of Political Philosophy* 191; Alexander Green, 'A Philosophical Taxonomy of European Human Rights Law' [2012] *EHRLR* 71; Nicolas Croquet, 'The Right to Self-representation under the ECHR: What Role for the Limitation Analysis?' [2012] *EHRLR* 292.

[260] For a useful overview, see Lazarus, Goold and Swiney, *Public Protection, Proportionality, and the Search for Balance* (n 259 above) 1–2.

[261] ibid 29–34.

context. As such, when I refer to proportionality or balancing in this section those terms are being used as shorthand for the idea expressed by Stumer above, rather than to any particular technical meaning.

Thus, the goal of this section is to identify elements of reasoning in Article 6 cases that involve attempts to limit Article 6 rights by reference to the community interest: cases that explicitly or implicitly reflect reasoning found in proportionality analysis. A reference to 'explicitly' reflecting proportionality reasoning means cases in which the parties or the Court have directly assessed an application at least partially by using proportionality. A reference to implicitly reflecting proportionality, on the other hand, refers to cases in which the Court uses forms of argument and analysis commonly used in proportionality analysis: for example, this section reviews many cases in which the Court assesses to what extent pressing societal needs and problems are relevant when it assesses whether a particular restriction on Article 6 rights is justifiable.

Some authors appear to unquestioningly accept the application of proportionality in the Article 6 context,[262] but, as will be shown in this section, the case law is much more complex. Indeed, this part demonstrates that, in many cases, the European Court is firmly against the use of public interest arguments in any sort of proportionality or balancing analysis. It then contrasts those cases with a series of cases in which the Court has been willing to 'balance away' Article 6 rights as part of a proportionality-style analysis. This part then turns to a series of cases in which the Court performs public interest balancing but places constraints and limits on its applicability, before turning to a series of cases in which those limits are undermined or disregarded. In this section, as in previous sections in this part, I argue that the use of these techniques to assess potential violations of Article 6 has been inconsistent, but also internally incoherent. My argument is that these cases reflect deep uncertainty about whether public interest concerns, filtered through a proportionality or balancing framework, are relevant in assessing Article 6 violations. More broadly, in making these arguments, this section also advances the two macro-arguments of internal incoherence and inconsistency with other analytical tools.

E.6.1 In Many Cases the European Court is Firmly Against the Use of Public Interest Arguments

There are many cases in which the European Court has rejected the use of public interest balancing arguments in assessing Article 6 violations. In these cases, the

[262] van Dijk and van Hoof, *Theory and Practice of the European Convention on Human Rights* (n 5 above) 573; and, with respect to implied rights specifically, Clayton and Tomlinson, *Fair Trial Rights* (n 5 above) 121. Others accept this with regret: Hoyano, 'What is Balanced on the Scales of Justice?' (n 10 above) 6. Note that, as will be seen below, the European Court has on occasion used the language of 'proportionality' itself (eg *Poitrimol v France* (App 14032/88) (1994) 18 EHRR 130, para 38; *Khalfaoui v France* (App 34791/97) (2001) 31 EHRR 42, para 39; *Ong v France* (App 348/03) (14 November 2006) para 43).

Court has resisted government arguments that restrictions on Article 6 could be justified in the name of some broader societal policy interest through the use of some sort of proportionality-style analysis.[263]

In *Kostovski v Netherlands*, for example, the Dutch government argued 'that case-law and practice in the Netherlands in the matter of anonymous evidence stemmed from an increase in the intimidation of witnesses and were based on a balancing of the interests of society, the accused and the witnesses'.[264] The Court stated that it did not

> underestimate the importance of the struggle against organised crime. Yet the Government's line of argument, whilst not without force, is not decisive. Although the growth in organised crime doubtless demands the introduction of appropriate measures, the Government's submissions appear to the Court to lay insufficient weight on what the applicant's counsel described as 'the interest of everybody in a civilised society in a controllable and fair judicial procedure'. The right to a fair administration of justice holds so prominent a place in a democratic society that it cannot be sacrificed to expediency.[265]

As such, the European Court rejected Dutch attempts to diminish the applicant's rights in the name of the public interest, and found a violation of Article 6(3)(d) taken together with Article 6(1).[266]

Then, in *Funke v France*, the European Court rejected the notion that the 'special features of customs law' could justify a measure placing restrictions on Article 6 guarantees:[267] an infringement of the silence and self-incrimination guarantees could not be justified by the public interest in maintaining a customs regime. It is worth noting, however, the reasoning of the Commission in the same case. The Commission, by a majority of seven to five, had concluded there was *no* violation of Article 6: the Commission could not 'choose to ignore the special character of inquiries of an economic and financial nature', especially given the authorities' 'aim of protecting the country's vital economic interests'. [268] The Commission described the Convention system as characterised by '*an inherent balance* between the legitimate interests of the community, on the one hand, and the individual rights it protects on the other'.[269] Its reasoning, ultimately rejected by the European Court, thus represented a rather different vision of Article 6.

[263] See Greer, *The European Convention on Human Rights* (n 46 above) 248; Ashworth, *Human Rights, Serious Crime and Criminal Procedure* (n 131 above) 69; cf Hoyano, 'What is Balanced on the Scales of Justice?' (n 10 above).

[264] *Kostovski v Netherlands* (n 59 above) para 44. See Greer, *The European Convention on Human Rights* (n 46 above) 252.

[265] *Kostovski v Netherlands* (n 59 above) para 44, citing *Ciulla v Italy* (App 16839/90) (1991) 13 EHRR 346, para 41. In *Ciulla*, the European Court rejected the use of public interest arguments on the basis of its past rulings that 'the exhaustive list of permissible exceptions in [Art 5(1)] must be interpreted strictly'.

[266] It may be noted, however, that the *Kostovski* Court (n 59 above) at para 44 characterised the government's argument as being 'not without force'.

[267] *Funke v France* (n 216 above) para 44.

[268] ibid para 35 of the European Court's judgment, quoting paras 63–64 of the Commission's decision.

[269] ibid para 35 of the European Court's judgment, quoting paras 63–64 of the Commission's decision (emphasis added).

Similar issues were raised in *Saidi v France.* The applicant argued that he had been denied a fair trial because he had been unable to confront witnesses who had given evidence against him. Their evidence had been the sole evidence against the applicant. In finding a violation of Article 6(1) and Article 6(3)(d), the Court stated that it was

> fully aware of the undeniable difficulties of the fight against drug-trafficking – in particular with regard to obtaining and producing evidence – and of the ravages caused to society by the drug problem, but such considerations cannot justify restricting to this extent the rights of the defence of 'everyone charged with a criminal offence'.[270]

Notably, while the *Saidi* Court rejects reasoning on the basis of broader societal interests, its language ('cannot justify restricting *to this extent*') suggests that there is at least a possibility that considerations of the difficulties of the fight against drug-trafficking may justify restricting the rights of the defence *to a lesser extent.* A firm statement rejecting government arguments along these lines came in *Saunders v United Kingdom,* where the Court stated that it did not

> accept the Government's argument that the complexity of corporate fraud and the vital public interest in the investigation of such fraud and the punishment of those responsible could justify such a marked departure . . . from one of the basic principles of a fair procedure . . . the general requirements of fairness contained in Article 6, including the right not to incriminate oneself, apply to criminal proceedings in respect of all types of criminal offences without distinction from the most simple to the most complex.[271]

This passage is a clear statement that the assessment of the public interest, and the nature of the particular crime, will have no impact on the extent of Article 6 guarantees.

A similar rejection of these sorts of public interest arguments came in *Teixeira de Castro v Portugal,* where the European Court rejected an argument that evidence obtained as a result of police incitement could be justified by the public interest:

> The use of undercover agents must be restricted and safeguards put in place even in cases concerning the fight against drug trafficking. While the rise in organised crime undoubtedly requires that appropriate measures be taken, the right to a fair administration of justice nevertheless holds such a prominent place that it cannot be sacrificed for the sake of expedience. The general requirements of fairness embodied in Article 6 apply to proceedings concerning all types of criminal offence, from the most straightforward to the most complex. The public interest cannot justify the use of evidence obtained as a result of police incitement.[272]

[270] *Saidi v France* (n 233 above) para 44.

[271] *Saunders v United Kingdom* (n 16 above) para 74. See Lord Hoffman, 'The Universality of Human Rights' (Judicial Studies Board Annual Lecture, 19 March 2009) paras 27–29; Trechsel, *Human Rights in Criminal Proceedings* (n 5 above) 342; van Dijk and van Hoof, *Theory and Practice of the European Convention on Human Rights* (n 5 above) 593.

[272] *Teixeira de Castro v Portugal* (App 25829/94) (1999) 28 EHRR 101, para 36. See also Andrew Ashworth, 'The Exclusion of Evidence Obtained by Violating a Fundamental Right: Pragmatism before Principle in the Strasbourg Jurisprudence' in P Roberts and J Hunter (eds), *Criminal Evidence and Human Rights* (Hart Publishing, 2012).

The Court has referred to this passage in subsequent cases, such as in *Edwards and Lewis v United Kingdom*.[273]

Further, the European Court has repeatedly indicated that concerns over national security or terrorism are incapable of justifying restrictions of Article 6. In *Hulki Gunes v Turkey*, for example, the Court stated that it was

> fully aware of the undeniable difficulties of combating terrorism – in particular with regard to obtaining and producing evidence – and of the ravages caused to society by this problem, but considers that *such factors cannot justify* restricting to this extent the rights of the defence of any person charged with a criminal offence.[274]

The *Hulki Gunes* Court found a violation of Article 6(1) and Article 6(3)(d). Similarly, in *Heaney and McGuinness v Ireland* and *Shannon v United Kingdom*, the European Court was unwilling to accept the notion that the security context justified a restriction on the Article 6 silence and self-incrimination guarantees. It stated in *Shannon* that:

> The Court recalls that in *Heaney and McGuinness* it found that the security context of the relevant provision in that case could not justify a provision which 'extinguishes the very essence of the . . . right to silence and . . . right not to incriminate [oneself]' . . . The security context – the special problems of investigating crime in Northern Ireland – cannot justify the application of the 1996 Order in the present case any more than could that in *Heaney and McGuinness*.[275]

The *Shannon* Court found a violation of Article 6(1). It should be noted that in these cases, the Court indicated that national security efforts could not justify restrictions 'to this extent'[276] and that national security efforts could not justify restrictions extinguishing 'the very essence' of the right.[277] I will return to the effect of these qualifications later in this section.

This general approach extends even to the most serious crimes. In *Papon v France*, the applicant had been convicted of 'offences that constituted crimes against humanity'; he argued that the French Code of Criminal Procedure had the effect of interfering with his right of access to a court under Article 6.[278] The Court stated once again that any limitation of the right to a court must not impair 'the very essence of the right' and that there must be 'a reasonable relationship of proportionality' between the measure and a legitimate aim (which will be returned to below).[279] And yet the Court rejected an argument based on the proportionality of the measure relative to the seriousness of the offence:

[273] *Edwards and Lewis v United Kingdom* (n 125 above) para 49.

[274] *Hulki Gunes v Turkey* (n 202 above) para 96 (emphasis added); cp *Saidi v France* (n 233 above) para 44.

[275] *Shannon v United Kingdom* (App 6563/03) (2006) 42 EHRR 31, para 38. See also *Heaney and McGuinness v Ireland* (App 34720/97) (2001) 33 EHRR 12, paras 56–58.

[276] *Hulki Gunes v Turkey* (n 202 above) para 96.

[277] *Shannon v United Kingdom* (n 275 above) para 38.

[278] *Papon v France* (App 54210/00) (2004) 39 EHRR 10, paras 71, 84.

[279] ibid para 90.

> As to the Government's argument based on the extreme seriousness of the offences of which the applicant stood accused, the Court does not overlook the fact. However, the fact that the applicant was prosecuted for and convicted of aiding and abetting crimes against humanity does not deprive him of the guarantee of his rights and freedoms under the Convention.[280]

If the seriousness of the offence was not relevant to assessing the proportionality of a restriction when the offences were *crimes against humanity*, then the *Papon* Court is making a firm statement about its reluctance to take into account public interest considerations. As the *Salduz* Court put it more recently, 'it is in the face of the heaviest penalties that respect for the right to a fair trial is to be ensured to the highest possible degree by democratic societies'.[281] Such statements are, perhaps, of particular significance in an age when many governments might find such public interest arguments attractive.[282]

In its decision in *Ramanauskas*, regarded as 'the leading authority on entrapment',[283] the Court included this emphatic passage:

> While the rise in organised crime requires that appropriate measures be taken, the right to a fair trial, from which the requirement of the proper administration of justice is to be inferred, nevertheless applies to all types of criminal offence, from the most straightforward to the most complex. *The right to the fair administration of justice holds so prominent a place in a democratic society that it cannot be sacrificed for the sake of expedience.* Furthermore, while the use of undercover agents may be tolerated provided that it is subject to clear restrictions and safeguards, *the public interest cannot justify the use of evidence obtained as a result of police incitement*, as to do so would expose the accused to the risk of being definitively deprived of a fair trial from the outset.[284]

Thus, the Court again adopted a robust view of the extent to which public interest considerations are relevant to determining the level of protection afforded by Article 6.

This section, therefore, has examined a significant number of cases in which the European Court refuses to allow the public interest to be used as a justification for restrictions on Article 6 rights.[285] In attempting to solve the puzzle created by Article 6's lack of an express meta-principle for analysing infringements, these

[280] ibid para 98 citing *Koch v Germany* (Commission) (App 1270/61) (8 March 1962).

[281] *Salduz v Turkey* (n 190 above) para 50; see also, eg, *Oulahcene v France* (App 44446/10) (10 October 2013) para 43.

[282] See, for analysis of such trends, eg, Waldron, 'Security and Liberty' (n 60 above); C Gearty, *Civil Liberties* (Oxford University Press, 2007) 30–58.

[283] Harris, O'Boyle and Warbrick, *Law of the European Convention on Human Rights* (n 5 above) 264–65.

[284] *Ramanauskas v Lithuania* (App 74420/02) [2008] Crim LR 639, paras 53–54 (emphasis added). Note the discussion of the 'democratic catchphrase' at A.6, and that, picking up on the arguments made in that part, it might not be entirely clear here whether this rejection of expediency applies only to rights that hold such a 'prominent place', and, for that matter, precisely which Convention rights do *not* hold a prominent place in a democratic society.

[285] Further recent examples include *Hanzevacki v Croatia* (n 52 above) para 23; *Aleksandr Zaichenko v Russia* (n 77 above) para 39; *Bannikova v Russia* (App 18757/06) (4 November 2010) paras 33–35; *Erkapic v Croatia* (App 51198/08) (25 April 2013) para 73 (adopting an unusual interpretation of *Jalloh v Germany* (n 77 above)).

cases provide a clear and emphatic statement: the public interest cannot justify Article 6 restrictions. But, as will be seen in subsequent sections of this part, the statement has not been applied consistently.

E.6.2 The European Court's Case Law Allowing Balancing of Rights in Cases Involving Vulnerable Witnesses is Poorly Explained

In general, this part's analysis of proportionality and balancing focuses on what might be called public interest balancing. Public interest balancing provides useful insights into how the European Court views Article 6, and examples of various trends with respect to public interest balancing are common in the case law. This subsection, however, considers several examples of balancing in which the 'other factor' being balanced is something other than the public interest. Examples of this sort have also been considered elsewhere in the book.[286]

In cases involving vulnerable witnesses, victims, or complainants, the European Court has been willing to accept that the witnesses' interest in being protected may justify restrictions on applicants' Article 6 rights. In some cases, such as *Doorson*, this balancing is explained as being a balancing of the witnesses' Article 8 rights against the applicant's Article 6 rights:

> It is true that Article 6 does not explicitly require the interests of witnesses in general, and those of victims called upon to testify in particular, to be taken into consideration. However, their life, liberty or security of person may be at stake, as may interests coming generally within the ambit of Article 8 of the Convention . . . Against this background, principles of fair trial also require that in appropriate cases the interests of the defence are balanced against those of witnesses or victims called upon to testify.[287]

The *Doorson* Court did not provide further explanation for this approach to Article 6, nor did it explain whether Article 8 factors were the only ones against which the applicant's rights could be balanced (for example, could the public interest in protecting Article 10 rights be balanced against Article 6 rights?). More broadly, the *Doorson* judgment reflects a view that specific Article 6 rights should be interpreted in accordance with other Convention rights.

A number of cases have drawn on the logic in *Doorson* as a way of justifying restrictions on Article 6 in the name of particular individuals' interests. In *SN v Sweden*, for example, the applicant had been convicted of sexual abuse of a child. The European Court considered the extent to which the interest in protecting the complainant might affect the applicant's defence rights:

> The Court accepts that in criminal proceedings concerning sexual abuse certain measures may be taken for the purpose of protecting the victim, provided that such measures can be reconciled with an adequate and effective exercise of the rights of the defence.[288]

[286] See B.6, eg, which considered the under-explained relationship between Art 6 and Art 3.
[287] *Doorson v Netherlands* (n 118 above) para 70.
[288] *SN v Sweden* (n 120 above) para 47, citing *Baegen v Netherlands* (Commission) (App 16696/90) (20 October 1994) para 77. See also Brems, 'Conflicting Human Rights' (n 84 above) 319.

Unlike in *Doorson*, in *SN* the Court gave no indication that its balancing approach was linked to the need to protect other Convention rights. Its emphasis was simply on 'protecting the victim' rather than, for example, Article 8 rights. This book makes no argument that complainants in sexual offences cases are not in need of special consideration; the argument is simply that there is a lack of clarity in the European Court's approach to balancing the applicant's Article 6 rights with the complainant's. More specifically, in the absence of fuller explanation, these cases risk creating inconsistency with those cases in the previous section: the special features of sexual offences cases justified restrictions on an Article 6 guarantee in *SN*, even though the special features of terrorism, customs, and fraud cases did not. It may be noted that the *SN v Sweden* formulation has been subsequently cited or repeated.[289]

A similar approach was taken in *Krasniki v Czech Republic*, where the applicant 'complained that his conviction had been based exclusively on anonymous witness testimony' and that he had been 'denied the opportunity either to see the anonymous witnesses during their testimonies or to learn their identities'.[290] In this case the witnesses, who were involved in the drug world, were said to be fearful of reprisals. The *Krasniki* Court framed the relevant test as being, at least in part, whether 'the interest of the witnesses in remaining anonymous could justify limiting the rights of the applicant to such an extent'.[291] On the established facts in this case, however, the Court was not satisfied that the witness' interests justified limiting the rights of the applicant in this way.[292] Nevertheless, the *Krasniki* Court demonstrated a willingness to countenance balancing arguments.

The cases considered up to this point have involved vulnerable witnesses or complainants in sexual offences cases. The balancing approaches considered in these cases are arguably in tension with the cases considered in the previous section, in which the European Court stressed the prominent place that Article 6 rights held in a democratic society, and in which the Court warned against balancing away Article 6 rights.[293] One could, however, accept that cases involving the interests of particular individuals, such as witnesses or complainants, ought normatively to be considered differently to cases involving a broader public interest. One could argue that sexual offences, in particular, warrant special treatment. Clarity, however, demands that the European Court more fully articulate the rationale for this form of balancing and situate it more clearly with respect to its more general balancing case law. As matters stand, the applicability of this form of balancing to cases *other than* vulnerable witness cases remains unclear. This is

[289] *Bocos-Cuesta v Netherlands* (App 54789/00) (10 November 2005) paras 64–74 (no violation found); *WS v Poland* (App 21508/02) (19 June 2007) paras 53–64 (violation found); *Kovac v Croatia* (App 503/05) (12 July 2007) paras 27–33 (violation found); *Demski v Poland* (App 22695/03) (4 November 2008) paras 34–47 (violation found); *Breukoven v Czech Republic* (App 44438/06) (21 July 2011) paras 45–58 (violation found).

[290] *Krasniki v Czech Republic* (n 73 above) para 51.

[291] ibid para 83.

[292] ibid para 83.

[293] See, eg, *Ramanauskas v Lithuania* (n 284 above) paras 53–54.

especially so in light of poorly explained statements like this one in *Al-Khawaja and Tahery*, in which the Grand Chamber explained that its 'traditional' method of considering the proceedings as a whole was

> to weigh in the balance the competing interests of the defence, the victim, and witnesses, and the public interest in the effective administration of justice.[294]

In the remainder of this section, the focus returns to how the Court deploys balancing and proportionate analysis in the context of public interest balancing.

E.6.3 In Other Cases the European Court Allows the Use of Public Interest Arguments

In a number of Article 6 cases, the European Court has been explicitly willing to consider public interest arguments. When contrasted with the cases in part E.6.1 above, the cases in this section create the appearance of inconsistency and incoherence in the Court's case law. Looking at cases since the turn of this century, one can point to a number of cases as examples of this willingness.[295]

The first example is provided by *Janosevic v Sweden. Janosevic* sought to interpret the Court's oft-cited statement in *Salabiaku* that Article 6(2) requires presumptions of fact or law to be confined 'within reasonable limits which take into account the importance of what is at stake and maintain the rights of the defence'.[296] The *Salabiaku* Court had not made it expressly plain what it meant by 'the importance of what is at stake', but a string of subsequent cases indicate that the Court generally regarded the phrase as meaning what is at stake *for the applicant.*[297] In cases such as *Janosevic*, however, the Court uses 'what is at stake' as a way to introduce public interest considerations when assessing a potential infringement of Article 6 rights.[298] The *Janosevic* Court purported to apply *Salabiaku*, and summarised its effect in this way:

[294] *Al-Khawaja and Tahery v United Kingdom* (Grand Chamber) (n 109 above) para 146.

[295] Stumer has argued that it is only in the context of Art 6(2) rights that the European Court has allowed 'attempts to limit Article 6 rights by reference to the community interest': Stumer, *The Presumption of Innocence* (n 258 above) 110. In this and the following sections it is argued that there are also examples from elsewhere in Art 6. See also Abenaa Owusu-Bempah, 'Defence Participation through Pre-trial Disclosure: Issues and Implications' (2013) *International Journal of Evidence and Proof* 183, 193.

[296] *Salabiaku v France* (n 135 above) para 28. On *Salabiaku* presumptions, see Stumer, *The Presumption of Innocence* (n 258 above) 98–102; *R v G* [2008] UKHL 37, [2009] 1 AC 92, para 5.

[297] While the European Court does not always identify what is in fact 'at stake' when it cites the *Salabiaku* test, we can refer, eg, to *Pham Hoang v France* (App 13191/87) (1993) 16 EHRR 53, paras 32–33 (seriousness of potential sentence); *Phillips v United Kingdom* (App 41087/98) 11 BHRC 280, paras 42–47 (seriousness of a fine compared to a conviction); *Helmers v Sweden* (n 166 above) para 38 (professional reputation and career at stake); *Matyjek v Poland* (App 38184/03) (24 April 2007) para 59 (applicant's 'good name' and political career at stake); *Portington v Greece* (App 28523/95) (23 September 1998) paras 21, 34, 125 (death sentence); *Rasmussen v Poland* (n 56 above) para 39 (applicant's 'good name' and 'her special status as a retired judge'); *Shilbergs v Russia* (App 20075/03) (17 December 2009) para 122 (lengthy sentence). See van Dijk and van Hoof, *Theory and Practice of the European Convention on Human Rights* (n 5 above) 608–9.

[298] On this point, see Stumer, *The Presumption of Innocence* (n 258 above) 108.

> Thus, in employing presumptions in criminal law, the Contracting States are required to strike a balance between the importance of what is at stake and the rights of the defence; in other words, the means employed have to be reasonably proportionate to the legitimate aim sought to be achieved.[299]

For the *Janosevic* Court, therefore, the logical implication is that the 'what is at stake' element does not assess what was at stake *for the applicant* but what is at stake *for broader society*. Indeed, the Court was clearly willing to countenance a balancing exercise, outlining the interest of the state in organising an effective system of taxation:

> The Court also has regard to the financial interests of the State in tax matters, taxes being the State's main source of income. A system of taxation principally based on information supplied by the taxpayer would not function properly without some form of sanction against the provision of incorrect or incomplete information, and the large number of tax returns that are processed annually coupled with the interest in ensuring a foreseeable and uniform application of such sanctions undoubtedly require that they be imposed according to standardised rules.
>
> In view of what has been stated above, in particular the fact that the relevant rules on tax surcharges provide certain means of defence based on subjective elements and that an efficient system of taxation is important to the State's financial interests, the Court considers that the presumptions applied in Swedish law with regard to surcharges are confined within reasonable limits.[300]

Having considered these public interest arguments, the Court ultimately found that there had been no violation in this case. Similar public interest reasoning via the 'what is at stake' route was deployed in *Vastberga Taxi AB* and *Radio France*.[301] In this way, 'what is at stake' provided the Trojan horse for community interest balancing. This reasoning creates a degree of confusion and incoherence when contrasted with the general trend of the Court's 'what is at stake' jurisprudence. But most importantly for present purposes, this sort of reasoning sits inconsistently with the cases considered in part E.6.1.

In *Jussila*, the Court outlined an approach that allowed it to afford greater Article 6 protection to more serious criminal offences and lesser protection to less serious offences. In summarising a number of civil cases in which the Court had held that the obligation to hold a hearing 'is not absolute', the *Jussila* Court then focused its argument on the notion that oral hearings could be dispensed with in the name of 'efficiency and economy' in civil hearings.[302] There was no rule, it held, that an oral hearing could be dispensed with 'only in rare cases'.[303] Having framed its approach based on civil cases, the *Jussila* Court then turned its attention to criminal cases:

[299] *Janosevic v Sweden* (App 34619/97) (2004) 38 EHRR 22, para 101.

[300] ibid paras 103–4.

[301] *Vastberga Taxi AB and Vulic v Sweden* (App 36985/97) (23 July 2002) paras 113–22 (see Stumer, *The Presumption of Innocence* (n 258 above) 108); *Radio France and others v France* (App 53984/00) (30 March 2004) para 24.

[302] *Jussila v Finland* (App 73053/01) (2007) 45 EHRR 39, paras 41–42.

[303] ibid para 42.

> While it may be noted that . . . the requirements of a fair hearing are the most strict in the sphere of criminal law, the Court would not exclude that in the criminal sphere the nature of the issues to be dealt with before the tribunal or court may not require an oral hearing. Notwithstanding the consideration that a certain gravity attaches to criminal proceedings, which are concerned with the allocation of criminal responsibility and the imposition of a punitive and deterrent sanction, *it is self-evident that there are criminal cases which do not carry any significant degree of stigma. There are clearly 'criminal charges' of differing weight.* What is more, the autonomous interpretation adopted by the Convention institutions of the notion of a 'criminal charge' by applying the Engel criteria have underpinned a gradual broadening of the criminal head to cases not strictly belonging to the traditional categories of the criminal law . . . Tax surcharges differ from the hard core of criminal law; consequently, the criminal-head guarantees will not necessarily apply with their full stringency.[304]

In this extraordinary passage, the Court noted that its own 'autonomous interpretation' case law has led to 'criminal charge' being construed broadly. It then determinedly undermined the long line of *Engel* case law by indicating that a reduced level of protection will be afforded to some less weighty criminal proceedings. In linking a reduced level of protection in criminal proceedings to broader considerations of seriousness, efficiency, and economy, the Court adopted a form of reasoning radically different from that in part E.6.1. Judge Loucaides noted this departure in a strident dissent:

> This is the first time the Court has found that an oral hearing may not be required in a criminal case. The Court previously found that the obligation to hold such a hearing was not absolute in respect of certain civil proceedings. Without entering into the question whether the approach regarding civil proceedings was justified or not by the terms of Article 6, I must, from the outset, stress the point that there is a great difference between civil proceedings and criminal proceedings in many respects affecting the requirement of an oral hearing.[305]

The *Jussila* majority's willingness to adjust levels of Article 6 protection in response to public interest considerations is evident in a number of other cases.[306]

Indeed, in the third example, *Marcello Viola v Italy*, the Court concluded that the public interest in fighting the organised crime 'scourge' might justify restrictions on Article 6 rights:

> At the same time it should be pointed out that the applicant was accused of serious crimes related to the Mafia's activities. The fight against that scourge may, in certain cases, require the adoption of measures intended to protect, in particular, public safety and order and to prevent other criminal offences . . .
>
> In the light of the foregoing, the Court considers that the applicant's participation in the appeal hearings by videoconference pursued legitimate aims under the Convention,

[304] ibid para 43 (emphasis added) citing, inter alia, *Bendenoun v France* (App 12547/86) (1994) 18 EHRR 54 and *Janosevic v Sweden* (n 299 above).

[305] *Jussila v Finland* (n 302 above) para O–II 2.

[306] See, for further expansion of this approach in the criminal context, *Kammerer v Austria* (App 32435/06) (12 May 2010) paras 26–31.

> namely, prevention of disorder, prevention of crime, protection of witnesses and victims of offences in respect of their rights to life, freedom and security, and compliance with the 'reasonable time' requirement in judicial proceedings. It remains to be considered whether the arrangements for the conduct of the proceedings respected the rights of the defence . . .
>
> That being so, the Court finds that the applicant's participation by videoconference in the appeal hearings during the second set of criminal proceedings did not put the defence at a substantial disadvantage as compared with the other parties to the proceedings, and that the applicant had an opportunity to exercise the rights and entitlements inherent in the concept of a fair trial, as enshrined in Article 6.
>
> It follows that there has been no violation of Article 6 of the Convention.[307]

Thus, in this passage the European Court has indicated that the special characteristics of the Mafia may justify measures restricting the rights of a defendant where those measures pursue 'legitimate aims' and where the arrangements 'respected the rights of the defence'. This latter qualification adds some uncertainty to the Court's reasoning: if 'the rights of the defence' is simply synonymous with Article 6 rights, is the Court effectively simply saying that a measure will violate Article 6 rights if it violates Article 6? If so, perhaps it is similar to those counterbalancing cases in which the Court provides a circumlocution masking a simpler question. But more generally, this is an instance of the Court plainly accepting restrictions on Article 6 rights in the name of the public interest, and doing so with a formulation ('legitimate aims') that reflects a proportionality analysis.

In *Jalloh*, the European Court made several statements about the role that 'public interest' considerations can play in assessing Article 6 infringements. At this point, I simply note one such statement:

> In order to determine whether the applicant's right not to incriminate himself has been violated, the Court will have regard, in turn, to the following factors: the nature and degree of compulsion used to obtain the evidence; *the weight of the public interest in the investigation and punishment of the offence in issue; the existence of any relevant safeguards in the procedure*; and the use to which any material so obtained is put.[308]

But *Jalloh* and other related cases also made statements about the relationship between public interest arguments and the 'very essence' of Article 6 rights, which will be considered in a moment.

The penultimate example is *Heglas*, in which the European Court considered the extent to which public interest considerations might define the extent of Article 6 guarantees. Invoking *Heaney and McGuinness*, the Court stated:

> The general requirements of fairness provided in [Article 6] apply to all criminal proceedings, regardless of the type of offence. Nevertheless, in order to determine whether

[307] *Marcello Viola v Italy* (App 45106/04) (5 October 2006) paras 71–77. In the course of its analysis the European Court relied on two Art 5 decisions in which concessions had been made in light of a Mafia context: *Pantano v Italy* (App 60851/00) (6 November 2003) para 69 and *Contrada v Italy* (App 27143/95) (24 August 1998) para 67; the *Marcello Viola* Court did not note that these were Art 5 decisions.

[308] *Jalloh v Germany* (n 77 above) para 117 (emphasis added).

> the proceedings as a whole have been fair, *the weight of the public interest in the prosecution of a particular offence and the sanction of its author may be taken into consideration and put in the balance with the interest of the individual that evidence against him be gathered lawfully.* However, the considerations of public interest cannot justify measures emptying an applicant's rights of defence of their very substance, including the privilege against self-incrimination guaranteed by Article 6.[309]

In applying this statement of the law, the Court considered various factors as part of its 'weighing up', including the seriousness of the offence, the injuries caused to a third party, and the length of the prison sentence ultimately imposed on the applicant.[310] As a result of this and other factors, the Court held that 'the use of the recording complained of as well as of the list of telephone conversations by the national courts did not infringe the applicant's right to a fair trial' and there had been no violation of Article 6.[311] Plainly, this sort of reasoning contradicts those cases considered in part E.6.1. But from *Heglas* one also gains a complicated sense of the workings of the Court's tests. It seems the Court intended there to be an analytical safeguard provided by sternly indicating that the public interest cannot justify a measure destroying the very substance of the right. Yet at no point does the *Heglas* Court *even ask* whether the very substance of the right has been extinguished. We will return to notions of the 'very substance' or 'very essence' later in this part.

Finally, it is worth reiterating the willingness of the Grand Chamber in *Al-Khawaja and Tahery* to countenance public interest arguments as part of its assessment of the proceedings as a whole:

> [T]he traditional way in which the Court approaches the issue of the overall fairness of the proceedings, namely to weigh in the balance the competing interests of the defence, the victim, and witnesses, and *the public interest* in the effective administration of justice.[312]

The *Al-Khawaja and Tahery* judgment leaves open the question of precisely what infringements the public interest in the effective administration of justice is capable of justifying, but there is no doubt that it regards the public interest as a factor to be taken into account in assessing the overall fairness of the proceedings.[313] This passage thus provides further evidence of the vast flexibility that the 'pro-

[309] *Heglas v Czech Republic* (App 5935/02) (2009) 48 EHRR 44, para 87 (translated) (emphasis added).

[310] ibid para 91. For broadly similar analysis, see *Sandor Lajos Kiss v Hungary* (App 26958/05) (29 September 2009) paras 22–24; *Talaber v Hungary* (App 37376/05) (29 September 2009) paras 25–26; cf *Leonid Lazarenko v Ukraine* (App 22313/04) (28 October 2010) para 50.

[311] *Heglas v Czech Republic* (n 309 above) paras 92–93.

[312] *Al-Khawaja and Tahery v United Kingdom* (Grand Chamber) (n 109 above) para 146 (emphasis added). This passage drew upon language used in *Gafgen v Germany* (Grand Chamber) (n 189 above) para 175 ('There is no doubt that the victims of crime and their families as well as the public have an interest in the prosecution and punishment of criminals, and in the present case that interest was of high importance').

[313] Indeed, the passage is framed in broad terms about 'questions of fairness': *Al-Khawaja and Tahery v United Kingdom* (Grand Chamber) (n 109 above) para 146.

ceedings as a whole' test allows the Court in conducting broad-brush balancing exercises, especially when that test is combined with a 'taken together' approach. This passage from *Al-Khawaja and Tahery* has subsequently been repeatedly cited by the Court.[314]

In concluding this section, it is worth noting that in a long series of recent cases, touching on a variety of Article 6 rights and a variety of public interests, the European Court has demonstrated a willingness to consider public interest arguments as justifying restrictions on Article 6.[315] It has done so notwithstanding, and without acknowledging, the extensive case law to the contrary. The ability of this case law to provide any form of predictable guidance must be questioned.

E.6.4 In Other Cases the European Court Allows the Use of Public Interest Arguments Subject to Some Form of Safeguard

This section, building on the analysis above, considers those cases in which the European Court purports to allow the use of public interest arguments, but only within certain limits. It begins by considering the Court's poorly explained references to the 'very essence' of Article 6 rights. It moves on to analyse how, in a number of cases, the Court has used the 'very essence' tool as a way to limit the applicability of public interest arguments. It considers cases in which the Court appears to state that the public interest may be used to justify some restrictions on Article 6, but *not* to justify restrictions that go so far as to extinguish the very essence of the relevant Article 6 right.

To begin, an example of the 'very essence' test. While the test has been used in a number of Article 6 civil cases since the mid-1980s,[316] one of its first uses in a

[314] See, eg, *Chmura v Poland* (App 18475/05) (3 April 2012) paras 46, 51 (alleged violations of Art 6(1), (3)(b) and (3)(d)); *Ellis and Simms v United Kingdom (Admissibility)* (n 241 above) para 71 (Art 6(1) and (3)(d)); *Sarkizov and others v Bulgaria* (App 37981/06) (17 April 2012) para 53 (Art 6(1) and (3)(d)); *Fafrowicz v Poland* (App 43609/07) (17 April 2012) para 53 (Art 6(1) and (3)(d)); *Vidgen v Netherlands* (App 29353/06) (10 July 2012) para 38 (Art 6(1) and (3)(d)); *Hummer v Germany* (n 109 above) para 37 (Art 6(1) and (3)(d)); *Sievert v Germany* (App 29881/07) (19 July 2012) para 58 (Art 6(1) (3)(b) and (3)(d)); *Beggs v United Kingdom* (App 15499/10) (16 October 2012) paras 151–152 (Art 6(3)(d)); *Sellick and Sellick v United Kingdom* (App 18743/06) (16 October 2012) para 40 (Art 6(1) and (3)(d)); *Pichugin v Russia* (n 109 above) para 194 (Art 6(3)(d)); *Stefancic v Slovenia* (n 109 above) para 36 (Art 6(1) and (3)(d)); *Pesukic v Switzerland* (n 156 above) para 43 (Art 6(1) and (3)(d)); *Mesesnel v Slovenia* (App 22163/08) (28 February 2013) para 34 (Art 6(1) and (3)(d)); *Garofolo v Switzerland* (App 4380/09) (2 April 2013) para 45 (Art 6(1), (3)(a) and (3)(d)); *Kostecki v Poland* (n 130 above) para 59 (Art 6(1) and (3)(d)); *Brzuszczynski v Poland* (App 23789/09) (17 September 2013) para 79 (Art 6(1) and (3)(d)); *Donohoe v Ireland* (App 19165/08) (12 December 2013) para 73 ('Art 6').

[315] For further examples, see the discussion of *Jussila v Finland* (n 302 above) and *Hermi v Italy* (App 18114/02) (2008) 46 EHRR 46 in A Mowbray, 'No Violations but Interesting: a Study of the Strasbourg Court's Jurisprudence in Cases where No Breach of the Convention has been Found' (2008) 14 *European Public Law* 237, 243–45.

[316] See, eg, *Ashingdane v United Kingdom* (App 8225/78) (28 May 1985) para 57. See also *Lithgow and others v United Kingdom* (App 9006/80) (1986) 8 EHRR 329, para 194; *Fayed v United Kingdom* (App 17101/90) (1994) 18 EHRR 393, para 65; *Philis v Greece* (App 12750/87) (1991) 13 EHRR 741, para 69; *De Geouffre De La Pradelle v France* (App 12964/87) (16 December 1992) para 28; *Holy Monasteries v Greece* (App 13092/87) (1995) 20 EHRR 1, para 83; *Tolstoy Miloslavsky v United Kingdom* (App

criminal case appears to have been in *John Murray*. In that case the European Court referred to 'a degree of compulsion' that 'destroyed the very essence of the privilege against self-incrimination'.[317] The *John Murray* Court did not define what constituted 'the very essence' or identify the non-essential parts of the privilege. The closest that the Court came to identifying the 'very essence' of the privilege was to identify two essential elements outlined by the applicant in that case: 'the right to remain silent in the face of police questioning and not to have to testify against oneself at trial'; and 'that the exercise of the right by an accused would not be used as evidence against him in his trial'.[318] It is hard to imagine that these descriptions allow much room for *non*-essential content of the right to silence or the privilege against self-incrimination.

Although it is beyond the scope of this book to chart the history of the use of 'the very essence' as a judicial tool more generally,[319] one may note that the 'very essence' test has its supporters. Indeed, the 'very essence' test has been said to have 'spawned . . . dynamic and insightful methods of analysis' on a satisfactorily 'ad hoc basis'.[320] Others, however, including Alexy and Rivers, have argued that in most cases the 'very essence' test simply boils down to a circumlocutive restatement of a proportionality analysis.[321] The 'very essence' test, Rivers argues, is thus 'practically useless'.[322]

18139/91) (1995) 20 EHRR 442, para 59; *Bellet v France* (App 23805/94) (20 November 1995) para 31; *A v United Kingdom* (App 35373/97) (2003) 36 EHRR 51, para 74; *Bakan v Turkey* (App 50939/99) (12 June 2007) para 66.

[317] *John Murray v United Kingdom* (n 16 above) para 49. See, for later examples, *Heaney and McGuinness v Ireland* (n 275 above) para 48; *Quinn v Ireland* (App 36887/97) (21 December 2000) para 48; *Allan v United Kingdom* (n 88 above) para 44; *Jalloh v Germany* (n 77 above) paras 97, 101; *O'Halloran and Francis v United Kingdom* (n 250 above) para 49; *Salduz v Turkey* (n 190 above) para 54; *Bykov v Russia* (n 55 above) para 92; *Marttinen v Finland* (App 19235/03) (21 April 2009) para 75; *Pishchalnikov v Russia* (App 7025/04) (24 September 2009) para 69; *Ozcan Colak v Turkey* (App 30235/03) (6 October 2009) para 44; *Aleksandr Zaichenko v Russia* (n 77 above) para 38; *Hakan Duman v Turkey* (n 189 above) para 47; *Pavlenko v Russia* (App 42371/02) (1 April 2010) paras 100–101; *Baran and Hun v Turkey* (App 30685/05) (20 May 2010) para 68. On compulsion, see also A Choo, 'Give Us What You Have: Information, Compulsion and the Privilege Against Self-Incrimination as a Human Right' in P Roberts and J Hunter (eds), *Criminal Evidence and Human Rights* (Hart Publishing, 2012).

[318] *John Murray v United Kingdom* (n 16 above) para 41; cf Brems' assertion that notions such as 'essence' 'regularly appear in the case law of the [European Court, albeit not so often in the context of the right to a fair trial': Brems, 'Conflicting Human Rights' (n 84 above) 304.

[319] For more general discussion of the 'very essence' tool, see D Grimm, 'Proportionality in Canadian and German Constitutional Jurisprudence' (2007) 57 *U Toronto Law Journal* 383, 384–87; David Currie, *The Constitution of the Federal Republic of Germany* (University of Chicago Press, 1994) 178; Brems, 'Conflicting Human Rights' (n 84 above) 303–4; Stumer, *The Presumption of Innocence* (n 258 above) 114–18; Emmerson, Ashworth and Macdonald, *Human Rights and Criminal Justice* (n 7 above) 77; Rivers, 'Proportionality and Variable Intensity of Review' (n 2 above) 186–87; Lazarus, Goold and Swiney, *Public Protection, Proportionality, and the Search for Balance* (n 259 above) 11–12; E Brems, *Human Rights: Universality and Diversity* (Martinus Nijhoff, 2001) 368–71; *State v Makwanyane and another* [1995] ZACC 3, paras 132–34.

[320] Yutaka Arai-Takahashi, *The Margin of Appreciation Doctrine and the Principle of Proportionality in the Jurisprudence of the ECHR* (Intersentia, 2002) 36; Brems, *Human Rights: Universality and Diversity* (n 319 above) 369.

[321] Alexy, *A Theory of Constitutional Rights* (n 1 above) 192–96; Rivers, 'Proportionality and Variable Intensity of Review' (n 2 above) 186–87.

[322] Rivers, 'Proportionality and Variable Intensity of Review' (n 2 above) 187.

To what extent do these theoretical criticisms reflect the European Court's use of the 'very essence' test in the Article 6 context? In this section, I explore some of the ways in which the 'very essence' has been used to analyse alleged violations of Article 6. If the Court is to continue to use the 'very essence' as a useful or meaningful test, the interests of the rule of law demand that it define what is involved in the essence of the guarantees, and what is part of the guarantee but nonetheless may be regarded as peripheral or non-essential.[323] The European Court has occasionally been willing to identify particular rights, or aspects of rights, as 'essential',[324] but unless *non-essential* content can be identified and defined, then referring to the 'very essence' of the guarantee is mere obfuscation.[325] Having established the vagueness of the 'very essence' as an analytical tool, I turn to the ways in which the Court has used that tool as a safeguard in the context of public interest balancing.

In *Heaney and McGuinness*, the applicants were convicted of 'failing to provide an account of their movements during a specified period', contrary to Irish legislation.[326] In arguing that the legislation did not violate the silence and self-incrimination guarantees, Ireland described the measure as 'a proportionate response to the subsisting terrorist and security threat given the need to ensure the proper administration of justice and the maintenance of public order and peace'.[327] The Court took notice of the Irish security situation, but did not accede to the government's argument:

> [T]he security and public order concerns relied on by the Government cannot justify a provision which extinguishes the very essence of the applicants' rights to silence and against self-incrimination guaranteed by [Article 6(1)].[328]

Importantly, therefore, the Court indicated that 'security and public order concerns' could not justify measures that extinguish the 'very essence' of the silence

[323] See Stumer, *The Presumption of Innocence* (n 258 above) ch 4; Rivers, 'Proportionality and Variable Intensity of Review' (n 2 above) 186–87; Hoyano, 'What is Balanced on the Scales of Justice?' (n 10 above) 24–28.

[324] Perhaps most commonly in the context of referring to 'the right of a criminal defendant to be present in the courtroom' as 'one of the essential requirements of Article 6': see, eg, *Stoichkov v Bulgaria* (App 9808/02) (2007) 44 EHRR 14, para 56; *Sejdovic v Italy* (n 212 above) para 82; *Hermi v Italy* (n 315 above) para 58; *Sidorova (Adukevich) v Russia* (App 4537/04) (14 February 2008) para 23; *Samokhvalov v Russia* (App 3891/03) (12 February 2009) para 42; *Sibgatullin v Russia* (App 32165/02) (23 April 2009) para 33; *Makarenko v Russia* (App 5962/03) (22 December 2009) para 131; *Sinichkin v Russia* (App 20508/03) (8 April 2010) para 30; *Abdulgadirov v Azerbaijan* (App 24510/06) (20 June 2013) para 33; *Kozlitin v Russia* (App 17092/04) (14 November 2013) para 52; cf *Belilos v Switzerland* (n 204 above) para 63 ('the proceedings before him satisfied the essential requirements of Article 6(1): a defendant could ask for inquiries to be made into the facts, and Mrs Belilos had successfully availed herself of that possibility; the Board always considered the evidence and had only limited powers of punishment').

[325] See Hoyano, What is Balanced on the Scales of Justice?' (n 10 above) 15. The vagueness of this approach is exacerbated when the Court refers to 'the very essence of an applicant's defence rights' instead of the 'very essence' of a *particular* right: see, eg, *Bykov v Russia* (n 55 above) para 93; *Othman (Abu Qatada) v United Kingdom* (App 8139/09) (2012) 55 EHRR 1, para 260.

[326] *Heaney and McGuinness v Ireland* (n 275 above) para 12.

[327] ibid para 56.

[328] ibid para 58. See, eg, T Ward and P Gardner, 'The Privilege Against Self-incrimination: In Search of Legal Certainty' [2003] *EHRLR* 388, 395–96.

and self-incrimination guarantees. *Quinn v Ireland*, decided the same day as *Heaney and McGuinness*, included a virtually identical passage, as did *Shannon v United Kingdom*.[329] One implication of this passage is that security concerns *may* justify a measure that infringes the silence and self-incrimination guarantees, provided that such a measure does not go so far as to extinguish the essence of the guarantees. The paragraph 58 implication, as will be seen, was taken up by the *Jalloh* Court.

Jalloh included a number of passages worthy of close scrutiny in this context. The first *Jalloh* statement drew on *Heaney and McGuinness*:

> 97. The general requirements of fairness contained in Article 6 apply to all criminal proceedings, irrespective of the type of offence in issue. Nevertheless, when determining whether the proceedings as a whole have been fair the weight of the public interest in the investigation and punishment of the particular offence in issue may be taken into consideration and be weighed against the individual interest that the evidence against him be gathered lawfully. However, public interest concerns cannot justify measures which extinguish the very essence of an applicant's defence rights, including the privilege against self-incrimination.[330]

With one paragraph, the Court thus reframed the *Heaney and McGuinness* formula, under which public interest concerns could not 'justify a provision which extinguishes the very essence' of a right, such that public interest concerns may be 'weighed against' individual rights *except* if the relevant measure extinguishes the very essence. The public interest cannot justify the very worst infringements, the *Jalloh* Court seemed to reason, but that means it can justify other infringements. The Court then offered this formulation of the circumstances in which the very essence of the privilege would be extinguished:

> 101. . . . the Court will have regard, in particular, to the following elements: the nature and degree of the compulsion, the existence of any relevant safeguards in the procedures and the use to which any material so obtained is put.[331]

One may note that the public interest was *not* listed as a relevant factor to the assessment of whether the very essence of the privilege had been extinguished; this fits with the Court's insistence that the public interest cannot justify measures extinguishing the very essence of a right. We will return to this point below.

The *Jalloh* Court made a further contribution to the use of the public interest in assessing violations. It stated:

> 117. In order to determine whether the applicant's right not to incriminate himself has been violated, the Court will have regard, in turn, to the following factors: the nature and degree of compulsion used to obtain the evidence; *the weight of the public interest in*

[329] *Quinn v Ireland* (n 317 above) paras 57–60; *Shannon v United Kingdom* (n 275 above) para 38.

[330] *Jalloh v Germany* (n 77 above) para 97, citing *Heaney and McGuinness v Ireland* (n 275 above) paras 57–58 (*mutatis mutandis*).

[331] *Jalloh v Germany* (n 77 above) para 101. This passage was applied in a curious way in *Sorokins and Sorokina v Latvia* (n 77 above) para 110, in which the European Court applied this test as though it related to the right itself rather than to the essence of the right.

> *the investigation and punishment of the offence in issue; the existence of any relevant safeguards in the procedure*; and the use to which any material so obtained is put.[332]

Crucially, therefore, 'the public interest' is relevant in the second test and not in the first. *Jalloh* offers no explanation for these 'factors', nor for the introduction of a public interest balancing test into the assessment of an Article 6 violation. In any event, in this case the 'public interest' conclusion was that 'the public interest in securing the applicant's conviction could not justify recourse to such a grave interference with his physical and mental integrity'.[333] And so the public interest could not justify the restrictions on Article 6 in *Jalloh*.

One possible summary of the *Jalloh* framework is this: the Court first requires that there be an assessment of whether or not the privilege has been infringed. For this assessment, a variety of factors, including the public interest, may be taken into account ('the paragraph 117 factors'). If the conclusion at the end of this balancing exercise is that the right has been violated, then that will be the end of the matter. If the conclusion at the end of this balancing exercise is that the right has *not* been violated, then a secondary question comes into play: has the very essence of the right been extinguished? On this account, for the secondary question, the Court may have regard to all the same factors to which it had regard for the primary question *apart from the public interest* ('the paragraph 101 factors'). It is important to emphasise that this sort of rationalisation for the Court's approach is entirely reverse-engineered: the Court itself does not provide any explanation through which its analysis may be understood.[334]

And yet if one turns from *Jalloh* to *O'Halloran and Francis*, it seems that any clarity capable of being discerned from *Jalloh* is perhaps illusory. In *O'Halloran and Francis* the Court stated:

> 53. . . . While the right to a fair trial under Article 6 is an unqualified right, what constitutes a fair trial cannot be the subject of a single unvarying rule but must depend on the circumstances of the particular case. This was confirmed in the specific context of the right to remain silent in the case of *Heaney and McGuinness* and, more recently, in the Court's *Jalloh* judgment, in which the Court identified the factors to which it would have regard in determining whether the applicant's privilege against self-incrimination had been violated . . .

[332] *Jalloh v Germany* (n 77 above) para 117 (emphasis added). See Andrew Ashworth and Mike Redmayne, *The Criminal Process*, 4th edn (Oxford University Press, 2010) para 5.6.

[333] *Jalloh v Germany* (n 77 above) para 119. Compare the Concurring and Dissenting Opinions: see the Concurring Opinion of Judge Bratza; Joint Dissenting Opinion of Judges Ress, Pellonpaa, Baka and Sikuta.

[334] Indeed, it could be approached another way: one could also argue that the effect of the passages is that if a government (or, indeed, the European Court) wishes to take into account public interest factors in assessing an alleged violation, it need only state that the measure does not extinguish the very essence, thereby allowing public interest considerations to come into play. This fluid process is, of course, made both more complex and more opaque by the fact that the European Court has never provided a working definition of what falls inside and outside the very essence of the guarantees. See also John Jackson, 'Re-conceptualizing the Right of Silence as an Effective Fair Trial Standard' (2009) 58 *International and Comparative Law Quarterly* 835; Jenny McEwan, 'Truth, Efficiency, and Cooperation in Modern Criminal Justice' (2013) *Current Legal Problems* 1, 25; in terms of the clarity of the judgment, cf A Lester, 'The European Court of Human Rights after 50 Years' [2009] *EHRLR* 461, 474.

> 55. In the light of the principles contained in its *Jalloh* judgment, and in order to determine whether the essence of the applicants' right to remain silent and privilege against self-incrimination was infringed, the Court will focus on the nature and degree of compulsion used to obtain the evidence, the existence of any relevant safeguards in the procedure, and the use to which any material so obtained was put.[335]

There are two things to note here. First, the Court appears to go back and forth between referring to a violation of the privilege and referring to a violation of *the essence of* the privilege. There is no sense here that there may be a distinction between the two. The focus of the *O'Halloran* analysis is very much on the essence of the privilege rather than the right itself. The significance of this analytical choice, however, is never explained.

Second, the factors listed in *O'Halloran* as relevant to the essence of the right reflect those in *Jalloh*.[336] However, in *O'Halloran*, the Court additionally considered several public interest factors in the course of assessing whether the essence of the privilege had been violated. Principally, the *O'Halloran and Francis* Court identified the public interest in a 'regulatory regime' affecting drivers, and the 'limited nature of the inquiry which the police were authorised to undertake'.[337] These public interest factors were used as the basis for a conclusion that 'the essence of the applicants' right to remain silent and their privilege against self-incrimination has not been destroyed' and that as a result there had 'been no violation'.[338] Leaving to one side the question of whether the Court should be having regard to public interest considerations in determining whether or not there has been a violation of Article 6, it certainly seems that even under the formulation adopted in *Jalloh*, this sort of public interest considerations should not have been considered in answering the question of whether or not *the essence of the right* had been destroyed. The *Jalloh* Court did not regard the public interest as relevant to assessing a violation of the *essence* of the right. *O'Halloran and Francis* did. In *Jalloh*, at least, it appeared that the inquiry about the essence of the right may have been designed as a safeguard against excessive consideration of public interest factors. If one accepts that reading of *Jalloh*, the *O'Halloran and Francis* Court has undermined that analytical safeguard.[339] The potentially farcical result

[335] *O'Halloran and Francis v United Kingdom* (n 250 above) paras 53–55; see also Ashworth, 'Self-Incrimination in European Human Rights Law' (n 245 above) ; A Choo, *Compelling the Provision of Information: the Privilege Against Self-incrimination as a Human Right*, University of Warwick Legal Studies Research Paper Series 2010-20 (2010); cf Lord Hoffman, 'The Universality of Human Rights' (n 271 above) para 29.

[336] See *Jalloh v Germany* (n 77 above) para 101; cf *O'Halloran and Francis v United Kingdom* (n 250 above) para 55.

[337] *O'Halloran and Francis v United Kingdom* (n 250 above) paras 57–58. The points made were similar to those originally raised by Lord Bingham in the Privy Council in *Brown v Stott* [2003] 1 AC 681, 705–6.

[338] *O'Halloran and Francis v United Kingdom* (n 250 above) paras 62–63.

[339] Hoyano suggests that, after *Al-Khawaja and Tahery v United Kingdom* (Grand Chamber) (n 109 above) 'the "essence of the right" constraint seems no longer to exist in substance' (see Hoyano, 'What is Balanced on the Scales of Justice?' (n 10 above) 6). The analysis above suggests its demise may have come about even earlier than Hoyano thought.

is that the Court's case law allows public interest factors to be taken into account so long as the essence of the right is not violated, but it allows public interest factors to affect its conclusion on whether or not the essence of the right has been violated. It should also be noted that the decision in *Grayson and Barnham v United Kingdom* echoes the reasoning adopted in *O'Halloran and Francis.*[340]

The flimsiness of the European Court's use of the 'very essence' as a possible limitation on public interest arguments is also seen in *Bykov.* In that case, the Court made an enigmatically brief statement about the role for public interest concerns:

> 93. The general requirements of fairness contained in Article 6 apply to all criminal proceedings, irrespective of the type of offence at issue. Public-interest concerns cannot justify measures which extinguish the very essence of an applicant's defence rights, including the privilege against self-incrimination.[341]

This ostensibly-straightforward statement is, however, problematic. If the logic of the first sentence holds, then the second sentence's scope should not be limited to measures which extinguish the *very essence* of defence rights but rather should apply to measures which extinguish *defence rights*, regardless of whether or not the very essence of the right is extinguished. If the logic of the first sentence is to be extended, the second sentence of paragraph 93 should perhaps have read something like:

> Public-interest concerns cannot justify measures *which extinguish an applicant's defence rights*, including the privilege against self-incrimination.

Stating the law in the way it has done in *Bykov* adds nothing to the clarity or predictability of the European Court's jurisprudence. Moreover, after having established the relevant test as being whether 'the very essence of . . . defence rights' had been extinguished, the *Bykov* Court made no further reference whatsoever to the 'very essence' of the right. Even in reaching its conclusion the *Bykov* Court omitted any reference to the very essence of the right and simply concluded that the alleged violating actions 'were not contrary to the requirements of a fair trial'.[342] It is acknowledged that this distinction may not be of significance in many cases. But if the Court's 'very essence' test is to mean anything more than simply 'was there a violation?', and if the 'very essence' test is to act as a check on the creeping influence of public interest considerations, then the onus of justifications means it is incumbent on the Court to be clear and consistent in explaining, applying and reaching decisions about the 'very essence' test. On the other hand, if the Court regards the public interest as relevant to both the infringement of the right *and* to the infringement of the very essence of the right, the Court ought to own up to this and say so plainly. In either situation, the Court will need to explicitly recon-

[340] See *Grayson and Barnham v United Kingdom* (n 134 above) para 49.
[341] *Bykov v Russia* (n 55 above) para 93.
[342] ibid para 104.

cile its approach to these cases with its approach to the cases considered earlier in part E.[343]

There is one final example of a case in which the European Court appears to open the door for public interest arguments, albeit with a limitation, and a limitation different to the 'very essence' approach. In *Salduz v Turkey*, the Court adopted a robust view of the circumstances in which the public interest might be able to be taken into account:

> Any exception to the enjoyment of [the right of a detainee to have access to legal advice] should be *clearly circumscribed* and its application *strictly limited* in time. These principles are particularly called for in the case of serious charges, for it is in the face of the heaviest penalties that respect for the right to a fair trial is to be ensured to the highest possible degree by democratic societies.[344]

Having articulated this position, the Court went on to offer a somewhat opaque description of the approach to be taken when considering whether confidential access to a lawyer can be restricted:

> [T]he Court finds that in order for the right to a fair trial to remain sufficiently practical and effective [Article 6(1)] requires that, as a rule, access to a lawyer should be provided as from the first interrogation of a suspect by the police, unless it is demonstrated in the light of the particular circumstances of each case that there are *compelling reasons to restrict this right.* Even where compelling reasons may exceptionally justify denial of access to a lawyer, such restriction – whatever its justification – must not unduly prejudice the rights of the accused under Article 6. The rights of the defence will in principle be irretrievably prejudiced when incriminating statements made during police interrogation without access to a lawyer are used for a conviction.[345]

This passage, which has been repeatedly cited by the European Court, is worth disaggregating.[346] The Court appears to acknowledge that, in exceptional circum-

[343] Including *Al-Khawaja and Tahery v United Kingdom* (Grand Chamber) (n 109 above) which Hoyano criticises for its failure to incorporate an 'essence of the right' analysis: Hoyano, 'What is Balanced on the Scales of Justice?' (n 10 above) 6–7.

[344] *Salduz v Turkey* (n 190 above) para 54 (emphasis added). See also *Oulahcene v France* (n 281 above) para 43. This 'strict' approach bears some similarities to that used in the 'trial within a trial' cases considered at E.2.3 above.

[345] *Salduz v Turkey* (n 190 above) para 55 (emphasis added). For more on *Salduz*, see Jackson, 'Re-conceptualizing the Right of Silence' (n 334 above); R Pattenden, 'Case Comment: Right to Counsel at the Police Station' (2011) 15(1) *International Journal of Evidence and Proof* 70; TAHM van de Laar and RL de Graaff, '*Salduz* and *Miranda*: Is the US Supreme Court Pointing the Way?' [2011] *EHRLR* 304; W Wu, 'Interrogational Fairness under the European Convention on Human Rights' (2011) 39 *International Journal of Law, Crime and Justice* 37; Bjorge, 'Exceptionalism and Internationalism in the Supreme Court' (n 228 above); Bratza, 'The Relationship between the UK Courts and Strasbourg' (n 155 above); cf the reference to 'exceptional circumstances' in *Flisar v Slovenia* (App 3127/09) (29 September 2011) para 34.

[346] This passage has been cited in, eg, *Plonka v Poland* (App 20310/02) (31 March 2009) para 35; *Pishchalnikov v Russia* (n 317 above) para 70 (on *Pishchalnikov*, see Wu, 'Interrogational Fairness under the European Convention on Human Rights' (n 345 above) 52); *Pavlenko v Russia* (n 317 above) para 97; *Sharkunov and Mezentsev v Russia* (App 75330/01) (10 June 2010) para 97; *Lopata v Russia* (App 72250/01) (13 July 2010) para 130; *Mader v Croatia* (App 56185/07) (21 June 2011) para 149; *Sebalj v Croatia* (n 77 above) para 250; *Mehmet Serif Oner v Turkey* (App 50356/08) (13 September 2011) paras 18–23; *Diroz v Turkey* (App 38560/04) (31 May 2012) para 30; *Khayrov v Ukraine* (App 19157/06) (15 November 2012) paras 73–79; *Zamfresko v Ukraine* (App 30075/06) (15 November 2012) paras 60–65.

stances, compelling reasons may justify denial of access to a lawyer. It does not identify any such compelling reasons. The Court then goes on to say that such a denial must not 'unduly prejudice' the rights of the accused. This statement seems self-defeating, insofar as the *rights* of the accused under Article 6(3)(c) will, by definition, be prejudiced by a denial of access to a lawyer. The trial, or the result of the trial, may not *necessarily* be prejudiced, but the accused's *rights* will be. But leaving those objections to one side, the Court complicates the matter further by indicating that, 'in principle', the rights of the defence will be 'irretrievably prejudiced' when incriminating statements made during interrogation without access to a lawyer are used for a conviction. The cumulative effect of these three statements, therefore, would appear to indicate that even 'compelling reasons' in 'exceptional circumstances' cannot justify the use in evidence of incriminating statements made during police interrogation without access to lawyer. This cumulative effect makes one wonder whether there was any significant content at all to the Court's apparent concession with respect to 'exceptional' circumstances.

E.6.5 In Another Class of Cases, the European Court Appears to Regard Measures Infringing the 'Very Essence' of a Right as Synonymous with Disproportionality

There is another class of case: cases in which the European Court appears to define 'a restriction infringing the very essence of the right' as effectively meaning 'a disproportionate restriction'.[347] In these cases, the Court implicitly identifies the proportionality or 'fair balance' of a restriction as being decisive to the question of whether the restriction has infringed the very essence of a right. In taking this step, the Court implicitly acknowledges that public interest factors, capable of being made part of any proportionality or fair balance exercise, may be taken into account when determining whether a restriction has infringed the very essence of a right. The logical implication of this move is that public interest factors may be capable of justifying a measure that *might otherwise have infringed the very essence of a right.* In other cases, of course, the European Court has strenuously indicated that the public interest is not relevant to assessments of Article 6 violations,[348] or that if it *is* relevant, the public interest cannot justify measures infringing the very essence of a right.[349] And yet those stringent indications are robbed of much of their force if public interest considerations can be relevant to the assessment of whether a restriction has infringed the very essence of a right. As will be seen, however, in a number of cases the Court has clearly indicated a view that a restriction will infringe the very essence of a right if it is disproportionate.

[347] On this point, see Rivers, 'Proportionality and Variable Intensity of Review' (n 2 above) 186–87; Alexy, *A Theory of Constitutional Rights* (n 1 above) 193–96; Arai-Takahashi, *The Margin of Appreciation Doctrine and the Principle of Proportionality* (n 320 above) 36–37.

[348] See E.6.1 above.

[349] See E.6.3 above.

I turn first to the judgments in *Omar* and *Guerin*, both decided on the same day. These applications concerned a French procedure that the applicants argued 'had infringed their right of access to a court'.[350] The Court drew on a number of civil cases as it 'reiterated' its approach to the right to a court:

> 34. The Court reiterates that the right to a court, of which the right of access is one aspect, is not absolute; it may be subject to limitations permitted by implication, particularly regarding the conditions of admissibility of an appeal. However, these limitations must not restrict exercise of the right in such a way or to such an extent that the very essence of the right is impaired. They must pursue a legitimate aim and there must be a reasonable proportionality between the means employed and the aim sought to be achieved.[351]

The Court thus uses the 'very essence' as a way of confining the scope of limitations on rights. Notably, the Court's statement here also openly articulated a proportionality analysis as the method through which to assess Article 6 violations. But in this passage the Court does not make it entirely clear how the 'very essence' rule interacts with the proportionality rule outlined in the following sentence, or whether one takes precedence over the other. The Court's conclusion provided some indication of how the two statements might interact:

> [The restriction] impairs the very essence of the right of appeal, by imposing a disproportionate burden on the appellant, thus upsetting the fair balance that must be struck between the legitimate concern to ensure that judicial decisions are enforced, on the one hand, and the right of access to the Court of Cassation and exercise of the rights of the defence on the other.[352]

In this passage, therefore, the European Court indicates that a restriction will impair the very essence of a right if that restriction is disproportionate. It goes on to note that such a disproportionate restriction would upset the balance between societal and individual interests. If 'impairing the very essence of the right' simply means 'disproportionate', then it is unclear why the Court complicates its analysis by apparently adding the 'very essence' as an additional criterion in paragraph 34. If 'impairing the very essence of the right' means something different to this, then

[350] *Omar v France* (App 24767/94) (2000) 29 EHRR 210, para 31. See also *Guerin v France* (App 25201/94) (29 July 1998) para 34.

[351] *Omar v France* (n 350 above) para 34, citing *Levages Prestations Services v France* (App 21920/93) (1997) 24 EHRR 351, para 40; *Bellet v France* (n 316 above) para 31; *Tolstoy Miloslavsky v United Kingdom* (n 316 above) para 59; *Fayed v United Kingdom* (n 316 above) para 65. See also *Guerin v France* (n 350 above) para 37; *Sporrong and Lonnroth v Sweden* (App 7151/75) (1983) 5 EHRR 35, para 69; *Belgian Linguistic Case (No 2)* (App 1474/62) (1968) 1 EHRR 252, para 5 of 'Interpretation adopted by the Court'; *Lithgow and others v United Kingdom* (n 316 above) para 194; *Ashingdane v United Kingdom* (n 316 above) para 57. It should be noted that the cases referred to by the European Court in this passage (and the cases referred to by *those* cases) do not offer an explanation as to why this sort of proportionality analysis should be deployed in the specific context of Art 6. Indeed, ultimately the cases appear to rest on cases making general statements about balance being 'inherent in the whole of the Convention' or statements about rights other than Art 6.

[352] *Omar v France* (n 350 above) para 40. See also *Guerin v France* (n 350 above) para 43. In both *Omar* and *Guerin* the European Court went on to find a violation of Art 6(1): *Omar v France* (n 350 above) para 44; *Guerin v France* (n 350 above) para 47.

the Court has obscured that meaning by framing its analysis in this way. Approaches similar to that of *Omar* and *Guerin* have been utilised in a number of Article 6 criminal cases.[353]

Less than four years after *Omar* and *Guerin* came *Eliazer v Netherlands*, a case in which the applicant argued he had been denied access to the Court of Cassation due to regulations preventing appeals in cassation against judgments given *in absentia*.[354] The European Court regarded the facts of *Eliazer* as different from those in *Omar*,[355] but for present purposes one may note one curious aspect of the Court's analysis. The Court established the relevant test as including the 'very essence' requirement:

> [T]he right to a court . . . may be subject to limitations . . . However, these limitations must not restrict exercise of the right in such a way or to such an extent that the very essence of the right is impaired. They must pursue a legitimate aim and there must be a reasonable proportionality between the means employed and the aim sought to be achieved.[356]

And yet the Court made no reference whatsoever to the 'very essence' requirement when it concluded that there had not been a violation of Article 6. Instead, it focused on proportionality:

> The decision declaring the applicant's appeal in cassation inadmissible cannot, therefore, be considered as a disproportionate limitation on the applicant's right of access to a court or one that deprived him of a fair trial. Accordingly, there has been no violation.[357]

The terse conclusion in *Eliazer*, therefore, lends support to the notion that this series of cases appears to regard proportionality as decisive of whether the very essence of a right had been infringed. On that version, perhaps it was unnecessary for the Court to make any reference at all to the essence of the right in reaching its conclusion.[358] One might even wonder if, under this logic, the 'very essence' test is relevant at all or whether it is a circumlocution that simply amounts to a proportionality test.[359]

[353] *Khalfaoui v France* (n 262 above) paras 27, 36, 40; *Osu v Italy* (App 36534/97) (11 July 2002) para 31; *Pelevin v Ukraine* (App 24402/02) (20 May 2010) para 27; *Peltier v France* (n 17 above) para 35; *Zvolsky and Zvolska v Czech Republic* (App 46129/99) (12 November 2002) paras 47, 54; *Celice v France* (App 14166/09) (8 March 2012) para 33. *Guerin*-type approaches are also cited and applied in civil cases such as *Fogarty v United Kingdom* (App 37112/97) (2002) 34 EHRR 12, para 33; *Beles and others v Czech Republic* (App 47273/99) (12 November 2002) paras 61, 68; *Ernst and others v Belgium* (App 33400/96) (2004) 39 EHRR 35, para 48; *Melnyk v Ukraine* (App 23436/03) (28 March 2006) paras 22, 31; and *Jesina v Czech Republic* (App 18806/02) (26 July 2007) paras 25–30. But note that, despite ostensibly adopting the *Omar* and *Guerin* tests, the *Khalfoui* Court did not expressly reach a conclusion on proportionality.

[354] See *Eliazer v Netherlands* (App 38055/97) (2003) 37 EHRR 45, paras 22–24.

[355] ibid para 33.

[356] See, eg, ibid para 30; van Dijk and van Hoof, *Theory and Practice of the European Convention on Human Rights* (n 5 above) 574–75.

[357] *Eliazer v Netherlands* (n 354 above) para 36; see also paras 34–35.

[358] cf *Guerin: Guerin v France* (n 350 above) para 43.

[359] Very similar reasoning can be seen in the civil case of *Osman v United Kingdom* (App 23452/94) (2000) 29 EHRR 245, eg, paras 147, 154.

In *Nikitin v Russia*, the European Court used the 'very essence' analytical tool in a different context, namely, for assessing the extent to which reopening a criminal case for review after acquittal complies with Article 6:

> [C]ertain special circumstances of the case may reveal that the actual manner in which [a case was reopened] impaired the very essence of a fair trial. In particular, the Court has to assess whether, in a given case, the power to launch and conduct a supervisory review was exercised by the authorities so as to strike, to the maximum extent possible, a fair balance between the interests of the individual and the need to ensure the effectiveness of the system of criminal justice.[360]

Most importantly for present purposes, *Nikitin* constitutes a further example of a case in which the Court describes 'the very essence' as being virtually synonymous with concepts of balancing and proportionality in a broad sense ('a fair balance between the interests of the individual and the need to ensure the effectiveness of the system').[361]

This section, therefore, has considered a line of cases in which the European Court appears to equate 'restricting the very essence of a right' with 'a disproportionate restriction'. This is important for several reasons. First, it suggests that on this logic the 'very essence' test may be capable of being regarded as an unnecessary circumlocution that could be jettisoned in favour of a proportionality test. Second, it suggests that public interest considerations (which would be relevant to the proportionality of a measure) may have an analytical impact on assessing whether a measure has infringed the very essence of a right. Third, and more broadly, this line of cases does not sit well with those cases considered above, especially those in which the Court sternly warns against the use of public interest balancing. Indeed, the approaches adopted in the categories of cases discussed above, most notably those cases in which the very essence of a right is intended to act as a safeguard on proportionality analysis, appear to contradict the approach adopted in the cases considered in this section. Either 'restrictions on the very essence of a right' are simply disproportionate restrictions, or they are restrictions that are identified as unacceptable following an analysis conducted in the absence of public interest and proportionality considerations. The European Court appears to be having it both ways.

E.7 Building the Foundations for a New Approach to Assessing Violations of Article 6

This part has charted the European Court's attempts to solve the puzzle of Article 6: how ought we assess alleged violations of Article 6 in the absence of an express

[360] *Nikitin v Russia* (App 50178/99) (2005) 41 EHRR 10, para 57. See Mowbray, 'A Study of the Principle of Fair Balance in the Jurisprudence of the ECtHR' (n 259 above).

[361] Among further examples, see *Abdelali v France* (App 43353/07) (11 October 2012) paras 55–56. See also Mowbray, 'A Study of the Principle of Fair Balance in the Jurisprudence of the ECtHR' (n 259 above) 302–3, 308–11.

meta-principle guiding that assessment? After identifying the origins of this puzzle in the *travaux*, this part charted a series of Court attempts to solve it. Moving from the 'proceedings as a whole' test through counterbalancing and defect-curing to the 'never fair' jurisprudence, this part demonstrated inconsistency between, and incoherence within, these analytical tools. This part then looked at how the Court has dealt with the extent to which the public interest may justify restrictions on Article 6, and how this has played out in the context of various inconsistent attempts to clarify the place of balancing and proportionality analysis in Article 6 cases. It demonstrated a variety of approaches to public interest balancing that were in tension with the text of Article 6, and of the Convention more generally.[362]

Indeed, as the macro-arguments made in this part demonstrated, the European Court's assessment of alleged violations of Article 6 involves the use of a variety of analytical tools, seemingly chosen and deployed with minimal explanation of why one tool is used in one situation and another is used in another situation, and often without acknowledging that the alternative tools even exist. Moreover, looking at each of these analytical tools in isolation demonstrated considerable uncertainty and incoherence within each tool.

If the European Court wished to design a finely-calibrated and nuanced analytical framework in which particular methods of analysis were tailored to particular violations, it could do so. But even then, the interests of predictability and coherence demand that there be an explanation for why one method of assessment is appropriate in one Article 6 context but not another, and why using alternative methods for seemingly-similar violations is not inconsistent. In any event, the European Court has not done either of these things.

The above criticisms having been made, how ought the European Court to analyse alleged violations of Article 6? In framing its inquiry, the Court ought to follow the normative arguments made earlier in this book, especially the argument made in part C.5 that any Article 6 analysis must begin with analysis of the specific component right that is said to have been violated, rather than with consideration of more general notions of a fair trial.[363] Once that starting point is secured, there is less need for reference to ideas such as the proceedings as a whole, counterbalancing and defect-curing, or irretrievable unfairness. If, for example, the question is whether or not the applicant had 'the free assistance of an interpreter' under Article 6(3)(e), the Court's initial focus ought to be solely on that question. This, in turn, would render much less relevant any consideration of whatever else happened in the proceedings, any counterbalancing mechanism, and any need for a 'never fair' principle.

[362] As one example of the latter, the Convention is structured such that, at least on its face, Art 6 is unqualified but derogable. See Ashworth, 'Security, Terrorism and the Value of Human Rights' (n 8 above). Yet if the effect of the European Court's case law has been to interpret Art 6 as, effectively, a qualified right, one might wonder whether the formal structures of derogation under Art 15 have been subverted to some extent by providing an alternative 'out' to states wishing to restrict Art 6 rights.

[363] In addition to the normative arguments made at C.5, see, too, A.7, B.7 and D.5.

Building on this analysis, I suggest that it is time for the European Court to state clearly that public interest balancing and proportionality have no place in the assessment of whether or not Article 6 has been violated. If Article 6 applies, any infringement ought to amount to a violation incapable of justification.[364] Given the status of Article 6 as an unqualified but derogable right, such a statement would be a more faithful interpretation of the text of Article 6 in the context of the Convention. This approach need not be regarded as revolutionary. Indeed, while rejecting balancing and proportionality would amount to a repudiation of the cases discussed in parts E.6.3, E.6.4, and E.6.5, it would constitute a reiteration of the case law considered in part E.6.1.

The repudiation of public interest balancing and proportionality has also featured in other aspects of the European Court's jurisprudence. Most notably, the Court's Article 3 case law is characterised by emphatic statements about the 'absolute' nature of Article 3.[365] The Court is, therefore, familiar with this sort of approach. As has been the case with the Article 3 jurisprudence, it is likely that the approach outlined above would generate scholarly and judicial arguments about 'which are the legitimate factors and circumstances to be taken into account in the interpretation and application of'[366] Article 6, and about the appropriate definitions to be adopted for each of the Article 6 guarantees.[367] It is beyond the scope of this book to offer a conceptual definition of the various Article 6 guarantees here, but the arguments made throughout parts A to E have offered considerable normative guidance as to the factors and circumstances which ought to be taken into account in shaping, interpreting and applying those guarantees.

There is a further important nuance to add to this account. Unlike the situation with respect to Article 3, it should not be forgotten that forbidding public interest balancing in the context of Article 6 does *not* leave the contracting states entirely powerless to act contrary to the Article 6 guarantees. Indeed, the text and structure of the Convention provides for the possibility of derogation from Article 6 obligations in the event of 'war or other public emergency threatening the life of the nation'.[368] Where a contracting state considers that such an emergency warrants action that would otherwise amount to an infringement of Article 6, let the relevant government pursue a derogation under the Article 15 procedure, with all the accountability that that mechanism entails. Such an approach would better reflect the text of the Convention, reduce the extent to which reasoning inspired by public interest balancing can infect the European Court's Article 6 case law, and hold contracting states to a clearer standard than the existing poorly-defined balancing case law.

[364] cp Natasa Mavronicola, 'What is an "Absolute Right"? Deciphering Absoluteness in the Context of Article 3 of the ECHR' (2012) *Human Rights Law Review* (Advance Access) 1, 8.

[365] See ibid; cf *Jalloh v Germany* (n 77 above).

[366] Natasa Mavronicola and Francesco Messineo, 'Relatively Absolute? The Undermining of Article 3 ECHR in *Ahmad v UK*' (2013) 76 *Modern Law Review* 589, 593.

[367] Such definitions would need to be crafted with awareness of the possibility that contracting states may attempt to smuggle public interest considerations into the process of definition. See, eg, ibid.

[368] See Art 15 of the Convention.

But in the event that the European Court felt reluctant to revise its case law in this way, or believed that some form of public interest balancing at the violation stage was essential to the contemporary operation of Article 6, there would nonetheless remain considerable room for improvement. For example, the Court ought to refrain from purporting to analyse the proceedings as a whole unless it is actually willing to analyse the proceedings as a whole. The use of counterbalancing and defect-curing should be rendered more transparent through greater and more precise explanation of how the Court understands these mechanisms to work. The notion that criminal proceedings can be irretrievably prejudiced by some forms of violation should be clarified, and its relationship with the 'proceedings as a whole' doctrine and counterbalancing principles rationalised. And finally, if public interest balancing was to be thought inevitable, then it would be incumbent on the European Court to reject unstructured broad-brush balancing in favour of a form of rigorously-structured proportionality reasoning appropriate for the Article 6 rights, and to use that form of reasoning consistently across all Article 6 criminal cases. Such rigour would enhance the extent to which the Court's decisions can provide meaningful guidance. The Court could also make any such proportionality test more rigorous and robust by implementing a requirement of *strict* or *compelling* necessity as part of that analysis.[369] If the notion of the very essence of the right were to continue to be employed as a notional safeguard, it would be incumbent on the European Court to identify the essential *and* non-essential elements of Article 6 in order to make sense of its utility. All these arguments are, of course, advanced on the presumption that the Court is unwilling to adopt my more sweeping suggestions above.

In any event, even if the European Court is reluctant to adopt *any* of the specific normative recommendations outlined in this section, it is to be hoped that the Court might adopt the broader normative arguments made throughout this part: that the Article 6 case law ought to be more consistent, more coherent, and better explained.

[369] As in, eg, *Salduz v Turkey* (n 190 above) para 55.

Conclusion

The questions outlined at the beginning of this book were these: how does the European Court's criminal fair trial case law fare in relation to the book's measuring stick? To what extent is the case law consistent, predictable, locally coherent, and capable of acting as a guide to citizens, lawyers, officials, and judges? The book considered these questions in the context of how the European Court interprets Article 6, how the European Court sees its role in Article 6 cases, how the Court approaches the internal structure of Article 6, the Court's implied rights jurisprudence, and how the Court assesses alleged violations of Article 6. In this conclusion, I gather together the various strands of argument.

The primary aim of this book was to describe and critique the existing case law. The argument, based on an extensive survey of the Article 6 criminal case law, was presented in five parts. Part A laid the foundations for what followed by examining the Court's interpretative approaches through two principal lines of inquiry. The part considered various general interpretative approaches and demonstrated uncertainty about the rationales for these approaches, and uncertainty as to when one should be preferred over another. In particular, part A considered the democratic catchphrase and established that the catchphrase was used in an under-reasoned and poorly explained way.

Part B demonstrated that despite the Court's rhetorically-emphatic descriptions of its own role, the Court's sense of its own role is poorly defined and poorly explained. Moreover, particularly in the context of the fourth instance doctrine and the Court's approach to evidence, the book demonstrated significant incongruence between the Court's stated view of its own role and the way in which the case law suggests the Court operates in reality. The fourth instance doctrine was shown to be riddled with largely unacknowledged exceptions and qualifications.

Part C continued the broad macro-arguments that run throughout the book, focusing on the Court's approach to the internal structure of Article 6. In particular, it was demonstrated that the European Court has adopted a series of different approaches to Article 6, and that these approaches offer irreconcilable alternatives to the correct way to view the relationship between Article 6(1) and Article 6 as a whole, the correct way to view the relationship between the various component parts of Article 6, and to whether alleged violations of multiple provisions should be taken separately or together. Moreover, part C demonstrated that the Court has no clear sense of what it means to 'take together' multiple violations. As was the case with so many other sections of the book, part C established that it is difficult to find reasoned, predictable explanations of why certain classes of case fall under one approach, while other classes do not.

In part D the argument on the internal structure of Article 6 continued, albeit with a focus on the implied rights. Part D established the European Court's failure to rationalise and explain its implied rights jurisprudence in any coherent or consistent way, by exploring the various foundations for those rights, their relationship with the explicit rights, and the 'dogs that did not bark'.

The largest element of the book was part E, which evaluated the Court's attempts to solve what was described as the puzzle of Article 6: how should violations of Article 6 be assessed in the absence of an express meta-principle? Having sketched the foundations of this puzzle, part E analysed the Court's attempts to resolve the puzzle. The part established radical uncertainty within, and considerable inconsistency between, notions such as the 'proceedings as a whole' test, counterbalancing and defect-curing, and the 'never fair' jurisprudence. In considering the extent to which the public interest may justify restrictions on Article 6, and how this has played out in the context of attempts to carry out structured balancing and proportionality analysis, the part established further incoherence.

Running through all of these parts were the two broad classes of argument set out in the Introduction. First, the book established that there was incoherence and uncertainty *within* each of the various tools and approaches used by the European Court. Second, throughout the book, it was demonstrated that there was significant inconsistency *between* those approaches. These two macro-arguments, interrelated and running throughout the book, combine to demonstrate significant ways in which the European Court's criminal fair trial rights case law has failed to provide guidance of the sort required by the measuring stick of predictability, coherence, and consistency.

What is the significance of these arguments? I suggest that this book has established that the European Court's Article 6 case law is incoherent to an extent that raises real questions about its ability to provide guidance. Indeed, I have shown that the Court's case law provides flawed guidance on how the Court chooses between one interpretative approach or another in a given case; how the Court views its role; how the Court views the internal structure of Article 6; how the Court conceptualises the implied rights; and how the Court assesses alleged violations of Article 6. The case law, as described in the book, is marked by this sense of irrational flexibility.

This irrational flexibility means that the Court can approach an individual application in an unpredictable multitude of ways: the Court may be deferential or not; the relevant test may be said to be one part of Article 6 or several; the relevant basis for the implied rights may be said to be one thing or another; and the alleged violation may be assessed using any one of a number of incoherent approaches. The consequences of choices to adopt a 'taken together' approach combined with a 'proceedings as a whole' test and a willingness to consider community interest balancing arguments will look very different from the consequences of a choice to adopt a 'minimum guarantee' approach combined with a 'never fair' assessment and a rejection of expedient public interest balancing. Any one of these areas of uncertainty would be problematic. Read as a whole, what the book shows is that these areas of uncertainty have the potential to act as cogs turning one another, generating uncertainty and incoherence greater than the sum of the individual parts. Of course, as has been emphasised throughout, there is nothing wrong with flexibility, and the rule of law and guidance measuring stick does not preclude a degree of flexibility. If the Court wished to deploy different approaches in similar situations, or different approaches in different situations, the interests of predictability and consistency simply demand that it adequately explain itself.

Some may seek to cite institutional and political factors in defence of the Article 6 case law criticised in this book. Undoubtedly there is much scope for future research into, and discussion of, the effect of institutional and political factors on the Article 6 case law. But let that discussion now proceed on the basis of frank acknowledgments that the case law is incoherent and inconsistent, rather than on the basis of assertions that 'the judgments of the Court are exceptionally well reasoned'[1] and praise for the Court's 'impressive case law' on Article 6.[2]

While the primary aim of this book was description and criticism rather than normative prescription, the book may nonetheless be read as a robust and targeted call for the European Court to adopt in this area of law a renewed, rejuvenated approach that is more consistent, more coherent, and better explained. This book is a call for a jurisprudence capable of providing the citizens of Europe with vital guidance on their rights, and a jurisprudence that meets the onus of justification. For a provision as heavily-litigated as Article 6, and one that thus affects so many people in day to day lives, it is particularly crucial that the European Court make its views clear and predictable. At the end of each part of this book, I offered more specific normative suggestions as to how the Court might begin to implement these more general normative arguments.[3] No attempt will be made to summarise those arguments here, but it should be noted that many of the building blocks of those arguments are already present in the case law of the European Court; the challenge is to shed the inconsistent and incoherent case law that sits alongside those building blocks. And so it is hoped that the specific normative suggestions in this book, together with the criticisms made above, have helped to lay the foundations for future normative work by scholars, practitioners, and judges. Ultimately, even if none of these *specific* arguments are adopted by the European Court, it is hoped that recognition of the more *general* concerns about coherence and predictability will produce an Article 6 case law that is better able to provide a sense of guidance.

[1] Francois Ost, 'The Original Canons of Interpretation of the European Court of Human Rights' in Mireille Delmas-Marty and Christine Chodkiewicz (eds), *The European Convention for the Protection of Human Rights: International Protection Versus National Restrictions* (Martinus Nijhoff, 1992) 284.

[2] Paul Lemmens, 'The Right to a Fair Trial and its Multiple Manifestations' in E Brems and Janneke Gerards (eds), *Shaping Rights in the ECHR* (Cambridge University Press, 2013) para 2.3.4.

[3] See A.7, B.7, C.5, D.5 and E.7.

Unless there is change it will, unfortunately, remain hard to envisage how a potential applicant might attempt to make sense of the Court's Article 6 case law. It is time for the European Court to take criminal fair trial rights more seriously.

BIBLIOGRAPHY

Books

Alexy, R, *A Theory of Constitutional Rights* (Oxford University Press, 2002)

Arai-Takahashi, Y, *The Margin of Appreciation Doctrine and the Principle of Proportionality in the Jurisprudence of the ECHR* (Intersentia, 2002)

Ashworth, A, *Human Rights, Serious Crime and Criminal Procedure* (Sweet & Maxwell, 2002)

Ashworth, A and Redmayne, M, *The Criminal Process*, 4th edn (Oxford University Press, 2010)

Bingham, T, *The Rule of Law* (Penguin, 2011)

Brady, ADP, *Proportionality and Deference under the UK HRA: An Institutionally Sensitive Approach* (Cambridge University Press, 2012)

Brems, E, *Human Rights: Universality and Diversity* (Martinus Nijhoff, 2001)

Cane, P, *Administrative Law*, 5th edn (Oxford University Press, 2011)

Christoffersen, J, *Fair Balance: Proportionality, Subsidiarity and Primarity in the ECHR* (Martinus Nijhoff, 2009)

Clayton, R and Tomlinson, H (eds), *The Law of Human Rights*, 2nd edn (Oxford University Press, 2009)

—— *Fair Trial Rights*, 2nd edn (Oxford University Press, 2010)

Council of Europe, *Collected Edition of the Travaux Préparatoires* (Martinus Nijhoff, 1975) vol I

—— *Collected Edition of the Travaux Préparatoires* (Martinus Nijhoff, 1975) vol II

—— *Collected Edition of the Travaux Préparatoires* (Martinus Nijhoff, 1976) vol III

—— *Collected Edition of the Travaux Préparatoires* (Martinus Nijhoff, 1977) vol IV

—— *Collected Edition of the Travaux Préparatoires* (Martinus Nijhoff, 1979) vol V

Craig, P, *Administrative Law*, 7th edn (Sweet & Maxwell, 2012)

Currie, D, *The Constitution of the Federal Republic of Germany* (University of Chicago Press, 1994)

Dembour, M-B, *Who Believes in Human Rights?* (Cambridge University Press, 2006)

Dennis, I, *The Law of Evidence*, 3rd edn (Sweet & Maxwell, 2007)

Dworkin, R, *Law's Empire* (Hart Publishing, 1998)

Emmerson, B, Ashworth, A and Macdonald, A, *Human Rights and Criminal Justice*, 3rd edn (Sweet & Maxwell, 2012)

Endicott, T, *Administrative Law*, 2nd edn (Oxford University Press, 2011)

European Commission of Human Rights, *Preparatory Work on Article 6 of the European Convention* (DH(56)11, Council of Europe, 1956)

European Court of Human Rights, *Preparatory Work on Article 6 of the European Convention* (CDH(68)3, Council of Europe, 1968)

—— *The European Court of Human Rights: Some Facts and Figures: 1959–2009* (Council of Europe, 2009)

European Court of Human Rights, *The European Court of Human Rights in Facts and Figures: 2013* (Council of Europe, 2014)
Foster, S, *Human Rights and Civil Liberties*, 2nd edn (Pearson Education, 2008)
Fuller, L, *The Morality of Law* (Yale University Press, 1964)
Gearty, C, *Principles of Human Rights Adjudication* (Oxford University Press, 2004)
—— *Can Human Rights Survive?* (Cambridge University Press, 2006)
—— *Civil Liberties* (Oxford University Press, 2007)
Greer, S, *The European Convention on Human Rights: Achievements, Problems and Prospects*, 2nd edn (Cambridge University Press, 2006)
Harris, D, O'Boyle, M and Warbrick, C, *Law of the European Convention on Human Rights*, 2nd edn (Oxford University Press, 2009)
Hayek, F, *The Road to Serfdom* (Routledge Classics, 2001)
Jennings, I, *The Law and the Constitution*, 5th edn (University of London Press, 1959)
Lasser, M, *Judicial Transformations: the Rights Revolution in the Courts of Europe* (Oxford University Press, 2009)
Lazarus, L, Goold, B and Swiney, G, *Public Protection, Proportionality, and the Search for Balance*, Ministry of Justice Research Series 10/07 (2007)
Legg, A, *The Margin of Appreciation in International Human Rights Law* (Oxford University Press, 2012)
Mahoney, P et al, *Statement on Case-Overload at the ECtHR* (European Law Institute, 2012)
Merrills, J, *The Development of International Law by the European Court of Human Rights*, 2nd edn (Manchester University Press, 1995)
Möller, K, *The Global Model of Constitutional Rights* (Hart Publishing, 2012)
Mowbray, A, *Cases, Materials, and Commentary on the European Convention on Human Rights*, 3rd edn (Oxford University Press, 2012)
Murphy, P, *Murphy on Evidence*, 10th edn (Oxford University Press, 2008)
Ovey, C and White, R, *Jacobs and White: The European Convention on Human Rights*, 4th edn (Oxford University Press, 2006)
Pinto-Duschinsky, M, *Bringing Rights Back Home* (Policy Exchange, 2011)
Raz, J, *The Authority of Law: Essays on Law and Morality* (Clarendon Press, 2002)
Rundle, K, *Forms Liberate: Reclaiming the Jurisprudence of Lon L Fuller* (Hart Publishing, 2012)
Simpson, AWB, *Human Rights and the End of Empire* (Oxford University Press, 2001)
Stavros, S, *The Guarantees for Accused Persons under Article 6 of the European Convention on Human Rights* (Martinus Nijhoff, 1993)
Stumer, AC, *The Presumption of Innocence* (Hart Publishing, 2010)
Sullivan, ET and Frase, RS, *Proportionality Principles in American Law* (Oxford University Press, 2008)
Summers, SJ, *Fair Trials: the European Criminal Procedural Tradition and the European Court of Human Rights* (Hart Publishing, 2007)
Svensson-McCarthy, A-L, *The International Law of Human Rights and States of Exception* (Martinus Nijhoff, 1998)
Tamanaha, B, *On the Rule of Law* (Cambridge University Press, 2004)
Tapper, C, *Cross and Tapper on Evidence*, 12th edn (Oxford University Press, 2010)
Trechsel, S, *Human Rights in Criminal Proceedings* (Oxford University Press, 2006)
van Dijk, P and van Hoof, GJH, *Theory and Practice of the European Convention on Human Rights*, 4th edn (Intersentia, 2006)
Wade, W and Forsyth, C, *Administrative Law*, 10th edn (Oxford University Press, 2009)

Wolfrum, R and Deutsch, U (eds), *The European Court of Human Rights Overwhelmed by Applications: Problems and Possible Solutions* (Springer, 2009)

Chapters of Books

Arai-Takahashi, Y, 'The Margin of Appreciation Doctrine: a Theoretical Analysis of Strasbourg's Variable Geometry' in A Follesdal, B Peters and G Ulfstein (eds), *Constituting Europe* (Cambridge University Press, 2013)

Ashworth, A, 'Security, Terrorism and the Value of Human Rights' in B Goold and L Lazarus (eds), *Security and Human Rights*, 2nd edn (Hart Publishing, 2007)

——'The Exclusion of Evidence Obtained by Violating a Fundamental Right: Pragmatism before Principle in the Strasbourg Jurisprudence' in P Roberts and J Hunter (eds), *Criminal Evidence and Human Rights* (Hart Publishing, 2012)

Bernhardt, R, 'Thoughts on the Interpretation of Human-Rights Treaties' in F Matscher (ed), *Protecting Human Rights: the European Dimension*, 2nd edn (Carl Heymanns Verlag KG, 1990)

Choo, A, 'Give Us What You Have: Information, Compulsion and the Privilege Against Self-incrimination as a Human Right' in P Roberts and J Hunter (eds), *Criminal Evidence and Human Rights* (Hart Publishing, 2012)

Conan Doyle, A, 'Silver Blaze' in A Conan Doyle (ed), *The Memoirs of Sherlock Holmes* (Penguin, 1950)

Costa, J-P, 'The Authority of the Jurisprudence of the ECtHR' in Steering Committee for Human Rights (ed), *Reforming the European Convention on Human Rights: A Work in Progress* (Council of Europe Publishing, 2009)

Delmas-Marty, M, 'The Richness of Underlying Legal Reasoning' in M Delmas-Marty and C Chodkiewicz (eds), *The European Convention for the Protection of Human Rights: International Protection Versus National Restrictions* (Martinus Nijhoff, 1992)

Golsong, H, 'The European Court of Human Rights and the National Law-maker' in F Matscher (ed), *Protecting Human Rights: the European Dimension*, 2nd edn (Carl Heymanns Verlag KG, 1990)

——'Interpreting the European Convention on Human Rights Beyond the Confines of the Vienna Convention' in R Macdonald, F Matscher and H Petzold (eds), *The European System for the Protection of Human Rights* (Martinus Nijhoff, 1993)

Jacot-Guillarmod, O, 'Rights related to Good Administration of Justice' in R Macdonald, F Matscher and H Petzold (eds), *The European System for the Protection of Human Rights* (Martinus Nijhoff, 1993)

Lazarus, L, 'Mapping the Right to Security' in B Goold and L Lazarus (eds), *Security and Human Rights*, 2nd edn (Hart Publishing, 2007)

Lemmens, P, 'The Right to a Fair Trial and its Multiple Manifestations' in E Brems and J Gerards (eds), *Shaping Rights in the ECHR* (Cambridge University Press, 2013)

Letsas, G, 'The ECHR as Living Instrument: Its Meaning and Legitimacy' in A Follesdal, B Peters and G Ulfstein (eds), *Constituting Europe* (Cambridge University Press, 2013)

Matscher, F, 'Methods of Interpretation of the Convention' in R Macdonald, F Matscher and H Petzold (eds), *The European System for the Protection of Human Rights* (Martinus Nijhoff, 1993)

McBride, J, 'Proportionality and the European Convention on Human Rights' in E Ellis (ed), *The Principle of Proportionality in the Laws of Europe* (Hart Publishing, 1999)

Mountfield, H, 'The Concept of a Lawful Interference with Fundamental Rights' in J Jowell and J Cooper (eds), *Understanding Human Rights Principles* (Hart Publishing, 2001)

Norrie, A, 'Criminal Justice, Judicial Interpretation, Legal Right' in T Campbell, K Ewing and A Tomkins (eds), *Sceptical Essays on Human Rights* (Oxford University Press, 2001)

Ost, F, 'The Original Canons of Interpretation of the European Court of Human Rights' in M Delmas-Marty and C Chodkiewicz (eds), *The European Convention for the Protection of Human Rights: International Protection Versus National Restrictions* (Martinus Nijhoff, 1992)

Petzold, H, 'The Convention and the Principle of Subsidiarity' in R Macdonald, F Matscher and H Petzold (eds), T*he European System for the Protection of Human Rights* (Martinus Nijhoff, 1993)

Raz, J, 'The Relevance of Coherence' in J Raz (ed), *Ethics in the Public Domain: Essays in the Morality of Law and Politics* (Clarendon Press, 1995)

Redmayne, M, 'Confronting Confrontation' in P Roberts and J Hunter (eds), *Criminal Evidence and Human Rights* (Hart Publishing, 2012)

van Dijk, P, 'The Interpretation of Civil Rights and Obligations by the European Court of Human Rights' in F Matscher (ed), *Protecting Human Rights: the European Dimension*, 2nd edn (Carl Heymanns Verlag KG, 1990)

Journal Articles, etc

Ambrus, M, 'Comparative Law Method in the Jurisprudence of the European Court of Human Rights in the Light of the Rule of Law' (2009) 2(3) *Erasmus Law Review* 354

Arato, J, 'Constitutional Transformation in the ECtHR: Strasbourg's Expansive Recourse to External Rules of International Law' (2012) 37(2) *Brooklyn Journal of International Law* 304

Ashworth, A, 'Self-incrimination in European Human Rights Law: a Pregnant Pragmatism?' (2008) 30 *Cardozo Law Review* 751

Ast, S, 'The Gafgen Judgment of the ECtHR: On the Consequences of the Threat of Torture for Criminal Proceedings' (2010) 11(12) *German Law Journal* 1393

Badar, ME, 'Basic Principles Governing Limitations on Individual Rights, and Freedoms in Human Rights Instruments' (2003) 7 *International Journal of Human Rights* 63

Barber, N, 'Must Legalistic Conceptions of the Rule of Law Have a Social Dimension?' (2004) 17 *Ratio Juris* 474

—— *Self-Defence for Institutions*, Oxford Legal Studies Research Paper No 61/2012 (2012)

Battjes, H, 'In Search of a Fair Balance: the Absolute Character of the Prohibition of Refoulement under Article 3 ECHR Reassessed' (2009) 22 *Leiden Journal of International Law* 583

Bjorge, E, 'Exceptionalism and Internationalism in the Supreme Court: *Horncastle* and *Cadder*' (2011) *Public Law* 475

Bratza N, 'The Relationship Between the UK Courts and Strasbourg' [2011] *EHRLR* 505

Brems, E, 'The Margin of Appreciation Doctrine in the Case-Law of the ECtHR' (1996) 56 *Zeitschrift für Ausländisches Öffentliches Recht und Völkerrecht* 240

——'Conflicting Human Rights: an Exploration in the Context of the Right to a Fair Trial in the European Convention on Human Rights' (2005) 27 *Human Rights Quarterly* 294

Briant, S, 'Dialogue, Diplomacy and Defiance: Prisoners' Voting Rights at Home and in Strasbourg' [2011] *EHRLR* 243

Cali, B, 'The Purposes of the European Human Rights System: One or Many?' [2008] *EHRLR* 299

Choo, A, *Compelling the Provision of Information: the Privilege Against Self- incrimination as a Human Right*, University of Warwick Legal Studies Research Paper Series 2010–20 (2010)

Clayton, G and Wray, H, 'Editorial: *Othman v United Kingdom* (2012)' (2012) 26 *Journal of Immigration, Asylum and Nationality Law* 2

Coen, M, 'Hearsay, Bad Character and Trust in the Jury: Irish and English Contrasts' (2013) 17 *International Journal of Evidence and Proof* 250

——'"With Cat-like Tread": Jury Trial and the European Court of Human Rights' (2014) *Human Rights Law Review* (Advance Access) 1

Croquet, N, 'The Right to Self-representation under the ECHR: What role for the Limitation Analysis?' [2012] *EHRLR* 292

Daly, A, 'The Right of Children to be Heard in Civil Proceedings and the Emerging Law of the ECHR' (2010) *International Journal of Human Rights* 1

Dembour, M-B, '"Finishing Off" Cases: the Radical Solution to the Problem of the Expanding European Court of Human Rights Caseload' [2002] *EHRLR* 604

Dembour, M-B and Krzyzanowska-Mierzewska, M, 'Ten Years On: the Voluminous and Interesting Polish Case Law' [2004] *EHRLR* 517

Dennis, I, 'Fair Trials and Safe Convictions' (2003) 56 *Current Legal Problems* 211

Doobay, A, 'The Right to a Fair Trial in Light of the Recent ECtHR and CJEU Case-law' (2013) (Online) *Academy of European Law ERA Forum*

Dzehtsiarou, K, *Consensus from Within the Palace Walls*, University College Dublin Working Papers in Law, Criminology and Socio-Legal Studies Paper 40/2010 (2010)

Elliott, M, *Proportionality and Deference: the Importance of a Structured Approach*, Cambridge Legal Studies Research Paper Series Paper No 32/2013 (2013)

Endicott, T, 'The Impossibility of the Rule of Law' (1999) 19 *Oxford Journal of Legal Studies* 1

Feingold, CS, 'The Doctrine of Margin of Appreciation and the European Convention on Human Rights' (1977–78) 53 *Notre Dame Lawyer* 90

Gearty, C, 'The European Court of Human Rights and the Protection of Civil Liberties: an Overview' (1993) 52 *Cambridge Law Journal* 89

——'Democracy and Human Rights in the European Court of Human Rights: a Critical Appraisal' (2000) 51 *Northern Ireland Legal Quarterly* 381

——'The Human Rights Act: an Academic Sceptic Changes his Mind but Not his Heart' [2010] *EHRLR* 582

Gerards, J and Senden, H, 'The Structure of Fundamental Rights and the European Court of Human Rights' (2009) 7 *International Journal of Constitutional Law* 619

Green, A, 'A Philosophical Taxonomy of European Human Rights Law' [2012] *EHRLR* 71

Greer, S, 'Constitutionalising Adjudication under the European Convention on Human Rights' (2003) *Oxford Journal of Legal Studies* 405

——'Should Police Threats to Torture Suspects Always be Severely Punished? Reflections on the *Gafgen* Case' (2011) 11(1) *Human Rights Law Review* 67

Greer, S and Wildhaber, L, 'Reflections of a Former President of the European Court of Human Rights' [2010] *EHRLR* 165

Grimm, D, 'Proportionality in Canadian and German Constitutional Jurisprudence' (2007) 57 *U Toronto Law Journal* 383

Harmsen, R, 'The European Convention on Human Rights after Enlargement' (2001) 5 *International Journal of Human Rights* 18

Helfer, L, 'Consensus, Coherence and the ECHR' (1993) 26 *Cornell Int'l LJ* 133

Hickman, T, 'Proportionality: Comparative Law Lessons' (2007) *Judicial Review* 31

Hoyano, L, 'What is Balanced on the Scales of Justice? In Search of the Essence of the Right to a Fair Trial' [2014] Crim LR 4

Hutchinson, MR, 'The Margin of Appreciation Doctrine in the European Court of Human Rights' (1999) 48 *International and Comparative Law Quarterly* 638

Jackson, J, 'Re-conceptualizing the Right of Silence as an Effective Fair Trial Standard' (2009) 58 *International and Comparative Law Quarterly* 835

Kolb, R, 'The Jurisprudence of the ECHR on Detention and Fair Trial in Criminal Matters from 1992–1998' (2000) 21 *Human Rights Law Journal* 348

Kuijer, M, 'The Right to a Fair Trial and the Council of Europe's Efforts to Ensure Effective Remedies on a Domestic Level for Excessively Lengthy Proceedings' (2013) 13(4) *Human Rights Law Review* 777

Lavender, N, 'The Problem of the Margin of Appreciation' (1997) 4 *EHRLR* 380

Lazarus, L, 'Conceptions of Liberty Deprivation' (2006) 69 *Modern Law Review* 738

Lester, A, 'The European Court of Human Rights after 50 Years' [2009] *EHRLR* 461

——'The ECtHR and the HRA: British Concerns' (2012) 17 *Judicial Review* 1

Letsas, G, *Judge Rozakis's Separate Opinions and the Strasbourg Dilemma*, SSRN Working Paper Series (2011)

——'Rescuing Proportionality' in Rowan Cruft and Massimo Renzo (eds), *Philosophical Foundations of Human Rights* (Oxford University Press, 2013)

Levenbook, BB, 'The Role of Coherence in Legal Reasoning' (1984) 3 *Law and Philosophy* 355

Lupu, Y and Voeten, E, 'Precedent in International Courts: a Network Analysis of Case Citations by the European Court of Human Rights' (2011) *British Journal of Political Science* 1

Mahoney, P, 'Judicial Activism and Judicial Restraint in the ECHR' (1990) 11 *Human Rights Law Journal* 57

Marks, S, 'The European Convention on Human Rights and its "Democratic Society"' (1995) 66 *British Yearbook of International Law* 209

Mavronicola, N, 'What is an "Absolute Right"? Deciphering Absoluteness in the Context of Article 3 of the ECHR' (2012) *Human Rights Law Review* (Advance Access) 1

Mavronicola, N and Messineo, F, 'Relatively Absolute? The Undermining of Article 3 ECHR in *Ahmad v UK*' (2013) 76 *Modern Law Review* 589

McEwan, J, 'Truth, Efficiency, and Cooperation in Modern Criminal Justice' (2013) *Current Legal Problems* 1

McHarg, A, 'Reconciling Human Rights and the Public Interest: Conceptual Problems and Doctrinal Uncertainty in the Jurisprudence of the European Court of Human Rights' (1999) 62 *Modern Law Review* 671

McInerney-Lankford, S, 'Fragmentation of International Law Redux: the Case of Strasbourg' (2012) 32(3) *OJLS* 609

Moral Soriano, L, 'A Modest Notion of Coherence in Legal Reasoning: a Model for the ECJ' (2003) 16 *Ratio Juris* 296

Mowbray, A, 'The Role of the ECHR in the Promotion of Democracy' (1999) *Public Law* 703

——'No Violations but Interesting: a Study of the Strasbourg Court's Jurisprudence in Cases where No Breach of the Convention has been Found' (2008) 14 *European Public Law* 237

——'An Examination of the European Court of Human Rights' Approach to Overruling its Previous Case Law' (2009) 9 *Human Rights Law Review* 179

——'A Study of the Principle of Fair Balance in the Jurisprudence of the ECtHR' (2010) 10 *Human Rights Law Review* 289

Mureinik, E, 'A Bridge to Where? Introducing the Interim Bill of Rights' (1994) 10 *South African Journal on Human Rights* 31

Murphy, C, *Human Rights Law and the Challenges of Explicit Judicial Dialogue*, Jean Monnet Working Paper No 10/2012

Nicol, D, 'Original Intent and the European Convention on Human Rights' (2005) *Public Law* 152

Nifosi-Sutton, I, 'The Power of the ECHR to Order Specific Non-monetary Relief: a Critical Appraisal from a Right to Health Perspective' (2010) 23 *Harvard HR Journal* 51

O'Brian, B, *Confrontation: the Defiance of the English Courts*, 2010–09 University of Warwick School of Law Legal Studies Research Paper 1 (2010)

Owusu-Bempah, A, 'Defence Participation through Pre-trial Disclosure: Issues and Implications' (2013) *International Journal of Evidence and Proof* 183

Pattenden, R, 'Case Comment: Right to Counsel at the Police Station' (2011) 15(1) *International Journal of Evidence and Proof* 70

Rivers, J, 'Proportionality and Variable Intensity of Review' (2006) 65 *Cambridge Law Journal* 174

Roberts, P, 'Does Article 6 of the European Convention on Human Rights Require Reasoned Verdicts in Criminal Trials?' (2011) *Human Rights Law Review* 1

Sauer, H and Trilsch, M, '*Gafgen v Germany* (Case Comment)' (2011) 105 *American Journal of International Law* 313

Schokkenbroek, J, 'The Basis, Nature and Application of the Margin of Appreciation Doctrine in the Case Law of the European Court of Human Rights' (1998) 19 *Human Rights Law Journal* 30

Spurrier, M, '*Gafgen v Germany*: Fruit of the Poisonous Tree' [2010] *EHRLR* 513

Tobin, J, 'Seeking to Persuade: a Constructive Approach to Human Rights Treaty Interpretation' (2010) *Harvard HR Journal* 1

van de Laar, T and de Graaff, R, '*Salduz* and *Miranda*: Is the US Supreme Court Pointing the Way?' [2011] *EHRLR* 304

Voeten, E, 'The Impartiality of International Judges: Evidence from the European Court of Human Rights' (2008) 102(4) *American Political Science Review* 417

Waldron, J, 'Security and Liberty: the Image of Balance' (2003) (11)2 *Journal of Political Philosophy* 191

Wallace, S, 'The Empire Strikes Back: Hearsay Rules in Common Law Legal Systems and the Jurisprudence of the ECtHR' [2010] *EHRLR* 408

Ward, T and Gardner, P, 'The Privilege against Self-incrimination: In Search of Legal Certainty' [2003] *EHRLR* 388

White, R, *Judgments in the Strasbourg Court: Some Reflections*, SSRN Working Paper Series (2009)

White, R and Boussiakou, I, 'Separate Opinions in the European Court of Human Rights' (2009) 9(1) *Human Rights Law Review* 37

Wu, W, 'Interrogational Fairness under the European Convention on Human Rights' (2011) 39 *International Journal of Law, Crime and Justice* 37

News Articles, Speeches, etc

BBC News, 'Human rights row: UK quitting would be disaster – ECHR head',14 January 2014, available at www.bbc.co.uk/news/uk-politics-25726319

Gearty, C, 'Al-Khawaja and Tahery v United Kingdom', UK Constitutional Law Group Blog, 9 January 2012, http://ukconstitutionallaw.org/2012/01/09/conor-gearty-al-khawaja-and-tahery-v-united-kingdom/

Lord Hoffman, 'The Universality of Human Rights' (Judicial Studies Board Annual Lecture, 19 March 2009)

Lord Neuberger, 'The British and Europe' (Cambridge Freshfields Annual Law Lecture, 12 February 2014)

Russia Today, 'ECtHR decisions may become invalid in Russia', 24 December 2013, available at http://rt.com/politics/court-constitution-echr-law-726/

Sumption, J, QC, 'Judicial and Political Decision-making: the Uncertain Boundary' (FA Mann Lecture, 8 November 2011)

Watt, N and Bowcott, O, 'David Cameron calls for reform of ECtHR', *Guardian*, 26 January 2012, available at www.theguardian.com/law/2012/jan/25/david-cameron-reform-human-rights

INDEX

www.ingramcontent.com/pod-product-compliance
Lightning Source LLC
LaVergne TN
LVHW052308200926
848481LV00002B/498
9781509909865